FARM KELLY

THE LAST WAR TRAIL

THE UTES AND THE SETTLEMENT OF COLORADO

ROBERT EMMITT

with an Introduction by Andrew Gulliford, an Afterword by Charles Wilkinson, and drawings by Bettina Steinke

frontispiece art by Clifford Duncan, Uncompahgre-Yampatika Ute

UNIVERSITY PRESS OF COLORADO

Copyright © 2000 by the University Press of Colorado
International Standard Book Number 0-87081-540-7

Published by the University Press of Colorado
5589 Arapahoe Avenue, Suite 206C
Boulder, Colorado 80303

The University Press of Colorado is a cooperative publishing enterprise
supported, in part, by Adams State College, Colorado State University, Fort
Lewis College, Mesa State College, Metropolitan State College of Denver,
University of Colorado, University of Northern Colorado, University of
Southern Colorado, and Western State College of Colorado.

The paper used in this publication meets the minimum requirements of the
American National Standard for Information Sciences–Permanence of
Paper for Printed Library Materials. ANSI Z39.48-1984

Library of Congress Cataloging-in-Publication Data

Emmitt, Robert.
    The last war trail : the Utes and the settlement of Colorado / Robert
    Emmitt.
        p. cm.
    Originally published: Norman : Univ. of Oklahoma Press, 1954, in
    series: Civilization
of the American Indian series ; v. 40.
    Includes bibliographical references and index.
    ISBN 0-87081-540-7
    1. Ute Indians–Wars, 1879. 2. Meeker, Nathan Cook, 1814–1879. I.
    Title.

E83.879 .E5 2000
973.8–dc21   99-088013

09 08 07 06 05 04 03 02 01 00   10 9 8 7 6 5 4 3 2 1

CONTENTS

ILLUSTRATIONS

vii

MAPS

INTRODUCTION

by ANDREW GULLIFORD

To understand the importance of Robert Emmitt's unique writing style and his significant book *The Last War Trail: The Utes and the Settlement of Colorado*, Ute Indian history must first be put into historical perspective. By the time Colorado attained statehood in 1876, most Native Americans had been confined to small reservations or forced to relocate to Indian Territory in present-day Oklahoma. The Plains Indians had been moved away from Denver, but the Utes of Western Colorado – unlike the Arapaho and Cheyenne, who fought against both settlers and the U.S. Army – were peaceful. They practiced diplomacy, got along well with their neighbors, and did not fight other tribes or the occasional white man who ventured deep into their lands. By 1876, the Utes remained sovereign and in control of over one third of Colorado – roughly twelve million acres of deep forests, swift rivers, high meadows, and steep canyons – and Colorado's elected officials remained vexed because the state had too many peaceful Utes.

After the 1858 discovery of Colorado gold, hordes of miners poured into Ute territory, so the federal government requested a treaty designating Ute reservation boundaries. The Tabeguache Treaty of 1863 recognized Ouray as head of the Utes, though he only represented the Tabeguache Band.[1] The Northern Utes and other bands did not ratify the Tabeguache Treaty, so it was not until the treaty of 1868 that the seven bands of Utes received title to the western third of Colorado territory.[2] Considering that the Ute population probably never exceeded 5,000, their defense of their mountain homeland against other Indian tribes and white incursions is remarkable.[3]

In January of 1868, Ouray, Mouache Chief Kaneache, White River subchiefs Captain Jack and Sowerich, the late Chief Nevava's nephew Piah, and five other chiefs traveled to Washington to sign a treaty that defined Ute territorial boundaries.[4] According to this treaty, the Indians had the right to bar any whites from entering the Western Slope and the peaks they called "The Shining Mountains." Though Chief Ouray had negotiated a remarkable treaty and was at the height of his diplomatic powers, he told reporters, "Agreements the Indian makes with the government are like the agreement a buffalo makes with the hunter after it has been pierced by many arrows. All it can do is lie down and give in." Ouray demanded that the treaty be made "final and forever."[5]

D.C. Oakes had been appointed head agent of the White River Utes in May of 1865, and he maintained good relations with the Utes as he began to build up the agency that, according to the 1868 treaty, was to include a warehouse, schoolhouse, and houses for the agent, a farmer, a blacksmith, and a miller. The agent was to distribute annuities and adjudicate Ute complaints.

As White River Agency construction got under way in 1868, other log cabins were being built by a scientific crew fifteen miles downriver from the agency. Beginning in mid-October, John Wesley Powell, a one-armed veteran of the Civil War battle at Shiloh, Tennessee, spent the winter on the Ute Reservation with his wife and other members of a scientific expedition intent on floating down Wyoming's Green River to the confluence of the Colorado River and then into the unknown.[6] Major Powell came to know the White River band of Antero and Douglas. Though he spent weeks learning their language and customs, he was almost killed for pounding a row of survey stakes into the ground near the Utes' race track on what became known as Powell Bottoms or Powell Park. Wisely, he withdrew the stakes.[7]

The Major developed a close friendship with the Utes, especially with Chief Douglas. The beadwork and other handmade items he acquired became the start of the Bureau of Ethnography, and one of the first Indian collections for the Smithsonian Institution's National Museum of Natural History.[8] In mid-March of 1869, the rising White River flooded Powell's winter quarters. The log cabins, along with the exploring party's possessions, were soaked. Two months later, on May 24, 1869 – only fourteen days after completion of the transcontinental railroad – Powell's crew shoved off in wooden boats from Green River, Wyoming territory for their rendezvous with destiny in the Grand Canyon.

His closeness to the White River Band that winter on Powell Bottoms stood him in good stead. Unlike most other adventurers, Powell never went armed among Indians during his twenty-year career in the West, and undoubtedly he knew and used the many Ute trails that transected the White River country. Powell later established the United States Geological Survey, and it was survey teams from Washington, D.C., that came to the White River in the summer of 1873 to map Colorado and to survey boundaries for the Ute Reservation.[9]

The U.S. Government Commission appointed to negotiate the 1873 Brunot Treaty for the San Juan cession met in western Colorado, because gold had been discovered in the southwest part of the reservation. During treaty talks, Utes expressed concern over the presence of surveyors on land which had been deeded to them in the treaty of 1868. Ute chiefs were justifiably troubled over the surveyors' presence. The commission noted, "One division of Professor Hayden's exploring party has spent some time upon their reservation, making surveys and taking observations which excited the suspicions of the Indians."[10]

The White River Utes, or *Nupartka*, lived north of the Colorado River and hunted across northwest Colorado and portions of southern Wyoming. The Utes did not understand the surveyors, but they did not harass them. Much to the consternation of empire-builders like Colorado Governor Frederick Pitkin and *Rocky Mountain News* editor William Byers, approximately 2,500 Utes lived on one third of the state and would not be dislodged. The Utes, unlike the often-troublesome Plains tribes, abided by the law and the treaty terms that had established their reservation. However, that delicate peace would be shattered with the arrival of Indian agent Nathan C. Meeker on May 15, 1878. The conflict with Meeker is the painful turning point in Ute-white relations, and it is described in detail in Robert Emmitt's *The Last War Trail*.

The Last War Trail: The Utes and the Settlement of Colorado is a richly researched, deeply felt book that portrays Ute life from an insider's perspective based on valuable interviews the author conducted near Whiterocks, Utah in the late 1940s. Omer C. Stewart, in his *American Anthropologist* review of *The Last War Trail*, wrote that "Old White River Ute informants may have given Emmitt some additional facts about the Massacre and War. Saponise Cuch, who served as informant, participated in the battle as a boy of fifteen." Just as Black Elk supposedly said to poet John Neihardt who wrote *Black Elk Speaks*, "I have known you were coming. Why have you taken so long?" In August 1948, Saponise Cuch, Chief of the White River Utes, said to Robert Emmitt, "I am an old man now, and I am the only one left who remembers this. I have known that someone would come to tell this story; now you will write it out, as I have told it to you."

Originally published by the University of Oklahoma Press in 1954, *The Last War Trail* is based on careful research, a fine writing style, and a sensitivity not only to historical documents but also to Ute oral traditions and storytelling. The book is a marvelous blend of primary source materials such as letters and telegrams from Secretary of Interior Carl Schurz, Indian Commissioner Edward A. Hayt, Indian Agent Nathan Meeker, and Major Thomas Tipton Thornburgh. Robert Emmitt catches the flavor of the Ute language and makes judicious use of Ute words such as *maricat'z* (whites), *tawacz viem* (chief), and Ute place names such as Smoking Earth River for what is now known as the White River.

The Last War Trail describes western Colorado as a living land for the Ute people, "a life where the good play of the hunt brought food, and the pleasure of the dance brought a man a wife, a woman a husband; a life where a man owned little and belonged to everything." With skill he refined as a former newspaperman and university press editor, Robert Emmitt crafted an ethnographic portrait of a people caught between cultural values. Unlike so many descriptions of Indian-white conflicts, Emmitt writes eloquently and subjectively from the Native American perspective in a contemporary non-fiction style.

LeRoy R. Hafen, reviewing *The Last War Trail* in the *American Historical Review*, explained that Emmitt "presents an incident or a phase of the story from the documents, then tells it from the Ute point of view and in picturesque Indian language and figures of speech. By daring to express the thoughts of the Indian actors and supplying imaginary conversation, the author gives a dramatic and effective portrayal." Robert Athearn in the *Pacific Historical Review* noted that "Emmitt's major contribution here is not that he has introduced new evidence or added much to the familiar story of Ute removal, but that he has presented the Indian's point of view in a manner that is moving and forceful." Stanley Vestal wrote, "it is refreshing to find a serious, scholarly and readable historian who takes no stock in the old myth that Indian testimony is necessarily unreliable."

Robert Emmitt attended the University of Colorado, and worked for the Boulder *Daily Camera*. He also worked for the New York *Herald Tribune*, which was founded by Horace Greeley, who also funded Nathan Meeker's Western dreams. Emmitt also reported for the Toronto *Telegram* and the Tucson *Citizen* before becoming managing editor of Vanderbilt University Press in Nashville. He authored several books, and once wrote that he was "concerned with the total condition of estrangement, and, as an American historian, with the problem of man's estrangement from his natural environment."

Emmitt died in Colorado in 1984, but his legacy will live on with this reprint of *The Last War Trail*. In the book he clearly shares the Utes' love and respect for their land and language, which Emmitt says "flows like a smooth, deep river." His descriptions of the Bear Dance and other Ute traditions are in concise, careful prose, and he also describes in detail the political tenor of late nineteenth century Colorado. He explains Governor Pitkin's view that the Utes were "paralyzing the progress of a great new state," and he demonstrates Nathan Meeker's harsh assimilationist policies by quoting the Indian Agent's proposal "to cut every Indian to [a] bare starvation point if he will not work." In another letter the sanctimonious Meeker writes, "A savage can have no notion of the value of knowing many things. Besides, the savage family has no discipline, and the children are neither heirs nor successors of it. The only discipline exercised at this agency is when I get the men to work day after day; and this on the penalty of withholding extra rations . . . [but] with plenty of coffee, sugar, and dried peaches I can lead them forward to civilization."

The Utes killed Meeker on September 29, 1879, for his inability to understand the Indian people he was supposed to represent. They drove a barrel stave through his throat so in the afterlife he could not tell lies. Seven other agency men and three nearby whites died, three women and two children were taken hostage, and thirteen soldiers were killed in a chain of events which forced the Utes from their homeland in the Shining Mountains and into a new life on the high desert of eastern Utah.[11]

Three years after the publication of *The Last War Trail*, another journalist/historian, Marshall Sprague, wrote about the incident in his 1957 book *Massacre: The Tragedy at White River* (reprint 1980, University of Nebraska Press). Sprague's work is more of a conventional Western history, and it lacks Emmitt's richly textured attention to Indian detail, though Sprague did add valuable insight into a major source of Ute dislike of Meeker. Previous Indian agents had helped the Utes profit from trade in furs, hides, and horns. J. S. Littlefield, agent between 1871-1874, not satisfied with his monthly salary of $125, "doubled and tripled it by serving as commission man for the White River groups.

Several times a year his Indian Bureau wagons arrived at the
U.P. freight station in Rawlins with five or six tons of elk and
deer hide, antlers, and bones, which he auctioned to Omaha and
Chicago buyers."[12] The Utes made money and so did their agent,
but Meeker would have none of it. He was there to teach the
Indians to become farmers.

Recent scholarship on the Meeker killing and Major
Thornburgh's attempt to come to Meeker's rescue includes a
detailed analysis of the military's movements in *Hollow Victory:
The White River Expedition of 1879 and the Battle of Milk Creek*
(University Press of Colorado, 1997). The author, Wyoming State
Archaeologist Mark Miller, writes about the military actions of
Major Thornburgh and troops sent from Fort Steele, Wyoming,
at the request of Nathan Meeker, whose intransigence caused
him to fear for his life. *Hollow Victory* demonstrates excellent
research and writing from an archaeological perspective, but it
is interesting to note that both Emmitt in 1954 and Miller in
1997 failed to grasp an understanding of Major Thornburgh's
personality as advanced by Mari Sandoz in her review of *The
Last War Trail.*

She wrote that "although he has worked deep into Ute history, Mr. Emmitt does not seem to realize that the Ute troubles
were part of a general protest against the starvation and removal
policy of the government, including the Nez Perce flight in 1877
and those of the Poncas and the Northern Cheyennes in 1878.
Thornburgh had to bear much criticism for his failure to capture the Cheyennes, although he had made a real effort. . . .
[L]ess than a year later, he was faced with the Ute problem and
he was determined that this time there would be no charge of
hesitation. So he moved in swiftly and died a hero, and with him
the agent and others."[13] Perhaps future historians will delve more
deeply into Thornburgh's career and motivations.

Thornburgh's death came because of deep-seated Ute fears
of soldiers invading their villages and what the "blue coats"
would do to Indian women. The Utes probably knew what had
happened at Bear River, Idaho, where in 1862 General Patrick

E. Connor attacked a sleeping Shoshone village and killed over 400 people. The Northern Utes also knew of Col. John M. Chivington's November 1864 attack at Sand Creek, where Black Kettle's Cheyenne village had been surprised at dawn and over 200 men, women and children were killed. The Utes must have known that at the Sand Creek Massacre Chivington's soldiers hacked off women's breasts, cut out their vaginas, scalped them, and displayed the bloody trophies on stage at the Denver Opera House.[14]

Some of the Utes including Nicaagat, also known as Captain Jack, had worked as scouts for General Crook during the Sioux Wars and knew full well what might happen if soldiers entered the reservation. When Thornburgh's troops tried to advance across Milk Creek, Utes perceived it as an invasion of their reservation and an act of war. According to Saponise Cuch, a small group of fifty Utes kept the army from advancing. All of the details and nuances of this tragedy are laid out in *The Last War Trail* in a masterful and sympathetic retelling of a complicated tale.

Though it has been more than a century, the events of the Thornburgh battle and killings at the White River Agency happened as if they were yesterday for the descendants of the Northern Utes living on the Uintah and Ouray Reservation in eastern Utah, and the pain and isolation of removal is acutely felt. The Utes want other Americans to know that Indian Agent Nathan Meeker had threatened them, lied to them, withheld food, provisions and annuities from them, and thoroughly misunderstood their culture and their ways. The 1868 treaty provisions included the stipulation, insisted upon by the Utes, that "The United States now solemnly agree(s) that no person except those employes (sic) of the Government as may be authorized by law, shall ever be permitted to pass over, settle upon, or reside in the territory." As far as the Utes were concerned, this included the United States military, which had violated its own treaty by attempting to enter reservation land without Ute consent.

Over the decades, the historic sites described in *The Last War Trail* have been altered. Only a few stone buildings remain at what once was Fort Steele, from which Major Thornburgh's troops rode out. At Powell Bottoms, where Nathan Meeker ignored the Ute discomfort that had earlier convinced John Wesley Powell to pull up his surveying stakes, irrigated alfalfa grows, just as Meeker wanted. He paid for his stubbornness with his life, and today a highway sign points south to where his agency burned.

At the Thornburgh battle site a granite monument lists the names of soldiers killed, but a new marker tells the story from a different perspective. The etched metal tablet reads:

Dedicated to the Ute Indians Who Were
Involved in the Battle of Milk Creek
Ute Indian Tribes of Utah
29 September 1879

Let us not forget the Whiteriver Utes who gave their lives and those who were wounded in the battle of Milk Creek on September 29, 1879. Nathan Meeker, Indian Agent, did not understand the Utes and knew very little about their traditions and culture. Resentment toward Meeker's policy of farming resulted in a fight between "Johnson," a Ute, and Agent Meeker. This was the beginning of the problems that ensued. Because of the battles at Whiteriver and Meeker, Colorado, the Whiterivers and Uncomphagres were forced by gun-point to the reservation in Utah, leaving behind their beautiful land in Colorado. However, the Uncompahgres had nothing to do with those events. Under the 14th amendment, their rights were ignored.

Ute Tribal Business Committee
Uintah & Ouray Meeker Monument Committee
Title V Parent Advisory Committee
Colorado Historical Society
Uintah School District
29 September 1993

Though Northern Utes lost their lands in Colorado, they returned to the high country to hunt, and they continued to gather deer and elk skins as they had for centuries. Eventually, though, Colorado game laws resulted in an end to their hide trade. At the turn of the century, game wardens tried to prosecute Ute Indians for violating the law. Interestingly, in 1901 a jury in Meeker, Colorado, refused to convict their Native American neighbors.[15]

Today Utes in Utah, whose ancestors lived in the Shining Mountains, are several hours away by car, but they return as often as they can. Like many tribes, the Northern Utes have established a cultural rights and protections office. Even though they have lost possession of their mountain lands, Ute cultural and spiritual leaders can have a say in forest management. Under federal laws including the National Historic Preservation Act (1966, amended 1992); the Archaeological Resources and Protection Act (1979, amended 1989); the Native American Graves Protection and Repatriation Act (1990); and Presidential Executive Order 13007 Protecting Native American Sacred Sites (1996), the Utes assert influence over forest management policies, particularly as those policies affect sacred sites near the prehistoric and historic Ute Indian trail, which is remarkably intact along a fifty-seven-mile corridor from the confluence of the Eagle and Colorado Rivers at Dotsero, northwest to the original Ute Agency on the White River.

The Ute Trail at one point ascends 4,000 feet over ten miles, providing spectacular views of the Colorado River Valley and rows of snow-capped peaks.[16] The fifty-seven mile route goes up and over the Flat Tops, a beautiful 10,000-foot mountain range with lush meadows, high peaks, and numerous lakes, creeks, and canyons. Though perhaps three-fourths of the trail has been discovered, its exact location will always remain a mystery, and there are many research riddles that will never be solved. Some sacred sites close to the trail have been identified, while others will probably remain unknown and hopefully undisturbed.[17] Few other Indian trails in the central Rocky Mountains are in such pristine condition and present such an opportunity for a part-nership in preservation involving the three Ute tribes, the United States Forest Service, the Bureau of Land Management, and private landowners.

Understanding the trail and migratory patterns of the Ute Indians requires stepping back in time half a millennium. Walking the trail today represents a unique wilderness experience – in places the trail widens to almost three miles and then funnels down to narrow thirty-yard passageways between ecotones, where open meadows and small aspen groves give way to thick, dark spruce. From a hundred yards away, the trail is invisible until the opening in the forest is discovered.

A key to finding and identifying the Ute Trail is to think about the forest as excellent summer range for small bands of Ute families who came to the Flat Tops from the south up the Roaring Fork River Valley and from Utah to the west from the Uintah and Piceance Creek Basins.[18] These close-knit family bands came to hunt, fish, gather berries and seeds, collect eagle feathers, and worship in the high mountain meadows and among the tall stands of Englemann spruce.[19] Ute use of the forest was part of an age-old rhythmic cycle that began in the spring and ended around the first of November, when early snows closed off the high country. The Utes used the lush mountain meadows in the summer and then descended in the winter to the warmer basin and plateau country of 5,000 feet in elevation.

In the final chapter of *The Last War Trail*, Robert Emmitt writes, "The Land is the body; the People are the spirit. When the Land and the People are cut apart, this is death." But now there is a re-birth as a younger Ute generation seeks to know the ancient homeland of its ancestors and to re-establish ties to the land and the landscape that was theirs centuries before the white man came. Betsy Chapoose and Clifford Duncan of the Northern Utes work with other tribal members, including Kenny Frost of the Southern Utes, to help preserve and protect Ute sacred sites.[20]

This recent edition of *The Last War Trail* includes an afterword by Charles Wilkinson, the Moses Lasky Professor of Law at the University of Colorado at Boulder. An expert on Indian legal issues, Wilkinson wrote about Nicaagat, or "Captain Jack," in a chapter titled "The Betrayal of Jack," for *Heart of the Land*, a volume on unique American ecosystems published by the Nature Conservancy. Wilkinson writes about the Ferry Carpenter Ranch's Morgan Bottoms on the Yampa River just east of Hayden, Colorado, which is traditional Ute land now owned by the Nature Conservancy. Professor Wilkinson writes movingly about the Ute troubles on the White River, and he does so in a modern environmental context. He concludes that "Betrayals, and all the lasting things that we learn from them, die out when our memories die. This is why the forceful but careful and restrained, even gentle reminders from the modern Utes matter so."

Emmitt ends *The Last War Trail* with a manuscript excerpt by Captain James Parker of the Fourth Cavalry, who in March of 1880 helped force Utes out of Colorado by gunpoint. Parker wrote, "As we pushed the Indians onward, we permitted the whites to follow, and in three days the rich lands of the Uncompahgre were all occupied, towns were being laid out and lots being sold at high prices." On the Colorado, White, and Yampa Rivers the process took longer, but settlement continued in mountain valleys until the land was set aside by President Harrison as the White River Forest Reserve in 1891, which is the second oldest in the nation after the Yellowstone Forest Reserve.

Arthur Carhart, a young U.S. Forest Service landscape architect, came to the head of the White River in the summer of 1917 to survey Trapper's Lake for cabin sites to be leased to summer vacationers. Struck by the beauty and solitude of the lake, Arthur Carhart had difficulty planning to carve up the lake shore into cabin sites. One evening at twilight as he left a cook tent and a conversation with visiting fishermen, Carhart recalled, "The hushed stillness of a late summer day in the mountains filled the cliff girt basin holding [the] placid waters of

Trappers Lake. The lake's surface reflected upside down images of surrounding spruce trees and of serrated rimrock standing in multicolored high-rise masses above the forest."

He wrote, "Here, as I loafed along the trail, was a place, a moment, when one could explore his thoughts. Suddenly a strange sibilance filled the basin. I halted, I listened. The soft eerie whispers came clearly through the sun drenched air. I glanced in all directions, hoping to discover their source. I failed."

"Silence returned quickly."

"Abruptly the strange sound returned, increased, dimmed, and in a moment was gone."[21]

Arthur Carhart had experienced a moment of revelation and realized that the shoreline of Trapper's Lake, considered sacred for centuries by Utes, should not be marred by tourist cabins. Prior to that time no U.S. Forest Service official had conceived of leaving land in its natural state because the credo of the forest service was one of multiple use. The concept of protecting wilderness areas in national forests was born on ancient Ute lands. Contemporary Ute spiritual leaders would argue that Indian guardian spirits had spoken directly to Carhart, and because of the spirits' soft voices Trapper's Lake is now known as the cradle of the American wilderness movement. Trapper's Lake, on sacred Ute lands, inspired the concept of wilderness – land without roads or development in which humans will always be visitors, never permanent residents.

At the end of his life Carhart wrote, "As I have looked back along many trails, I recognize that incident at Trapper's Lake was in truth a moment when I stepped across a threshold. I discovered true wilderness and reached the conviction that without the sanctuary found in our wildlands, without the experience of living as a part of it, this nation might perish from the earth."[22] Arthur Carhart may have heard Ute spirits at the water's edge of Trapper's Lake. Carhart's wilderness insight born of "a strange sibilance" and "soft eerie whispers" began a conservation movement which has helped to set aside millions of acres of wild land across America. He wrote to his supervisors in 1919 about special pristine places on public land "that should be preserved for all time for people of the nation and the world."

Arthur Carhart received his inspiration at Trapper's Lake, and the famous conservationist Aldo Leopold, after meeting Carhart in the office of the regional forester in Denver, adopted the wilderness ethic in 1924 and set aside the first wilderness area in the nation in the Gila National Forest of New Mexico. In 1964 Congress passed the Wilderness Act, which established special sanctuaries for native plants and animals and required high standards for clean air and water. In 1975, Trapper's Lake itself and 196,360 acres of the Flat Tops Mountains became congressionally designated federal wilderness areas with access only by foot or on horseback.

Like Carhart, we have much to learn from the Utes about their ancestral homelands. *The Last War Trail* puts into poignant perspective how Colorado's original inhabitants came to be displaced by confusion, arrogance, and misguided attempts to force farming upon a people who already lived in balance with their natural world. Charles Wilkinson writes, "We know now that we came on too hard and fast for the Utes. We could have accommodated settlement by non-Indians and also allowed for the Northern Utes to hold good land in the Yampa and White country. We could have allowed for the hunt."

Historian Patricia Limerick writes, "There is no clearer fact in American history than the fact of conquest. The land was occupied by native peoples; whites entered as invaders; as soon as the whites wanted permanent possession of the land, they drove the Indians from their homes, sometimes with treaties and negotiations, oftentimes with pure force." Limerick challenges us by stating, "Americans ought to know what acts of violence brought them their right to own land, build homes, use resources, and travel freely in North America. Americans ought to know what happened on the ground they stand on; they surely have some obligations to know where they are."[23]

Unlike so much that has been written about Native Americans and their dispossession, Robert Emmitt's *The Last War Trail*

tells about life in the high country from the Ute perspective. No
other book so clearly spells out the contradictions and cultural
conflicts which drove the Utes from western Colorado. By holding on as long as they did, by living deep within their Shining
Mountains, they helped to preserve their forest landscape. A
modern conservation movement had begun in the east, and ten
years after the Utes' forced removal, President Harrison set aside
1.2 million acres of what would become the 2.5 million acre White
River National Forest.

A century later, the Flat Tops Mountains still shine in the
sun with thick blankets of winter snow as late as May, and one of
the largest elk herds in North America still lives between the
Colorado and White rivers. In summer the high alpine meadows are ablaze with purple, yellow, red, and blue wildflowers,
and trout jump in numerous creeks like Elk Creek, Deep Creek,
Grizzly Creek and the South Fork of the White River. No wonder the Utes were baffled by Nathan Meeker's attempts to make
them farmers. No wonder they fired upon Thornburgh's troops.

We owe the Utes a great debt for protecting the high country
as long as they did. In 1993, when Ute Indians returned to the
Milk Creek battle site to erect their monument, citizens of
Meeker, Colorado, the town that had grown up near the second
Ute Indian Agency, invited tribal members to a banquet as an
offering of peace. The rest of us should welcome the Utes back,
too. *The Last War Trail* is part of that welcome, because the University Press of Colorado seeks to share Ute culture and history
with a new generation of readers who will find Robert Emmitt's
eloquence a vivid account of a tragic event in Western history.

NOTES

1. P. David Smith, *Ouray: Chief of the Utes* (Ridgway, Colorado:
   Wayfinder Press, 1986), 62.
2. Thomas K. Cree, "Report of the Commission Appointed
   Under Act of Congress Approved April 23, 1873 to Negotiate
   with the Ute Indians in Colorado Territory" (Washington: Government Printing Office, 1873), 5. See Charles S. Marsh, *People of*

the Shining Mountains (Boulder: Pruett Press, 1982),67-68, Smith, *Ouray: Chief of the Utes,* 72-78, and Robert W. Delaney, *Ute Mountain Utes* (University of New Mexico Press, 1989), 33. In 1868, the tribe had approximately 16 million acres, but with the Brunot Cession of 1873, they lost 4 million acres for a total of 12 million acres in 1876.

3. Population statistics are from Cree, "Report of the 1873 Commission." The commission noted on page 6, "The number of Indians occupying the same (reservation) is relatively small, not exceeding, according to the most reliable data obtainable, more than four or five thousand souls." Also see Marsh, p. 24 and p. 68. The exact population of the Utes at any one time is very hard to determine, because bands moved from place to place throughout Western Colorado. A September 1878 census of the Yampa and Grand River Utes proved that all groups visited north to south and frequented the White River Agency. Though sizable numbers of Utes lived in the Uintah Basin of northeast Utah after 1820, the population of Colorado Utes probably varied from 4,000-6,000. For various historical accounts see Julian H. Steward, *Aboriginal and Historical Groups of the Ute Indians of Utah: An Analysis with Supplement, Indian Claims Commission* (New York: Garland Publishing, 1974). In 1879 the Ute population is reported as 2,000 at the Los Pinos Agency, 1,307 at the Southern Agency and 900 at the White River Agency. See *46th Congress, 3rd Session, Executive Document No. 31, U.S. Secretary of the Interior, Report of the Ute Commission, 1881,* 18.

4. Marshall Sprague, *Massacre: The Tragedy at White River* (Lincoln: University of Nebraska Press, 1980), 90-92.

5. Marsh, *People of the Shining Mountains,* 64 and 68.

6. John Wesley Powell, *The Exploration of the Colorado River and Its Canyons* (New York: Dover reprint, 1961, originally 1895).

7. Wallace Stegner, *Beyond the Hundredth Meridian: John Wesley Powell and the Second Opening of the West* (Lincoln: University of Nebraska Press, 1982), 39-40. Though originally published in 1953, this remains the definitive historical treatment of Powell and his immense contributions.

8. For an excellent analysis of Powell and his many scientific contributions, including the work of his photographers, see Don D. Fowler, *Myself in the Water: The Western Photographs of John K. Hillers* (Washington, D.C.: Smithsonian Institution Press, 1982).

This writer has seen Ute materials in the collections of the Smithsonian's National Museum of Natural History originally collected by both Powell and Capt. Gunnison. This beadwork still has original accession tags written by both men.

9. Though the Ute reservation had been established with the treaty of 1868 and reaffirmed with the treaty of 1873 and the Brunot "Map of Colorado Territory," which delineated the "proposed purchase," the actual Ute boundaries had not been surveyed. They existed on the map only as land stretching east to west from 107 to 109 degrees longitude and from 37 degrees to 41 degrees north latitude.

10. Cree, "Report of the 1873 Commission",19. The report would be published as F.V. Hayden, *Tenth Annual Report of the United States Geological and Geographical Survey of the Territories Embracing Colorado and Parts of Adjacent Territories* (Washington, D.C.: U.S. Government Printing Office, 1878).

11. That new life included farming. See the section on the Northern Utes in David Rich Lewis, *Neither Wolf Nor Dog: American Indians, Environment & Agrarian Change* (New York: Oxford University Press, 1994).

12. Sprague, *Massacre*, 117.

13. Mari Sandoz's review of *The Last War Trail* was syndicated and appeared in many newspapers. The year before, in 1953, she had published *Cheyenne Autumn*, which has several pages in the index that specifically refer to Thornburgh chasing the Cheyennes.

14. Robert M. Utley, *The Indian Frontier of the American West 1846-1890* (Albuquerque: University of New Mexico Press, 1984), 92-93. Helen Hunt Jackson wrote *A Century of Dishonor* in 1881 deploring the government's disregard for its treaty obligations. In the appendix pp.343-358 she reprints letters published in the *New York Tribune* in 1879 which are an exchange of commentaries between herself and William Byers, editor of the *Rocky Mountain News*, on the Sand Creek Massacre and the killings on the White River. She complains that the errors of a few have brought starvation to many Utes. Helen Hunt Jackson explains that the Utes "attempted by force of arms, to restrain the entrance upon their own lands–lands bought, owned and paid for–of soldiers that the Government had sent there, to be ready to make war upon them, in case the agent thought it best to do so! . . . And

now the Secretary of the Interior has stopped the issue of rations to 1,000 of these helpless creatures; rations, be it understood, which are not, and never were, a charity, but are the Utes' rightful dues, on account of lands by them sold; dues which the Government promised to pay 'annually forever.'"

15. George Feltner, *A Look Back: A 75-Year History of the Colorado Game, Fish and Parks Division* (Denver: Colorado Game, Fish & Parks, 1972), 14.

16. Surveyors, miners, settlers, and cowboys all referred to the trail as the Old Ute Trail. Marshall Sprague in *Massacre: The Tragedy at White River* also calls it "the Back White River Trail" on p. 162. Lena M. Urquhart in *The Cold Snows of Carbonate* on page 1 explains that prospectors "came from Leadville down the Eagle River to where it joined with the Grand (since named the Colorado River). Here they left the valley to follow the age-old Ute Indian Trail which climbed out onto the Flat Tops, then crested the divide between the White and Colorado Rivers." She continues "all along that Ute Indian Trail men continued to come prospecting" p. 3. Because low grade silver was discovered at Carbonate, the trail became known as The Carbonate Trail.

17. Sacred sites in the area and their locations are classified and protected under provisions of the National Historic Preservation Act as amended in 1992. Staff archaeologists for the White River National Forest consider that information to be Ute intellectual property. For a general overview of contemporary Indian attitudes towards preserving their sacred landscapes, see Andrew Gulliford, *Sacred Objects and Sacred Places: Preserving Tribal Traditions* (University Press of Colorado, 2000).

18. See Steward, *Aboriginal and Historical Groups of the Ute Indians of Utah* and Floyd A. O'Neil and John D. Sylvester, eds. *Ute People: An Historical Study* (Salt Lake City: University of Utah, 1970).

19. See Charles S. Marsh, *People of the Shining Mountains* (Boulder: Pruett Publishing, 1982) and Jan Petit, *Utes: The Mountain People* (Boulder: Johnson Books, 1990). For an excellent look at Ute oral tradition see Anne M. Smith, *Ute Tales* (Salt Lake City: University of Utah Press, 1992).

20. See Jon Klusmire, "Ute Indians return to their homeland," *High Country News,* May 17, 1993. Extensive coverage of Ute research into their sacred sites, done in connection with Heritage Resources Manager Bill Kight of the White River National Forest,

has been described by Nan Johnson of the Glenwood Springs, Colorado *Glenwood Post.* See Nan Johnson, "On the Ute Trail: History is being preserved," *Glenwood Post,* August 30, 1989; "In search of . . . the Ute Trail," *Glenwood Post,* September 3, 1993; and "In the cradle of the wilderness," *Glenwood Post,* August 22, 1997.

21. Arthur Carhart Papers, Series 2, Manuscripts, Box 2:100; Folder 2 biography "This Way to Wilderness," p. 65-66. Western History/Genealogy, Denver Public Library, Conservation Collection.

22. Ibid.

23. Patricia Limerick "Haunted America," in Drex Brooks, *Sweet Medicine: Sites of Indian Massacres, Battlefields, and Treaties* (Albuquerque: University of New Mexico Press, 1995), 120 and 125.

THE LAST WAR TRAIL

I am an old man now, and I am the only one left who remembers this. I have known that someone would come to tell this story; now you will write it out, as I have told it to you.

SAPONISE CUCH
(Chief of the
White River Utes)

White Rocks, Utah
Uintah and Ouray Ute
  Indian Reservation
August, 1948

1. THE PEOPLE

DEEP in the Rocky Mountains of western Colorado, a long time ago, there lived a nation of laughing people who called themselves *Nünt'z*, "the People." They were the Utes, and they named their country the Shining Mountains.

The country of the Shining Mountains was a great, living land: a tumbling, climbing country that sloped downward from the rock and wind-powdered snow, its lifting and heaving back thick coated with forest; a green country sparkling with lakes and rivers sloping gently down to the brush and high desert, beyond the long reach of the snow. It was a country constantly seeping out life like threads of water from the melting white meadows—forests filled with deer, bear, elk; antelope bunched in the open country below the forests; long-haired, shaggy buffalo grazing half-buried in the grass of the high parks, bringing meat, clothes, and warm walls to wrap around new-cut saplings to make homes.

For the People, it was a life with little hunger and want, where play and humor were taught to smother pain, sickness, and death; a life where the good play of the hunt brought food, and the pleasure of the dance brought a man a wife, a woman a husband; a life where a man owned little and belonged to everything.

For as long as anyone could remember, the People had lived in the mountains. They went down to the plains to hunt buffalo or to steal from their enemies, the Cheyenne and Sioux, but they always returned quickly to their high peaks. Sometimes other

3

people came to live for a while in the mountains, but they did not love the land and they did not stay. Then one day a new people, the white man, came across the plains into the mountains, and they did not go away.

In the year 1858 the nation was recovering from a panic. For more than two years people had been watching and listening for something to come out of the West, for it was from that direction, in times of crisis, that the right word usually came. The word was sounded: "Pikes Peak!" It was the name of a mountain which poked its head up out of the Great American Desert, far out across the big rivers. In a way, it could be said that the name of Pikes Peak, repeated over and over again in print, on the streets, and in the places where workless men loaf and hope, was a sort of invocation that whisked away hard times.

Panic was only part of it: the ebb and flow of luck and ambition, as regular in the days of an expanding America as the changing of the moon. With it came long doses of humility, until a man became first drugged, then drunk on it. Good and drunk, he needed to holler. He was given the word "Pikes Peak" and he hollered it.

They were good and jolly men, the hosts who threw the spree that ended the Panic of '57 and '58. They knew the right places to go and the right things to say. They had learned it all back in 1849. Not that most of them had ever been to California; but what had been learned in '49 could be applied in '59, and the two important principles were these: first, you don't need gold to make a gold rush, and second, the ones who get the gold aren't usually the ones who dig and pan.

They printed their invitations in the newspapers.

First came the information about the Russell Party, who brought back sacks of gold they had picked up out that way. That was in the fall of 1858, and shortly afterward came more stories.

Some told of Pikes Peak itself: a massive mountain of solid gold where men built bobsleds with knife-edged runners, which they pulled to the top of the slope then took a joyous ride to

the bottom to shovel up the gold shavings peeled off by the sled runners.

Other stories were more conservative, telling only about lumps of gold that lay around on the ground out there, mostly no larger than hens' eggs but worth the while of an industrious man with a shovel and cart.

Those who read the first stories in the papers thought and waited, but the men who had fitted the stories to print were busy. That fall some of them went far out to the abrupt end of the plains where Kansas Territory, rolling, brown, and treeless, bent upward; where the mountains and deserts of Utah Territory began. About twelve miles from the high western wall of the Rocky Mountains they found a little creek, lined with a grove of cottonwoods, and off the hot, dry plains they crept into the shade and laid out a city with stakes and string. Some of them crossed to the other bank of the creek and laid out an-

5

other city. One they called Aurora for the shining lure, and the other they named Denver after the Governor of Kansas Territory.

Then, with winter about to blow out of the mountains, they went home to Chicago and Omaha and all the established, comfortable cities, leaving the uninhabited towns to sleep under the cottonwoods and wait out the winter, for spring to bring their budding.

Throughout the winter such men as D. C. Oakes, of Kansas City, and William N. Byers, of Omaha, kept the presses busy. The stories took a practical turn: where to go, how to get there, what to take, where to buy it; and the nation, still deep in hard times, was believing in gold, thinking about Pikes Peak.

With the first thaws of spring the invasion drove forward again. Spring wagons, hand carts, wheelbarrows, horses, mules, oxen, dogs, chickens, children, they streamed out: up the river, down the river, across the river, they flooded Leavenworth and St. Louis. They fought and argued, bought and paid for, lost and stole. Stores at the jumping off places offered practical guide books to the gold fields with maps showing the shortest route and lists of necessary equipment. One was written by D. C. Oakes, recommending the southern route through Kansas; the other, by W. N. Byers, suggested the Platte River trail, through Nebraska Territory. Merchants on both routes enjoyed a brisk trade.

A solid river of people flowed across the brown, rolling plains. They came to the barrier of the Rockies and the cities planted in the shade beside Cherry Creek, without buildings or inhabitants; and in the middle of the Great American Desert, owned by no man, they bought town lots. They built shacks with dirt floors and made trips to the tent stores to buy food and whisky at exorbitant prices.

Then they went out to look for gold and they found none.

Wild enthusiasm turned to dull, drumming anger. The immigrants left their newly-purchased real estate under the cottonwoods and their money in the pockets of the city-builders and began the retreat across the brown short grass.

The river of invaders had turned; it flowed eastward. Along

the trail, on a lone tree, hung a rag-stuffed suit marked with a bitter epitaph:

> *Here lies the body of D. C. Oakes,*
> *Who was the starter of this damn hoax.*

But a trickle of the optimistic or desperate still pushed westward, into the mountains, up a canyon where white water boiled over the rocks. They shoveled at the creek beds with their pans until the clear water sparkled with clouds of sand. They swung their picks against the quartz rock until the canyon floors and walls were pitted with test diggings. Early summer warmed the mountain air and they worked on. Tents and sluice boxes sprouted along the banks. The nameless creeks were known by the names they were to bear from that time on: Clear Creek, Chicago Creek. Tents became shacks, shacks became towns: Payne's Bar, Mountain City, Blackhawk, Nevada City. The river flowing east across the plains turned and flowed west again, swelling, rising by the minute.

They had found gold; they had really found it! The architects of the gold rush were amazed.

Among the scattering of tents and shacks that was called

Denver, William Byers took a deep breath then moved his printing press into a log building standing on thin stilts over the creek and founded a newspaper. He printed it on brown wrapping paper and called it the *Rocky Mountain News*.

Now there were logs where there had been canvas, and from the new city on the plains the gold civilization spread like a fan to the west, into the wild summer of the mountains. There were new names: Boulder City, Colorado City, Silver Plume, Breckenridge, Georgetown, Oro City. The snow came and covered everything, ten feet deep. Then spring and mud and white water, and the clear pools of the mountain streams were foul with bitter gray tailings, while the stamp mills thumped through the night.

Out of the western end of Kansas Territory and the eastern part of Utah Territory a new political entity was carved. It was a huge rectangle, humped down the middle by the snaky ridgepole of the Continental Divide. At first its new citizens called it Jefferson Territory; but when the territorial charter was issued in 1860, it was in the name of Colorado.

Gold turned to silver and the streams of prospectors pushed on across the snow and rock tundra of the Divide. Denver gathered in the goods rolling on tarp-covered wagons from the east and performed the lucrative duty of distributing them to the men who lived with the gold and silver. The fever burrowed deeper into the mountains, and Denver fattened like a well-fed scion. Its transplanted citizens grew homesick and hungry for traditions and moods of the older cities of the East: and since they were ambitious they studied short cuts to maturity. Soon Denver became a city of diamond stickpins, opera capes, and finger bowls.

The scourings of the mining camps mingled with the tall, respectable hats on the streets, and the blanketed Indians who moved among them were a vivid reminder of the roots of prairie grass hardly dry under the foundations of the new buildings.

The Indians were the proud, good-humored people who lived deep in the Rocky Mountains. They came to Denver to watch in amusement the frantic scrambling of the white men, to trade a little at the stores and taste lightly of the strange and intriguing new civilization, and to gather in the presents that were often there for them from Washington.

They were the Utes, and their country was the splendid and forbidding wilderness of peaks which they called the Shining Mountains. The invasion of the white men had flowed around them. For many years the Indians of the plains had fought it, and by the time Denver had become a maturing city their war was all but lost; but the Utes lived apart in their mountains, took what they wanted from the white man and saw little of the rest. They had not yet met him as the enemy.

In 1876 Colorado became a state. Civilization-conscious Denver was anxious to remove the Indians from its streets and public places. The agency which distributed goods from Washington to the Utes was taken away from Denver, and agencies were established on the Ute Reservation, which filled most of the western half of the state.

The invasion, the sprouting of the white man's civilization which now surrounded the Ute country had been too rapid. The Utes did not know that a line had been drawn around them, nor were they conscious of another line, which had been crossed when the presents given them twice a year by Washington had become necessities—when the curiosity and pleasure found in the white man's stores had become need.

After 1876 they seldom went to Denver. They settled back into their Shining Mountains, ignoring as well as they could the changes which had crept into their old life. Even now, their great, silent country still lay west of the invasion. But on the Eastern Slope, the Colorado settlers and miners were watching the Utes and thinking of the fertile, mineral-rich land in the Shining Mountains. Unmindful of the watchful eyes and the threat that was building up around them as 1877 came to a close, the Utes were thinking of the white man only in terms of the rations from Washington which they now relied on to help carry them through the harsh winter.

2. THE NATION

I T WAS a winter of cold, hunger, and waiting, and it was only beginning. There had never before been such a winter, even in the words of the oldest stories.

In many other years, within the memory of those living and the stories of those dead, the snow moons had brought cold, hunger, and sickness, and there had been waiting—waiting for the first thunder, when the land wakes and shakes off the snow like old blankets.

But this winter the cold and hunger had come to them earlier, and sickness paced silently, fearsomely among them, never once leaving.

And the waiting itself was something different. The waiting was given to them in the form of a word not known to the old stories or the memories of the Old People—Washington.

On the trail to the north the Shining Mountains sank slowly into the brush-covered hills, and the hills sank into the rolling prairies of the buffalo country. Often during the summer moons, and sometimes during the First Fall Moon, hunting parties would take that trail for buffalo hunts. But this was now the middle of the Last Fall Moon, and the snow was already flying down from the tall standing mountains far on the other side of the buffalo prairies, and the prairies themselves were empty and white, and the trees stood like dead sticks stuck upright in the snow along the two rivers of the buffalo country of the north.

It was no time of the year for the *Nüpartka*, that band of the

People who lived in the country of Smoking Earth River, to be traveling with their families to the buffalo country; but it was the only thing left to do.

At that time when bright color pushed the summer green from the tiny leaves of the quaking aspens, when the leaves of the cottonwoods showed a dip of yellow on their tips and the sweet nuts were falling to the ground under the low brush forest, the People had come from all corners of their land, pack ponies heavy from the late hunts and the trading at the stores, to gather around the agency on Smoking Earth River, their *carniva* growing up along the river like a grove of trees. They went to the agency, as they had done every year during the three years since the agency had been put in their country by Washington, to receive those presents which Washington had given them each fall. The women waited there, as they had waited throughout the summer for the food which Washington had promised to give them every month; but the agent, a man with good eyes who always talked with one mouth, could only tell them every day that Washington had sent them nothing. The presents, like the food rations, had never come to the agency, and all the words the agent had sent to Washington had done no good.

Not many snows ago, in a time remembered well by all the older ones of the Nüpartka, the country of the People had been so huge that few men had ever seen all of it during a lifetime. On the east it ended only with the last upturned wall of the Shining Mountains, which stood up and looked out over the plains and which showed the beginning of the country claimed by the plains enemies; it stretched south to the place called Taos, where the people lived in houses of mud and stones and grew their food from the ground; it extended west to the Great Salt Lake, beyond which lay a country nobody wanted, and north it ended with the last of the trees, where the mountains become swells on the buffalo prairie. Theirs was a rich country of many trees, high grasses, and so much game that nobody ever feared hunger. Deer and elk grew fat, and sometimes hunting parties of the People rode out of the last sloping canyons to kill buffalo in the country of the enemies.

11

Then the *Maricat'z* came—a few at first, then, suddenly, many. They brought presents—clothes that were not made of buckskin; food that tasted strange, then good; and rifles and saddles and bright things that flashed back at the sun.

So slowly that few could say when it started or how it happened, the country of the People grew smaller. The People began to eat the bread and wear the clothes of the Maricat'z, and to sell the hides from their hunts at the Maricat'z stores, because the stores held things that could never be found on hunts. Then it became known, as it was known with hunger and pain this winter, that if the People did not get the Maricat'z presents which were given by Washington, they were hungry and cold and sick.

It was this hunger, this cold, this sickness that took them now to the greater cold of the buffalo country—out of the shelter of their mountains where the snow fell through still, bright air, to that country without trees, where the snow was sharp and hard and driven on great, long winds.

It was a long, two-sleep trip to the Maricat'z village called Rawlins from the Smoking Earth River. The trail curled up steep slopes, wound through deep canyons, and plunged into wide rivers; and now the land was covered with the new snow of the Last Fall Moon. At first only a few men—those of the People who could talk best to the Maricat'z—made the trip to Rawlins to ask for the presents.

Through the village of Rawlins passed *panakarpo*, "the railroad," carrying the fast-spinning wheels from Washington to the end of the world, far to the west. It was at Rawlins that the wheels stopped to leave the presents from Washington—the flour, the blankets, the grain, the clothing and tobacco—for the Maricat'z wagons to carry them to the agency on Smoking Earth River, called the White River by the Maricat'z. It was at Rawlins that the presents had lain for a long time, and nobody, not the agent nor anybody, could come and take them away.

A little while after the first of the men went to Rawlins and came back home with none of the presents, others went; and the women and children went with them, dragging their carniva and driving their pack ponies; and soon villages of the Nüpart-

ka, which belonged in the country of Smoking Earth River, grew
up in the snow on the banks of the two rivers in the buffalo
country.

Day after day some of the men rode out to each of the two
villages and traveled hopefully to Rawlins to ask again for the
presents. They always returned to their villages to tell about
talks with Maricat'z who said they knew Washington but never
seemed able to do anything for the People.

Quinkent, the man whom Washington had said was *tawacz
viem*—"the chief"—of the Nüpartka, came back one day and told
the people of his village about a man in Rawlins who had a little
machine which shot words to Washington as fast as bullets.
Quinkent said he had given words to this man to send to Washington telling about the hunger and the cold and how the People
had not been given any presents. He told his people, as he had
many times before, that Washington was his best friend and
would listen to his words—that now something would be done.
But another day went past and still nothing was given out at
Rawlins.

The carniva of those who followed Quinkent stood on the
northernmost of the two rivers nearer Rawlins. Each day Quinkent rode into Rawlins and talked to the Maricat'z there, and
each night he returned to his village on the river, called the

Sweetwater by the Maricat'z, to tell the hungry families that another sun would not pass without the giving out of the presents from Washington; for he, Quinkent, of all the men of the Nüpartka, was respected and admired by Washington.

A tawacz viem, a "chief," among the People became so only because he had shown himself capable of leading those who chose to follow him into fulfillment of their needs, and he remained tawacz viem only as long as he kept proving that he was able to lead. When people quit following a man, he can no longer claim to be a leader.

Quinkent, more than anything else, had always wanted to keep his position. One time he had been given the power of talk, and he talked long and well to many. His words felt like drums and singing, and people came to hear him as they would have come to a dance. At this time he became tawacz viem, and he took the name of a great Maricat'z talking chief—"Douglas"; and it was by this name that Washington knew him as chief of the Nüpartka. But Quinkent could not remain tawacz viem if his people did not follow him, no matter what Washington believed. So Quinkent went each day to Rawlins, and he returned with fine talk, to which any man would stop to listen because he told of little machines for shooting words and of the great Maricat'z in Washington with whom he talked.

A second village had grown on the river farther south— farther from Rawlins and nearer to the Smoking Earth River and the country of the Nüpartka. This river was called the Little Snake, because "Snake" was the Maricat'z word for Shoshoni, and this river was on the edge of the country of the Shoshoni. The village on the Little Snake had grown up around the carniv of another leader among the Nüpartka. This man, Nicaagat, had known perhaps fifteen fewer snows than Quinkent. He was a large man with wide shoulders, a strong jaw, and a well-made nose that seemed to lift his face and tilt it a little backward. He was greatly admired among the Nüpartka and among other bands of the People, for he had returned only a short time before from riding with General Crook and fighting and defeating the Sioux enemy.

That the village on the Little Snake was much larger than

14

the one on the Sweetwater was a thought that Quinkent did not like to hold in his head.

Quinkent had seen sixty snows. He wore his hair cut close to his head and often dressed in Maricat'z clothes, for this seemed to please the good friends of Washington who sometimes visited the White River Agency. His eyes were small, round, and very bright, and tiny gray points of a mustache stuck out on either side of his upper lip.

Five days had passed and Quinkent had still not received words from Washington in return for those words of his own he had given the man at Rawlins to shoot away on the little machine. The great winds came again, pushing, whipping, strengthening the cold, which was always still like the stars in the country of the Smoking Earth River. Those who had come to the buffalo country became more anxious to return with the presents from Washington. The First Winter Moon would rise soon, and those presents meant warmth, full bellies, and life. The children whimpered in the carniva, and fathers and mothers became angry with the winds, with Rawlins, and with Washington himself. Quinkent, like most of the others, stayed in his carniv as the wind rose, his little eyes shining like hard, black berries as he stared into the fire, while the cold sneaked in through the hides and pressed against his back.

That day the winds returned, Quinkent had a visitor. It was Nicaagat. Quinkent never visited the carniv of Nicaagat, but Nicaagat sometimes came to Quinkent for talk on matters important to all the Nüpartka. This Nicaagat was a man who knew a great deal of the Maricat'z ways and had more of their words than any of the People, except, perhaps, Ouray, that one whom Washington had said was tawacz viem over all the People and who lived in a Maricat'z house halfway between the bands of the north and the south. It was known to Quinkent that Nicaagat had been talking to the chief of the soldiers, who lived in a village of their own just outside Rawlins; and Nicaagat was a friend of the soldiers. Although Quinkent gave no sign of friendship toward Nicaagat, he was anxious to know what this man had learned and to gain some word of hope, which Quinkent might pass on to his own people to still their impatience.

Like a prime bull buffalo Nicaagat pushed through the door of Quinkent's carniv and stood tall beside the center fire, warming his back and hands. The proud lift of his head was prouder because of the backward slope of his forehead, on which rested the sliver ornament of one who leads others. His two braids hung like strong ropes over the fine buckskin coat which his *piwán* had made for him after the last summer hunt.

"*Maiquas.*" They exchanged greetings, and Nicaagat settled himself down on the opposite side of the fire from Quinkent.

Being the host, Quinkent brought out the sack of *quap* and the husks for rolling cigarettes. There was only a little left in the sack; tobacco was one of the presents from Washington lying locked inside the building at Rawlins.

They rolled their cigarettes and lit them from coals on the edge of the fire. Then began the smoke which must come before such a talk. Each drew in a great puff of smoke then let a stream crawl slowly from his mouth. With great gasps they drew the smoke back into their mouths and on down, close to their hearts, where they held it for a long time. Then, with a loose swing of their heads, they blew the smoke out in big circles around them on the ground. They repeated this, and the second puffs they blew straight upward, so that the smoke from their hearts mingled with the smoke from the fire and passed out through the ears of the carniv toward the sky. They had now given the truth of their hearts to the earth and the sky; and although these two men were not good friends, only good could come from their talk.

After sitting a while longer with his own thoughts, Quinkent spoke:

"Washington is great and kind. Washington wants all people to live in peace, and he wants no man, woman, or child to be cold, hungry, or lonely. But because Washington holds this good feeling for all people, he is sometimes fooled.

"Sometimes men go to Washington who are poor and hungry. They are sad and they cry before Washington; and because Washington is kind he wants to do something to help these men. He makes them Indian agents.

"Washington sends these Maricat'z who are poor and hungry

16

to us. They have nothing, and they steal the presents Washington sends us. Then it is as now: they have something and we have nothing.

"I will tell Washington about this. I will tell Washington to send us men for agents who are not poor—men who have something of their own. Such men would not steal the presents Washington sends. They would give these presents to us, as they are supposed to do. Then all would be well."

It took a long time for Quinkent to say this. He spoke in the Old Language, which flows like a smooth, deep river, filling men's heads.

Nicaagat carefully took his time to think about Quinkent's words. He waited until the deep feeling stirred by the music of Quinkent's talk no longer mixed into his thinking; and when he spoke he made no reply to what Quinkent had said about agents. During the few snows that the agency had been at White River, there had been several agents sent there by Washington. Nicaagat had been a good friend to all of them, but there were none among those Maricat'z he knew who was a better friend to him than this present agent, whose name was Danforth. This man believed and lived all the best teachings of his God, and the good teachings of any God were the same—any man of any color could understand them. This agent wanted to do the right things for the People of Smoking Earth River, and his piwán spent much time with the women, teaching them the best of her people's ways and learning the best of their ways. This was the way all things should be between the People and the Maricat'z.

Nicaagat had talked long with the agent about this trouble which held back the presents from Washington. Nicaagat understood about it and he had tried to explain it to his people. It was the railroad that carried the goods from Washington to Rawlins, and for this work Washington paid money to the railroad. This time the railroad had not been paid. Washington had sent out the money for the railroad, but somebody—perhaps those Maricat'z who carried the presents from Rawlins to the agency in their wagons—had taken the money and used it for themselves, or lost it. So the railroad was holding the presents in a big locked building at Rawlins, while Washington was trying to find out about the lost money.

Nicaagat repeated all this to Quinkent, although he had heard it before, and he added something new. Nicaagat had been talking to an officer at the soldiers' camp, and this officer had said he would arrange with Washington to give the People some of the food and blankets that were for the soldiers. This would probably be all right, since presents for the soldiers also came from Washington. The officer would give the People enough flour, sugar, coffee, tobacco, blankets, and oats for the ponies so that they could go on a good winter hunt in the buffalo country. When they returned, Nicaagat believed, Washington would have found a way to get the railroad to give out the presents.

The officer of the soldiers had first said the People should come and live at the soldiers' camp until the snow went away, but this, Nicaagat knew, would not be a good thing. The People did not like to be around close to the soldiers. Soldiers are not like well-grown men should be—they are always chasing after women.

Nicaagat finished by saying that Quinkent should go with him to Rawlins in a day or two. When the officer of the soldiers gave them food and things, it would have to be Quinkent who put a mark on a paper to show the People had received them, since Washington had called Quinkent tawacz viem of the Nü-partka. To this Quinkent said, "Unh," without hesitating. He liked to have his name—his Maricat'z name—sent to Washington as often as possible. Also, perhaps Washington had sent an answer to him on the little machine.

The talk ended. Outside the carniv the wind had quieted. The sky was big and blue and the land was white and cold. The sun had gone a long way toward where the river began, and it would soon be dark. Nicaagat untied his pony and started south toward his own village.

All the way he watched through narrow, squinted eyes for game, and sometimes his hand moved toward his rifle when a speck of lone cedar or piñon seemed to be a moving thing on a long, white hillside. But the sky and the land were empty. The game had gone to shelter among the rocks and canyons of the lower country.

The sun was just going away behind the long, low hills when he came to that other river where the carniva of those who stayed with him grew out of the snow. Smoke rose from the pointed tips of the houses and mixed with the gathering dusk.

Nicaagat had not been back to his village since the day before. His piwán had been given some coffee by one of the women, and now, as he dismounted and pushed his head into the warmth of the carniv, he saw her hurrying to put a large pot of water on the fire. Before the coffee boiled, three of Nicaagat's good friends had come to sit with him and hear what he had done in Rawlins. First came Sowówic and Acarí. Next came Colorow—the one of the large belly and big frowning face who was always hungry—whom Nicaagat suspected had smelled the boiling coffee while sitting before the fire in his own carniv, away on the other side of the village.

Nicaagat told them what he had told Quinkent earlier, while his three friends sipped loudly at their hot coffee. When he had finished each one expressed approval of what Nicaagat had done the day before—except Colorow who, seeing that the coffee was gone and that there was no other food in the carniv, stood up, muttering something about going to visit a friend, and lumbered slowly and heavily outside. They heard his pony squeaking away through the snow and knew that he had meant what he said— that he would soon be riding up to one of the Maricat'z houses down the river, then, seeing that there were not too many people in that house, would walk inside, stomping heavily and telling stories about himself as the great fighter and a mean man. He would then ask for something to eat, and those Maricat'z, who would be greatly scared by Colorow's stories, would feed him; and he would stay in that house until there was no more food there.

After a while Acarí and Sowówic went home, and Nicaagat, his legs and back tired from so much riding, his brain tired from so much talking, and his eyes heavy, rolled in his warm blankets with his piwán and went to sleep.

Old Coyote howled with a thousand voices that night, complaining of the snow—of the cold that was now and the greater cold that would come with the winter moons. Cold and snow and wind, until *Quigat*, "the bear," heard the first thunder of spring and awoke; then the People would wake with their land, knowing it was again time for Bear Dance.

During the night the singing from one carniv in the village mingled with the voice of Old Coyote. The medicine song whined, then shrieked. Someone was sick in that carniv, and the medicine song continued throughout the night, growing as members of the sick one's family gathered at the bedside.

In the morning the piwán and an old woman of that carniv were laying down the lodge poles and folding the skins. Soon their hair would be cut off and their faces smeared with ashes. Before *tavi-mois*, "sunrise," a small boy had died in that carniv, and the family had taken him away and dug a little cave for him to lie in. A family must not stay in a place where someone has died, so the women were rolling the household into bundles ready to pack the ponies and move. The few little things that had belonged to the child were left there for distribution among living children.

The sun had risen into a blue sky. Already it beat gently against the white land, and before the day was ended much of the snow would be melted. More would come, but that would not be until tomorrow, perhaps the next day, or the next. Today warm sun would limber stiffened limbs of the old and would bring the young out to run and push and play by the bank of the river, still flowing and not yet bound by ice. It was not the way of the People to remain unhappy or angry for long.

Soon the presents from Washington would be given out, and the People could go back to the Shining Mountains and deep valleys of their country, their ponies loaded with meat from hunts. There the waiting was better, for the cold stood still like the stars; and the thunder would come, the sun would stand tall again, and the bear would awake, to tell the People of Smoking Earth River it was again time for Bear Dance.

« II »

In the territorial years, and through the first years of statehood, Colorado had a vexing Indian problem. It was a problem common during the settlement of America but little noted today, for it lacks the drama, the overt dynamics which keep Indian stories alive. It was the problem of friendly Indians.

W. B. Vickers, private secretary of Colorado's first elected governor, summed up the whole frustrating situation in the first sentence of his article entitled, "Lo, The Poor Indian": "Western Colorado, though undoubtedly the finest part of the state, is practically unproductive, owing to Indian occupation."

And Governor Pitkin, who was elected shortly after Colorado was made a state in 1876, himself described the problem in more detail in a statement before the legislature:

Along the western borders of the State, and on the Pacific Slope, lies a vast tract occupied by the tribe of Ute Indians, as their reservation. It contains about twelve million acres and is nearly three times as large as the State of Massachusetts. It is watered by large streams and rivers, and contains many rich valleys, and a large number of fertile plains. The climate is milder than in most localities of the same altitude on the Atlantic slope. Grasses grow there in great luxuriance, and nearly every kind of grain and vegetables can be raised without difficulty.

This tract contains nearly one-third of the arable land of Colorado, and no portion of the State is better adapted for agricultural and grazing purposes than many portions of this reservation. Within its limits are large mountains, from most of which explorers have been excluded by Indians. Prospectors, however, have explored some portions of the country, and found valuable lode and placer claims, and there is reason to believe that it contains great mineral wealth.

The number of Indians who occupy this reservation is about three thousand. If the land was divided up between individual members of the tribe, it would give every man, woman, and child a homestead of between three and four

thousand acres. It has been claimed that the entire tribe
have had in cultivation about fifty acres of land, and from
some personal knowledge of the subject I believe that one
able-bodied white settler would cultivate more land than the
whole tribe of Utes. These Indians are fed by the government, are allowed ponies without number, and except when
engaged in an occasional hunt, their most serious employ-
ment is horse-racing. If this reservation could be extin-
guished, and the land thrown open to settlers, it will furnish
homes to thousands of the people of the state who desire
homes.

The Utes—the high mountain people who had been called
"the Switzers of America"—were the gravest problem of the
young state. They were Colorado's friendly Indians.

The tribes who fought—the makers of war who had resisted
white settlers from its beginning on the North American Continent—were problems too, but problems of a very different kind.
They were problems moving visibly toward solution, for the
Indians who fought were inevitably conquered and removed as
obstacles to progress. It was the tribes who insisted on being
friends and allies—allies when the white men needed them most
—who eventually became the kind of problem that Colorado
now faced.

The tribes of the Colorado plains had bitterly resisted every
step of the advancing white invasion, and before the end of the
sixties they had been successfully removed. A highlight of this
clean-up campaign occurred near Denver in 1864 when Colonel
J. W. Chivington, a former minister, led a force against the Cheyenne village of Black Kettle in what was known as the Sand
Creek Battle. The Cheyenne men were holding a religious dance
and were not expecting an attack. It was easy for the troopers
to wipe out the village. Chivington, surprising one of his soldiers in the act of trying to hide a small Cheyenne boy, reminded his men that "nits become lice"; his words became famous among the Indian fighters and settlers of the West.

In these plains wars the Utes were allied with the whites.
They were traditional enemies of the plains tribes. After the

Cheyenne and Arapaho were taken on the trail to Indian Territory in 1867, the Utes enjoyed the freedom of hunting buffalo on the plains. They rode their ponies down the dusty streets of Denver, loafed in front of the trading stores, and camped on the shady banks of Cherry Creek. Their presence was lucrative for many Denver merchants who traded in buffalo hides and meat.

Governor Pitkin, from the time he took office, looked upon the Utes as a force paralyzing the progress of a great new state; before, as a private citizen, Mr. Pitkin knew these Indians as an obstacle to personal progress. Like most of the leading citizens of early Colorado he was a man with heavy investment in mining interests. It was not until 1873 that the federal government was able to put into force a treaty with the Utes which opened the San Juan Mountains in the southwestern part of the state to mining; and it was the rich silver deposits of the San Juans that made Mr. Pitkin one of the most successful mining men in the state.

The first treaty with the Utes had been signed in 1863. This treaty gave the Utes all the land west of the Continental Divide, for at that time the white people had their hands full mining gold and settling the Eastern Slope. But settlement moved rapidly. In 1868 a new treaty united all Ute bands and established the first boundaries of the Ute reservation, now somewhat shrunken, compared with the vague boundaries of the old

Ute Nation. No generally recognized chief could be found among the Utes, and the Indian Bureau chose a man who had done some interpreting in both Spanish and English. He was treated, during the Civil War, to a trip to the seat of the Great White Father in Washington, where he was impressed with the armed strength of the United States. He was then sent home to Colorado with an annual salary of $1,000, a collection of medals and trinkets, and the title of Chief Ouray.

The invasion spilled over the Continental Divide. The tales which have always lived among prospectors and miners came back—rich placers, glittering veins, and rubies as big as marbles. All on the forbidden reservation of the Utes. More ventured over, came back unharmed by the savages, and returned taking more with them.

Government surveyors came with the compasses, chains, and stakes. Scrambling over high, bare rocks, sighting through dense pine forests, crawling under thick sagebrush in the lower valleys, and followed everywhere by curious Indians, they laid out the boundaries of the new reservation.

When the imaginary lines were at last made, the Utes discovered that some of their best hunting country—the high parks near the Divide—was now part of the White Man's land. Chief Ouray protested to Washington and refused to put his name on the ratification of the survey. He also complained that settlers were edging over the reservation line in many places.

A delegation was sent to reason with Ouray. They argued and pleaded, often unpleasantly amazed at the quick, sharp mind of Washington's "Ute Chief." Ouray finally gave in and accepted the survey with a promise from the delegation that soldiers would be sent to drive out the squatters from the reservation.

A detachment of cavalry was ordered out, but a great protest rose from citizens of the Territory. The troops were recalled and never again dispatched.

Then another delegation was sent to Ouray. Headed by General Edward Hatch of the United States Army, the delegation was to offer the Utes several alternatives: to move voluntarily to Indian Territory, to sell the entire southern portion of their reservation and concentrate in the north, or to give over the areas of the reservation now illegally occupied by the whites.

Ouray and the other headmen of the tribe would not even discuss the first two proposals. As to the third—giving over the land now occupied by squatters which the soldiers had failed to drive out as agreed—Ouray asked General Hatch: "Is not the United States Government strong enough to keep its treaties with us?"

Hatch's plea that only by giving in to this final proposal could the Utes avoid eventual collision with the illegal squatters and serious trouble with the government eventually forced Ouray and the Ute chiefs to agree to relinquishment of this land.

With the 1868 treaty an agency had been established in Denver, where the Utes gathered to receive their "presents" from Washington. But Denver was growing into self-conscious adolescence, and the presence of Indians on the streets was an unbecoming crudity. In 1873 three agencies were set up on the reservation. One, the northernmost, was on the White River; a middle agency was located on the Gunnison and later moved to the Uncompahgre; and the southern agency was near the border of New Mexico.

The Utes, most of them, disappeared from Denver; but Colorado still had its friendly Indians. Feeling toward the Utes throughout the state was well-expressed by Governor Pitkin's secretary, Mr. Vickers:

25

Though not particularly quarrelsome or dangerous, the Utes are exceedingly disagreeable neighbors. Even if they would be content to live on their princely reservation, it would not be so bad, but they have a disgusting habit of ranging all over the state, stealing horses, killing off game, and carelessly firing forests in the dry summer season.

The Government should be shamed to foster and encourage these Utes in their idleness and wanton waste of property. Living off the bounty of a paternal but idiotic Indian Bureau, they actually become too lazy to draw their rations in the regular way, but insist on taking what they want wherever they find it. But for the fact that they are arrant cowards, as well as arrant knaves, the Western Slope of Colorado would be untenanted by the white race. Almost every year they threaten some of the white settlers with certain death if they do not leave the country, and, in some instances, they have tried to drive off white citizens, but the latter pay little attention to their vaporings.

The degeneration of the Utes has been very rapid ever since the first settlement of the country. Formerly, they were a warlike tribe, and held their own with the fierce Arapahoes of the east and the savage Cheyennes of the north, whether upon the mountains or the plains. As civilization advanced the plains Indians retreated before it, and after the Sand Creek fight in 1864, the plains were almost deserted by the wild hordes which, until then, had been the terror of all travelers to and from Pikes Peak and California.

The continuous and ever-increasing intercourse between Colorado and the East has long since dispelled the ancient idea that Denver was situated in the heart of the Indian country, but the presence of Indians in the State still constitutes an obstacle to the advancement of Colorado, for even those who do not fear the Utes dislike them, and would be glad to see them banished to some more appropriate retreat than the garden of our ever-growing state.

To this end, Congress and the Interior Department have been, and are continually, besieged to provide for the extinguishment of Indian title to the reservation lands, and in this movement the military commanders on our frontier are earnestly interested. General Pope, commanding the department, is particularly anxious to have the Utes massed at a more convenient point. At present they have three agencies on their reservation. Both White River and the Uncompahgre agencies are remote from railways and supplies, as well as from the military posts, which are so necessary to keep the savages in check. Removed to the Indian Territory, the Utes could be fed and clothed for about one-half what it now costs the government.

Philanthropists down East and abroad may mourn over the decadence of this once powerful tribe of Indians, but even a philanthropist would fail to find any occasion for regret if he came to Colorado and made a study of Ute character and habits. Though better in some high (and low) respects than the Digger Indians of Arizona, or the Piutes of Nevada, the Colorado Utes have nothing in common with the Indians of history and romance, whose "wrongs" have been so tearfully portrayed by half-baked authors. The strongest prejudices of Eastern people in favor of the Indians give way before the strong disgust inspired by closer acquaintance.

《 III 》

Spring came; the land awoke and laughed.

The hungry winter was passing away. The snow and the cold crawled farther and farther up the river, toward the mountains with flat heads, which would still be wearing snow in the Last Spring Moon.

The People of Smoking Earth River had stayed too long in the white, windy buffalo country. Little by little the presents from Washington had come—not all of them, and never enough —and there had been much talk, with the loud and crowded words of the Maricat'z, many papers on which little marks had to be made, and many words flying back and forth from Washington on the little machine.

27

But by the end of the Last Winter Moon—the Maricat'z call it February—most of the People were back in their own country; and now the time for which winter waited was with them, and they looked to the spring hunts. The snow was creeping away like a dying coyote, leaving the great valleys and meadows bright, young, green. The hard black winter pines wore soft feathers on the tips of their branches. White water bounced high against rocks and dived into the rivers, sliding down frozen slopes into the lower country. The Smoking Earth River, white and cold, chewed its way through dirty, earth-streaked chunks of snow on its way to the desert.

The People laughed with their land: they had waited with the winter, now they laughed with the spring. Winter was dead, and it was not good to think about the dead. *Iniput'z,* the "ghosts of the dead," draw close if a person thinks too much about them; and these ghosts, if they are allowed to come too close to the present, can make dead that which is alive.

Although the laughter of spring was already with them, it was a quiet time, with spring moving slowly into their valleys; for the People were listening. They were waiting and listening for the first thunder, which would awaken the sleepy bear in

his winter den and awaken the spirit of the bear in the People. Awaken their feet and their hearts and bring music among them. This was the time for Bear Dance.

As the time came closer the men talked much of hunting, and the women began to prepare their men for the early hunts. As each hunting party left the villages the women, children, and the old men (some of whom had seen their last hunts only the year before) followed to the edge of the village, and as the men rode out into the thin, clear sunshine, shouts, chants, squeals of children, and barking of dogs followed them, wishing them good luck. The hunters returned the shouts, and loudest of all were the voices of those young men going on their first hunt.

The hunters returned, driving ponies loaded with fresh meat, and they saw that the time had come, and that their fresh meat would be used well; for those who had stayed behind had been cutting young trees and brush to build the *avinkwep,* the "cave of sticks" in which the bear dance would be held.

Around the avinkwep, down in the lower valley where the ponies were pastured through the winter, carniva grew up like new grass; and all the villages grew together into one great one, which kept on growing with the avinkwep. The great cave of sticks was taking shape, with its wide opening facing the afternoon sun in the southwest; for the bear always chooses a winter den into which the sun will shine part of the day.

The carniva in the great growing village were not all those of the Nüpartka. Some belonged to families of other bands of the People, and some to people of other tribes. At Bear Dance, the country of the Nüpartka was visited by many who were not fortunate enough to live in these high mountains where the snow kills the land and makes it live again. The Nüpartka were a happy people who lived with a country of high peaks and fast water, a country that knew how to laugh. They were good to visit. At Bear Dance people traveled from far away places and spent many sleeps on the trail to come to Smoking Earth River.

Nünt'z, "the People," were a great nation, and there were many bands other than the one on Smoking Earth River. The People were called *Yuta* by their friends the Shoshoni and Co-manche, whose languages were much like their own. The Cheyenne and Sioux enemy called them Black Faces, and the white men called them Utes.

The Nüpartka of the Smoking Earth River country had been caled *Yampatika*, "Root Eaters," by the Shoshoni, because in the days before they rode ponies their women often dug roots for food during the long winters in their country.

There were other bands of the People farther to the south, beside the tall mountains which the *Quat'z*, the "Spanish people," had long ago named the San Juan. These bands now lived on a river which the Maricat'z called the Uncompahgre River, because they could not say the right word, *Acapagad'r,* "where the red light shines on the water." These southern bands had their own Bear Dance, but many of them came to the Bear Dance on the Smoking Earth River, because at this time of year the country of the Nüpartka is the finest of all, where the deer are fattest and the grass is tallest and greenest.

Far to the west across the desert, near the village of Ta'bo, called Brigham Young by his own people, was another range of high mountains. Here was the home of another band of the People, the *Uintah,* those who lived "at the edge of three trees." Those of the Uintah band who came to the Smoking Earth River for Bear Dance always brought with them people of smaller nations who lived in the country to the west. These were called the Bannocks, Paiutes, and Gosiutes.

From the great dry open country to the south and west came people of another nation. These were the Hopi, who were also good friends to the People and who spoke a language much like that of the People. But they lived very differently. Their houses of mud and stones were built high on mesas, and they grew many good things to eat in the ground at the foot of these mesas. They made fine bowls and jars of clay, and these they filled with good things from the ground when they came to visit the People at Bear Dance.

A long time ago these Hopi and others who lived as they did on top of mesas feared the People. This was because the People often went to their country and took things away from them. There had been great battles, and one of the old stories told of such a battle in which the ancestors of the People defeated those who lived on the high rocks, and turned them into fishes. But a time came when the People made a long peace with the Hopi, and since that time the Hopi came to the mountains at Bear Dance and traded the corn and beans and gourds for meat and skins and baskets. The corn and beans, squash and gourds of the Hopi were welcome for the great feast which followed the Bear Dance.

But the Hopi, who lived far to the south and west, mostly visited the southern bands. Of the people from other nations who visited the Smoking Earth River for Bear Dance, the greatest number of all were from the Shoshoni, who, although they were hunters of buffalo, were not like the enemy peoples who lived on the frowning plains to the east of the Shining Mountains. Those plains people, even in the oldest stories, had been enemies of the People. None of these ever came to Bear Dance.

The People had always lived in the mountains, and the mountains and the plains were two worlds, as any man who had ever ridden his pony out of the doorway of one of those last canyons knew. The change-over between the two worlds was sudden and complete. A man whose world was the mountains would not stay long, open and exposed, on that land mashed flat and treeless. The plains were good for nothing, except buffalo; and when a hunter of the mountains had gotten what he wanted there—the meat and hide of the buffalo, and perhaps a few ponies of some Cheyenne or Arapaho village—he wanted only to return to his own world. With his good, fast ponies he could return quickly and seldom have to meet and fight the plains enemy.

Since ponies came to them long, long time ago, the People hunted buffalo often in the country of the enemy. But the old stories told of a time when there were no ponies. Those stories made a strange picture of the People. A thousand walking on foot in long lines, with the women walking in front and along the sides, carrying shields made of three thicknesses of buffalo hides—so that no arrows or spears could go through them; men walking along carrying their bows, spears, and knives in their hands, ready to use them; and between these lines of men walked the old men, old women, and the children. Also in the

31

center walked the great dogs, carrying the carniva, poles, and packs.

No living person had ever seen one of these great pack dogs. They had all died or gone away when the ponies came. The ponies came with the Quat'z, the Iron Shirts. It was the People and the Apache who first met the Quat'z and traded hides and meat for their ponies. When they first got these ponies, the stories told, the People did not know what to do with them. They first used them as they did the great dogs, and they did not ride them for a long time. They traded their ponies with people of other nations, and soon the pony was spread over the plains and throughout the mountain country. Then the People learned to ride their ponies and from them the others learned; life changed a great deal.

The stories also told of a time when the hunting grounds of the People spread far out from the mountains, out onto the buffalo plains of the south. It was this way for many years, when the People joined with the *Komant'z*, called Comanche by the Maricat'z, and the war they made was too terrible for the Apache and the other fighting nations. It was a good time, until bad blood came between the Komant'z and the People, and the People went back into their mountains.

Still the People went often to the plains to hunt buffalo. Their ponies had grown strong and fast, living in the high mountains, climbing among the rocks, and eating the fine mountain grasses. The People hunted and raided villages on the plains, and their ponies could easily outrun those of the plains people, who usually knew better than to follow them into their mountains. The People grew richer and stronger, and the family groups were growing together into a great nation when the Maricat'z came.

Those people who had lived out on the plains—the Arapaho and Cheyenne, the Sioux and the Kiowa, who had been driven away by the words and rifles of the Maricat'z—had some strange ways, which were almost as hard to understand as some of the ways of the Maricat'z. They were always having wars. They had wars the way some people might have games or dances. They were always getting hurt and killed in these wars, when they could easily have taken what their enemies had and run away. In the time before the Maricat'z came, the People hunted and raided on the plains, ready to fight if they had to; but it was much better to take what they wanted and go on home, without wasting time or getting anyone hurt in one of those silly wars. It used to make the plains people angry because the People would go home after a raid and would not stay for a war.

Yet there were many stories of wars. There were brave stories of strong warriors and funny stories of those young men who belonged to the Dog Society, the ones who lived in camps of their own outside the main villages and practiced for war.

But the wars, like the time when there were no ponies, had passed. The Maricat'z had come, and most of the plains enemies had been crowded and pushed down into the prison land of hot sun, red dust, and sickness. And now, at last, the People had the plains to themselves, whenever they wanted to go there. They could go and put up their carniva beside the Maricat'z villages, hunt the buffalo, and trade for guns and other fine things which the Maricat'z had in their stores.

Although the Maricat'z had been good to the People, giving them presents and helping them fight away the plains enemies, there were things about them that were troublesome. Often, after they had given some presents away, they would try to get the People to let them come into their country, dig in the ground for rocks, and build their houses, bring in their cattle, and drive away the game. Most of the People would not listen to such talk, but often some of the Maricat'z would go to the house of Ouray, down on the Uncompahgre, and after they left, the People would hear that a piece of their country no longer belonged to them, and the Maricat'z would come with their digging tools, spoil the water and the grass, cut down the trees, and build their strange houses, which could never be moved from the place they were first built. This thing had happened with the high parks—Middle and North Park, which had been some of the best hunting country in all of the Shining Mountains. Some of the People, especially among the Nüpartka, were angry about this and they talked with Ouray; but he would only say something about the many soldiers of the Maricat'z. The

33

Nüpartka knew that this was foolish talk; the soldiers came only to the enemies—the Sioux, Cheyenne, and Arapaho.

Still, it was nothing to get too angry about, since the People could still hunt in the parks. The Maricat'z had promised this. But many said that Ouray was not a good man to talk with Washington. When talking to Maricat'z, a man must never say too much, and he should just keep saying "No" until the Maricat'z get tired and go away. It was not so bad to have Maricat'z around. They were very funny.

Now, in the winter valley of the Smoking Earth River, spring pushed preparations for Bear Dance, which, in turn, would help spring come into the country. The avinkwep grew to its full and proper size, as great bundles of brush and new spring foliage from the banks of the river and the hillsides walked into the village on the small, strong legs of children and the feeble legs of old men. The game ground grew up beside the growing avinkwep, and the men gathered around blankets to play games

with the Maricat'z cards. Lines formed along logs for *nia*, the old hand game, men chanting as they beat their sticks on the log, sharp eyes watching to see which man held the marked stick. Fast ponies beat their way down the long race track, and fine possessions were won and lost. The women found time away from preparing food for the great feast which would follow the Bear Dance to form little knots of monte games. The People played furiously now, for there would be no games during Bear Dance.

Already the brush rattled and rustled here and there with the giggling of young girls as they found their partners for Bear Dance. A man must stay throughout the dance with the woman who plucked his blanket. Some of these couples would stay together only a little while after the dancing; others would stay together through many snows.

Slowly the spirit and life of the game ground was shifting to the avinkwep.

At one end of the cave of sticks a group of men dug a round hole, and when the hole was deep enough they reached back under the ground and scooped out dirt with their hands, until the hole became an entrance to a small underground cave. Then the singers came carrying a basket which they fitted upside down, closing the entrance of the little cave. The People began to gather in the avinkwep, forming lines, with the men on one side and the women on the other.

The last of the singers entered carrying the *w'ni thokunup*, the instrument around which the music of Bear Dance is built. It was a long stick, shaped like the jawbone of a great animal, notched along one side, and with a small bear's head carved on one end.

The music was about to begin. The one who was to play the w'ni thokunup, which the Quat'z called a *morache*, placed one end of his music-maker on top of the basket, holding the other end in his lap. With a smaller stick he rubbed up and down over the notches, and the little thunder sounded deep in the cave, spreading out over the awakening land and rumbling in the spring air. The song of the other singers closed around the first thunder, and the first song of Bear Dance was made.

The female bear chooses her mate. Now, as the first dance was about to begin, the women had already plucked the blankets of the men they had chosen and had again taken their places in the line, which was now moving forward, stepping with the music and the throbbing of the w'ni thokunup, toward the line of men. They halted before their partners, then the line moved backward two steps. The line of men followed, each man carefully covering with his foot the spot from which his partner's foot had just been withdrawn. Then the men moved backward three steps, the women following, watching that they did not touch their partners' feet. If this happened to a woman, it would be like telling everybody that she wanted this man in the blanket with her, and a great shout of laughter would arise and mix well with the music.

The two neat, straight lines glided forward and backward with the three steps of the dance, the men, as they moved forward, pawing the air like bears. The *machutagogeta*, the two old men whose job it was to keep the lines straight, to see that no one came into the avinkwep who did not dance, and to keep dogs and ponies outside, marched up and down the lines with their sticks, their sharp eyes watching for missteps and mistakes. Now a stick thumped for the first time against the legs of a man who had touched his partner. It was good for a long, loud laugh from all the dancers. Again the stick filled the air with a loud crack against the fattest part of the fattest woman, who was having trouble keeping herself in line. Another shout of laughter.

The first little thunder of the w'ni thokunup trembled in the winter dens of the bears. They stirred sluggishly, fighting for wakefulness, but fighting against it. The bears were a long time waking from their long sleep. The People, wanting to make it as easy as possible for the bears, never danced long on the first day of Bear Dance. There was no feasting and no playing of games after the dancing was finished. All the dancers went away to their carniva for quiet talk.

On the second day the sleepy bears had not left their dens, but they had begun to see, hear, and feel; and the first thoughts of feeding and mating were in them. The dancing lasted longer and the stiff, formal movements of the first day of dancing began to relax. The dancing lasted all day, and at sundown the bears finally left their dens, the females beginning to dance now to trees, the first feelings of mating growing big in them.

Night came and the dancing stopped. It began again with the dawn. This was the third day, and dancing would go on all day without stopping. Thick sleepiness was gone from the heads of the bears now, and they were filled with strong thoughts of food and mating. As the day moved on, the dance became less and less a line of women dancing to a line of men. Couples were dancing together, hugging like bears and varying in many skillful ways the three steps of Bear Dance. Children danced in pairs among their fathers and mothers. The cubs, who had only thoughts of food, nevertheless imitated the old bears in their hugging.

Sometimes during the three days a dancer fell. This could mean evil, unless a man with great powers of bear medicine—a *m'sut t'quigat*—came with the w'ni thokunup and stick to drive away the bad spirits that had made the fall. When a dancer fell, the music stopped, and the fallen one did not move until the m'sut t'quigat had brought the w'ni thokunup and stick, making

motions to push the evil out of his feet and chase it off toward the sky.

At sunset the singing stopped while the dancers rested and ate a meal; then when dark came into the valley all those who had danced, all the musicians who had sung during the three days of the dance gathered in the avinkwep. Then the finest part of Bear Dance—the night dance—began. The great fires lighted the dancing couples and filled the night with a huge circle of red light. The bears now, hungry both for mates and food, wandered the forests all night, and the spirit of the bear filled the night inside the avinkwep. Now and then men and women came into the avinkwep with heaps of dry branches to pile on the fires, and the song lifted with the sudden daylight of flames and sparks. Sometimes a couple—usually a young man and woman—would leave the dance and take their blankets up into the brush on the hillside to let out the spirit of the bear and the thunder of spring that had grown too strong in them to be held back any longer.

As with all dances of the People there were many healings at Bear Dance. Several times during the third day and during the night one of those men who kept the lines straight during the first days waved his stick. Instantly a great silence fell across the avinkwep. The men stood quietly in a line, as on the first day, and the women took seats on the other side of the avinkwep. Then the m'sut t'quigat, usually Canávish, whose medicine was the most powerful among the Nüpartka, came forward to tell of the ceremony that was to come. He would hand a bunch of corn husks and a pouch of *pöra*, "medicine tobacco," to the one who played the w'ni thokunup, and that one, after softly chanting a prayer to Sunáwiv, the God, rolled a cigarette, passing the pöra and husks to the next singer. When each of the singers had rolled a cigarette there was a long time of silence, then the prayer was chanted again by all the singers together. Then they lit their cigarettes and blew smoke to the sky.

Once during the third day and twice during the night a handsome beaded pipe, filled with the sweet-smelling kinnikinnick leaves, was brought to the dance, lighted, and passed around from one man to another. Each man dancer took three puffs, rubbing his fingers over the pipe as though bringing music from it, and blew his smoke to the sky. This would protect the dancers from sicknesses that enter the chest.

A greater, quieter light spread across the sky over the broad, flat tops of the mountains in the east. The pale dawn drew away into the desert. The dance went on through the morning, until the sun stood at its full height. The dance was ended; it was time for the great feast to begin.

At one time during every Bear Dance, Nicaagat went away to sit alone for a while. It was during a Bear Dance on Smoking Earth River that he had first seen the country of his people, and the strong medicine of spring had given him a home, a country, and a piwán. It was the power of his name—Nicaagat, "Leaves Becoming Green."

There was the time that went before. The Quat'z had taken him from his own people and sold him to that family who lived in one of the villages of the Mormons. He had lived in the house of those people all the years he was growing up; he had gone to their school and to their church; he had read their Book and been dipped into their water. Then there were the other children—the white children who belonged to those people. Although he had been too small to remember when he was taken from his own people, he had always known that he did not belong in that house, or in the school or the church where he was made to go. Those people explained to him that their God had made his people dark long ago because they did bad things. They said that if he tried to be a good Saint, he might some day become white; but Nicaagat always knew that he did not want to become white.

Then came that last day when he faced, as he had many times, the anger of the woman, holding her long buggy whip in her hand; that day the anger came into him also, and he was holding a knife in his hand and telling the woman to come no closer. Then the knife was on the floor. He had flung it away, and was running out the door toward the saddled horse standing tied beside the house.

For many days he had wandered in the mountains. He found other people, dark-skinned like himself, ate with them, slept in

39

their houses, then wandered on, deeper into the desert—on toward the great mountains over which the sun always rose in the morning. And at last it was spring, and he had come to the country of the Smoking Earth River.

It had been Bear Dance then, and a girl had chosen him for her partner. After the dancing and the feasting he had gone with that girl to the carniv of her father and mother and had drunk with her from the same cup. They became piwán to each other. The Nüpartka on Smoking Earth River became his people.

Nicaagat never talked about those days before he came to that first Bear Dance. Bit by bit the Maricat'z language slipped away from him and he did not try to bring it back.

The last day of Bear Dance ended with the sun high in the middle of the sky. The feasting began. Many new couples had been made; some had left old mates and found new ones; some were young men and women finding the first mates of their lives. These new couples passed the drinking cup between them and went away to make new carniva.

The People and their visitors ate at the feasts until they could eat no more; then they slept until they could sleep no more. Great chunks of red meat splashed into the boiling kettles. The tall coffee pots were emptied and filled again, and the pieces of *po-pana* and the flat, hard cakes of chokeberry and sunflower seed meal were passed around and around, until there were no more.

When the feasting had ended, it was time to begin thinking about going away. The great village around the avinkwep would soon break apart, and those fragments, which would become the hunting camps scattered out over the high meadows, the many streams, and the buffalo country of the north, would be tied together by the strong cord which bound this time to the first thunder of the next spring.

This breaking apart of the big village into hunting camps did not happen in a few days. Bear Dance makes men and women want to rest, and think, and talk for a long time. The spring sun grew warmer every day, and it soaked through the skin, into muscles tired from dancing; bodies were lazily absorbing the sun from the outside and the good food of the Bear Dance feast from the inside.

The men who usually led hunting parties gathered in small groups to talk about where they would go for the early summer hunts, but before any serious plans could be made a game usually grew up in the middle of the group, and talk, if any was left in them, drifted to other things.

A group of Nicaagat's friends gathered around him, and Nicaagat told them he planned to go up to the Shoshoni country and hunt buffalo. Some of the Shoshoni who had come for Bear Dance were getting ready to go home, and Nicaagat planned to go with them, taking his hunting camp along.

This was an invitation for his friends to come with him on the hunt; so there was a time of no talk, while the others thought about it.

Acarí, one of Nicaagat's closest friends, said he too would like to go hunting with the Shoshoni. His son, Saponise, who was now turning into a man, should be having his first buffalo hunt.

Sowówic did not have to tell his plans. He always went with Nicaagat, and he also had a son who was of age to try out in a buffalo chase, for buffalo hunting, like no other kind, had the power to help the man form around the seedling of man, which is the boy.

Colorow said he had decided to go into North Park this year. There were still a few of the shaggy mountain buffalo there, over which the People and the Arapaho had fought some hard

wars in days which could still be remembered. There were also plenty of antelope and deer and elk.

Colorow had heard that some Maricat'z settlers had come into North Park recently to build their houses. They had many cattle with them, and those Maricat'z who had cattle always had plenty of food. It was the ones who had no cattle who often had little food. Colorow would go to North Park to see if those new settlers were going to be good to the People and if their women could make good food; he would probably do little hunting.

Acarí began teasing Colorow, saying that he would probably not hunt at all but would spend all his time eating the food of the Maricat'z and trying to scare them with long stories about himself. It was Colorow's last son that did this thing to him. When that son was born, it was suspected that Colorow did not do as a man should and walk in the forest and make the motions of hunting. For this he had paid in becoming lazy.

Colorow went on talking as though he had heard nothing Acarí said. He told stories about the greatest hunter in all the mountains and plains—Colorow. Colorow's stories had been many and long in recent days. They were always best at Bear Dance time; there were many visitors around who did not know him very well.

Piah, a man some place between the age of Nicaagat and Acarí's son, Saponise, had joined the group. Piah was a strong young man and he was brave and a good hunter, but his years had not yet carried him into wisdom. He had come to join the group so that he would not have to stay alone in his carniv. The swelling and shrinking of the moon had drawn blood from his piwán, and at such times the woman must make a camp by herself, away from the carniv, for the blood of this woman-magic can spoil a man's hunting power. Piah listened to what Colorow had to say about going into North Park, and he said he would join this hunt.

It was at this time that Quinkent, who had been wandering around the village all day, busy about something and stopping wherever men had gathered for a game or talk, came to Nicaagat's group. He had saved it until last. He stopped, staring out across the river, the grin on his face so wide that the little gray points of his mustache pointed straight outward. A bright fire behind his small eyes was burning hot, and something seemed to be turning over and over inside his head, like meat roasting on a stick.

Quinkent always wore this look when he had something to tell. It always made Quinkent a little angry when some important news came and another person heard of it first and told it around. Now he was happy; he was the one who carried news.

Another new agent was coming in a few days, Quinkent told them. Now, perhaps, things would be better, for this new agent was a good friend to Washington. There would be no more holding up of the presents from Washington, for this new agent would know how to get them and would give them out to the People at the right time, before they were caught by the snow. Quinkent said he would see this new agent as soon as he came to Smoking Earth River, and he would tell that agent what he must do. Then the People would always have their presents from Washington, and they would never again have to go up to the railroad in the snow and cold.

Quinkent finished talking and walked on to find another group of men. Nobody in Nicaagat's group had anything to say about Quinkent's news. There had been several agents here since the agency had been built on Smoking Earth River, and although the things from Washington were sometimes long in coming, the People would get them after a while, no matter what agent was living in that house in the upper valley. The agents whom Washington sent to Smoking Earth River were certainly better than the ones who used to give out the presents in Denver. These who now came here to the People always gave out all the presents sent from Washington, while those in Denver kept some of them for themselves or made the People give skins and furs in trade for them. But it was the way with Washington to send an agent, then, as soon as the People were beginning to know that agent, to take him away. Agents came and agents went; things changed little.

As soon as Quinkent walked away, the men went back to talking about the early summer hunts.

43

3. THE PLAN

IN THE books of school children of the mid-nineteenth century a map of the half-formed nation of the United States showed a great, blank triangle between the thin lines of the Oregon Trail and the Santa Fe Trail; and this vast wedge in the map was usually filled only with widely spaced letters, "GREAT AMERICAN DESERT."

The name stuck, even after the first gold camps were built in the Pikes Peak region; then slowly, gradually, it began to pass away, and a man who contributed much toward erasing this forbidding label was an agriculturist from Ohio, Nathan Cook Meeker, who brought the magic of irrigation to Colorado.

Meeker was born in the small town of Euclid, Ohio, near the Lake Erie port city of Cleveland, in 1818. Nathan's family used to tell often, with pride, the story of Nathan's first quarter. He had acquired a whole round silver twenty-five cent piece. Eagerly he took it to the store and returned with a spelling book.

Why had he bought a spelling book? Because, the small boy explained to his parents, he was going to be a writer.

Writing absorbed him, as a youth and as a young man. For a year he attended Oberlin College, the shockingly progressive school in northern Ohio which was to cause world-wide talk by admitting women students, calling itself coeducational. After the year at Oberlin, Nathan finished his education at Western Reserve University in Cleveland.

His literary output was tireless in those days: mostly poetry, occasionally an article. Newspapers, notably the Cleveland

44

Plain Dealer, published some of his work, without compensation; but Nathan thought little of money at that time. It was enough to see his name and his work in print.

Before he turned twenty the restlessness grew great in him. It would not let him stay in Ohio. He set out for New Orleans, mostly on foot, and there took a job as a cub reporter for the *Picayune.* He stayed in New Orleans a year and nearly starved. It was on the return trip to Ohio that he pitched down the companionway of a river boat, landing on his head, which was fortunately protected by a high hat full of manuscripts of poems. It was the only good service his poetry had ever done him, Meeker remarked in later years, and this was often cited by his friends as a rare lapse. Meeker was a man of many genuine virtues; a sense of humor was not one of them.

Young Meeker was known as a visionary dreamer who thought a great deal and took himself quite seriously. Born into the most stable era of American history, he was racked by conflict. Radicalism and Orthodoxy fought tirelessly for possession of his soul, the solid and sanctioned side usually on top. But the stubborn, wiry radical streak would not be quieted.

Then Orthodoxy won a great victory. A very proper young lady several years his senior became intrigued with the state of the troubled soul.

Arvella was the daughter of a retired New England sea captain who had brought his family to Ohio. She was born to, and steeped in, the New England variety of Christianity, and the sensitive, unconventionel young Meeker was a puzzle, a challenge to her. She married him. Immediately she began to put the soul in order.

He gave up writing poetry and joined Arvella's church. But the Radical still struggled feebly; it never, throughout his life, quite gave up.

Meeker and many other young intellectuals of that day were interested in the theories of the French philosopher Fourier, who advocated agrarian socialism in co-operative phalanges. Such a phalanx—a branch of New England's Brook Farm—was being established near Warren, Ohio, and was called the Trumbull Phalanx. Meeker and his new wife joined the phalanx, and

Meeker was made librarian because of his "literary leanings." But after three years the community went to pieces, crushed by the surrounding American economy of few people, huge resources, and free speculation. "I learned then how much co-operation people would bear," Meeker liked to say later.

The economics of the Meeker family remained turbulent. Meeker grasped with one hand at a living for his growing family and with the other strove to hold fast his ideals. He continued writing, selling little or nothing, and the children kept coming.

The Meekers moved next to Hiram, Ohio, where the Campbellite sect was establishing Hiram College. Here Meeker set up a store and wrote a book called *The Adventures of Captain Armstrong,* the story of an extraordinary seaman wrecked on a south sea island who taught the natives all the practical wonders of the Christian world, including steam power—all the advantages of modern civilization with none of the vices.

But Meeker's principles were again interfering with his family's subsistence; credit at Meeker's store was too easy. He made little effort to collect, and he gave away almost as much merchandise as he sold. As bankruptcy approached, Arvella took hold of the situation with her firm, Yankee hand. She turned the store over to her two sons, who ran it successfully.

The Panic of 1857 nearly ruined Meeker. He sold the store at Hiram and opened another at Dongola, in Southern Illinois, where he also had a fruit farm. That year the last of his children was born, a girl who was named Josephine.

Meeker continued to write. At the outbreak of the Civil War he found himself a strong abolitionist in an area that was almost totally in sympathy with the Confederacy. He wrote and published many articles and reports.

In New York City, Horace Greeley, editor and publisher of the *New York Tribune,* read Meeker's articles. He was impressed. The views were like his own, and Meeker wrote fearlessly, refusing to leave his home in the hostile southern community. Greeley wired his correspondent at Cairo, Illinois, "Meeker is the man we want." And Meeker became war correspondent for the *Tribune.*

The years that followed were different. After the war Meeker

became agricultural editor for the *Tribune*. No longer a floun-
dering dreamer, his intellect had come under the aegis of a
man who knew how to guide the energies of other men. Greeley,
founder of the great *Tribune*, became Meeker's balance wheel;
his life ran on a straight, smooth course.

Meeker became a national authority on agriculture. His advice was sought, through his column, by farmers all over the
nation. He wrote a series on the experimental community at
Oneida, New York, and another book called *Life in the West:
Stories of the Mississippi Valley*. Then in 1869 he started on a
tour of the real West, his plans calling for the trip to end in
Utah where he could get a look at the farm and community
life of the Mormons.

The long trip over a new pair of steel rails that spanned the
continent was cut short at Cheyenne, where a blizzard had
piled snow deep across the tracks for many miles. The train did
not go on. Meeker turned south, toward Denver; but instead of
the infant city and the Pikes Peak gold diggings, he became
intrigued with the vast, empty grasslands east of the mountains.

Meeker returned to New York filled with a plan, certain he
had knowledge and experience to make the plan work. When
he first suggested an agricultural community on the Great
American Desert to Arvella, she was cool. She remembered the
uncertain years of life in experimental communities; they compared unfavorably with the present security, with the head of
the Meeker family drawing a steady, comfortable salary from
the *Tribune*, supporting a pleasant home in the New York sub-
urbs.

Greeley was all enthusiasm. He had long had plans for the
West, and again he saw the great canal of immigration crossing
the continent, with the overflow—the surplus manpower from
mills and factories of the East—passing through this huge drain-
age ditch. In the West they would find homes and farms; new
workers would come from Europe to fill the factories of the East.
But with the great western outlet there would never be too
many workers and too few jobs. There would never be another
panic, and America would prosper, East and West.

At a press dinner in the elegant main dining room of Delmonico's Restaurant, Meeker first presented his plan to Greeley. He was assured of Greeley's support; Greeley even stated rather wistfully his wish that he could join the colony, but his responsibilities were too great in New York and his eyes were still cast toward the Presidency of the United States.

Meeker's choice of a location in Colorado was partly influenced by the writings of William N. Byers, Denver newspaperman and selling agent for the vast lands of the Denver Pacific and Kansas Pacific Railroads, given the companies by the United States government. In the promotional magazine *Star of Empire,* Byers wrote glowingly of prospects for development and agriculture on the plains of Colorado.

December 4, 1869, Meeker announced through a *Tribune* article his plan for the new colony, wherein the investors would have building lots in the community and tracts of farm land adjacent to the town. He asked for men to join him: "temperance men, and ambitious to establish good society." Answers and inquiries flooded in. A few days later he called the first meeting to form a company for colonization and adopted the name "Union Colony." Meeker was elected president and Greeley treasurer.

The first year the colony, located on the Cache la Poudre River and far out on the plains, came close to disaster—so close that many members sold out and went home to the East. The second year was rescued by mistakes and lessons of the first. The irrigation ditch, originally dug too small, was enlarged, the waters of the Cache la Poudre flooded the fields, crops more suited to the severe climate were planted, and the fields yielded a good harvest. It was the first large-scale success of irrigation outside Utah.

Meeker, president of the colony, devoted all his time to the project and served without compensation. He refused the proposal to have the town named after him and insisted it be called "Greeley." The community prospered, and those who had invested prospered with it; but Meeker, who had neither time nor money for speculation, found himself in debt.

In the first year Meeker poured his savings into building the largest house in the colony to demonstrate his faith in the plan.

His single business was the newspaper, the *Greeley Tribune*, the instrument through which he guided the community to success. It was a financial failure. A rival paper was established and Meeker was urged to sell out, but Greeley offered a loan of $1,000 to bolster the fortunes of the *Greeley Tribune*. Meeker was to repay only when he was again in good financial condition.

In 1872, Greeley died unexpectedly and tragically, and his heirs, a wife and two daughters, immediately sued for the debt. The colony had deeded Meeker forty acres in appreciation for his services as president. He sold the tract—his only holding in the community other than his house and the paper—and paid only part of the sum. Other debts were pressing him; more accumulated.

When, in 1877, Meeker was offered an appointment as agent to the White River Utes—the most inaccessible of all the Ute agencies, which had seen many an agent come and go in a few years—he saw it as a way to obtain a steady income and clear his debts. He also had a long-standing theory on the Indian problem, and here was a chance to put it into practice.

Meeker's appointment as Indian agent broke an important precedent. It had been the policy of the Indian Bureau to seek recommendation of men for the agencies through various religious denominations. Meeker was not recommended by a church; his name was handed to the Indian Bureau by President Rutherford B. Hayes.

The seed of Meeker's interest in civilizing Indians, planted many years before, germinated rapidly in Colorado. He had studied the development of "severalty" or "land allotment" policy as led by Carl Schurz, Secretary of the Interior. The military was pressing to have the Indian Bureau transferred from the Interior Department to the War Department. "Severalty" was the plan for absorbing Indians as individuals into the American society, eventually extinguishing the concept of separate tribes.

Schurz and his followers saw the tribal unit and the communally held land as an enemy of individual freedom for members of the tribe. They proposed to settle each family on a separate plot, comparable in size to a white family's farm, then sell off the remaining lands and devote the money to establishing

49

the Indians as farmers or ranchers. Each Indian would then be released from government supervision to compete as an equal with the white man.

The success of the policy depended on education. A new plan grew in Meeker's mind: something of a Union Colony, but for Indians. It was a way to bypass two or three centuries, to take the long jump from hunting, through herding, to agriculture—the process of centuries crowded into months, years crowded into days.

Sixty years old, looking toward the new peak he could now see clearly with the enthusiasm of a boy who had walked to New Orleans, Meeker started off in May of 1878 for the wilderness of the White River Country.

The Cache la Poudre River poured down out of the mountains and flowed eastward across the prairies; the White River rose in the high country over the Continental Divide and flowed west, winding through the diminishing mountains toward the desert of Utah Territory. Between Greeley and the White River Ute Agency jutted the highest mountain ranges on the North American Continent. It was necessary to make a great circle to the north in order for Nathan Meeker to reach his new post on White River from his home at Greeley.

He traveled north to Cheyenne where he boarded a train and crossed a piece of the bleak, butted alkali plains of southern Wyoming to Rawlins, the nearest railroad station to White River. From that frontier cattle and railroad settlement, he again turned south toward the tumbled mountains of Colorado.

The spring wagon he rode fell into the two ruts that were the road to White River and trundled on over the 170 miles of wilderness, fording rivers and streams, swollen from melting snows, wheels sinking deep into the spring mud and jolting on outcropping rocks. Except for Bagg's Ranch at the crossing of Little Snake River and Peck's Store at Windsor on the Bear River, there were no settlements, no homes, along the entire route. Two nights they camped on the frosty ground. From Bear River on, theirs was the first wagon for nine months.

Out of the narrow canyon, bursting into the wide park, divided by the White River, Meeker saw the cluster of log buildings that was the White River Agency. Like a jungle the wilderness pushed up to the doors and foundations of the bleached log buildings. A plowed and planted field of about twenty acres, ravaged by insects and choked with weeds, lay a short distance from the agency headquarters; and a fence, lying flat on the ground or half-supported by rotting cottonwood posts, surrounded the field. Meeker, agriculturist and new agent to the White River Utes, surveyed his headquarters with tired eyes. Inside the house he found three-legged stools for chairs, crude tables, bedsteads made hastily by carpenters pressed by greater tasks around the agency.

Meeker, who had just finished raising a civilization out of a patch of prairie wilderness, now stood at the beginning of another, similar labor. The strangeness of those first weeks at his new job gripped him; he wrote an article for his *Tribune*, back home at Greeley, and gave it the one-word title, "Lonely."

> Altogether there are six of us, one a lady, four employes, often during the day all are gone [the article began].
>
> So the sun goes down over the mountains, covered with grass to the top, and one looks down the narrow valley which opens a little a mile or so to the north, looks along the wagon road where only one track has been made this year, as if some one were coming, tired and ready for a warm supper, looks out through the gap in the range as if a four-horse team might be discovered in a hurry to make the five or six miles before dark, but not a soul is seen, nothing moves.
>
> If there were neighbors five miles away, or ten or twenty, it would be quite cheerful, and one could ride over for a visit once a month, but it is sixty-five miles to the nearest house, where, by the way, no family is now living, the woman having gone east because it was so lonely. . . .

Of course they had Indians: ". . . have them until you can't rest." Meeker saw the Indians in their own country now, saw how they dressed, how their clothes were put together, what they did when they got up in the morning, how long they waited for breakfast, what they had to eat and how they ate it, what kind of society they had, and how they enjoyed themselves.

". . . But after you do know them and things are not as you think they might be, a change comes; it is lonely . . . . However," he added, "it is only when we stop to think that loneliness appears, for we have enough to do to keep busy all day long."

Although Indian camps lined the river above and below the agency, Meeker learned that these were only a small part of all the families registered at the White River Agency. He soon understood the meaning of previous reports complaining of "the roving character of these Indians." Between the reservation and agency as Meeker first saw it and the civilized agricultural community he envisioned lay a long, hard way.

The wants of the Indian Bureau were clear enough, and Meeker's plan, conforming to that policy, was equally clear.

He was to teach the Indians agriculture, establish a school, build them homes on parcels of land assigned to each family, and start them on the road to civilization. But to accomplish this he must first have Indians.

Meeker found that H. E. Danforth, the agent who preceded him, reported that an "unusual number" of Indians had been away from the reservation the year before. Anxious to learn more about this, Meeker studied Danforth's report.

There are several reasons for this [Danforth wrote]. The annuities and supplies furnished these Indians amount to, at a liberal estimate, not over one-half that required for their support. None of their annuity goods and but part of their supplies have reached this agency during the year. Goods purchased in August of last year have been lying in the railroad depot, 175 miles away, since November last, a period of over nine months. Flour, purchased the first of June is still at Rawlins, no clothing, blankets, implements, or utensils of any kind have been issued at this agency for nearly two years. . . . In addition to the proportion of their subsistance which the Indians provide for themselves, they had this great deficiency to make up wholly or in part, in some way. With the exception of a few families the only way in which the Indians know how to provide for themselves is by hunting. By regulation of the department the sale of arms and ammunition on the reservation has been prohibited. At the same time the Indians have only to go off their reservation to obtain all the arms and ammunition, both loose and fixed, which they desire, a number of trading posts being accessible, and no white man refusing to furnish these articles to the Indians—a pretty good evidence, when there is no feeling in the community against it, that the people do not stand in any great fear of the Indians. Many settlers have made it their principal business to trade with the Indians during the past year, and have offered every inducement for them to leave the reservation.

Later Meeker thought he had made a start on keeping his

Indians close to the agency. The annuity goods which had been held at Rawlins through a mix-up over payment of shipping charges were released and brought to the agency. As though the entire reservation and surrounding country were threaded with telegraph lines, Indians appeared in great numbers, all in good humor. Meeker sought to make the best of this situation.

Shortly after Meeker's arrival there had appeared at the agency a grinning-faced Indian, somewhere between twenty-five and forty-five years of age, who opened his mouth and proudly peppered the air with misplaced and misshapen English words. Meeker listened with difficulty to Henry Jim's story of how he had been interpreter for other agents and decided that this was probably the best he could do for now.

At Meeker's request Henry Jim went out to the village and brought the White River chief to the agency. This man's name was Douglas.

Douglas' appearance, his dress, and his manner gave Meeker encouragement. Here was the chief, and he was dressed in civilized clothing and spoke understandable English. He wore blue denim pants, a work shirt, and his hair was cropped off just below the ears. From the sides of his upper lip projected two neat points of a mustache.

Douglas talked freely, until Meeker began to explain something of his plan. This talk was met with silence. Meeker thought possibly Douglas did not understand these ideas, or that he was being cautious, wanting to know more about it before he spoke. Meeker painted a picture of the rich life awaiting those Utes who followed Meeker's plan, and of the approval that Washington would heap upon them. Abruptly, as though excited about something, Douglas announced that he must leave. Meeker invited the chief to return for other talks, but Douglas was gone.

With all the Indians gathered around the agency, Meeker looked forward to beginning immediately on his farming and educational program; but as soon as the last of the goods were passed out, all but a few of the Indians folded their lodges, packed their belongings on ponies, and disappeared. The few who remained near the agency were the followers of Chief Douglas, and with disappointment Meeker learned that although Douglas was the official chief, so listed in the records of the Indian Bureau, the larger body of the White River Utes followed another chief, whose name was Captain Jack.

Meeker became interested in learning all he could about this "Jack." He inquired of the employees and he questioned Henry Jim. Meeker did not meet Jack for many months, but as time went on Jack became a part of the plan at the agency as though he had been there all the time. The most puzzling thing Meeker learned about Jack was that he was probably the best educated of all the White River Utes, yet he was the strongest in resisting progress. He had been raised by a Mormon family. He had been sent to school and church; yet, according to Henry Jim, Jack did not believe in Indians farming, working, living in houses, or going to schools or churches.

Though most of the Indians were away from the reservation, the most important piece of raw material at this point lay waiting. That was the land; Meeker rode out and looked it over.

The agency was situated in a broad, high valley, and the White River flowed down from the mountains, crossed the valley, and made its exit through the narrow rock gateway at the lower end. Beyond the gateway was another valley, bordered by low ranges covered with cedar and scrub oak. This lower valley was level, and the drop in elevation would stretch any growing season for many weeks. It was irrigable from the river. This valley, which was called Powell's Valley or Powell's Park, Meeker decided was the place to begin farming, and consequently the place where the agency should be. He wrote Indian Commissioner Hayt for permission to move the agency, and permission was given.

Meeker's mind—the mind of an agricultural strategist—laid out the irrigation ditches, the fields and fences. When the plan was complete, he talked to Douglas about it.

Douglas did not want the change. Meeker talked and talked, describing fine homes and rich harvests, but Douglas kept saying, "No," and, "No good." Finally Meeker told Douglas that these were orders from the commissioner and Washington, and that Washington would not like it if the agency were not moved. In this Meeker made an important discovery: the word Washington was magic. Douglas consented.

55

Later, Douglas was able to provide a working crew of young Indians to clear the land, build fences, and begin work on the main irrigating canal. Meeker put the agency plowman to work, opening the hard sod of the valley floor to receive the river's water. The moving of the agency was begun, but Meeker soon saw that his large task would not be completed that summer. Most of it would have to be done in the spring, when the river was high and logs could be floated down from the old agency to the new site.

During the second week in July, Meeker's wife and youngest daughter, Josephine, arrived at the agency.

Josephine was now twenty and just out of Oberlin. She had grown into a tall, slender, assured young woman—not pretty, but with a vivid, alert face; she was the true heir of her father's intelligence, and his single-mindedness. She was an "emancipated" woman—her dark blonde hair was cut short at the shoulder—yet the center of her world was still her adored father.

Arvella Meeker's face was wrinkled and her eyes, though still sharp, held something of weariness and old age. Now sixty-four, she had struggled through the years of failure and discouragement, and even the better years had called upon her New England firmness as she worked at the side of her husband. As with all women of her time and place, her life, her identity were in her husband. She was ready to begin, with him, a new and strange task.

Mrs. Meeker immediately took hold of the domestic affairs of the agency. Gradually the house in the wilderness became the home of the Meeker family, as had happened with many other houses in many places. Her services to the Indians included attending to their medical needs, although this work was, according to the rules of the Bureau, supposed to be assigned to the teacher. Josephine was listed as "teacher and physician," but would work only with the school.

Her background also fitted Mrs. Meeker to take over the religious education of the Indians; when she obtained a house servant, a young Indian woman called Jane, who had been raised by a white family and spoke good English, Mrs. Meeker spent

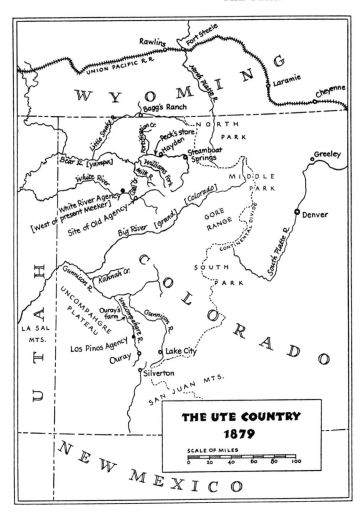

THE UTE COUNTRY
1879

SCALE OF MILES
0   20   40   60   80   100

many hours trying to interest her in the Bible and the Christian way of life.

Josephine's first weeks at the agency were spent in getting acquainted with Indian families. She rode out to the camps with Henry Jim and for the first time tasted *pana* and boiled jerked meat. She became absorbed in learning about Ute customs, and she talked at home about the things she had learned and seen among the Indians. When she brought home a pair of moccasins that one of the women had made for her, Meeker was forced to remind her gently but firmly that she was here to teach, not to learn, and should set a careful example of the American way. She dutifully put the moccasins away to be shown later in Greeley.

In the camps she tried to talk to the Indian women about her school and to make them see advantages in having sons, and even daughters, who could read, write, and work with numbers. She finally succeeded in getting three children for her school, which was conducted in the agency house since the new school building was part of the vision of the Indian town in Powell's Valley. One of the children was Douglas' youngest son, Freddie, one was a son of one of Jack's subchiefs, and one was a little girl whose mother had died recently and whose father was happy to have Josephine care for her.

Meeker, as he saw his plan taking visible form in Powell's Valley, thought about ways to keep the Indians at home. The stores on the borders of the reservation were, beyond doubt, the main attraction outside the reservation. They must buy guns and ammunition for their hunting; these were the only needs not available at the agency. Meeker looked upon hunting as a distraction from progress, but he conceded that the jump from the hunting to the agricultural stage could not be too abrupt. Besides, they could not be totally provided for by agency supplies. If limited hunting was necessary for a time, they should be able to buy hunting needs at the agency; then the Indians would stay at home and hunting could be controlled.

He wrote the commissioner asking that the Bureau's rule against sale of arms or ammunition within reservations be suspended in the case of the White River Agency. A store could be established at the agency where the Indians could purchase what they needed without having to go away. He asked that the army stop the illegal trade with Indians at outside stores; it was well known that these merchants took in goods issued at the agency and sold the Indians whisky. This trade was harmful, but Meeker argued that stopping sale of arms altogether was "to forbid the Indians from pursuing the only industry they now engage in."

Hayt answered, reminding Meeker that it was "not the policy to encourage the Indians to engage in these hunting expeditions, but use all legitimate means to induce them to abandon the hunt and engage in agricultural pursuits for a living." Hayt further ordered Meeker to "take stringent measures" to prevent the Indians from leaving the reservation, except by special permit from the agent when traveling Indians should be "accompanied by a police escort."

Meeker kept on trying to stop the trade at the stores. He made remarks about it in nearly all his letters to Hayt, but he met with silence. He visited merchants in person, but they countered his arguments with such answers as, "I never heard that an Indian agent had any authority outside the reservation."

His final resort was a visit to the deputy U. S. Marshal for the district, but the marshal's office took no action on the illegal Indian trade. Meeker later learned that the marshal himself was engaged in profitable trade with the Indians.

Still, as autumn approached, Meeker's hope and enthusiasm ran high. A tiny patch of civilization had appeared on the face of wild, beautiful Powell's Valley, and a large part of the work had been done by the Indians themselves.

"The Ute Indians are peaceable," Meeker wrote in a monthly report to Washington, "respectors of the right of property, and with few exceptions amiable and prepossessing in appearance. There are no quarrelsome outbreaks, no robberies, and perhaps not half a dozen who pilfer, and these are well known. The marriage relation is strictly observed, at least for the time it continues, and polygamy is practiced to but a limited extent. On the whole, this agent is impressed with the idea that if the proper methods can be hit upon they can be made to develop many useful and manly qualities and be elevated to a state of absolute independence."

<< II >>

As the early spring turned to summer and the sun was crossing the center of the sky so that it stood directly overhead at midday, the country around Smoking Earth River held only a few carniva.

Most of the families were away on the hunts, and the ground around the Bear Dance enclosure was covered with wide, brown circles where carniva had stood. Now those same carniva stood in smaller villages on Bear River, in Middle and North Parks, on the Sweetwater River, in the Buffalo Country, and around the stores on the Little Snake River. The hunts were good. The rain stopped at just the right time and the game gathered in great bunches to eat the good grass. There was meat to be eaten while it was red, and more meat to be dried on the racks. There were hides to trade at the stores.

The few carniva that remained on Smoking Earth River were those of the families who followed Quinkent. Some of Quinkent's people had gone on short hunts, but most of them had stayed near the agency.

This new Agent was a man a little older than Quinkent; his face was soft, beardless, and very white. He did not talk to the People but he spent a great deal of time with Quinkent, and Quinkent had told his band a great deal about this new Agent and what the People should do if they were going to please Washington, receive many presents, and get many fine new things.

There had been protest from Quinkent's people when he told them of the Agent's plan to move the agency buildings down into the winter valley, and some asked Quinkent to tell the Agent he must not do this. The valley below, where the Agent planned to move, seldom saw much snow, and good grass stayed there all winter. The winter camps were always made there, and the dancing and game grounds and the racing track were in the center of it. Those who had many ponies always left them there through the snow moons; it was these people who objected most to the move.

But Quinkent, with his fine words, had quieted them. He had told them that he, Quinkent, was speaking to Washington through this Agent; that this Agent was the closest friend of Washington, and that the People must please Washington if they were ever going to have anything. He hold them this Agent was going to have more feed for the ponies. He was going to raise good things in the ground and give them to the People to eat, and he going to keep cows and give the People milk. Quinkent also told his band that this Agent had straightened out with Washington this business about the presents being held up, and that soon they would have those presents, and many more.

Among the People a tawacz viem held his position only as long as he helped them to get the things they wanted and needed. Few men cared whether they ever were called chief or not, but sometimes there were men like this Quinkent, who wanted it more than anything else. All of the People, even those who followed Quinkent, knew this about him; but those who followed him were those who believed him when he said he was the friend of Washington and could get things for them. If Quinkent could do as he said, and get fine new things from Washington through this Agent, many more of the People would soon be following him.

One day Quinkent came down from the agency house and began talking around about the Agent having some money from Washington to give to those young men who did not have rifles to hunt with, or ponies to race on the race track. There were many such young men among Quinkent's people, and a few older ones, and this talk caused great excitement. Soon all of those who wanted to know how they were to get this money came to Quinkent's carniv to ask about it. Quinkent repeated that it was true; that this Agent did have money for them.

Then he told them what they must do to get this money, and most of them said they were no longer interested. Quinkent told them that first they must take up those shovels and long knives on sticks and such Maricat'z tools, and do what the white man calls "work." Most of those who had come to Quinkent's carniv

61

to find out about the money began to leave, some a little angry, but Quinkent called them back. He told them they would not have to do this work long and that when they were finished they would have money to buy guns and ponies. How, he asked them, did they ever expect to live well if they did not even have guns to hunt with?

After a while most of them said they would do this work for a while, but none of them liked it. Only a man who wanted and needed something very badly would put himself in the place of a white man. As soon as he had finished talking to them, Quinkent went back to the agency house.

In a few days some of the men, led by Quinkent, went down to the winter valley. There they began digging in the ground, cutting brush with long knives, and digging out stumps, as the Agent showed them how to do. Before long, a long patch of ground down there was a strange, naked looking thing. Then along came another white man with a different kind of a knife, pulled along behind two horses, which cut into the ground.

The older people did not like this business. A big piece of the winter valley was changing its face, and it seemed wrong. They spoke again to Quinkent about it, but Quinkent only repeated that this was part of what Washington wanted, and that they would see that it was a good thing, when Washington began giving away many presents.

The wrongness of it, the older people felt, had nothing to do with presents. A man could be given the finest presents, and he could give fine things in exchange for them; but doing such things to the land was another matter.

Then one day the older people saw proof of their belief that the wrongness of this thing was far beyond any of the People, or anything they might get from Washington. They called Quinkent to them, and showed him. He too squinted upward, and saw what they were looking at: a piece was gone out of the sun.

Even as they watched, their eyes aching from the glare of the naked, broken sun, the missing piece became larger. The sun was going away.

Those who watched were afraid, and they were not ashamed of their fear. It was easy to see that Quinkent too was afraid.

Such things had happened to the sun before, and a few of the older people could remember seeing it once or twice. The stories, even back to the oldest ones, told of this; but every time that it had happened it made people afraid. The sun, from which all good power came, was being eaten up; only the greatest, the strongest of all good powers could fight off the bad powers that tried to kill the sun.

Twilight, then dusk, fell over the country: over the mountains and the river, over the piece of the valley where the men had been doing the agent's work. Quinkent turned to his people; his fear seemed to be gone. He said he would go out by himself and use his powers to bring the sun back.

Quinkent walked off. In the near-darkness they could see him walking up a low hill. They saw him standing on top of the hill and pointing his feather to the sky. They heard his voice, chanting, and they knew that he had spoken his name to Sunáwiv, the God. Only at such a time should a man ever say his own name out loud. They knew he was calling to the sun to come back.

The sun was a black circle in the sky. Then an edge of brightness began to show at one side, and little by little the sun became whole again.

When the sun was again standing round, naked, and hot overhead Quinkent came down from the hill. He said nothing to the group—a large group now—who had been standing and watching him. He walked back toward the place where he and the others had been working, and those who had been working with him followed.

Later in the summer word was passed around that the presents which had been held at the railroad were being brought to the agency. Those who had gone on the hunts, many of whom had already been to the stores to trade, began coming in to the agency. One by one the carniva appeared again on Smoking Earth River, and every day families rode in, driving loaded ponies; the hunts had been good.

Those returning from the hunts heard about the men who were working in the winter valley and many went down there to see them. They were very funny, digging around with those white man tools and sweating. Men, women and children gathered in groups to watch them and laugh.

"Never mind," a young man said to some of his friends who were laughing at him. "You are laughing now, but soon I will finish this work. Then the Agent will give me money, and I am going to go and buy one of those rifles that shoots many times. Then you can laugh. I will not care."

"Cut'z-t' sawa," said one of the watchers, still laughing, "you are a big fool. While you are doing this you are not hunting. Your family will need food, the same as mine. You will have to spend this money for food, instead of buying a rifle. Then you will have to work some more. Pretty soon you will be living just like a Maricat'z."

The men who worked for the Agent in the winter valley found it hard to keep on, with so many standing laughing at them all the time. One by one they quit. Soon even Quinkent quit; for when his people would not follow him, even such a man as Quinkent believed it was best to follow his people for a while.

Then something new happened. A Maricat'z, whom all of the People knew and who was called Curtis, came to the agency. This Curtis had been at the agency many times before. He was not like most of the Maricat'z. He spoke the language of the People well—almost as well as one of their own children—and

he played games and told good, funny stories with the People. In meetings with white men from Washington, Curtis sat with the People and interpreted for them, and told the white men what they had to say. He helped the People in their business with Washington, and he did not lie, like so many of the Maricat'z.

Once Curtis had gotten some fine things from the soldiers to give to some of the men. This had happened while Nicaagat was with the general and his soldiers, fighting the Sioux. Some of the men told Curtis they would like to see Nicaagat, so Curtis took a lot of them and started up there to find him. When they reached the railroad, near the place where many of the soldiers stayed, they showed Curtis that their rifles were old and that they did not have good, warm clothes to go up into that north country. Curtis took them to where the soldiers lived, and he got some of the soldiers' rifles and some of their coats and shoes and gave them to the men.

Then they went on toward the Sioux country. Soon many of the men found that they were sick in their bellies. This, they told Curtis, would not be good for fighting Sioux, and these men went home. Then the others told Curtis that the ponies would not eat this grass up here, and if they did not eat the grass they would not be good for fighting Sioux. After a while everybody went home and Curtis went with them. They had not found Nicaagat, but they all had new rifles and warm clothing. The People still told this story in the camps; it was a very good story.

Shortly after Curtis came, Quinkent again went to the agency house. When he came back Curtis was with him. He called together all the men who had been working and told them that Curtis had come here to help them. He said there was not so much left to do, and that now they would be working with Curtis, not for the Agent. All the men went back to work. The others would not laugh so much now, since they were not working for the Agent. Soon they would be finished and would have the money to buy their rifles and some fine ponies.

At that time when the sun is hottest and brightest and the grass turns dark green and the hills turn brown, two white women came to the agency. One was a very old woman. Some said this was the Agent's mother and others said she was his piwán. Quinkent told his people that this one had come to give Maricat'z medicine to the sick and to read to them from the white man's Spirit Book.

The other was a young woman. She was long past the age when a woman should have a man with her, but this woman, who was the Agent's daughter, had no man. Quinkent said this woman had come to be with the children. He said she would be like a big sister to all the children.

Pa-veet'z, the "big sister," came out often and talked with the women. She told them something about taking the children into her house and caring for them and teaching them. She said the childen would learn all the things the Maricat'z children learn, and when they grew to men and women they would live just like the Maricat'z.

There was something about this woman that made a person like her. She was sad, the women said, because she had no man to be with. They felt sorry for her, and they listened to her talk because they did not want to hurt her feelings.

They told this woman they would ask their children if they wanted to go and live with her. When they asked them, the children always said, "No." They would tell Pa-veet'z this, and she would tell the women to ask the children again. The women said they would, but they did not. Pa-veet'z did not understand that the women would not make the children do what they did not want to do. The People thought the Maricat'z were very cruel to their children, always making them do things they did not want to do.

After the presents from Washington were passed out most of the People left the agency again, some to trade at the stores and some to start out on new hunts. The First Fall Moon was not far away, and those who had not gotten enough meat for the winter on the early hunts were going again.

The friends of Nicaagat had gone down to the agency to receive their presents, but Nicaagat stayed on Bear River. He had sent his piwán down to the agency for the goods. Everybody had heard about the work the agent was doing down there, and all except the few who stayed with Quinkent disapproved of it—

most of all Nicaagat. He did not want to go to the agency because he knew that if he did go there this new Agent would
probably want to talk to him.

The Maricat'z way had gotten inside Nicaagat when he was
a boy growing up, and as he turned into a man it had left him.
A man who has had such a thing happen to him wants to stay
away from those Maricat'z who are always trying to make others
live in the way of Maricat'z.

When his friends returned, Nicaagat listened as they told
him about what the Agent was doing in the winter valley; but
Nicaagat only listened. He had nothing to say about it now, and
he did not want to go down to Smoking Earth River to see these
things. He did not need to see them to understand and to know
what they might mean to the People. Many moons passed before
he saw them. The summer and fall moons passed and the snow
came and went before Nicaagat again saw Smoking Earth River.

« III »

The winter of 1878 came down and sealed everything. Day after
day it spread its whiteness and left life beating slowly under-
neath; then the sun stood in the bleak blue sky and the white
land gave back its harsh light. And at night snow filled the air
again.

Once a week the team came up to the agency from the lower
valley, bringing a load of coal and returning with lumber or some
other articles to be moved to the new agency site. Coal from new
mines on the reservation, opened by Meeker, burned in the fire-
places and stoves. Josephine spent most of her time with her
three brown-faced children, washing, dressing, feeding, teaching them. Meeker noticed with interest and pride the great
change in these children. The little girl was clothed as well as a
"girl of good family living in the city." They had learned rapidly
to read, write, and do simple sums; and they spoke English well,
although they used it with diffidence, especially before their own
people. On Christmas Eve their stockings were hung in over the
fireplace, and in the morning they giggled and squealed as they

pulled out gift after gift, while the Meeker family looked on, smiling.

On the evening before Christmas Eve, with sounds of children being washed and prepared for bed coming from another room, Meeker sat in his study writing. It was a long letter, to Senator Teller, a member of Colorado's first representation in the United States Congress; a holder of considerable mining and railroad interests in Colorado, Teller had from the beginning shown a great deal of interest in Meeker's work with the Utes.

I arrived here last May to take charge of these White River Utes [Meeker began]. Seeing how unsuitable is the location of the agency, by reason of its great elevation, and entire lack of land that can be tilled within several miles, I made application to have the location changed, which was granted, and a selection was made in Powell Valley, fifteen miles below. This valley comprises not less than 3,500 acres of excellent land, with cottonwood along the river, abundance of cedar on all the mountains, and about two months ago I discovered coal at the head of the valley, which, on further investigation, extends at least ten miles, in veins from six to ten feet thick, and often three to five of these veins above each other, all having a surface outcrop, and remarkably accessible. The stock-range on every hand is good, and I judge that it is sufficient for 10,000 head of cattle, which can live well the year round on the grass alone.

The valley was divided into four parts by streets running straight, one street through the length of the valley being seven miles long, and where the other street crosses the agency buildings are to be erected. As a preliminary, four or five log structures have been built for the use of the employes, for stabling and blacksmith shop, and a 40 acre field has been plowed on which wheat is to be sown next spring, while it is intended to plow at least one hundred acres more for the growing of corn, potatoes, pease, and vegetables next season. A grist-mill is to be built next year, and I think that in year after next, all the food required by these Indians will be grown here.

68

At first the Indians were decidedly opposed to the occupancy of Powell Valley for the agency, because they had always used it for their winter encampment, particularly for pasturing their horses, since snow seldom lies there more than a few days, while here it lies for five months, and they were perfectly willing to come up to this location once a week to draw rations, when they would immediately return. Their only idea of an agency is that it shall be a place where they get supplies, since no crops had ever been grown here, and only a sprinkle of vegetables, watered from pails, and they had only a vague idea what it is to engage in farming; in short, they protested against any change.

But that important work of furnishing water supply was undertaken by having the irrigating ditch surveyed, for which Congress made an appropriation, and then everything stopped because the Indians were opposed to moving the agency, and some of them threatened, while they generally declared they would not live there, and not one of them would have anything to do with farming, because Indians were never made to work, but white men were. All they wanted was their regular supply of rations and annuity goods. In consequence, at least two months' most valuable time was lost.

Meanwhile, I could only study the situation, and try to come to a decided resolution. A great embarrassment arose from the necessity for getting the Indians to consent to the expenditure of the $3000, appropriated for building the irrigation ditch, and I wrote fully to the Commissioner that their objection was to the removal at all, not to the ditch; for even they know, ignorant as they are, that if the removal was to be made it was for the purpose of having farming land, and in this case the water supply of the ditch would follow as a matter of course, and as much so as a well for getting drinking water.

Further, these Indians are divided into two parties, Douglas, the chief of all, and Jack, an aspirant to his place, so that if one side consents to any measure the other side is sure to oppose; therefore, to get the consent of the whole to any

69

measure, particularly a government one, was entirely out of the question, and to propose a government measure is to press the government between them, so that to ask that they shall agree upon a policy or measure is just as absurd as to ask that the Democrats and Republicans shall in like manner agree, for government is run, when it runs at all, by the party in power, and cannot be blocked by the party out of power. Apparently in response to such a statement of the case, the Commissioner sent me $1000 for the construction of the irrigating ditch.

By this I was encouraged, for I supposed, of course, the Commissioner waived the obtaining of the Indians' consent, since the agency was to be moved whether or no, and water must be had, and accordingly I told Douglas and other leaders that the Commissioner would get a "heap mad, by and by," and they had better not object to moving to Powell Valley. Then they surrendered and agreed we might move.

Upon this, I made agreement with Mr. Lithgow, on Bear River, to execute the first 2,000 feet on the line of the ditch, through a cottonwood forest, and requiring the most resolute work to grub out the big trees and clean out a perfect jungle of willow thicket, and he came on with teams and went ahead.

About this time Curtis came to the agency, having been employed by the Ute Commissioners at Los Pinos, and seeing the state of affairs, he proposed to employ a band of Indians to dig the remainder of the ditch. Of course I agreed to this at once, for it would follow that if they should work themselves, their 'consent' to the expenditure of the $3000 was obtained. . . . But we had no small job before us, for, when Douglas and his band proposed to work, Jack and his party opposed, and Douglas drew off; and so two or three weeks were spent; Jack's position was this, that Indians ought not to work, that it was the white man's business, and that they should dig the ditch.

In this dilemma I sent for Jack's right-hand man, Sowerwick, and told him that this opposition to the rest of the Indians working must stop or I would write the Commissioner and tell him about him. Upon this Sowerwick said they might go to work, and Jack coming around, he agreed also.

Thereupon Douglas and his band went to work under Curtis, who is an old hand at digging ditches, the contract being this, that Curtis was to have 25 cents a yard and the Indians $15 a month and double rations. Curtis made a machine by which there was a vast saving of labor, when the cut is only a foot or so, and he ate and slept and lived with the Indians, and worked early and late. Twenty-five Indians were at work fully a month, when freezing weather came and stopped all operations for this year, and they worked in a most faithful manner. They completed over 5,000 feet, most of the way about a foot deep, and the remainder from three to five feet deep, and I venture to say that the same number of average white men would not have done better.

The Indians' work came to $303, which was paid them in cash, and Curtis to about $200, from which should be deducted $20 or $30 which he paid for dried fruit and other things in his own money. I think the Indians were fully paid and Curtis did not have too much; indeed, I feel as if I could have been willing to pay him $100 out of my own little salary to secure such a great success. The ditch, so far finished, will water about 1,000 acres, all we shall want in two years. The result of all this is that as many Indians want to go to farming next year, and to have farm implements and houses, as I can possibly provide for; in fact, while working on the ditch all the tools that could be got together were in use, and more would have worked if I had tools.

I am absolutely embarrassed by their needs, for they want wagons and plows, and harness, and corrals, and seed of all kinds, so that it seems to me there is no kind of question but what they will work, and be glad to, for they believe they will have something and be better off. It is true that these workers belong to a party, and fortunately to the "administration" and they take pride in being conquerors, and particularly so because they are on the side of the government, but I have no doubt but the other side will, in a year or so, come over, and then some other subject will be found to quarrel about.

Naturally I cannot but imagine what would be the result if I should retire and Army rule should come in. I think of a West Point officer taking charge of these Indians. He has a good knowledge of mathematics and general accounts; he has read some history and many novels; he is a judge of good wine, or thinks he is, and he is honorable, honest, and what is called a perfect gentleman. But he has a few deficiencies; he knows nothing of farming, and like all the rest of the Army, he has a profound conviction that this great interior is wholly unfitted for growing crops, for wherever he has been located in Montana, Idaho, Arizona, Colorado or New Mexico, none of the officers or men have ever raised their vegetables. He says it cannot be done; he has no knowledge of the primary wants of families, as they progress from one state to another—no idea of what is needed in the household to lessen women's labor, to command the obedience of children. He has not the remotest notion of the township or neighborhood organization by which schools, roads, and fences are established or regulated; and finally he knows little or nothing of what constitutes a day's work at rural industry—how much a man should do, or how he should do it; nothing as to how much seed is sown to an acre of any kind of grain, nor when it is to be sown or reaped; nothing of hot-beds nor of small-fruit culture, and simply because these things are not in his line, nor does he pretend they are. Possibly there may be some subordinate or private who understands such matters, or thinks or says he does; but if such is the case, he will not be likely to have enlisted, because with such qualities as would enable him to direct the Indians, undoubtedly the most difficult job a man can undertake, he would find it far more profitable to work on his own account.

I think it is true that at every military post there is a sutler's store, and that there liquor is sold. I think it is true that more than half of all soldiers drink when they can, and true because they have enlisted from a class that drink; so that the proposition to turn the Indians over to the Army amounts to this: that men who do not practice industry, or who have avoided it, are expected to make others love it; that intemperate, unchaste, and dissolute men are to inculcate temperance, chastity, and morality to those who are like themselves; that they are to learn others to make homes and to establish the domestic hearth, when they have none of their own, and to educate families in economy, cleanliness, household arts and household industries, while they have no families and no households; nor could they have had in the uncertainty as to their abiding places. In short, it seems required that the soldiers shall exercise all the qualities of experts in whatever relates to the civilized and social state, except in the solitary branch which they understand; as if, when one wants his watch repaired, he will go to a shoemaker, or his piano tuned, he will go to a lawyer. . . .

Another thing I think of when I consider this subject, which is, the Indians fear soldiers and are prejudiced against them more than one can be told, and I judge, so far as I can learn, they are afraid their women will be led astray. Even if the soldiers were every way competent to civilize the Indians I think this prejudice will stand in the way for years, and if the plan so proposed shall be carried out I certainly expect outbreaks on the part of the Indians, even among these peaceable Utes—while I am certain there could be no progress in farming nor education.

Now note, I am only speaking from my knowledge and experience, and labor and success with the White River Indians, and I say it would be a cruel and unwise thing to bring soldiers here and break up what seems so happily begun. Of the wild Indians of the Upper Missouri I have nothing to say, except that whenever a tribe of Indians anywhere cannot by some means or other be brought into subjection, I think the taste of military rule for a few years would do them good, and I think all the Indian tribes had better be making up their minds pretty quick whether they are going to work or whether they propose to continue to be paupers.

When I get around to it, in a year or so if I stay as long, I shall propose to cut every Indian to bare starvation point if he will not work. The 'getting around to it' means to have plenty of tilled ground, plenty of work to do, and to have labor organized so that whoever will shall be able to earn his bread.

« IV »

The winter was past. The spring thunder and Bear Dance had come and gone. Now the sun climbed back toward its summer path through the middle of the sky, higher and warmer every day. The snow in the high country went away; the ground steamed. Soon the old pine needles and the old leaves were dry and crisp on the ground. Still no rain came. The old people said there would be no rain, that the summer would be a very dry one.

The early hunts went far. The People wanted to put away plenty of dried meat, in case the hunting was bad later in the summer. The old people told their families to use as little flour as possible, in case the flour from Washington was late in coming again. The Agent, Meeker, had been on the Smoking Earth River for almost a year now, and he might begin having trouble getting the presents, the way all the other agents had.

Nicaagat had not been near the agency since this Agent had come. Most of his friends had stayed away with him, going to the agency only once in a while to see what was happening there and coming back to tell about it. They said the Agent was still having all that digging in the ground, taking water out of the river, and making new buildings. Many of those who stayed with Nicaagat had hoped that the Agent would get tired of all that business before now and begin to act as agents are supposed to act. But the work down in the lower valley was still going on, and Quinkent and the Agent seemed to be good friends.

One warm day some of the men sat smoking their pipes and watching the women lay strips of red meat across the drying racks. The sides of many carniva were rolled up from the ground. It felt like summer here on Bear River. Here and there were families just arrived from the hunts, the naked frames of their carniva standing, shiny with new sap.

74

It was the kind of a day to be sitting around looking at the hills and trees, soaking in the late morning sunlight. Nicaagat and his friends talked little as they sat. Good friends can sit together on such a day, satisfied with their hunting, watching their women dry the meat and scrape the buckskins, and their thoughts gathering like the trickle of water from melting snows, joining together to make streams, joining together to make the river that flows past their little village. There were no plans for the coming days; there was only today.

A pony loped into the village. A voice called out, "Maiquas!" Nicaagat turned to see who was coming. It was the oldest son of Sowówic; the boy rode up to where they sat but did not dismount.

The boy was excited about something, although the long journey he had just finished showed in his tired face. Sowówic had left Bear River, after the early hunt, and had taken his family down to the agency, where his piwán planted some vegetables every year.

The boy brought a message from Sowówic to Nicaagat. Sowówic was having some kind of trouble with the Agent. It

had something to do with the Agent's wanting Sowówic to move his carniv to some other place. Yaminatz, leader of the band which stayed most of the time on Bear River and who had made good friends of the white settlers in this part of the country, was anxious to know more.

Feeling the importance of being the carrier of news to Nicaagat, the boy was anxious to tell more; but this same feeling of importance was making him careful to tell only that which he had seen and knew to be true—that no man might later accuse him, in his own mind, of telling something which he only believed to be true. He repeated that the Agent had taken the agency away. He said that when he went down to the agency with his father and mother, he had seen that the agency was not there any more. But he had seen the Agent there, and he had heard the Agent talking to his father. Afterward his father had told him to ride to Bear River for Nicaagat.

Nicaagat still did not fully understand this trouble, but he knew it was useless to try to get the boy to explain more. He also knew that Sowówic would not have sent his son this far if there had not been some kind of trouble that only Nicaagat could handle.

Nicaagat stood up. He told Sowówic's son to get off the horse and rest a while, and he started toward his carniv to tell his piwán to get his horse and a one-sleep camp ready for him. Acarí and Yaminatz said they would go too, and started off to their own carniva. Colorow said nothing, but at last he dragged his great body upward until he was standing. Then he lumbered away to get his horse and camp.

By the time the sun stood straight overhead the five of them were riding down the river, to a place below where they could wade their horses across and take the trail to the Smoking Earth River.

They rode long after dark, making only a small camp and starting again early in the morning. They rode hard; still it was not until past the middle of the day that they were riding down the long winding canyon into the upper valley.

Where the canyon opened out into the valley they halted their ponies. They could see down into the valley, and immediately each of them saw the strange empty place below, where the cluster of agency buildings had stood. They rode forward, and as they came closer they saw that scraps of wood and logs and rocks that had held up the buildings lay everywhere. Only part of one building was still standing.

Nicaagat had heard talk for several months that the Agent was planning to do some work below, in the winter valley. He had heard that some of the tools, wagons, and things from the agency had been taken down there. But he had heard nothing about the entire agency being moved.

Off to one side of the empty agency grounds they saw a single carniv with the sign of Sowówic on it. As they rode down the hill Sowówic came out and stood quietly in front of his house.

Three or four Maricat'z were working at the building which still stood. Two of them would lift a log from the wall and roll it until it splashed into the river. One of these Maricat'z saw them and came toward them across the bare ground.

Nicaagat had never seen the new Agent, but as soon as this man was close to them Nicaagat had no doubt that this was the one. What the others had said about him was true: he looked more like an old woman than an old man.

Nicaagat and his friends politely stopped their ponies as the Agent walked up to them. Sowówic waited beside his carniv.

The Agent approached, giving the Maricat'z greeting to Nicaagat. He was smiling. Now he stood beside Nicaagat's horse, talking rapidly. He was saying something about wanting Nicaagat to help him with something.

"You must help that Agent," said Colorow in the language of the People. "I think he is your grandmother."

The laughing that followed seemed to puzzle the Agent, who looked from one to another of them. The smile stayed on his face like something painted there. Then he turned to Nicaagat and went on talking.

Nicaagat looked at the Agent's face, stiff with a smile that had no part of laughter, and listened to the words spoken in the voice a man should use for children. Nicaagat was not using the Maricat'z language as he had learned to use it. He never did, before his own people, and he seldom did with Maricat'z, except when he needed to talk about something very important. Now, instead of answering the Agent, he turned to Acarí and told him to go with the others to the carniv of Sowówic, to wait for him there, and he would come later to tell of his talk with the Agent.

The others rode over to where Sowówic stood and dismounted. Nicaagat too had dismounted and was standing beside the Agent talking. Sowówic greeted each of his visitors and offered them tobacco, as they seated themselves outside his carniv.

Sowówic told them he had come to this place as he had every year at this time, at the end of Bear Dance, so that his piwán could take care of the vegetables she planted at the agency. Now, a few days ago, he had come with his family, his carniv, and his ponies; but when his piwán finished putting up the carniv, the Agent had come up from down in the winter valley, where he had been watching the work of his own Maricat'z and of Quinkent's people, and had told Sowówic that he must not put his carniv here—that he must take it down below, in the winter valley where the ponies were pastured through the snow. Sowówic, who understood little of the Maricat'z language, tried to ask the Agent something about this strange thing he had said, and the Agent had seemed to become angry. He had said that Washington had told him to make Sowówic do this. He told Sowówic that this was not his land here and that he would give him some land down below, in the winter valley. There, said the Agent, Sowówic must put his house. Sowówic told his friends now that he still did not understand this thing, and that if the

Agent had told the truth and Washington had really said such a thing, then something must be wrong with Washington.

Each man agreed with Sowówic. Then Yaminatz, who had many Maricat'z friends among those who had built their houses in the upper Bear River country, at the stinking springs which they had called Steamboat Springs, said perhaps it would be well to wait and try to understand more about this before saying more about it. The ways of the Maricat'z, although strange, were sometimes not so bad if a man took some time to understand them.

With this they began to talk of other things, forgetting the Agent and the agency, until they noticed that the sun was dropping toward the desert and that Nicaagat was walking toward them, leading his pony. The Agent had gone back to where the other Maricat'z were working, and all of them had climbed into a wagon and started down the road to the winter valley.

Nicaagat sat down; he did not wait long to begin talking:

"The Agent told me that we must all move down to the winter valley, where he has moved the agency," said Nicaagat.

"Unh," said Sowówic. "Unh," said each of the others.

"Then I answered him, 'You had better wait a little while before doing this, as we want to understand the reason for moving; I do not understand it.' I told him the place for the agency had been settled by treaty, and that I knew of no law or treaty that said anything about a new place. Then the Agent told me that we had better all move down below and that if we did not we would soon be made to; for this they have soldiers."

"Swerch!" came a whispered exclamation from one of the listeners. This Agent had spoken of soldiers. No other agent had ever spoken of such things. The interruption was excusable, for this was enough to excite the oldest and wisest man to bad manners. Nicaagat continued:

"I told the Agent that here was the agency, as the People had agreed with Washington that it should be; that we had agents before him, among others General Adams, who were all satisfied with the old place, and there the agency should stay. He said the place he has moved the agency to is better to grow things in the ground; that Adams was a man who knew nothing about farming and he had put the agency where they could do nothing of that kind; but he, Meeker, is a practical farmer and has moved it where something can be done."

Nicaagat waited again until each man signified he understood, then he continued:

"Then I said again to this Agent what I had said before, and I told him that it would be well if he grew things in the ground some other place. I told him we all have many horses, and we pasture them in that place during the Snow Moons. He then told me that Quinkent and Canávish had moved down to the winter valley, by the new agency, and that they, being important men, have been given pieces of ground they have chosen. He told me that I am an important man too, and that I may choose my own piece of land. He said all the People will have to move down there and take pieces of land, but the others will have to take what is left, after the important men have chosen."

What Nicaagat had said had to be thought over very carefully by each man. It was a strange idea this Agent had, and it was not easy to understand this kind of thinking. Each man there knew how the white men have strange ideas about the land; how they draw lines around pieces of it, and one man says, "This land inside this line is mine, and no other must come on it." But if a man looks he can see no line there at all.

But the agent had said something else which would be hard for any man to forget. He had talked of soldiers. Perhaps this Agent did not know what Washington had said when he called some of the important men of the People, and of other peoples, friends and enemies, to stand before him. He had said that now all tribes including the Maricat'z must live in peace with one another. To this all had agreed. The soldiers belonged to Washington, and Washington, who had talked of peace, would not send soldiers to the country of the People. This Agent had talked in a way to cause trouble; perhaps if Washington knew about it he would not like it.

Colorow wanted to tell a story. It was something the Agent had said that made Colorow think of a story. It was an old story, and they all listened as Colorow began:

"A long time ago, when the first Maricat'z came to our country, they saw an old man. They asked that old man if he were chief, and the old man told them he was chief. Then they told this old man they wanted to buy some of his land. They said they would give him many fine presents if he would give them some land. The old man looked at those presents, then he told them he would give them some land. They told him they wanted a great deal of land, so this old man asked them, 'Where will you take this land after I give it to you?' The Maricat'z answered that they would buy the land and leave it where it was. Then the old man told them, 'It is all right if I give you some land for these presents, but you must take this land away with you. We do not want your land lying around over our country.'"

The men sat thinking. It was a good story to tell at this time; that Agent had a great deal to learn if he were going to stay here.

Sowówic told them what he had seen down in the winter valley—the new buildings, the grass turned under, the cut and scarred land. Quinkent had been talking with this Agent a great deal—more than any other man. The bands down on the Uncompahgre and south of the tall mountains had lost much to the Maricat'z. It happened every time the Maricat'z came and talked to one man—to Ouray, who received the best presents of all from Washington. If one man becomes too big among a people, then he takes strength from the people, like a growth on the side of a tree; if there are too many such men among a tribe, then soon that tribe is no better off than the Maricat'z. Quinkent had been talking too much to this Agent. Perhaps soon all of the men of the Nüpartka would be doing this work, from which no good could come.

Nicaagat had waited for the others to talk about what he had told them. Now he had more to say about his talk with the Agent.

"Before the Agent left, I told him that perhaps I would go down there after a while and see what piece of land I would like. Perhaps we should all go down there now and see what he is doing."

They all mounted their horses and started down to the winter valley. They let the horses lope, for there was not much time until the sun would be gone. Soon the gently sloping ground flattened, and the white streaks faded from the river as it flowed more quietly. Then they saw the winter valley.

Down toward the river, by the big cottonwood trees where the race ground ran, were the agency buildings, almost as they had been up in the higher valley. In front of the buildings were two long strips where the good grass had been turned under; and the dry, brown earth lay face upward under the hot sun. Around these fields were thorny fences, which the Maricat'z used for keeping their cattle from going away, and which cut up ponies' feet and legs.

Nicaagat looked and his mind went back many snows, to that house where he had grown up, where the fields looked the same as this. He had run away. He had gotten angry and taken up a knife; then he had run away and wandered for many days in the mountains.

The Agent was not in sight, but as they rode into the agency grounds he came out of the house. He called to Nicaagat as he rode up and he began talking.

Nicaagat could not keep his mind on what the Agent was saying. He was still looking around him, at the plowed fields, at the land that had been stripped of brush farther down the river. He saw the points of two carniva down toward the river. One showed the medicine sign of Canávish, the sign of Quigat, the bear. The other carniv belonged to Quinkent.

Colorow was sitting thoughtfully on his pony, his belly hanging comfortably over the front of his saddle. "I think we had better go," he said, "before this Agent tries to make us dig in the ground; but perhaps if we only stay a little while he will give us food. This is the time all Maricat'z eat."

But Nicaagat could not stay here, even for a little while. He would go away as quickly as he could. He could not help things by staying, and it would be better if he went away where he could think.

"Go now," he said to the Agent.

Meeker stepped close to Nicaagat's horse, speaking softly, as though he did not want the others to hear what he was saying; but Nicaagat turned his pony around, anxious to get away. The Agent kept on talking, but Nicaagat was riding away, and the others followed. Soon they were climbing the dry, wrinkled hills; the river and plowed fields were below and behind them.

After a while they would all forget the Agent, what he had done to the winter valley, and all his talk. After a man goes away from talking to a Maricat'z, he can almost never remember what that Maricat'z has said.

4. TALK

THROUGH the cool days and chill nights of June, too many of which brought frosts, Meeker suffered with the infant crops. July came, and with it came hot days. The soil dried and crumbled into powder, and grasses turned brown and curled under the sun. The season was unusually dry. There had been only one shower for three months. The level of the river began to fall, and soon it trickled between jutting rocks, which blocked the newly-sawed logs the agency workers attempted to float down from the high forests. Building at the agency came to a near standstill, and a short hay crop added to Meeker's worries.

The last snow had long since disappeared from the mountains, and the sun, dry wind, and trunks of the pines had sucked up the last drop of water from the forest floor. The carpet of needles was brown and brittle, and hot, dry breezes swept with a gentle roar through the boughs of the trees.

It was a season for fire, and fire came. Small fires grew over night into big fires. They joined until a great band of flame cut across the land. Fire rushed through the forests, mountains to desert, north to south, leaving behind great patches of blackened stumps.

The drought and the fires brought new trouble to the White River Agent, to dwarf those earlier griefs brought on by the unseasonable cold of early summer. At that time, as the White River rose to a boiling flood crest, with the strengthening sun melting the high mountain snows, the buildings of the old

84

agency had been taken apart and piece by piece floated down to the new site in Powell's Valley.

Work was resumed, early in the spring, on the irrigation canal, and by the beginning of summer Indians were working in the fields surrounding the agency with shovels, axes, and brush hooks, clearing the land for planting, while the plow turned over more and more of the wild sod.

Meeker reported to Commissioner Hayt:

Eighty acres have been substantially fenced with cedar posts, a heavy pole on top and two strings of barbed wire below. Twenty acres of wheat is now up and growing. Twenty acres of new, bottom land, intended for potatoes, is partly cleared, mostly done by Indian labor. . . .

Something over thirty Indians have been at work, but the average of steady laborers is from twelve to fifteen. These are induced to work by the influence of Douglas, their chief. They are his retainers, and they are more subject to him than they would be if they were slaves. He takes their rations and provides regular meals. . . . The remedy for this condition is to provide small allotments of land for each working Indian, whereby he will have a home of his own, and thus become independent of his chief, by which means this species of feudal system will be broken up and destroyed.

Work on the new schoolhouse was begun during June. While the agency was being moved to Powell's Valley, two of Josephine's pupils slipped away and returned to their families, leaving only Douglas' little boy. Meeker was thoroughly disappointed by this sudden loss of ground he had counted as gained, but he looked toward the completion of the new school building, certain that this would induce more families to send children to school.

The school building will be ready for occupancy in a few weeks, [Meeker told Hayt]; then it will be seen what can be done to establish a school among people who do not and can not think, who have but an imperfect idea of the value of money or in what wealth consists, who have neither literature nor history, and who are without ambition or a necessity to exercise it, because the government feeds and clothes them, and if it will not they can live nearly as well by hunting, or by foraging on white people's possessions.

Considering his total project, Meeker had other thoughts on the education of Indians:

It seems to me that work goes before education, and that only a working man can have an idea of the use of schooling. A savage can have no notion of the value of knowing many things. Besides, the savage family has no discipline, and the children are neither heirs nor successors of it. The only discipline exercised at this agency is when I get the men to work day after day; and this on the penalty of withholding extra rations. This, in fact, is the equivalent to "compulsory education," and it is the only power that can be made to operate. In other words, with plenty of coffee, sugar, and dried peaches I can lead them forward to civilization.

June passed and hot, dry July came; and with July came the fires. The newspapers of Denver and of every town in the state large enough to have a newspaper were filled with news of the fires sweeping the state.

The cause of the forest fires which were so unusually bad this season was, according to all the reports, the Ute Indians. The Utes were setting the fires deliberately, to drive out the settlers and destroy the ranches of the whites, or to drive game. Many of the stories also charged the Utes with a variety of other crimes, from killing white settlers to chasing off stock and terrifying women.

These complaints against the Utes were usually made public from the office of Governor Pitkin; their principal source seemed to be the Middle Park, where W. N. Byers, now Denver postmaster, owned a large ranch which was being managed by his son. The stories often quoted Pitkin, who in turn quoted from reports he received from citizens.

Photo of Ute warriors surrounding Chief Ouray. *Left to right:* Ankatosh, Warets, Ouray, Shavano and Gurerro. Courtesy of the Denver Public Library. X-30698.

An 1876 photo of Ute Indians from the Western Slope of Colorado as they tried to maintain peaceful relations with their white neighbors. Courtesy of the Colorado Historical Society. F-21,075.

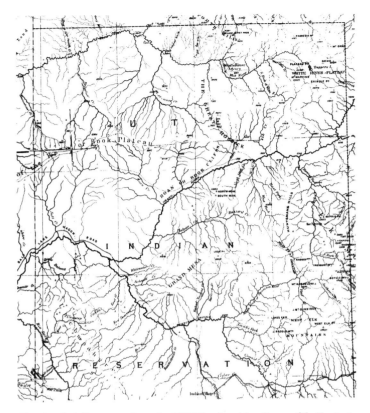

This detailed illustration from the 1878 Hayden Atlas *Survey of the Territories Embracing Colorado* clearly shows the Western Slope as the Ute Indian Reservation, though prospectors and others ignored those boundaries, especially after the discovery of gold in the San Juan mountains and silver ore in Leadville. A Western Slope copy of the original atlas is in the possession of Meeker attorney Frank G. Cooley.

Northern Utes, their agent and interpreter before the arrival of the controversial agent Nathan Meeker. Unlike Meeker, who insisted the Utes learn to farm, other agents helped the Utes transport and sell their deer horns and hides, which they had once traded as far south as the markets in Taos, New Mexico. Courtesy of the Denver Public Library. X-30633.

The Utes Must Go.

But don't forget to patronize the Pioneer Grocery of Colorado.
WOLFE LONDONER.

"The Utes Must Go"–this newspaper grocery ad symbolized the attitude of many whites in Colorado who insisted that the Utes be removed from the Western Slope though they remained remarkably peaceful during the exploration and settlement of the state. Courtesy of the Colorado Historical Society. F-44,177.

Likeness of Quinkent or Chief Douglas [sic], so named because he reminded whites of the black abolitionist Frederick Douglass. He was jailed for his role in Meeker's death, but he was later judged insane and released. Image probably from *Harper's Weekly*. Courtesy of the Denver Public Library. X-30704.

Likeness of Nicaagat or Captain Jack, probably from *Harper's Weekly*. Courtesy of the Denver Public Library. X-30703.

The Late Ute Outbreak at the White River Agency—the ruins after the fire and massacre of September 29, 1879, from a sketch by Lieutenant C.A.H. McCauley, Third U.S. Cavalry. Courtesy of the Denver Public Library. X-30699.

Though the death of Agent Meeker and others had occurred on the Northern Ute Reservation, all Utes lost land in Colorado. In this photo by Sumner W. Matteson, Ouray Utes have been ordered to leave Colorado hunting grounds. Courtesy of the Colorado Historical Society. F-15,557.

The Ute scare in Colorado in 1887, otherwise known as "Colorow's War," was a racist attempt to kill Indians. Chipeta and other Indian women were merely exercising their treaty rights and gathering berries near Buford on the White River when they were harassed and ridiculed by local cowboys. The so-called Colorow War cost the state $80,314.72 as over eager troops came on the Denver and Rio Grande Railroad to New Castle and then rode horseback over the old Ute Trail in pursuit of Utes who had already fled down river towards the Uintah and Ouray Reservation in Utah. The confrontation scene in this artist's drawing never occurred because cowboys never managed to catch the fleeing Utes. Courtesy of the Denver Public Library. X-30700.

Known as the Rocky Mountain Rifles, troops of soldiers—mostly from Leadville—and other volunteers gathered on the Western Slope to go kill Indians probably during the "Colorow War." Courtesy of the Denver Public Library. X-368.

Early in July Pitkin wrote a curt letter to Meeker, informing
him that his Indians were setting fires and molesting settlers
outside their reservation. He also warned Meeker that White
River Utes in North and Middle Parks had been ordering settlers
to leave, and threatening them with death if they did not obey.

On July 5 Pitkin sent a telegram to Commissioner Hayt:

REPORTS REACH ME DAILY THAT A BAND OF WHITE RIVER UTES
ARE OFF THEIR RESERVATION, DESTROYING FORESTS AND GAME
NEAR NORTH AND MIDDLE PARKS. THEY HAVE ALREADY BURNED
MILLIONS OF DOLLARS OF TIMBER, AND ARE INTIMIDATING
SETTLERS AND MINERS. HAVE WRITTEN AGENT MEEKER, BUT
FEAR LETTERS HAVE NOT REACHED HIM.

I RESPECTFULLY REQUEST YOU TO HAVE A TELEGRAPHIC ORDER
SENT TROOPS AT NEAREST POST TO REMOVE INDIANS TO THEIR
RESERVATION. IF GENERAL GOVERNMENT DOES NOT ACT
PROMPTLY THE STATE MUST. IMMENSE FORESTS ARE BURNING
THROUGHOUT WESTERN COLORADO, SUPPOSED TO HAVE BEEN
FIRED BY INDIANS.

I AM SATISFIED THERE IS AN ORGANIZED EFFORT ON THE PART
OF INDIANS TO DESTROY THE TIMBER OF COLORADO. THE LOSS
WILL BE IRREPLACEABLE. THESE SAVAGES SHOULD BE REMOVED
TO INDIAN TERRITORY WHERE THEY CAN NO LONGER DESTROY
THE FINEST FORESTS IN THIS STATE.

FREDERICK PITKIN, GOVERNOR OF COLORADO

Hayt was away from his Washington office, but Acting Commissioner E. J. Brooks immediately wired Meeker:

GOVERNOR OF COLORADO REPORTS YOUR INDIANS DEPREDATING
NEAR NORTH AND MIDDLE PARKS. IF CORRECT TAKE ACTIVE
STEPS TO SECURE THEIR RETURN TO RESERVATION. THE SECRE-
TARY DIRECTS THAT IF NECESSARY YOU WILL CALL UPON
NEAREST MILITARY POST FOR ASSISTANCE.

Since first taking over the White River Agency, Meeker had
felt that his greatest problem was that of the Indians' freedom
to roam as they pleased. He had tried to gain control over the

situation by direct persuasion, and by seeking aid from both
the Indian Bureau and the Army, without notable success. Now,
suddenly showered with these complaints, Meeker saw an opportunity to get the help he needed in keeping his charges at home.

> You are witness [he wrote Commissioner Hayt] that I have
> repeatedly reported to you of the absence of the Indians
> from their reservation, being generally on Snake and Bear
> Rivers; and I have, agreeably to your directions, often re-
> quested the military at Fort Steele, through the commandant,
> to clear those valleys, but no attention was paid, and no
> answers given. North Park is the best hunting ground in
> America, but it is too elevated for general farming. Recently
> gold discoveries have been made; a great many miners have
> gone in, and the Indians wish to occupy the ground. A col-
> lision is by no means improbable.

In his monthly report to the Indian Bureau Meeker explained
his view of the situation in detail:

> ... The great bulk of these Indians, or at least half of them,
> went over to the valleys of Snake and Bear Rivers last fall and
> have not returned. They have greatly annoyed the settlers by
> letting their horses run on their meadows and uplands, and
> by burning their timber, especially valuable in this almost
> treeless region. About two months ago many of them who
> remained here during the winter went off hunting, and I have
> had reports of their trespasses in Middle Park and elsewhere,
> though I positively forbade their going. An employe, H.
> Dresser, accompanied by Douglas, the chief, has now gone
> to Middle Park to bring them back, and as they belong to
> Douglas' band, they will probably come.
> Another collection of several bands, acknowledging no
> chief, is in North Park, threatening the miners and ranchmen.
> Whether the commandant at Fort Steele will pay any atten-
> tion to my request to drive them out of the park is doubtful,
> as hitherto he has paid no regard to my requests. Among these
> Indians in North Park are the worst of the whole tribe. Some

are well-known as horse thieves . . . all bad lots, and it seems to me inevitable that conflicts with the whites will result sooner or later. A most unfavorable characteristic of these Indians off the reservation is the burning of timber and their wanton destruction of game, and simply to get the skins. . . .

A few days later Douglas and Dresser returned from their errand to report that all Indians had vacated the parks. At that time Meeker informed Hayt that most of the Indians were now on Bear River, near the trading stores, "some of them begging food."

. . . In many parts of the Bear River Valley [Meeker wrote to the Washington office] and all the way up to its head in Egeria Park, the country is well burned over. At Hayden, where reside the families of Smarts and Thompson, the fires were so near the houses that the women, whose husbands were away, were on watch two days, and carried their household goods to a place of safety. . . .

The Thompsons, of Hayden, were the family of Major James B. Thompson, who had once served as general agent to the Utes in Denver. He, like Byers, had established a ranch on the Western Slope, but spent much of his time in Denver.

They are now drawing near the agency so as to be on hand at the yearly distribution of annuity goods. [Meeker continued]; after that they will depart, and roam over a country as large as New England, where settlers are struggling to make new homes, and the Indians think it all right because they are, as they boast, "peaceable Indians."

« II »

Quinkent had not gone on any of the hunts this year. He had stayed at the agency to see that the work which Washington ordered was done. Some of those who followed him had gone hunting, but Quinkent had stayed; and all those who were doing this work of digging the bed for the new little river and pulling the brush out of the ground had stayed.

There had not been the trouble this summer of getting the men to do this work. The Agent had given money to all those who worked last summer, and this had relieved Quinkent's mind a great deal; for the white man often promises money and presents and does not give them. Had the Agent not given as he promised, Quinkent would have had a lot of trouble explaining this to the men who had worked, and to their families.

But the Agent had given the money, and this summer, as Quinkent had promised, those who worked were getting extra presents from Washington—more coffee, sugar, and dried fruits than their families could use. Those who worked were beginning to feel that before very long they would become rich men, and Quinkent was greatly satisfied, knowing that these men were not sorry they had listened to Quinkent in the first place.

Even though he had gone on none of the hunts this year, Quinkent and his family had plenty of meat. Every time the white workers at the agency killed a steer the Agent gave Quinkent a big chunk of red meat, and when his piwán cooked it, nobody could tell that it was not buckskin meat. Quinkent and his family had all they needed to eat.

Every morning and every night his piwán went with some of the other women up to the corrals at the agency and took milk from the cows. They came home with their buckets full. They could not drink all this milk, and the women at the agency taught Quinkent's piwán and the other women to make the rich, sour, lumpy stuff that all the men and children liked to eat.

The Agent had made two wide roads that crossed each other in the valley, and he told Quinkent that the name of the most important one was "Douglas Avenue." The white workers had been sent to build a house of logs for Canávish and his family, and the Agent had said that soon Quinkent would have such a house, with an iron box inside to keep fire in, so that the house would always be warm through the snow months. Soon, the Agent had said, all of the People would have houses like this.

Quinkent was getting older; his bones were getting old. The

year before, when he had gone on a hunt in the high country where every morning the grass is white with dew, he could feel the aches deep inside him. When a man begins to reach this age, talk of houses that are warm all through the snow is good to hear. Perhaps the younger men would not listen to this talk, but it was the older ones who were important among the People. These men, when each of them had a warm, log house for his family, would know that Quinkent was the wise one for listening to Washington. They would know this, and they would always listen to Quinkent when he spoke; for they would know that Quinkent was the man who could bring a good and peaceful life to every man who listened to him. One by one the men who saw that those who had the finest horses, the best houses, and the most presents from Washington belonged to Quinkent's band would join those who followed Quinkent.

While Quinkent's plan would bring him many followers, it was also pleasing Washington. When Washington saw that Quinkent had more followers than any other man and that he was the wisest man and the one who listened to Washington, then Quinkent would be the most important man of all: perhaps even more important than Ouray, who now lived in a fine Maricat'z house, and who received the finest presents of all from Washington.

The summer began well for Quinkent; but later there had been some bad talk that troubled him a little. There had been many fires in the trees this year, and there was talk among some of the People that the Maricat'z were saying that the People started these fires.

Quinkent had worried about this talk at first, then some of his band came to him, asking what he thought of it. Quinkent said that this talk had started only because Washington was angry with those who had gone away and had not stayed at the agency and worked as Washington wanted them to do. Washington was angry with those who had not listened to Quinkent; but this talk was not about those who had stayed at the agency. This talk was for those who followed Nicaagat and disobeyed Washington, and perhaps these would get into trouble. Those who stayed at the agency with Quinkent would get into no trouble.

91

Those who had come to ask about this went away satisfied with what Quinkent had told them; he hoped that this would perhaps make more people leave Nicaagat and follow Quinkent. Nicaagat had led most of the families away from Quinkent when he came home from fighting the Sioux. The younger men admired him; it was mostly the older men who stayed with Quinkent.

This Nicaagat was not really one of the People, and there were bad stories about him. Some even said that he was part Maricat'z; others thought he was part Mexican, or Gosiute, or Paiute. Still, even after hearing these things, most of the People went with him. They came and listened to Quinkent talk, then they went away with Nicaagat.

At first Quinkent had been angry about this, but now he felt that he could wait. He was getting to be an old man, and even though their time is shorter it is easier for old men to wait.

Then one day the Agent called Quinkent to his office. He told Quinkent that some of the men were up in Middle Park, and that the white settlers up there were afraid of them. He asked Quinkent to go and bring them back to the agency.

At first Quinkent did not want to go. He thought of the stories the Maricat'z were telling about the People and the fires, and he was afraid some of the People might think that he was doing too many things for the Maricat'z, instead of for the People. Then he thought of Washington, and how Washington would think even more of Quinkent if he went there and brought these men back. Quinkent decided that he would go.

The Agent sent one of the white workers with him. Quinkent felt that it would have been more dignified to have gone without this man, but the Agent had insisted that the white man go too.

It was a long trip up into Middle Park. They found a small hunting camp near the Maricat'z village where Byers, that man the People called Pius, lived. The men did not like having their hunt interrupted like this. Some seemed a little angry with Quinkent, and one said he believed Quinkent was doing too many things just because the Agent told him to.

Quinkent answered that he had not come because the Agent sent him. He had come because Washington was angry with those who went away from the agency, and that he, Quinkent, had come here because he was afraid there might be trouble with Washington. After he said this the women began to pack the camps and get ready for the trip back to the agency.

On the way back they saw some soldiers. These were strange looking soldiers; they acted and dressed like ordinary soldiers, but they had black faces. These soldiers had been in Middle Park only a little while, and this was the first time Quinkent had ever seen them. He had heard about them from others; the People thought them very funny, and they called them Buffalo Soldiers, or *To-Maricat'z,* "Black-Whitemen."

The soldiers stopped in the road, and their general, who had an ordinary white face, talked to the white worker from the agency. Most of the People did not like soldiers and would not go near or talk to them, but Nicaagat was not afraid of them. He said the soldiers were his friends. When he thought of this, Quinkent made up his mind that he would talk to that general and show him that he was a good man. Then he could tell the People that he, too, had friends among the soldiers.

Quinkent edged his pony over beside the general's horse, and told him his Maricat'z name. The general was not difficult to talk to, and the black-faced soldiers, who sat on their horses and stared, did not bother Quinkent. He told that general that he was the man who always had been the friend to Washington and had always done everything the way Washington wanted. He told the general that he would never let the People do anything that Washington did not like.

The general seemed pleased to hear this, and he shook hands with Quinkent before he left. Quinkent too was pleased.

Now Quinkent was a friend of Washington's soldiers. There was no need for him to be afraid of them, for they would never hurt a good man like Quinkent.

« III »

Now, in 1879, the best and the worst were over for the soldiers of the frontier army posts. The work was more that of policing than of combat. The fierce Sioux had been subdued. A new reservation had been established for what was left of the runaway Cheyennes, and those few tribes that had not been taken to Indian Territory, where they were well controlled by Mackenzie's Fourth Cavalry at Fort Sill, were learning to live on their reservations. The Indian wars, it was being said every day now, were pretty much a thing of the past; but they were a thing of the very recent past. Hardly a man stationed in one of the western posts could say he had not participated in some Indian war or another; hardly a soldier was not an expert, self-styled or otherwise, on the ways and fighting style of this tribe or that tribe. The only lively Indian question left in the jurisdiction of the War Department was the proposition, gaining in popularity among the general staff members, to turn Indian Affairs completely over to their administration.

Major Thomas Tipton Thornburgh, commandant of Fort Fred Steele near Rawlins, Wyoming, was not at all in favor of this idea. He recalled vividly the Sioux campaigns, ably led by the Old Gray Fox, General Crook; he had participated in the pursuit of the runaway Cheyennes. Thornburgh still remembered too well those days and nights in the bleak Nebraska sand hills with his small command, tracking, trailing, but always a little too late and too far behind. He had been one relay in that long chain of Army units which chased the stubborn bands of Dull Knife and Little Wolf all the way from their reservation in Indian Territory to their old home in the Black Hills. When they created the new reservation for the remnants of the Cheyenne

94

bands in Montana, the Indian Bureau felt the matter was settled to their satisfaction; but to the Army the Cheyenne campaign was a degrading failure, a defeat.

Now Major Thornburgh, like other commanders of army posts in the Far West, was a keeper of the peace—a policeman who insured the safety of the frontier settlements. It was their duty to answer calls for aid from towns, settlements, agencies, ranches, and mining camps: to calm fears, to prevent bloodshed, to replace the panic of isolation with assurance of safety and security.

Major Thornburgh was well into his middle years. He was a graduate of West Point and had fought with the Army during the Civil War, but most of his military career had been spent as a professor of military science and tactics at various colleges. His sensitive, intelligent face, his round sad eyes fit the academic world better than the life of a frontier army post, but the bristling black sideburns and heavy dented chin were distinctly military.

Calls for police work drifted into Major Thornburgh's office now and then. He usually forwarded them to his immediate superior, George Crook, at Fort Omaha, Nebraska. If the request was urgent—and they seldom were, in recent years—action was taken. If there was no urgency, Major Thornburgh executed his duty by pushing them on up the chain of command and awaiting orders.

This latter was the action he took on a letter from Agent N. C. Meeker at the White River Ute Agency, in Colorado, which arrived on March 17, 1879. It read:

It is my duty to inform you that quite a large party of White River Utes are about to start north, perhaps for the scene of Indian troubles. Whether they intend to mix in is doubtful, but I think it entirely certain they will carry considerable supplies of ammunition for sale to their allies.

I have before reported to you that there are several stores on Snake and Bear Rivers which keep full supplies of ammunition. I would hereby request you to arrest all White River Utes bound north and either hold them or send them back to the reservation. They deserve a lesson. I wish also

95

the sale of ammunition as above kept be put an end to, agree-
ably to orders in such cases.

Meeker's letter was confusing. The "Indian troubles" he referred to must mean some of the Sioux, who were reported to be
showing some hostility. But "their allies" was truly a strange
choice of words. Major Thornburgh had heard General Crook
tell of the ferocity shown by the Ute and Shoshoni scouts in his
most recent campaign against the Sioux, the callous behavior of
one "Ute John" or "Captain Jack" shocking even the soldiers; an
"alliance" between the Utes and the Sioux was something to
make a man smile.

The Major asked some questions and discovered that a few
Utes had been hunting south of the Snake River, but settlers
reported that they had returned south.

Later in the spring, and early in the summer, Major Thornburgh began reading articles about the Utes in newspapers from
Denver and Cheyenne, Wyoming. Since his post was nearest
the country referred to in the articles, he was puzzled that he
had heard no reports of these Ute depredations. Major Thornburgh was a thorough man and a conscientious soldier. He wrote
letters to settlers he knew throughout the area which the papers
claimed was being ravaged by Utes, inquiring for details.

Toward the end of July Major Thornburgh received a message through the chain of command from the Secretary of War,
who said he had been advised by Secretary of the Interior Carl
Schurz of a complaint by Agent N. C. Meeker. This agent complained that he had repeatedly asked for military aid in keeping
his Indians on their reservation and putting a stop to their raids,
but that the commandant at Fort Steele had as repeatedly ignored his requests.

Major Thornburgh had his answer ready. On July 27 he wrote
to General Crook at Fort Omaha:

Sir:

I have the honor to submit the following report of the
recent visit of the Ute Indians from White River Agency to
this vicinity:

About the 25th of June a band of some 100 Indians from the White River Agency made their appearance at a mining camp on the divide near the head of Jack and Savoy Creeks, some 60 miles south of this post, and engaged in hunting and trading in this vicinity for about one week, when they departed (as they said) for their agency.

I did not learn of the presence of these Indians until after their departure, nor was I notified by the agent at White River that they had left their agency until July 11, when I received a communication from him dated July 7, stating that a considerable number of the Indians had left their reservation and were burning timber and wantonly destroying game along Bear and Snake Rivers, also warning all miners and ranchmen, and requesting me to cause them to return to their reservation. Upon receiving this letter I made inquiries and could not find such a state of affairs to exist but did find that the Indians had killed a great deal of game and used the skins for trade. The miners they visited in this section were not molested, but on the contrary were presented with an abundance of game. No stock was molested, and so far as I can learn no one attributes the burning of timber to these Indians.

Since I have been in command of this post (one year) Agent Meeker, of the White River Agency, has written me two letters. . . . These letters have usually come to me after the Indians had paid a flying but peaceful visit to this country and departed (as they always say) to their agency. The White River Agency is situated some 200 miles from this post, and there are very few settlers in the country between Fort Fred Steele and the agency, consequently I am not informed as soon as I should be of the movements of these Indians. Bear and Snake Rivers are about 100 miles from this post, and to reach them by traveling this distance would require the trip to be made through very rough country, impracticable for wagons, the only transportation available.

I have never received any orders from my superior to cause these Indians to remain on their reservation at the request of the agent, but am ready to attempt anything

97

required of me. I have been able to communicate with nearly every ranchman residing within 100 miles of this post in reference to the late visit of these Indians, and forward herewith letters received from them. Both the letters mentioned above as having been received from Agent Meeker were forwarded to higher authority, and instructions have been asked to guide me in this matter.

I am very respectfully, your obedient servant,
T. T. THORNBURGH
Major Fourth Infantry, commanding post.

Enclosed were eight other letters, variously scrawled and printed:

In regard to your inquiries of the Ute Indians on the Upper North Platte, would say that there was about 65 or 70 lodges, as near as I can ascertain; they camped on Jack Creek about the middle of June; they were evidently a hunting party doing no damage and seeming perfectly friendly. They had caught some elk calves which they wanted to trade for cartridges, but the ranchmen would not trade. They traded them some butter for furs and skins, and killed enough game for their own immediate use.

TAYLOR PENNOCK
Lake Creek, Carbon County, Wyoming
P.S. They went south towards North Park between the 3d and 5th of July, but done no damage nor made no threats.

. . . The Indians committed no depredations in this settlement beyond slaughtering game by the wholesale. No hostility was manifested toward any of the settlers, the Indians conducted themselves peaceably and quietly. No cattle was killed and no fires set.

Rumors of trouble in North Park have reached here from time to time, but I cannot vouch for their truthfulness. The Indians left this country for the North Park about the 3d of this month—at least not later than that time.

We have no one to blame for the Indians being in this

country but ourselves, for we were aware of the fact that if you had been notified of their presence that you would have at once taken steps to remove them.

J. T. CRAWFORD
Warm Springs, Wyo.

. . . about the last of June I had occasion to go to Spring Creek, some 12 miles farther south, and I found that a band of some 100 Indians had just left Wagner's Ranch, having remained there only two days, which time they used for trading horses, skins, &c.

These Indians are very friendly, and tried in every way not to get into trouble with any one. They killed considerable game, more than they could use, but that is not an uncommon thing in this country. I have heard of no acts of hostility, and in fact I know that none was committed, as I have seen nearly all the ranchmen in 100 miles of me since their departure. I have seen Mr. Jones, a miner, from North Park, who told me that a good many miners when they learned of the approach of the Indians, left and returned home.

No depredations were committed at the Park that I have ever heard of.

WM. BRANER
Lake Creek, Carbon County.

. . . I have just returned from seven days' journey through the country which the Ute Indians have been traveling and hunting. Being well acquainted with settlers of the country, have met and conversed with most of them, and have heard no complaints except the great slaughter of game. I traveled 30 or 40 miles along the base of the mountains on their trail and did not see where any prairie or timber fire had originated from their camps, or where there had been any recent fire. I learn from the ranchmen that the Indians left the North Park about July 1, and have heard nothing further of their movements.

NEWTON MAJOR
Fred Steele, Wyoming

... the band of Indians who were lately here left this country on the 1st instant, going south into Colorado. I don't think they have set out any fires or interfered with the settlers in any way whilst here, and I have had a good chance to know. They killed considerable game while here.

B. T. BRYAN
North Platte River, Wyo.

Regarding the Ute Indians, I do not think they set any of the fires in this part of the country, as the tie-men admitted to me that the fires on Brush and French Creeks caught from their camp fires. They crossed on Beaver Creek fifty miles south of Steele on June last or July 1st, going north.

W. B. HUGUS
Warm Springs, Wyo.

... I saw and traded with these Indians on or about the 8th of July, when they were on their way south toward their agency by way of North Park. These Indians—about fifty in number—were very peaceable and polite, and did not commit any depredations or show any hostility towards any of the settlers in this country. There were fires set about this time in the timber, but it is not know how they originated. I have, since their departure, learned from Mr. John LeFevre, of North Park, that another band of these Indians were in North Park in June, and that some of the miners talked of driving them off, but . . . they learned that the Indians did not wish trouble, and they immediately left. This is all I know or have ever heard of this subject.

GREY NICHOLS
Grand Encampment Creek

... a party of White River Ute Indians camped on Beaver Creek June 30, they being then on their way south, and they crossed the Colorado line July 1. During their stay on the Platte they killed considerable game, but offered no violence to settlers, nor did they, so far as I have been able to learn by diligent inquiry, set fire to any grass or timber in this country.

I have traveled all through the country referred to since the 1st of July, and am satisfied that had any violence been committed by the Indians, I should have heard of it.

J. M. Hugus
Fort Steele, Wyo.

« IV »

Some of the men had already been to the stores and had come back to their villages to tell about it. There were new things in the stores, as there were every year: things that interested the men, things that made the women talk among themselves and hope that the hunts would be good, and things that made the children eager.

For a long time—as long as the younger ones could remember—going to the stores had been part of the hunts. The Maricat'z wanted skins—skins from the winter hunts and skins from the summer hunts—and they would trade fine and interesting things for them; after a family had traded for things that made them look pretty and feel good, it was time to think about getting ammunition for the next hunt, and some flour and coffee and sugar to go with the meat.

Only the older people remembered how it was before the stores came, when the men went out to hunt and the women and children and old ones gathered berries and nuts and seeds, and dug roots. In those times the People took the skins—the ones they did not have to use to make their clothes and to keep them warm while they slept and to cover their houses—and traded with the Hopi and the others who lived down among the tall rocks: the people whom Sunáwiv, the God, had made to grow things in the ground, as He had made the People to hunt.

But in that time if a man or woman wanted something pretty to wear they had to make it for themselves. If the children wanted something to play with, their father or mother or one of the old ones of the family had to make it for them. Now all such things, and many more, could be bought in the stores.

As the days stretched out toward their greatest length, the men began preparing for more hunts. Still no rain came. Now and then, around the summer villages, there was talk about a great fire in the trees. Sometimes the fire would be far away, among the highest peaks; sometimes it would be so close to the village that the smoke could be seen covering a great piece of the sky. Some said it would not be good to go too far on the summer hunts this year. The lack of rain would mean that green grass for the ponies would be hard to find, especially up north, toward the buffalo country, and there might be trouble finding water for their hunting camps. In the nearby mountain country, game would be easy to kill because the deer and antelope and elk would crowd around the running streams and the springs that had not gone dry, and the fires in the forests would drive the game out into the open.

Those who had ridden out from the villages said there were many white men in the mountains this year. They said the Maricat'z were building a railroad, like the one that now passed through the buffalo country. They told about the Maricat'z working on their railroad. The Maricat'z, they said, first laid out pieces of wood on the ground in a line, like the women lay out porcupine quills to sew on a piece of buckskin. Then other white men came behind, carrying long, shiny poles, longer than lodgepoles, and laid them down across the porcupine quills. Then after they set the poles down, they took hammers and pounded and made a terrible noise.

Wherever these white men went they had fires to keep them warm in the early morning and again at night—great big fires that could never keep a man warm because he would have to stand back too far from them. Sometimes these fires ran away into the trees.

Many more Maricat'z had also come into the mountains this summer to dig in the ground and carry rocks away on wagons. These people were very funny—always digging great holes and dipping pans into the water, for nothing but rocks and dirt.

These Maricat'z talked too loud, made a great deal of noise, and killed too much game, and there were some of the People who said they did not like to have these diggers in the country.

Those Maricat'z who came into the country to build houses and raise cattle were all right, but too many of those who dug in the ground were coming in. Most of the People, however, said it was nothing to think or talk about. Those rocks the Maricat'z took away were no good to anybody, and soon they would get tired of that business and go home.

At night the heat lightning danced over the tips of the high mountains, and sometimes it would rumble, deep and low. Some nights the lightning got mixed up with the long, red glow of a fire burning far away in the mountains.

Band after band rode out of the villages for the hunts. They rode into the high forests, up the winding, climbing canyon, and into the high, level park country. Soon many were riding back into the lower country of Snake and Bear Rivers, driving pack ponies ahead of them, loaded with meat bundled in skins. The women were busy at the drying racks, putting up the great harvest of meat, and camps began to grow up around the stores, where storemen piled skins high on their counters.

As they finished with the hunts and the trading that followed, families gathered on the Smoking Earth River. It was again near time for the goods from Washington to be passed out at the agency.

As the village grew on Smoking Earth River the games, dancing, and horse racing began. The hunts had been good. There were heaps of red, fresh meat to be eaten, and every family had

a good store of dried meat for the winter. Much meat meant many skins to trade, and all the men, women, and children had new things from the stores to show around, especially to those who had stayed at the agency and worked instead of going on the hunts.

Nicaagat was one of the first to return from hunting. His piwán set up their carniv in a new place, halfway between the place of the old agency and the new one. His friends brought their families to that place and set up their carniva.

Colorow sometimes went down to the agency house and came back to tell jokes about the Agent and the other white people down there. Colorow told his friends after he returned from his first visit to the agency that he had seen that woman who was the Agent's piwán, or perhaps she was his mother; and he saw that one who was his daughter. He told those women that he must have something to eat—that he was very hungry. They said they had just finished eating and that he might come in and eat what they had left.

This was not good. Those people might stay at the agency a long time, and it was not good for them to get into bad ways. Colorow went away and found some men who were playing cards, and he waited until the Agent and his family were ready to eat again. Then he went to the window and looked in. He saw them sitting down to the table, so he went in and sat down with them. There was much good food on that table and he ate well. Now the Agent and his family would be good people to eat with. Colorow had made friends of them.

Colorow always returned from the agency with a good story. Those who lived around Nicaagat's carniv knew much about what went on at the agency without ever having to go down there. Another evening he came back and told a story about the white employees. Some of them went up into the canyon where they had dug some holes in the side of the hill. They went into these holes as the Agent told them to do, and they came out carrying the black rock that burns. Their faces were black as the holes. They would come into the agency and try to wash the black from their faces, but some always stayed on, around their eyes and noses. They looked like owls. This is what happened to men who went under the ground. Only snakes, worms, and Paiutes belonged under the ground.

Somebody asked Colorow whether their faces were as black as the faces of the soldiers he had seen up in Middle Park, and Colorow told again about the Buffalo Soldiers—the ones with black faces he and some of the others had seen on the summer hunts. These To-Maricat'z were led by a white general, and the black soldiers seemed very much afraid of their general. But they were more afraid of Colorow. No man could doubt that. All soldiers were funny, but these were the funniest soldiers Colorow or any man had ever seen.

A little later Colorow went down to the Los Pinos Agency for a few days, where the bands who were called the Uncompahgre received their presents from Washington. Colorow had given his name to the agent at Los Pinos, so that he could go down there when the presents from Washington were given out. In this way he received gifts from Washington at Los Pinos, as well as from the White River Agency.

Those people down there had been having a great deal of trouble with Maricat'z settling on their land, bringing in their many cattle to eat up the grass, and digging holes in the ground. This was the way the story was told:

Some of the men from the Uncompahgre bands were out hunting and they saw many cattle on their land. Some Maricat'z were with those cattle. These men told those Maricat'z that they must take their cattle and go away. They then went away to hunt and did not come back until the next day. They saw those same Maricat'z there with their cattle. They pointed their guns at those Maricat'z and told them to stand on their hands and knees, like cows, and eat the grass. They said, "You like the grass of our country. Now you may eat as much of it as you like." Those Maricat'z ate much grass that day.

One afternoon Nicaagat was sitting by his carniv smoking while most of the others were playing games or taking their horses down to the racing track, when he saw two men riding toward him. One was the man everybody called the Little Boy, because he never went hunting or played games with the other men, but stayed around the agency; he was supposed to help this Agent to understand the People when they spoke to him and to tell the People things the Agent wanted to say to them. With the Little Boy was a Maricat'z whom Nicaagat had not seen before.

As they came near the Little Boy told Nicaagat that the Agent wanted him to come and talk. The Maricat'z who ride into the agency on a horse had brought the Agent a paper, and the Agent had read it. Something in that paper had made him angry.

Nicaagat had hoped he would not have to talk to the Agent again, yet he had known that sometime another talk would have to come. Now he called to his piwán to get his saddle ready and, picking up his bridle, he started toward his horse which was hobbled nearby.

When they reached the agency, the Little Boy took Nicaagat inside, to the room where the Agent sat, and left. Nicaagat stood beside the big desk with papers scattered over the top of it. The Agent picked up one of these papers, looked at it, then looked up at Nicaagat. His face was tired, and the lines between his eyebrows were deep.

"I am going home," he said.

Then he eyed Nicaagat a moment and added, "Home to my house in Greeley."

He waited as though he wanted Nicaagat to say something; then he looked back at the paper in his hand.

"I have a letter here which complains of Indians setting fires in the forests. Many people have complained about this lately, but now something very bad has happened."

Nicaagat knew he was supposed to ask about what had happened, and this was why he said nothing. The Maricat'z always want a man to ask them questions; but it was best to wait for them to talk. After a while they always say what they have to say.

Soon the Agent continued: "I came here to help your people. I came here to teach them a good life and to save them from trouble, but it seems of no use. They insist on bringing trouble upon themselves. This letter says that two Indians have burned down a white man's home on Bear River."

"Where dey burn dis house?" asked Nicaagat.

"On Bear River," said the Agent again. Then he added, "At the Hayden settlement. Not only one but several houses have been burned."

"We ride up dere tomorrow," Nicaagat said. "You, me better go see if dese houses burned. You see dem?"

"I don't need to go any place to see," said the Agent. "This letter tells me. Besides, it's not my business to see about such things."

"How iss dis not your business?" Nicaagat asked. "You are Indian agent."

"It's not my business," repeated the Agent. "I am an Indian agent, but that does not mean that it is my business to try to get criminals and bad men out of trouble. The Indians who set those fires are bad men, and they should get out of it the best way they can."

"Iss no good dat you talk like dat," said Nicaagat. "Washington put you here for Indian agent. Somebody make paper, say Indians bad men. You go see—maybe bad, maybe not. Maybe paper lie."

Nicaagat's words were doing little good. The Agent had set his mind. He believed words on papers. Talk was of no use.

"I am not going to say any more about this," he said. "I am going home."

"You do, say something about dis trouble, den you go home," said Nicaagat.

"I have nothing to say." The Agent had taken up a pen and had dipped it in the ink, ready to write something. "Let the government handle it. Let the Indian Commissioner handle it. I am leaving for home tomorrow."

Nicaagat tried to say something more, but the Agent did not look up or answer. Nicaagat turned and went out of the room.

In front of the agency house, Acarí and Sowówic were waiting for him. They had heard that the Agent had called for Nicaagat, and they wanted to know if there were some kind of trouble. The three of them walked in silence to where the ponies were tied.

As they rode back toward their carniva Nicaagat said: "I think this Agent is a strange man . . . and he is old and unhappy."

Nicaagat could not forget about his talk with the Agent and what the Agent had said about the fires—the houses burned on Bear River and the fires in the trees. He made up his mind that night that in the morning he would ride up to Bear River himself, since the Agent had refused to go, and see what houses were burned, perhaps find out more about it, and what kind of talk the settlers up there were making about the People.

In the morning, while his piwán was getting his things ready, Acarí and Sowówic walked over to his carniv. They saw that his piwán was filling his saddlebags with jerked meat and pouches of potato gruel. Nicaagat told them only that he was going to the store on Bear River. But Acarí and Sowówic knew what the Agent had said about the fires the day before; they wanted to go with Nicaagat, wherever he was going.

When the sun had cleared the mountains and was throwing its first warmth into the valley, they started. It was a long ride up to Bear River, and the country changed many times; it was the kind of a trip a man with a good pony could enjoy. Along the way Sowówic saw a buck and shot it, and they stopped to skin it and pack the meat. It was always good to have fresh meat for the camp.

By the middle of the next day they were riding through the oak brush and chokecherry scrub, across the top of the last long gray hill. Below them the Bear River cut through the green valley floor. There was the store, and the little cluster of buildings around it.

If they had been younger men they might have made noises like coyotes and wolves, and raced their ponies down the slope to tell their Maricat'z friends they were coming. Only a few snows back they were all young enough for such games. But now they paused and looked at the log buildings below, then they let their tired ponies choose their own gait—a slow trot down the gentle slope.

A small white boy was in front of the store, watching them as they came. When they were close the boy turned and ran into the house to tell his father, the storeman, that people were coming to the store.

A long bench crossed the front of the building, on which white settlers and ranch hands usually sat, talking, whittling, and spitting tobacco juice. Today the bench was empty. They tied their ponies and went into the store. It too was empty. They waited, and soon they heard someone come out of the house. The storeman walked in and greeted them all, calling Nicaagat by his Maricat'z name.

While Nicaagat and the storeman talked, Acarí and Sowówic walked up and down the store, looking into the barrels that stood in a row, handling and feeling of the harnesses, bridles, and saddles along the wall.

Nicaagat and the storeman had a long talk. When they were finished Nicaagat said goodbye to the storeman and shook hands with him. He walked out of the store, and Acarí and Sowówic followed him. They untied their ponies, mounted, and started away; Nicaagat was taking the trail north, directly up the river.

They rode along for a time in silence, Acarí and Sowówic waiting for Nicaagat to tell them where he was going and what the storeman had said to him. At last he began to tell them.

That storeman did not like the Agent. The storeman said that the Agent was always trying to stop the People from coming to his store. The Agent had been writing letters to Washington trying to get soldiers to stop the People from coming to that store.

That was one of the bad things about the Agent: he was always writing letters—always writing and sending papers away.

The storeman had showed Nicaagat one of those papers. They came to this store; then they were sent to wherever the Agent wanted them to go. The one the storeman had showed Nicaagat during their talk said bad things about the People. Nicaagat saw this, then he heard the storeman tell him that this was not the first such letter that had been sent out; some had gone to the Governor, in Denver; some had gone to Washington.

Nicaagat then asked the storeman about this house the Agent said had been burned by two of the People, and the storeman said that this house had not been burned. He said that this house was standing beside the Bear River as it had since it was built, and nobody—none of the People, none of the Maricat'z—had burned it or tried to burn it.

Somebody had made a lie. Nicaagat and his friends would see for themselves, for they were going to pass that way.

They had taken the brush-lined trail up the Bear River. Ahead the oak-brush hills were swelling into pine and aspen covered mountains, where the trail climbed into the rugged string of peaks called the Gore Range by the Maricat'z. It led through the flaming canyon and into Middle Park, over the divide, and down the last long slope to the plains, where the buffalo hunting used to be good and where a man, in the old days, would glance sharply around him for smoke from a village of Arapaho or Cheyenne before riding on.

This was the trail they were taking. At last Nicaagat told them more about his talk with the storeman. After they had talked a while about the Agent, the storeman had told Nicaagat that he had better go to Denver to see the Governor. He should tell the Governor, who had heard all these lies about the People, the truth. Then, perhaps, the Governor would write Washington and say that this Agent had better be taken away and another one sent to the People. Washington, like the People, did not want trouble.

« V »

A Visit to White River
by R. D. Coxe, posseman

The Sheriff of Grand County, Mr. Marshall Bessey, with a posse of four men, left Hot Sulphur Springs at 1 o'clock p.m. August 22, and after a four-days' journey, through the rugged country that comprises the northern part of Middle Park and Egeria Park, and over the well-timbered Bear River bottom, the Sheriff camped at Pike's Agency, where Peck's store is located, 25 miles from the line of the reservation.

Mr. Bessey had a warrant for two Indians, by supposed name "Chinaman" and "Bennett" (for the burning of Major Thompson's house). We took some pains to inquire of the white people at Peck's store about these Indians, but could learn nothing. The dead, Sabbath calm of gossip, which is so noticeable among the Utes, extended even this far, and they were very ignorant of any crimes that might be alleged against the Indians.

We soon crossed the east line of the reservation, but traveled fully ten miles into the reservation before meeting an Indian. As we reached the top of a divide the trail led through a natural gateway of rocks, and from this point we saw in the distance Indians coming toward us. As they came nearer, we saw there were but three, and soon that they were a brave, a squaw, and a girl. As we met the brave extended his hand with the customary salute, "How?" I had learned enough Indian to answer him in his own language and found no hesitance in telling him *how!*

The brave was a jolly-looking fellow, easy to smile. He wore a straw hat (quite the thing among the Utes), and his locks were oiled and plaited. He was evidently dressed for a holiday, and so indeed it was for him, for he was taking his 'outfit', his home, his family and all his possessions, I judge, to the store, where the hides packed on his ponies were to be disposed of, and he was to get ammunition, possibly a gun for himself, and gewgaws for the squaw and children, for there was a papoose at the mother's knee, swinging to the saddle in one of those contrivances which take, with the Indians, the place of cradles.

We saw quite a number of Indians after passing this family, one of whom was standing on the mountain-side, with only a shirt on, his long hair flowing down his back, and his brown limbs exposed. He appeared to have struck washday, and he was at it with might and main. We passed about a quarter of a mile from him, but his pony took a liking to us and attempted to follow us. Then the savage within him roused, and he talked Ute to the horse like a father.

As we neared the White River we saw fleeting forms on horseback and, as long as we had a view of the road, they were noticeable. Indians dislike to walk a horse, and even the boys and girls of the tribe keep their ponies in a lope. We inquired the distance to the agency of an Indian girl, and she told us a mile. It was three, but anything short of five miles is a mile to an Indian.

Large camps lined the river-bank. The camps were mostly

composed of tepees; but once in a while was a tent, sometimes a log cabin, or shed with a brush roof.

All the Indians we met had on paint, a red smear over their faces; but we met one that was got up for pretty. His face was painted a drab color from forehead to chin; from ear to ear, his chin had a pink wash, and his eyelids were a bright vermilion. . . . He was very quiet—said nothing to us at all. I asked him if anyone was dead, but he did not reply.

The agency had been moved since any of the party had been there and as we came in sight of it, it presented a pretty picture to our eyes. The White River Valley at the agency is some half or ¾ of a mile in width, and is splendidly adapted to agriculture, as well by the ease with which it can be irrigated as by the natural qualities of the soil. Facing the agency buildings, under fence, was a field of about 50 acres, in which was growing corn and garden truck, and from which a good crop of wheat had been harvested. Around were the signs of a practical farmer, and under the sheds of the agency were the latest improvements in agricultural implements. Here, thought I, is the model; another generation will find our dusky neighbors tilling their ranches and pursuing the peaceful avocations of civilization, and the blessing will rest upon the head of N. C. Meeker. But a herd of horses skirted the fenced field, and it seemed to me they looked with a jealous eye upon the growing crops. On the hills, up on the other side of the river, were large herds of cattle, and everything looked pastoral and quiet.

It needed no introduction to tell us that the tall, angular, gray-headed man who welcomed us to the agency was "Father" Meeker. To look at him was to see plows and harrows and fence wire. He told us to unsaddle at the corral, and, after an eight hours' ride over a rough trail, we were not unwilling to do so.

As we approached the corral, a figure came toward us from the direction of the river, that I gazed at with increasing interest as it approached, dressed in what I call the fall attire of a workman in the states. I set myself to solve the problem of what nationality. White, red, or black? Once it was a sunburned white man, then a "nigger", but when it reached us the inevitable red smear betrayed it. It was an Indian, and moreover, an Indian who spoke respectable English. There was something I should describe as a reserved force in his manner (not matter) of speaking. Our conversation was trivial. I had put my estimate on him, and it was that he had grown civilized enough to doff the blanket (emblem of the aborigine) and to become generally no account. Imagine my surprise when the Sheriff turned to me and told me our visitor was Douglas. I had expected to find the great chief in a mud palace, exacting the reverence and homage of all comers. Instead, he is an Indian who would be taken for a respectable negro church-sexton in Kentucky, and he keeps up the likeness by his grave reticence and respectful curiosity as to what our mission is.

Douglas is a chief of ten years' standing, and, from, intercourse with the whites, as well as weight of years, has grown conservative and pliable. None can know better than he the futility of war with the whites. Since his chieftainship, the tribe has grown up. The boys that used to fight the Arapahoes are middle-aged, and among them is an aquiline-featured stalwart called Captain Jack. I am told that Capt. Jack, while nominally second chief, really commands the suffrage and good-will of far the larger portion of the tribe.

Douglas is about five feet seven inches in height, medium stature, and outrageously bow-legged. The most noticeable thing about him is that he shaves, but manages to escape an iron-gray growth of moustache on the sides of his mouth in that operation. In his dress he made no pretense to the gaudy—was satisfied with the substantial. While I was yet eyeing him, eager to hear some words of wisdom from this patriarch, the agent came out and told him he wanted to talk to him. Douglas followed him into the house, as did the Sheriff.

Mr. Bessey had already acquainted Mr. Meeker with the object of our visit, and Mr. Meeker had promised to do what he could to bring the criminal Utes to account. In the house, Mr. Bessey again went over the business and showed his warrant.

Douglas said the Utes were not on the reservation, and that therefore he could not give them up. Mr. Meeker said they could not be far away. Douglas did not know about that. Mr. Meeker then told Douglas it was his duty to send Utes with the Sheriff to identify the Indians specified in the warrant. For some time, Douglas made no reply to this, but with a reed which he had, made figures on the floor. Finally he looked up, and a thundercloud was on his brow. He told the agent decidedly and emphatically that he would not do it. This ended the council, and Douglas soon departed. . . .

During this time Miss Josie Meeker and Mrs. Price had been preparing dinner for us, and to this we were now invited. We had had our breakfast at 6 a.m., and it was a very slim breakfast we had. It was now nearly 4 p.m., and the dinner was fit for an epicure. It was the unanimous verdict of the party that the dinner was worth $10. . . .

Our business at the agency was complete. We saddled up for a return, bade farewell to the Meekers and started through the villages of tepees homeward bound. We found great commotion in every band. At every camp we were interviewed. Antelope's band was camped nearest the agency, and his brother, Powitz, and his squaw, Jane, hailed us with the customary, "How?" Our reply of "How" led them to ask, "What yer come for?" We told them we came to see Meeker. Douglas told them we had come for two Utes, Chinaman and another (whom they did not seem to recognize by the name of Bennett). We did not affirm or deny but passed on. This conversation was repeated eight or ten times in the three miles our road bordered the river. It was late when we struck the trail, and we saw no more Indians till we reached Peck's.

The fires and burned forests extended from the Springs to the Agency. At nightfall, on the day we left the Agency, we saw a large fire started not ten miles from the Agency. We constantly saw the smoke of fires, and many times they were quite close to our road. A large fire was sweeping the forests on Gore Range. The atmosphere was blue with smoke, and on every hand we heard complaints of the fires started by the Utes.

« VI »

Denver, the place where many Maricat'z lived huddled close together, had changed much since the last time these three men

114

had been there. It had been three, perhaps four, snows since the People had all come here together; now only a few ever came to Denver, and these were not the best of the men on Smoking Earth River. They were the ones who hunted little, drank a great deal of whisky, and now and then, it was said, stole a horse. There was no need to come here any more, with stores on Bear and Snake Rivers and an agency to give out the goods from Washington. Denver was crowded with white people, and it smelled bad. There was too much noise.

The face of this Maricat'z village had changed. The buildings were taller and some of the streets were hard, like rock. They hurt a man's feet to walk on them. The white people they saw all around them did not look like the white people they usually saw. They wore tall hats and fine clothes. They rode around in little wagons with funny little black tents over the top of them. There were many stores, and the things the stores sold were put in the windows, so that a man could look at them while he walked along the street. It seemed to Nicaagat that they would never get to see the Governor, for Acarí and Sowówic were always stopping to look in these windows.

Nicaagat had asked somebody where the Governor stayed and after a while they found the building. Inside, everything was shiny, and the floor was like a frozen lake. They went into a room where a man sat alone. He had a thin white face and his beard, like a beaver tail, hopped up and down as he talked to Nicaagat.

Acarí and Sowówic thought at first that this man was the Governor, but after a while Nicaagat turned to them and said they would have to find another white man to take them to the Governor. This man had told him that it would take an important man to help them see the Governor and that the man named Byers, the one with a ranch in Middle Park, the man that the People called Pius, might be able to help them. Acarí and Sowówic followed Nicaagat out of the building. They did not understand why they must find another man to take them to the Governor, but it was the business of Nicaagat to understand the Maricat'z.

They came to another building and went into another room, and there they saw the big, square face of Pius come out of a door. He shook hands with all of them, and he went with them back to the building where the Governor stayed.

Pius left them sitting on a long bench, went away for a while, then came back with another white man. After they had all shaken hands again, Nicaagat told Acarí and Sowówic that this man whom Pius had brought in was one of the men who made newspapers. Perhaps, Nicaagat said, he knows something about the things the newspapers have been saying about the People.

Now the little man with the beaver tail beard made a motion with his hand, and they all went into another room. A man sat there in a big chair behind a desk, and when they came in he stood up and held out his hand.

This one, Nicaagat told his friends, was the Governor.

They all had to shake hands again because Maricat'z do not like to talk to people, even their good friends, until they have shaken hands. This, the old people said, is because they are all afraid of each other.

Nicaagat stood in front of the table as the Governor sat down again. He did not want to sit in the chair they offered him, and Acarí and Sowówic did not sit down either. Nicaagat did not like to have so many other Maricat'z in here while he was talking to the Governor. Perhaps too many of them would want to talk, and he would not get to say anything. But he decided that since he had come here to find out about the lies in the papers and tell them the truth, it was better that all of them should hear him. Maricat'z like to talk around about what somebody has said, and it would be well if a lot of them could know that the People were good and did not want trouble.

"Tell me how things are going at the White River Agency," said the Governor when all were seated.

Nicaagat could not answer this. It would take a long time, and he was not sure of the right words to say.

"I have been receiving a lot of complaints about the White River Utes lately. I have just returned from a trip to my mines in the San Juan region, and I found everything peaceful among the Utes there. Tell me, what is the trouble at White River?"

They noticed that the man who made the newspaper had taken out a piece of paper, and was writing on it.

"Dis Agent, he iss no good," said Nicaagat.

"You are dissatisfied with your agent?" asked the Governor.

"Iss no good," said Nicaagat again. "We want new agent."

The Governor looked around the room at the others. The man with the paper looked up, then wrote something else down.

"The papers are saying a great deal about the Utes," said the Governor.

"Somebody tell lies," said Nicaagat. "Lies go to papers."

"You say the papers are printing lies about you, Jack?" The Governor seemed to want to laugh about something and was having trouble making his face stay straight. "Mr. Woodbury here may be able to help you with that. He is editor of one of our leading newspapers. But why did you want to see me?"

"Iss lies. I come here to tell truth. Maybe you tell me what iss wrong. Maybe you tell me why iss somebody mad at Ute?"

"I don't think anybody is angry with your people, Jack. You have always been well treated by the white people."

"Ute want peace. Ute iss all time good friend to white man."

The Governor did not answer this, but picked up a letter lying beside his hand and looked at it.

"This is a letter from your agent," he said. "The agent says he is trying to do good things for your people and help them. He says some of you are making trouble for him and are staying away from the reservation. He says some of you do not help him in what he wants to do for his Indians."

"Agent write dat letter," said Nicaagat. "I no write letter. Agent write lies. I come to tell you d' truth."

The Governor turned the letter over carefully and laid it down on the desk.

"Mr. Meeker says he wants the Utes to learn how to farm and make their own living. He wants them to learn white man's ways so they can live in this world as they should. He wants you all to work, and he says most of you refuse to do this. He does not understand why you do not want to be helped. Maybe you can explain this to me, and maybe you can tell me why you say you do not like an agent who wants to do the best thing for you."

"Ute hunt," said Nicaagat. "Ute don' farm. Ute don' work like dat; dig in ground; spoil grass. Ute hunt and get food."

The newspaper man was making his pencil go fast. It was making a loud noise in the still room.

"We all have to work, Jack," said the Governor. He seemed to be enjoying himself. "All of us that are put on God's earth have to do something to earn our bread. Why are you better than anybody else?"

Jack looked at the Governor, and then around this fine room where the Governor stayed. Many white men work—dig in the ground, carry loads, chop wood, he thought. But there are some who do none of these things, and these live well; they seem to be the important men of their people. He pointed his finger at the Governor, like a white man, and said:

"You no work."

He looked around the room and he saw that Pius was looking at him, and he pointed his finger again. "He no work."

He saw that the man who made the newspaper, who had been writing hard, looked up quickly; and he pointed his finger again. "He no work."

Then Nicaagat turned his finger around and pointed at himself. "I no work."

What Nicaagat said made all the white men laugh; and Sowówic said, "You have made a good joke for them. I think now they will be friends and will do something for us."

"Perhaps," said Acarí, "you can tell them something about the Agent, and make them laugh again."

The Governor was still laughing when he said, "I suppose, Jack, you would be willing to be governor, or postmaster, or editor of a daily newspaper."

Nicaagat answered, "Yes," and they all laughed again.

Then he told Acarí and Sowówic what the Governor had said, and Acarí said that perhaps Nicaagat would be governor tomorrow, and sit in that chair.

In the midst of all the laughter the Governor got up and went over to one end of the room, where a big paper was hung on the wall. It had a lot of lines and colors on it.

"This is a map of the state of Colorado," the Governor said, as soon as everyone was quiet. He drew a circle on the paper with his finger. "This is your reservation—nearly one-third of the state. There are only about fourteen hundred Utes in all this land. If you learned to use land like the white man does, you could be rich with only a small part of what you now have."

Nicaagat was not sure what the Governor was trying to tell them, but he listened and watched the Governor's finger move around on the paper.

"There is probably more wealth on the land you now hold than in all the rest of the state," he was saying. "The San Juan region, which was recently opened to mining, has produced a lot of silver; and there is silver here in the Elk Mountains, which are in your section of the reservation. If you would permit white men to go in there and mine that area, you Utes would be better off. The more silver in circulation, the more the Indians will get, as well as the white men; if the white people are rich, the Indians will get more money."

Nicaagat had heard Maricat'z talk this way before. They always spoke this way when they were trying to get the People to do something they did not want to do, or sell them something they did not want.

"This Governor wants us to let more of those Maricat'z come to our country and dig in the ground. He says they will make us rich," he told Acarí and Sowówic.

The white men in the room were all watching the Governor, who was waiting with his finger up against the paper on the wall. Nicaagat had no answer. After a while the Governor dropped his hand, sighed, and came back and sat down again in his big leather chair.

"I am busy today," he said. "If you have more to say perhaps you can come back tomorrow."

The talk was finished. All the white men gathered around the Governor, and began talking to him; Nicaagat, Acarí and Sowówic left the room.

The next day they went back to the Governor. All the other white men, who had been there the day before, were there again; and when they were all sitting and listening, the Governor picked up a paper in his hand and began to talk.

"There is something in this letter from your agent that I want to bring up today," he said. "There was a fire at Hayden, on Bear River. The house of Major Thompson was recently burned to the ground. A posse has been dispatched to your agency to arrest two of the Utes from your band, who were identified as the men who set fire to the house."

Nicaagat spoke up without hesitation. This was the sort of thing he had wanted to talk to the Governor about.

"I come by Bear River. I go see dis house. Thompson house not burned. Iss lie."

"It is more than just that one incident," the Governor went on smoothly. "Many fires are reported around your reservation, and settlers and others have said they have seen the Indians start them."

"Iss many fires dere," said Nicaagat, "but iss not what Ute do. All dry—trees, grass. Fires burn easy. Lightning start fires. White men start fires. Den we hear dese lies dat Ute start fires. Dese lies must come from Agent. Dis Meeker iss bad man—iss man to make trouble. Today he say one thing, tomorrow he say something different. We ask you to write Washington, tell Washington take dis Agent back, send 'nodder one. We don' want man dat write lies and make trouble. You write Washington?"

The Governor did not answer. He did not seem to be listening. He was looking at Byers. Then he was looking at the newspaper man, who was still writing fast.

"You write Washington?"

Now the Denver *Times* man looked up at the Governor and there was a trace of a smile on his face. This time, the Governor seemed to hear.

"Yes, Jack," he said. "I will write Washington for you to-morrow."

This was what they had come here to do; it was enough.

"Dat iss all we have to say," said Nicaagat.

They had been to see the Governor and now they were going out the door—going home.

5. THE LAND

IN THE middle of August, 1879, Meeker sat down to write his annual report to the Indian Bureau. After detailing the things he had achieved, he got down to stating his views of the problems he faced.

"I am all the while conscious," he wrote, "that temporary though powerful obstacles to advancement stand in the way, and that if these could be removed the condition of the Indians would be more hopeful." Well-organized as usual, Meeker had these difficulties classified neatly under two major causes.

First is the facility presented for their leaving the reservation. They have long been in the habit, after receiving their annuity goods in the fall, of leaving for the frontier white settlements, trading off their clothing at the Indian stores, and of rambling hither and thither over a vast extent of country, half as large as their reservation, living by hunting, trading horses (perhaps horse stealing), racing, gambling, and begging. It is true that the whites having families dread their appearance, but other whites make them welcome, that they may barter and associate with them, and while this state of affairs lasts I can not bring influences to bear on them.

In close connection is the fact that they have large bands of horses, which they carefully increase; and to find fresh and wide pastures, they are induced, perhaps compelled, to roam. While they possess their horses, the care of them prevents their working, and it calls for the help of all the children who can be of service.

Meeker had first begun to be seriously annoyed by the Indians' regard for their horses early in the spring of that year. In March he had written to the Commissioner:

> The practice of these Indians in keeping and holding horses on an extensive scale is not only discouraging to farm industry, but is working most serious inconvenience, if not loss, to cattle interests. I estimate that these bands of Utes must have 4,000 horses and at least 2,000 are in Powell Valley, the new agency location, or vicinity; for, although fully half of the Indians are on Snake and Bear Rivers, they have many of their horses here, cared for by their friends. . . . Now, during all winter, these horses have occupied Powell's Valley . . . exclusively monopolizing the range that hitherto has been used by our cattle. . . . When the snow began to disappear the horses would be taken out from the river, and they covered all the sunny slopes and gulches, and now, at this writing, they occupy all the range within half a day's ride, except where they have eaten it out.
> The fact is, a conflict exists between the horses and cattle for the possession of the best part of the range. Similar conflicts have existed in all pastoral countries, from the days of Lot and Abraham, and one or the other must give way. For the increase of the horses is now not less than 500 a year, that of the cattle about the same; and it must be manifest to you that it is utterly impossible for both to occupy the same range —And now I have to say that, if the Indians are under no restraint, nor regulations in regard to occupancy of the range and increase of their horses, it will be impossible to hold the cattle on any of these ranges. . . . If we move to a remote range, the Indians would follow to get the beef, and wherever they go, they take their horses.

It seemed to Meeker that as his agriculture grew, spreading slowly over the face of the raw land, the Indians' horse herds grew with it. The problem which the horses created became more and more complex, as he exhausted possible solutions.

When the bands had gathered in the valley for some sort of

dancing celebration, Meeker had hoped to interest many of them in helping with the work, but they did not respond. It seemed to him that the pastime of horse racing, more than anything else, turned their thoughts away from the plowing of fields and growing of crops. Worse still, at the race ground idleness and play were accompanied by a third vice—gambling.

In April of 1879 Meeker wrote to Commissioner Hayt:

> It seems to me evident that the greatest obstacle to civilizing the majority of these Indians is their ownership of horses, which is proved by the fact that those who work have either few or no horses. An Indian who has a band of horses devotes all his time to them and to racing. Such a one will not work, nor will he sell any of his stock, but he is clamorous for goods and supplies, and, having influence by means of his possessions, he is an obstacle to progress.

Meeker's struggle against the "obstacle" represented by the horses finally came to focus upon one man: Johnson, the old medicine man, in whom Meeker had placed so much of his first hope of winning over the leaders of the tribe to his plan.

Johnson was one of the few older Indians who had showed any interest in "becoming civilized." He had, under careful direction, apparently made a fine start toward forming one of the family farm units which Meeker foresaw for all the Utes. Johnson, as Meeker said, "had promise."

In the previous fall Meeker had devoted a large part of an article for his *Greeley Tribune* to a lively description of Johnson and his family. Johnson was here characterized as a "considerable chief . . . who takes the lead in progress and enterprise":

> He is not given to politics at all, and he devotes his energies to improving his domestic affairs. He has three cows from which he has milk, butter, and cheese; and poultry and goats. A table has been made for him at which he and his eat; he has crockery, dishes, and if he had a house he would probably make things shine. Susan, Johnson's wife, is a good genius. She is a large, handsome woman, reminding one of

that Boston lady, Louise Chandler Moulton; she has dignity and good sense, and she makes her husband do as she bids. Her dress is of the finest buckskin ornamented with elaborate fringes and beadwork, costing fully as much as a good silk dress.

... Johnson is one of those men who lead from the savage to the barbaric life on the way to civilization. He is not quite as far advanced as Cedric the Saxon, master of Garth, in Scott's Ivanhoe, but he is probably equal to the best among the British chiefs who tried to withstand the invasion of Julius Caesar.

Before the snow started Meeker had ordered work begun on a house for Johnson, and by early spring it was completed. In a February letter to Hayt, Meeker reported:

One Indian, named Johnson, has requested us to break a pair of his horses, as he wants to do teaming, and he wants harness and wagon. The horses are under training, and I shall lend him a wagon and harness.

Meeker was delighted with the prospect of seeing the first of the Indian horses converted from objects of indolence to instruments of utility. But as the season advanced, he was faced with a different kind of report on Johnson:

I have been talking to the Indians ever since I arrived ... about their horses, telling them they must not keep so many, but it has no kind of effect. The Indian is wealthy, and he has standing, precisely as he owns horses. When a wife dies from two to five horses will be shot and six to ten dogs, but none are ever or seldom sold, and the only real use to which they are put, aside from riding purposes, is to run races. Horse-racing, and consequently gambling, is the main pursuit for nine months in the year, and the Indian who has not a horse to run is nobody.

Late in January a Ute named Johnson, always friendly with the agent, always wanting to be civilized and to have things, requested us to break a pair of horses for him, wanted a wagon, wanted a farm, and he must have a team to work. Accordingly the men spent a good deal of time in breaking the horses, he riding around and soon learning to drive, and of course we kept the horses on hay and grain, so that they would be in a condition to work. Last week I discovered he was in the habit of racing these horses in the afternoon, and it was evident that his object had been to get them in good heart so that he could beat his brethren of the turf, and I told him to take away his horses. . . .

Thus the most serious pursuit of these Indians is horse breeding and racing, and only these young men who have no horses will work. . . . It seems to me that they would rather give up the cattle than their horses.

Now, in August, as Meeker evaluated the work and progress of the past year, he found himself on one hand pleased with the amount of work accomplished—the many acres plowed and planted, many more acres plowed, or ready for plowing, and great squares of land under fence—but frustrated when he considered the progress which he might have made, had he found a solution to the horse problem earlier.

Twenty or thirty lodges are under my control, because there is pasturage in the vicinity, but no more can occupy the ground. At the same time, these horses, worth not exceeding an average of $15 a head, crowd out the cattle, and make their care more expensive and difficult. If the government would take away all the horses except such as could be useful, the Indians would not go abroad; and if cattle were given instead they would, or could, or should engage in a profitable industry, and one to which they take readily and naturally.

To permit any class of human beings to do as they please, and at the same time to be supplied with food, inevitably leads to demoralization. After I get hold of these Indians I can tell a great deal better what can be made of them. I should like to have plenty of land in cultivation, with tools all ready; take away their horses; then give the word that if they would not work they should have no rations.

As to how much they would work and produce in such a case, and as to how fast they would adopt a civilized life, is merely to speculate, but my impression is they would not starve.

« II »

Late one warm afternoon Quinkent sat smoking in front of his house. From where he sat he could watch the river, which seemed to move a little too slowly because of the many moons without rain. On the other side the wavy hills made another huge river which flowed in the other direction in the long low sunlight. The sky was grayed with smoke from the many fires that had been burning in the dry forests, and Quinkent could feel the smoke in his nose.

Up the other way from the river, toward the agency buildings, he could see the man with the two mules as he walked behind the big curved knife that shaved away the ground. He watched the knife cut away long strips of green grass, and the brown streaks of ground follow behind. This is the way the Maricat'z work. The Agent had told Quinkent and the others to watch this man and see how it was done, so that maybe after the next snow they too could do it.

The Agent had said that some of the others could take care of the cattle because that work was easy and they would not have to learn anything. Anybody could take care of cattle, just as even children can look after the ponies.

While Quinkent sat and watched the plow, two others came to sit with him. One was Pauvit'z, who lived on the piece of ground beside Quinkent, and the other was Tatit'z, son of Canávish. Pauvit'z was not much better than some of those who went with Nicaagat; he had stayed here mostly because he had hurt himself with his rifle and could not go hunting, and his piwán, who was called Jane, had worked up at the agency house. She knew something about Maricat'z, and she could talk to them; so the Agent had planted her a garden and given her some things. Pauvit'z, who was a very lazy young man, had stayed on because he could eat well here and do little.

Canávish had asked his sons to help take care of the cows and work in the garden, so Tatit'z and his younger brother Tim had gone only on the early hunts.

They had sat without talking for some time before Quinkent understood that they were disturbed about something. He started the talk by saying something about not seeing Canávish around the agency for two, three sleeps; Tatit'z answered that his father had gone away visiting for a little while and that he, Tatit'z, had come to talk for him.

Tatit'z, being still a very young man, was not the one to speak. The matter they had come to talk over was important. Pauvit'z took a long time to think before he made his talk, and when he did he stated his complaint with his first words: the Agent wanted to plow up more ground, including the ground he had given Quinkent's people for their houses and even the long track where they raced their ponies.

Quinkent thought about it for a while. Then he said: "I do not think you heard the Agent say this. I think somebody has told you he said this. It is always this way."

Both Pauvit'z and Tatit'z knew that it was true: they had not actually heard the Agent say this. They could make no answer to Quinkent. But after a while Pauvit'z said that the Agent had told these things to his piwán, and that perhaps, if Quinkent wanted it, she would come and tell him herself. Then Pauvit'z said he had heard others who were living in the winter valley say that they thought the Agent had plowed enough land—that little grass was left for the ponies and that there was hardly enough now to last through the next snow. Pauvit'z pointed away from the river, to where the ground sloped upward, wrinkled, gray, and covered with brush; this kind of land would be all right to plow up. There was no grass there.

Then Pauvit'z repeated what he had said about the Agent wanting to plow the places he had given families for their houses, after he had talked to them and told them it would be good to live in the kind of houses the Maricat'z built. The Agent was the kind of man who would say a thing many times then, one day, say something entirely different.

Quinkent was sure that everything Pauvit'z was saying his

127

piwán had said a little while before. A man can not always be doing things that women want done. Soon every man might be like this Pauvit'z—always going and telling other people things that his piwán had said.

Quinkent would go and talk to the Agent about this business, but he would think about it awhile first. Since the time when those Maricat'z came here and tried to make him find two men for them to take away and put in prison, Quinkent had not felt so sure about this Agent.

He said: "I do not believe this Agent will plow up the places he has given us for homes and for our ponies; this is all I have to say now."

After a while Tatit'z and Pauvit'z went away. Quinkent lit his pipe and went back to watching the Maricat'z with the plow.

Pauvit'z and Tatit'z walked back to their houses. Pauvit'z was thinking about what he would say to his piwán, and Tatit'z wondered if his father would go and talk to the Agent when he came back.

Quinkent probably would not go and talk to the Agent. Quinkent would probably not do anything until the Agent told his worker to plow up Quinkent's ground—his pony pasture and the place where he had put his carniv. Then Quinkent would be angry. He would want all the People to talk about it.

Tatit'z had trouble understanding this thing the Agent had done of giving families pieces of land where they were to make their houses. Perhaps it would be all right, since Canávish had never said much about it but had gone ahead and let the Agent's workers build him a house. The Agent had said that Washington wanted the People to have these pieces of land and that each family should take care of their own land. Now, Tatit'z thought, he must go back and watch his family's land, since Canávish was away, and stop anyone from plowing it up.

The place the Agent had given Canávish to make his house was farther away from the agency than Quinkent's. From the door of the carniv Tatit'z could not see the agency buildings. The log house the white men had built for Canávish was in the way, and Tatit'z had to go around to the other side of this house to watch the man who was plowing. He sat there until the sun went down and the worker led his mules away, with all those pieces of leather hanging down and dragging on the ground.

Then Tatit'z went back to the carniv where the women were making the food, but he did not tell any of them he was watching the land. Canávish would not have said anything about it to the women. But later in the dark, when his brother Tim came home, Tatit'z told him what he was doing. Tim, who was almost a man, was very excited about it, and he said tomorrow he would stay home and watch with Tatit'z.

When the edge of the sun pushed above the mountains in the east it flashed on the shiny plow blade. They watched the plow-man fastening his plow to the leathers that hung down from the mules; then they saw him take hold of the handles. Then he started out. Up and back, up and back. Now and then he shouted something to the mules, the way Maricat'z do.

When the sun was half way to the middle of the sky, Tim said he was tired of sitting there. He said he thought soon the man would get tired and quit. Any man, even a Maricat'z, would get tired of walking back and forth behind those mules. Soon he would want to go some place else, and he would take all those

crazy leather things off the mules and he would get up on one of them and ride fast. Maybe he would go hunting.

But the man kept on plowing, walking up and back, up and back. Each trip brought him closer.

"Soon he will be on the race track," said Tim. "If he cuts the race track with that knife our ponies will not be able to go fast over it any more. They will hit their feet on one of those big chunks of earth, and maybe fall and kill themselves."

The worker came to the end of his row, shouted at his mules, turned them around and started back again.

"I went on a hunt two moons ago," said Tatit'z. "I shot more antelope and buckskin than I have ever shot before."

"I wish I had gone on that hunt with you," said Tim.

"With that old rifle," continued Tatit'z. "And every time I shot I had to pour the powder in and push the bullet in with that stick. If I had had a better rifle maybe I would be rich now, with all the game I saw."

"They say a man can sell skins at the stores and get a new rifle," said Tim.

"I took my skins and counted them, then I went to that store."

The man with the plow had made another trip. He stopped and pulled a colored cloth out of his pocket and wiped his face. The sun was getting hot.

"If you had enough skins, you could buy a new rifle," said Tim.

They were quiet for a while, watching the man with the plow. Both of them were thinking of the stores—how the Maricat'z storeman gets angry when you keep buying things one at a time and make him run all over the place. It is fun to go to the stores.

"I took those skins to the stores," said Tatit'z.

The Maricat'z storeman always wants to buy the skins, but he always tries to make you take something you don't want. If you can keep making him wait he will get angry; then you can get things you want from him—things that he would not give you if he were not angry.

"And after a long time that man showed me a new rifle—one of those that goes 'chick, chick,' and there is another bullet in it."

"I have seen that rifle," said Tim.

"You have seen it," said Tatit'z, "but you have not seen me shoot it."

They sat and watched some more, and after a while Tatit'z got up and went away. He came back with his new rifle in his hand.

"I think you should shoot it at a mark," said Tim.

They looked around for something to shoot at, and the man with the plow came to the end of another row. He turned and started back toward the river.

"There is something shining far over there toward the carniv of Quinkent," said Tim, motioning with his lips and chin.

Tatit'z studied the thickness of the trees down toward the river. At last he said: "I can see something shining down there, but I do not know what it is."

"If a bullet hits it, perhaps we will see what it is."

The Maricat'z pushed along behind the mules. He was nearing the end of the row. Tatit'z stared down into the trees. "Chick, chick," went the new rifle.

Tatit'z stared into the trees. He looked down the barrel of the new rifle. A breeze was blowing, moving the trees; and now he could see the thing, now he could not. It twinkled like a star, and now the thick cloud of yellow smoke was between his eyes and the thing. He could not see at all, and the air was still full of the great noise of the rifle, rolling up one hillside and down another.

Brown clouds were coming up from the ground where the white worker had been plowing. They were coming up behind his running feet, and an even bigger cloud came from the plow, which the mules were dragging behind them as they ran. Then the plow jerked loose and rolled over on the ground, and the mules ran on across the field, with the crazy leather things flying out behind them.

131

« III »

United States Indian Service
White River Agency, Colorado
September 8, 1879

Edward A. Hayt
U.S. Indian Affairs Office
Washington, D.C.

Sir:

We had recently finished plowing an 80-acre field, all inclosed; then we irrigated a piece of adjoining land, and upon
which the agency buildings stand at a corner. This parcel lies
between the river and the street coming to the agency, and
embraces probably 200 acres, and the plan was to devote 50
acres next the street and the agency to tilled crops and the remainder to grass land, and to inclose the whole with one common
fence. First, it is necessary to have fields contiguous, that fences
may be watched and depredators kept in check, and also to make
the work of irrigation as inexpensive as possible, since to carry
water far involves heavy outlays, besides being attended with
the greatest difficulty by reason of uneven ground. In short, the
described parcel was every way fitted for the object stated, and
the new location of the agency was made with a view of utilizing
and improving this particular land.

When we commenced plowing last week, three or four
Indians objected. They had set their tents down towards the
river, and corrals had been built, though I had previously told
them the ground would be plowed. I offered to move their corrals by employes' labor, and showed them other places, of which
there are many equally good, but they refused to consider. This
land is good, and being close to the agency their horses are protected; in short, they simply need the ground for their horses.

Now, since it was evident that if I could have moved the
agency building two or three miles below they would come and
claim equal squatters' rights there also, and I told them so; to
which they replied that I had enough land plowed, and they

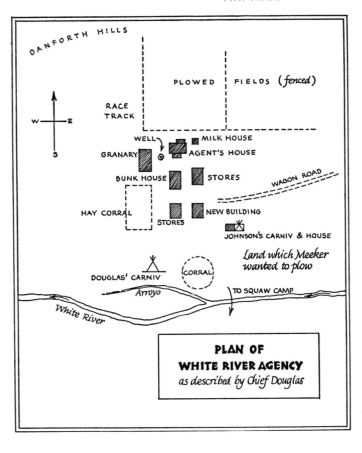

DANFORTH HILLS

PLOWED FIELDS (fenced)

RACE TRACK

W — E

S

WELL

MILK HOUSE

GRANARY

AGENT'S HOUSE

BUNK HOUSE

STORES

WAGON ROAD

HAY CORRAL

STORES

NEW BUILDING

JOHNSON'S CARNIV & HOUSE

Land which Meeker wanted to plow

DOUGLAS' CARNIV

CORRAL

Arroyo

TO SQUAW CAMP

White River

**PLAN OF
WHITE RIVER AGENCY**
as described by Chief Douglas

133

wanted all the rest for their horses. Still they did indicate that I might plow a piece farther away, covered with sage and grease wood, intersected by sloughs and badly developed alkali, while at best it would take three months to clear the surface. They would listen to nothing I could say, and seeing no help for it, since if they could drive me from one place they would quickly drive me from another, I ordered the plows to run as I had proposed.

The first bed had been laid out and watered, 100 feet wide and half a mile long, and when the plowman got to the upper end two Indians came out with guns and ordered him not to plow any more. This was reported to me, and I directed the plowing to proceed. When the plowman had made a few runs around the bed he was fired upon from a small cluster of sage-brush, and the ball passed close to his person.

Of course I ordered the plowing to stop. I went to Douglas, the chief, but he only repeated that they who claimed the land wanted it, and that I ought to plow somewhere else. Then I sent a messenger to Jack, a rival chieftain, ten miles up the river, who has a larger following than Douglas, and he and his friends came down speedily, and the whole subject was discussed at great length. The conclusion was, that Jack and his men did not care anything about it, but I might go on and plow that bed (100 feet wide and one-half mile long). I said that was of no use; that I wanted to plow 50 acres at least, and I wanted the rest for hay, as we had to go from 4 to 7 miles to do our haying, and even there the Indian horses eat much of the grass. Then they said I might go on and plow as I proposed.

This was either not understood or not assented to by the claimants, for when the plow started next morning they came out and threatened vengeance if any more than that bed was plowed. Immediately I sent again for Jack and his men, and the plow ran most of the forenoon, when I ordered it stopped, for by this time the employes were becoming scared.

Another long council was held, and I understood scarcely anything that was said, though I was present for hours, smothered with heat and smoke, and finally it was agreed that I might have the whole land and plow. half of it and inclose the rest, providing I would remove the corral, dig a well, help build a log house, and give a stove, to which I assented, for substantially the same had been promised before.

Altogether there were not more than four Indian men engaged in this outbreak; properly, there was only one family, the wife of which speaks good English, having been brought up in a white family; the remainder were relatives, and besides were several sympathizers, but by no means active.

During all this time I had a team in readiness to go to the railroad to ask instructions from you by telegraph, but the necessity for this seems, for the present, averted.

My impression is decided that it was the wish of all the Indians that the plowing might be stopped and that no more plowing at all shall be done, but that the conclusion which they reached was based upon the danger they ran in opposing the Government of the United States.

Plowing will proceed, but whether unmolested I cannot say. This is a bad lot of Indians. They have had free rations so long and have been flattered and petted so much, that they think themselves lords of all.

Respectfully, etc.,
N. C. MEEKER
Indian Agent

« IV »

The story went around, because it was a good story. Everyone who heard the story of Tatit'z and his new rifle told that story to someone else. It made everybody laugh. The old people, who sometimes forgot things, would tell the story two or three times to the same person, and that one would laugh every time, harder than before.

The man who had been plowing had rolled his clothes and bed up, and gone away. They said he went back over the high mountains to that place where the Agent had lived before he came here, and that place must have been the white worker's home because Maricat'z always run home when they are afraid.

The ones who had been angry about the plowing almost forgot about it now. When another man came to plow, some of the young men took their rifles and stood at the ends of the field. They did not talk; they just stood there. The man with the plow would see them as he walked along behind his mules, and when he came to the end of his row and turned around, he would see some more down at the other end. No matter which way he turned, he saw them; and after a while he walked behind his mules back to the agency.

The story got better and better. Around the morning fires the children told it and laughed. The women out cutting brushwood would think about it and start laughing, even though there was nobody there to laugh with them.

The Agent did not laugh, not even once. No one had ever seen this Agent laugh, and he did not laugh now. He was angry. Some who had seen him said he was angrier than he had ever been before, and that he was talking about bad things he was going to do. He had talked to Quinkent for a long time, and Quinkent went back to his carniv to think about it.

Quinkent had laughed with the others at the stories, and he had told them many times, for Quinkent enjoyed telling a story more than he did laughing at one when someone else told it; but now, after he had talked with the Agent, he would not talk to anyone. He said he would talk later, but now he had to think.

When Quinkent finally called some of the men to his carniv, he seemed unhappy. He seemed mixed up in his head, and he talked a long time before he said anything the others could make sense of. He started out by saying that he and this Agent had been good friends, but that now they would not be such good friends for a while.

Maybe sometime he would think some more about this and go up and shake hands with the Agent, but now they would not be friends. This Agent might know Washington better than any other Agent, but Quinkent knew Washington too. He knew Washington did not want to do anything the People did not like, and if the People would wait and listen to what Quinkent had to say, soon everything would be all right.

Quinkent talked on for a long time, and all of those listening to him wanted to know what the Agent had said to him and what he had said to the Agent; but Quinkent did not let anyone else talk.

The Agent told Quinkent a lie. He told Quinkent that the man who ran away when Tatit'z shot his new rifle had been killed. He said all the people were bad, and he said he would make some soldiers come to Smoking Earth River.

Now Quinkent waited while everybody talked over what he had said. Soldiers could bring great trouble to a place.

Then Quinkent said: "I told this Agent I do not want soldiers to come here. I told him that Washington wants us to live in peace and that there will be no soldiers coming here."

He waited again, seeing that they all felt better. Then he continued: "This Agent told me we must all move away from here. He said we must take our houses and go away because he wants to plow up all this land. He wants the land he had divided up for us to be plowed. I told him again that we need land for our ponies, and he said we have too many ponies and that we had better kill some of them. He said we had better kill part of our ponies and only save a few, so that he can have the land for plowing, and grass for the cows."

They were all quiet after Quinkent said this. Nobody had anything to say. These were bad, crazy things the Agent had said to Quinkent, and nobody wanted to talk about them now.

"I told the Agent he had better find some other land for plowing up. I did not answer him about the ponies; I only told him he should find some other land and not plow up the places he has already given us for our houses. He told me that anyhow the land is not ours. He said it was bought with blankets and goods he has given us; that the land was bought by Washington with blankets and such things. I could not talk to the Agent any more, and I came to my carniv to think about it."

Quinkent was finished. There was nothing to do but wait until Quinkent was again friends with the Agent and could talk some more to him; so they all forgot about it and sat for a smoke.

After they left Quinkent felt better. The People had listened to him, and they all knew, even those who went with Nicaagat, that Quinkent was the best one to talk to the Agent. He would wait awhile, and then he would call them all down to his carniv for a big talk.

Another morning came. The women took their pails up to the agency corrals to milk the cows. Quinkent heard the pounding begin up where the white workers were making a new building for the agency. But no man came out with the mules and plow. The fields, with the prickly fences around them half-finished, were empty. All morning Quinkent waited in his carniv, but no one came to tell him the Agent wanted to talk to him.

Then he saw some men on ponies riding fast toward the agency. They were coming from up above toward the old agency, and he saw soon that one of them was young Nicaagat. He watched them ride up in front of the agency house, and he saw Nicaagat get down and go in the house. The others waited outside, a long time.

Quinkent waited too. He went up from his carniv to a little strip that had not been plowed, where the sagebrush grew higher than a man, and he watched from there. He was worried. Perhaps now Nicaagat would do what Quinkent had planned to do in a day or two—make a bargain with the Agent that would make this thing all right with the People. Then the Agent would be friends with Nicaagat, and the People would think Nicaagat had done the thing better than Quinkent could have done it.

But when Nicaagat came out, Quinkent could see his face, and it did not look as though he felt good. He and the others rode away, and none of them seemed to be talking.

Quinkent spent the rest of the day trying to find out whether anyone had heard what the Agent and Nicaagat had talked about. Nobody at the agency had heard anything. Then he heard that there was going to be a council the next day, at which the Agent and Nicaagat would each talk.

A quiet excitement filled the camps along Smoking Earth River that night. There was little talk about the coming council but there was thought of little else. Now perhaps the puzzling things this Agent said and did would at least be understood and made clear. Perhaps now that Quinkent was angry with the Agent it would not be so easy to get the work done in the winter

138

valley. Perhaps soon Washington would find out about this Agent and would tell him to go home.

Quinkent waited through the night that would end in the big council, at which his power with words would meet a great test. The Agent would talk, and he would tell the People that the land must be plowed. Nicaagat would talk, and he would tell the People that the land must not be plowed. And now the People, even those who before had not much cared what this Agent did, were beginning to think and talk against this plowing. At one time Quinkent had agreed with the Agent and had told them that all things that the Agent wanted to do were good things. But there had been the Maricat'z lies about the fires; and the Maricat'z who came to take two of the men away to prison. There were the Buffalo Soldiers in Middle Park. And now the Agent wanted to plow up all the grass, the places he had given the People for their houses, and the race track. Quinkent would have to talk well tomorrow.

He turned his head and looked out under the side of the carniv, rolled up away from the ground, and he saw his breath against the gray light in the sky.

The fires burned up brightly all up and down the river. All the men in the village were getting ready to go to the council. While he was eating his meat and pana, Quinkent heard a group of men on ponies coming from up the valley. He thought he had better finish eating and leave for the agency. He wanted to be one of the first there.

The Agent had chosen a large, empty building, which had been built only a little while ago, for the council. There were no windows in the building, and it was like the inside of a carniv in the winter. The Agent had said he was going to put grain in the building.

The People gathered inside, making smaller and smaller circles, until soon there was only a little space in the middle where a man could stand and talk. Then the Agent came with the Little Boy, who would tell the People what the Agent said. The Little Boy was carrying a chair, which he put down in the middle of the floor for the Agent to sit on.

139

All the men lit pipes, and soon the top of the room was covered with a heavy cloud. Quinkent blew his smoke, and then got up and stood in the middle of the floor.

He began by talking about the old days. He told how it was before the People knew about Washington and before Washington knew about the People. That was when there were not many Maricat'z in the country.

In those times, the People fought with the Arapaho, and the Sioux, and the Cheyenne. The People fought with the Navajo and the Kiowa. All of those others fought among themselves, and many of them fought the Maricat'z.

Now Washington had come. Washington had great arms which stretched out far and embraced the People and all the other tribes. Washington was like a great father to them all, and there was peace because Washington wanted peace.

When this Agent came here, said Quinkent, he talked with the voice of Washington, but now some evil had taken hold of him and made him sick. Now he talked only with his own voice, but Quinkent still spoke with the voice of Washington, and perhaps soon this Agent would be well again and would talk right.

Now, Quinkent said, he would tell the People what Washington wanted them to do. He knew, he said, that Washington did not want them to kill their ponies. He knew that Washington had given them these pieces of land for their houses and that Washington did not talk with two voices—that what Washington said about the ground for the houses was the same as it had been, and that this Agent could not plow it up.

The brightest part of the morning came through the open door when Quinkent finished talking. The Agent had sat staring out the door while Quinkent spoke. Now and then the Little Boy would tell him something, but the Agent only sat and stared out into the sunshine.

Something big and alive rose up from the People—rose up with the cloud of smoke—when Nicaagat stood up.

He, too, talked about Washington at first. He talked about how he had gone to see the President a long time ago and that the President had given him the silver sun with his face on it, which Nicaagat still wore around his neck. That President had only one thing to say: he told the People to live in peace; since that time there had been no wars.

Nicaagat said many of the People were afraid of soldiers, but the soldiers were his friends. He said all the generals were his friends and the soldiers would not come here and hurt the People and scare the women and children.

He said this Agent was a bad man. This Agent talked bad, and he wanted to take everything away from the People. He wanted to take away their ponies and make them live like Mari-cat'z. He wrote bad things about the People to Washington.

Nicaagat said there were friends of his among the Maricat'z who would write to Washington. These were important men, and Washington would hear what they had to say. Soon Washington would know the truth, and this Agent would be taken away.

When Nicaagat finished talking and sat down, the Little Boy said something to the Agent, and the Agent stood up. He talked awhile, and the Little Boy told them what he had said.

"This Agent says he is going away soon," said the Little Boy. "He is going to the railroad and send some words to Washington. He is going to tell Washington that he is trying to do everything Washington wants him to do, but some of the People are bad and will not let him do it."

The Agent talked some more.

"He says he is the one who must say what land is to be plowed—that none of the People can say anything about it. He says he knows what Washington wants him to do, and if the People do not let him do it, Washington will be angry and send soldiers to us. Then some of us will go to prison and be tied up in chains and die."

When the Agent was finished it was time for others to talk. First the old ones said what they thought, then the younger men talked, and soon it became clear what the People wanted to do. They agreed that this Agent was a bad man, but they said that Washington did not know this yet, and perhaps if he went to the railroad and sent some words to Washington, these things would make Washington angry and there would be trouble before the truth came to Washington. Then Washington would be sad because this trouble had come. Then Washington would know the truth, but it would be too late.

The People decided that the Agent should go ahead and plow the land he wanted to plow, but he should not run the plow where the houses were, and he should not kill any ponies.

Nicaagat told the Agent what the People had said, and the Agent thought about it. He got up and talked again, and the Little Boy told them what he said:

"This Agent says he will start the man running the plow again today. He says we can stay where our houses are and soon he will build us all log houses, and we will have boxes in those houses to put our fires in. He says this is what we will have if we do as he says. He says all our country belongs to Washington and perhaps if we do not let Washington do as he wants with it, we will come to that place where many of the others are: that place where it is hot all the time and there is no water and not enough grass—that place the Maricat'z call Indian Territory."

By the time the Little Boy had finished talking the room was filled with a low, shaking rumble. It seemed to come out of the ground, but it came from the mouths of the People; and it started when the Agent said that word "Indian Territory." The word had reached out to all the People in the room, and the old people who knew no Maricat'z words felt it.

There might have been more talk, but the rumble of the voices rose. The Agent began to look the way Maricat'z look when someone is making a joke with them by trying to scare them. He stood up, looked around him, and in three large steps he was out the door.

The rumbling of voices did not quiet until Quinkent stood up. "This is all we have to say," he said.

« V »

During the days just before Bear Dance, Canávish had sat in the door of his carniv, smoking his long stone pipe, which was not like other stone pipes because it had some of the medicine

142

power of Canávish, and watched the white workers build the log house. When that new house was finished Canávish still sat and looked at it, because it was part of a very big joke.

Canávish, called Johnson by the Maricat'z, was getting almost old enough to be one of the old people. He seldom went hunting any more, but when he did he was still the best shot with a rifle of all the men on Smoking Earth River. His old rifle, one of those which the white man called a Sharps, was well known, and so was the hunting eye of Canávish.

But a man grown older enjoys a good joke even more than a good hunt, and this was why Canávish had spent so much of his time under the sleepy sun of the early spring days sitting and looking at the house.

Washington had built that house for Canávish because this Agent had told Washington that Canávish and his family should have a house. After it was finished, Canávish seldom went into the house. Everybody knew it was not a good idea to stay in a house that could not be picked up and moved away if something bad happened in the place where that house was put.

Canávish had done a lot of thinking about this new Agent, and because Cánavish was m'sut t'quigat, he understood more of him than most of the People did. A m'sut t'quigat is given power from Sunáwiv to cure sickness without herbs or berries or roots. And when he receives this power, a man is living outside himself, as well as inside.

Canávish had thought about these things the Agent said he wanted to do for the People—this plowing in the ground, building houses, working, and sending the children to school. The Agent wanted to do these things because he was an unhappy man, Canávish decided. He wanted his own people to see how he made the People do things; then he might be thought an important man among his own people. He was not a bad man, but he did not understand many things.

A little while after this Agent arrived on the Smoking Earth River, when he first began talking of moving the agency to the winter valley and when Quinkent was doing a great deal of talking to the People, Canávish had thought of this joke. It would be a fine joke for this Agent, and even for Washington.

143

Canávish went to this Agent and told him he liked to hear these things he talked about. He said he would do what the Agent and Washington wanted him to do, and he would have his sons and his piwán do all these things too. He talked a long time, and when he finished the Agent looked very pleased.

The next day the Agent showed Canávish a piece of land beside the river and near to where the new agency was then being built. The piece of land had good grass on it and Canávish told the Agent it was all right, that he would bring his carniv here; but the Agent said that Canávish and all his family were to live in a new carniv—the kind the white men live in—and that Washington would build this house because Canávish was a very good and a very important man.

In a little while the Agent gave Canávish two cows, because Canávish, being an important man, was head of a large family where there were many children. Then Canávish told this Agent that he had many ponies, and now some of these ponies would have to pull wagons and do hard work they had never done before—he said that ponies that are to do such work should have grain and hay. He told the Agent that he should start feeding his ponies oats and other grain now, so that they would be strong when it was time for them to work. So the Agent gave Canávish a sack of grain and some hay, and when that was all gone, he gave him some more.

While the People were getting ready for Bear Dance Canávish told his sons about the joke. He took them both outside and showed them the horses, which were shiny and strong from eating the oats.

Soon everybody would be talking about racing, and soon the racing would start. Canávish and his sons would tell everybody that they had horses that could beat any man's horse. This would make all the men want to race with them, and because they were all proud of their ponies they would bet fine things. Soon they would lose so much that they, too, would see the joke.

It was a very fine idea. After a while everybody would know it, and all of the People would be laughing. Then, perhaps, the Agent would see that all of those things he wanted were foolish, and he would laugh too.

As the first thunder of Bear Dance filled the spring days, the People began to gather along the race track. The men were bringing their finest ponies to race, and they were betting fine things, because every man thought no horse could outrun his. In the evenings Tim and Tatit'z would lead their horses home, covered with foam and wet all over, and with them they carried all the fine things they had won in the day's racing. When the ponies were cool, Tim and Tatit'z dipped out oats for them, and in the morning, before the races started, they fed them more oats.

Toward the end of the Bear Dance feasts, everyone saw the joke, and they laughed about it for a long time. Others said they would go and tell the Agent they too needed oats for their ponies.

Then one day that Agent came to the carniv of Canávish. He was not laughing. He told Canávish he was a bad man who lied and cheated. He said these things would some day bring him to prison, where he would be tied up, and that his sons would go to prison too. He said that Washington was very angry with Canávish and all his family and that now they would get nothing more —not even the food that the others got. Then he left.

Outside the carniv the Agent saw Tim and Tatit'z and he said the same bad things to them, and when the sons came inside they all sat down together and did not talk for a long time.

The way the Agent talked had made Canávish feel bad. He felt as though something had reached deep into his middle and stirred things around—the way it is when men are worried or afraid; however this feeling did not last long, for *pöorat*, the power Canávish had been given for curing sickness, soon took it away.

It was better, too, after Tim and Tatit'z came, and Tsashin, the piwán of Canávish, whom the Maricat'z called Susan, came and sat with them. Tim and Tatit'z were both strong, quiet, handsome young men. Most of the time they remembered they should not talk unless they had something to say. Tsashin always joined them for the council of the family; she was a sister of Ouray, who was a man with power whether a person agreed with his ways or not. Tsashin, like Ouray, was half Apache and was tall and strong like the Apache women. She was nearly as tall as her two boys, and she stood even with Canávish. When

145

Tsashin was a little girl she had been stolen by the Arapaho, and the soldiers had returned her to her home; she had learned much about Maricat'z and could talk to them.

Canávish took out his buckskin pouch, which Tsashin had beaded in yellow, green, blue, and white, and which held his stone pipe and tobacco. The smoke was rising out of his pipe like white horsehair, twisted to make a bridle, before he began to talk.

They had made a good joke. Everybody had laughed with them, but this Agent was angry. He was part of the joke and should laugh more than anybody, but he was angry. The trouble with this agent was that he did not laugh. When it was time for him to laugh, he was angry. When a man never laughs he becomes sick inside, and one big laugh would make all the sickness come out.

Canávish waited, for it seemed that Tsashin would have something to say. She knew the Maricat'z well. The People make their jokes, and the Maricat'z make trouble.

Tim and Tatit'z were looking at each other and grinning. Then they both sat up straight and pushed their chests out. They were acting like soldiers, and they thought it was very funny. Tatit'z held his arms out straight in front of him, jerking them up and down.

In this imitation of the *swerch,* the Maricat'z soldier, Tim was making a good laugh, and he was also showing that he would never be afraid of such men who, when their general shouted at them, were so afraid that they went, "Hump . . . hump, hump . . . hump, hump . . . hump," stepping with their feet all together. They were not like many men. They were like one creature with one great body; but they could be killed one at a time and the whole great body was dead. Tim held out his arms as though he were shooting a rifle. The soldiers were walking, "Hump . . . hump, hump . . . hump," their general was shouting at them and scaring them, and Tim was up behind a rock with his rifle. Both the boys laughed until their eyes shut up tight, and only little croaking sounds came out of their mouths.

Although his eyes seemed to be staring far away, Canávish

was listening to his sons, who were talking now more like boys than like young men.

It had only been a short time since Canávish had started talking to Tim and Tatit'z like men, and he had not told them most of the important things yet. Maybe he would never be able to tell them everything. Their few summers had given them men's bodies, but they were still growing into them; you could not tell how they would be when they were men all over.

Besides, there is only so much one man can tell another. The rest, if he is ever going to know it, must come from inside and outside of him. When a man has learned all he can from the words other men have given him, then perhaps the great wisdom will come to him; but the great wisdom does not come from other men, and if a man tries to tell another man about it, soon he finds that the words have tangled themselves around him like thick brush, and the other knows no more than he did before.

When Canávish received the power of the bear, he had a dream; when he woke he knew he had talked with Sunáwiv, but he could not tell his dream to other men, and soon he found that there was no need to speak of it. Everybody knew that Canávish had received the power.

Canávish knew that he could never tell another man what it was like to talk to Sunáwiv: His voice does not come from the sky, or from the ground, or from inside of a man. It comes from inside and outside all at once. Then a man knows both the inside and the outside, and he understands that they are both the same —that everything is one, like the circle a carniv makes on the ground. A man who has not talked with Sunáwiv can see only a little piece of the great circle at one time, and he may believe that it is straight. A man with power can only see a little piece of the great circle, but while he is seeing he knows that it goes on and on: the circle of the world, the sacred hoop of his People.

Before he had received the power Canávish had been bigger and stronger; but after that time the strength went out of his arms and legs and was changed into another kind of strength. He was a thin bony man now, with a dry, yellowed skin. His eyes were old, but they were not watery and dim. They were black and deep, as though they were always looking outside and inside at once: as though the things they saw outside were not the most important things to see.

A man who has this power can never go to sleep beside it and forget about it. He must never look at it without looking at the Great Circle. The power given by Sunáwiv can turn into a power for evil before the sun can move. Then it is the power to kill, not the power to heal; and soon it will destroy the man who has it.

Tim and Tatit'z knew nothing of wars and soldiers. They had never seen a war; for Washington had told the People many years ago that there would be peace. There would be no more wars—not with the Arapaho, the Cheyenne, the Sioux, the Kiowa, or the soldiers.

But the time comes when a young man thinks of war, and of women. This is the time when he should be given the wisdom of the old stories and the old people—the balancing of the land and the sky, of the inside and the outside.

Usually it is the grandfather, the oldest one in all the family, who tells the old stories to the young men; since Canávish was m'sut t'quigat, he had this power to instruct his sons. Now, he thought, was time to give them some of this wisdom.

Tim and Tatit'z were sitting quietly smoking now, so Canávish spoke aloud his secret name, and called out so that Sunáwiv might hear him.

Then he began that oldest story of all: what Sunáwiv did to make this world from nothing and darkness, how He became lonely living in it all by Himself and made a brother to live with Him—Sunáwigá, whom the Maricat'z call "Holy Ghost." Then the God made the animals, and in that time they could sing and dance and speak to one another, and the world was very good.

Sunáwiv told the animals that they should now put the world in order, and so they called a great council, which lasted many days and nights. In the night, when it was dark inside the carniv, Magpie painted a little white sun on his belly, and danced and sang, thumping it like a drum, and thus made light for them. During this council was settled the time of years, seasons, and days, the place of the directions, and many other things. When they were talking about the seasons, Hawk suggested having four moons in each season, but Quail, sitting on his three little toes, wanted three. And that was all right. So these matters were decided.

But Sunáwigá was always the busy one, always wanting to make things over to suit himself, and spoiling everything. In that time, when living creatures got old and tired, they only lay down for three days; then they would come alive again and be as good as new. Sunáwigá did not like this arrangement, and he said to Sunáwiv: "Brother, I think when the creatures lie down they should be dead, and their relatives should mourn them, and give away their belongings." The God said it should be that way. But Sunáwigá had a son, whom he loved very much, and the God said to him: "Now your son is the first one dead; go and mourn for him." Sunáwigá begged and cried, but the God would not change His word. So the world Sunáwiv made was changed to the world we now live in.

Canávish told his sons how Sunáwiv finally became tired of his brother spoiling the world, and He made him into Yorowit'z, Old Coyote. At that time He also changed the animals to the way they are today, and He allowed them each to choose how he would be: the color of feathers or fur, how he would eat and live. Some He made one way, and some another; in this same way some tribes were made to hunt, and others to go on water, and others to grow things in the ground.

Canávish told them something of the son of the God, Sunáwiv-ta'wat'z, who was so great among men that even the Maricat'z knew about him. Sunáwiv-ta'wat'z told men how Sunáwiv wanted them to live, and some who did not like this talk killed the God's son. It was not the People, or any of the others. The Maricat'z did not kill him. The old people knew who killed him, but they would not talk about it.

Canávish talked late into the night. Before he had finished, the fire had died to red coals, and it was getting black inside the carniv. The bite of late spring frost crept in through the doorway, and Canávish's eyelids were like heavy snow clouds sinking down between the mountains.

The next morning he sent Tim and Tatit'z out on a hunt with some of the other men. He did not go with them.

Canávish saw little of the Agent during the rest of that spring and through the summer moons, but he watched many things happening in the winter valley. Every day more of the good grass was turned under by the plow. Maricat'z—the same ones who had built the house for Canávish—worked on new buildings at the agency.

One day, near the beginning of the First Fall Moon, a woman and her son came from far away to Canávish's carniv. They carried with them the medicine sign of Quigat, the bear. This meant that Canávish was wanted at the camp of these people—that someone was sick there. Tsashin packed the medicine bundle for Canávish, and together they started out for this camp.

They were gone for many sleeps, and when they returned to Smoking Earth River Canávish was very tired. Pöwa'a, the tiny green man who carries the healing power inside a m'sut t'quigat, must draw strength from the body, and a medicine singing will always leave a man tired, especially one as long and difficult as this one had been. Tsashin, who had stayed by the side of Canávish through all the days and nights of the singing, and who had caught the sickness when it came out of the body and slapped it to death, as the piwán of a m'sut t'quigat must do, was also tired. Canávish had strong power in his bear-medicine, and the man for whom he had sung was already out of his blankets and ready to go on a hunt.

Canávish said he would sleep that night, and the next day go on a short hunt, so that new power could come back to him in case it was needed soon for some other sick person. But the next morning when the sun was showing its full face above the pine-edged slope up the river, Canávish looked out and saw Pauvit'z coming toward the carniv.

Pauvit'z had come to talk. When he was seated beside the breakfast fire, he told Canávish that a council had been held the day before with the Agent, and that it had to do with this business of turning the grass upside down. He said that Quinkent was not such good friends with the Agent any more, since Quinkent had built a big enclosure of logs for his ponies, and now that Agent wanted to plow up the ground. He said the Agent wanted to plow everything.

After Pauvit'z left, Canávish went out to look at his land.
There was plenty of grass for his ponies. He had nothing to com-
plain about. Quinkent and Pauvit'z would have to find other
grass for their ponies.

Then, as Canávish sat in front of his carniv, he saw what
looked like a strange animal coming toward him. He blinked his
eyes and looked again. He still could not see it clearly, so he
called Tsashin, who told him it was a man with two mules and
one of those knives to cut the ground. As they watched, the man
took down the wire fence around Canávish's piece of ground,
and made the mules step over it. Then he began fastening all
those straps, and soon the mules were walking along and the big
knife was cutting Canávish's grass and turning it under.

Canávish got to his feet; he said to Tsashin that he would go
to see this Agent and tell him he did not want his land spoiled
this way.

Canávish walked slowly up to the agency house and found
the Agent on the front porch. He was looking out past the corner
of the storehouse toward where the man was cutting up Canávish's grass. When he saw Canávish coming, he smiled and
nodded his head, then he looked back toward the man with the
plow.

Canávish thought perhaps the Agent had made a mistake,
had misunderstood about this. He thought that when he told the
Agent about it, he would make the plow stop.

"Man plow my ground," said Canávish.

"Yes, Johnson," said the Agent, still not looking at Canávish,
"a man is plowing your land."

"Don' want my piece torn up. Why he plow?"

"Because I told him to," said the Agent.

Canávish took a step toward the porch. He did not know
what to say to the Agent next. He did not understand about this.

"Why you tell man dat?" he asked.

The Agent kept looking toward the man with the plow. He
said: "Because, Johnson, we all had a council yesterday, and we
agreed that we should plow that piece."

"I don' say he can plow. Who say dat?"

"I told you," said the Agent, "we all had a council. It was

decided that we should go ahead and plow all the land that Washington wants plowed."

This did not sound right to Canávish. He had not been at any council, and none of the People would ever talk for someone who was not present. Nobody would tell this Agent that it was all right to spoil another man's grass.

"Don' want land plow," said Canávish.

"But you see, Johnson," said the Agent, as though speaking to a naughty child, "all of the Indians agreed to it. You can not go against everybody."

The Agent was saying something wrong. The rest of the People would not talk for one man; they would wait until he could speak for himself in council. So Canávish said:

"You lie."

The Agent looked directly at him for the first time, and he was angry.

"Don't stand there and accuse me of lying. Go and ask the others."

Canávish stepped up onto the porch beside the Agent.

"You lie," he said again, taking a step forward. "Don' want land plow."

The Agent was backing up and pointing his finger, the way Maricat'z do. His voice shook with anger.

"You take your lodge and your family and move out of here," he said. "Everything is settled. I'm through with troublesome Indians."

Canávish was standing right in front of the Agent.

"Washington give me land, build me house. I stay dere."

"I talked to you once, Johnson. I told you what would happen to you if you kept making trouble. Now do as I say, or you will go to prison."

The Agent was still backing up. Now he had one foot off the porch.

Canávish had not been angry with any person for many years. He had forgotten how anger pounces on a man suddenly, like a mountain lion dropping on a deer.

Canávish saw that his hand was clamped hard around the Agent's shoulder. His fingers were gripping the cloth of the

Agent's coat; and the Agent, now off the porch, was still backing up.

"Bad agent . . . very bad agent," he said. "You go away, new
agent come." The Agent took another step backward, and Canávish followed his step. The anger was holding onto him tight
now, and he could not shake it off. "Bad agent . . . very bad
agent."

When something like this is happening the feeling of it gets
into the air, and many others feel it. Neither Canávish nor the
Agent noticed that a few of the People were standing near and
that more were coming to watch.

"Bad agent . . . very bad agent. You go." The Agent backed
away and Canávish followed, his hand still holding the Agent's
coat. More people came, and they watched the Agent's face.
They saw that his eyes were very wide and now and then he
swallowed, but he did not say anything.

"Bad agent . . . you bring trouble. Very bad man."

Some of those who were watching looked at something just
behind the Agent. It was a lodge pole nailed across two posts,
where those who came to see the Agent tied their horses. One
by one they began to grin, as they looked at Canávish and the
Agent, who was still backing up, then at the hitching rail. Somebody made a loud whoop, then came another. Now there were
many sounds and they came together and made a song. As they
sang they bounced all together on bent knees, making their
hands go as though they were all beating a great drum.

Canávish kept saying things to the Agent, but the song made
so much noise that nobody could hear him.

Then the song cut off in a wild, shrill shriek. The Agent's
head went down and his feet shot up, straight toward the sky.
His legs made a big circle and almost kicked Canávish in the
face. Then the Agent was sprawled on the other side of the
hitching rail, on the ground. He was still for a minute, then his
head came up again, and he blinked and looked around him.
His mouth started to make words, but no one could hear him.
Many people were laughing, as hard as people can laugh.

Nobody noticed the two white workers who were coming.
They ran to where the Agent had fallen and lifted him by the

arms. He kept pointing at Canávish, but no one could hear what words were coming out of his mouth. Then the two Maricat'z were leading the Agent into his house.

Some place in the middle of the laughter the song started up again. Canávish was in the middle of the circle of people, their arms locked together, their bodies bouncing with the song. The whole circle turned slowly around Canávish, and his ears were so full of sound that he could only feel his mouth moving and the song coming up through his throat.

6. THE TROUBLE

« I »

THE MESSAGE moved slowly northward, jogging along in the saddlebag of the courier over the 170 miles of rocky ruts that were the road from the White River Agency to Rawlins.

At the railroad station in Rawlins the telegraph key clicked, and the message flashed across two-thirds of the continent to the central office of the Bureau of Indian Affairs in Washington, D.C.:

> SEPTEMBER 10, 1879
> I HAVE BEEN ASSAULTED BY A LEADING CHIEF, JOHNSON.
> FORCED OUT OF MY OWN HOUSE AND INJURED BADLY, BUT WAS
> RESCUED BY EMPLOYES. IT IS NOW REVEALED THAT JOHNSON
> ORIGINATED ALL THE TROUBLE STATED IN LETTER SEPT. 8; HIS
> SON SHOT AT PLOWMAN, AND OPPOSITION TO PLOWING IS WIDE;
> PLOWING STOPS; LIFE OF SELF, FAMILY, AND EMPLOYES NOT
> SAFE; WANT PROTECTION IMMEDIATELY; HAVE ASKED GOV.
> PITKIN TO CONFER WITH GEN. POPE.
>
> N. C. MEEKER, INDIAN AGENT

E. J. Brooks, still acting as Indian Commissioner in Hayt's absence, sent Meeker's telegram over to the office of Secretary of the Interior Carl Schurz, with a note of his own: ". . . I respectfully recommend that the matter be referred to the honorable Secretary of War."

In Washington a great gear that was the Interior Depart-

155

ment, turning slowly, began to swing on its axis toward another ring of teeth that was the War Department; the two meshed. Secretary Schurz passed the message from the Indian Bureau to the Secretary of War, and on September 16 an order left the Headquarters of the Army at Washington, bound for Lieutenant General P. H. Sheridan, commanding the Division of the Missouri at Chicago:

> ... Secretary of War approves request of Interior Department, just received, and General of the Army directs that necessary orders be given the nearest military commander to the agency to detail a sufficient number of troops to arrest such Indian chiefs as are insubordinate, and enforce obedience to the requirements of the agent, and afford him such protection as the exigency of the case requires; also that the ringleaders be held as prisoners until an investigation can be had.

Acting Commissioner Brooks then telegraphed Meeker:

SEPTEMBER 15, 1879

WAR DEPARTMENT REQUESTED COMMANDING OFFICER NEAREST POST TO SEND TROOPS FOR YOUR PROTECTION IMMEDIATELY. ON THEIR ARRIVAL CAUSE ARREST OF LEADERS IN LATE DISTURBANCE AND HAVE THEM HELD UNTIL FURTHER ORDERS FROM THIS OFFICE. REPORT FULL PARTICULARS AS SOON AS POSSIBLE.

E. J. BROOKS, ACTING COM'R

A large part of that day on which the message that set the biggest wheels in Washington in motion was sent, Meeker spent in letter writing. He had always been a man whose literary drive overflowed into copious correspondence, even during less eventful periods. Today, propped up on pillows, his aging bones and muscles sore and aching from the fall over the hitching rail, and his dignity smarting from the laughter, Meeker's pen flew. His first letter was to Governor Pitkin:

Sir:

We have plowed eighty acres, and the Indians object to any more being done, and to any more fencing. We shall stop plowing. One of the plowmen was shot at last week. On Monday I was assaulted in my own house, while my wife was present, by a leading chief named Johnson, and forced outdoors and considerably injured, as I was in a crippled condition, having previously met with an accident, a wagon falling over on me. The employes came to my rescue. I had built this Johnson a house, given him a wagon and harness, and fed him at my table many, many times. The trouble is, he had 150 horses, and wants the land for pasturage, although the agency was moved that this same land might be used, and the agency buildings are on it. I have had two days' council with the chiefs and headmen of the tribe, who concluded, after a sort of a way, that I might plow, but they will do nothing to permit me to, and they laugh at my being forced out of my house.

I have no confidence in any of them, and I feel that none of the white people are safe. I know they are not if we go on to perform work directed by the Commissioner of Indian Affairs. Here are my wife and daughter in this condition.

Confer with General Pope, Commissioner, and Senator Teller. At least 100 soldiers ought to come hither to protect us, and to keep the Utes on their reservation—should be more.

Don't let this application get in the papers, for I know the Indians will hear of it in a few days. Of course, what the Indians have done is a matter of news.

Truly,

N. C. MEEKER, Indian Agent

In another letter, Meeker told W. N. Byers:

. . . I think they will submit to nothing but force. How many are rebellious I do not know; but if only a few are, and the rest laugh at their outrages, as they do, and think nothing of it, all are complicated. I didn't come here to be kicked and hustled out of my own house by savages, and if the government can not protect me, let somebody else try it. You know the Indians and understand the situation. . . .

What the Indians did was, indeed, a "matter of news"; it "got in the papers." It got all over the papers. The doings of a busy young state, the news of a quiet, prosperous nation, were pushed into the background. From the papers it went into the streets, and from the streets into offices, stores, and homes. The popular picture of the Utes—"obstacle to progress"—began to take on fiercer colors.

Excited stories and editorials, built around Mr. Meeker's alarming letter with the colorful background of earlier reports from Mr. Byers' friends in Middle Park, again flowed from the Governor's office. As soon as the busy Governor found time away from his news conferences, he wrote General John Pope at Fort Leavenworth, Kansas:

> I have the honor to inclose herewith a communication from N. C. Meeker, esq., Indian Agent at the White River Agency, in which he details the feelings of the Utes at that point, and desires me to confer with you for the purpose of securing at least one hundred troops for the protection of the agency. . . .
>
> I received yesterday your dispatch advising me that a company of cavalry had been ordered to proceed at once to the White River Agency. Your letter concerning the disposition of the Utes, I presume, will reach me today. . . .

Meanwhile, before any reassuring word of the dispatch of troops was received at the agency, Meeker had again telegraphed the Indian Commissioner:

> SEPTEMBER 17, 1879
> (VIA RAWLINS, WYOMING)
>
> THERE IS NO PARTICULAR CHANGE, EITHER FOR WORSE OR BETTER. NO PLOWING IS DONE, NOR WILL IT TIL IT CAN BE DONE IN SAFETY. IT REMAINS TO BE SEEN WHETHER THE BUSINESS AND INDUSTRIES OF THIS AGENCY ARE TO BE CONDUCTED UNDER THE INDIANS OR YOURSELF.
>
> N. C. MEEKER, INDIAN AGENT

Secretary of the Interior Carl Schurz was by that time in Cheyenne, on his way to Denver to confer with Governor Pitkin about the "Ute Difficulty." On September 19, he telegraphed the Indian Office in Washington for any new details. Acting Commissioner Brooks answered that Commissioner Hayt was at the Palmer House in Chicago, and "all the official information we have is that White River agent was driven from agency building about 13th instant by Indians and seriously injured, but was rescued by employes on 15th. War Department ordered troops from Fort Steele to agency. Opinion is that Utes were driven to hostility largely by influx of miners. . . ."

Governor Pitkin met Schurz on his arrival in Denver. After talks with Pitkin, Byers, and others, Schurz sent further details to the Indian Office, where they were received by the now thoroughly confused Brooks:

Two Indian Utes, Bennett and Chinaman, have been identified as having burned down citizens' houses outside of reservation; warrants are out against them. Agent Meeker should be instructed to have them arrested and turned over to civil authorities; efforts should also be made to identify Indians having set fire to forests outside of reservation. On consultation with governor and others, I am advised that settlement of Utes in severalty will be possible on or near location now occupied by them, if properly managed. Steps to that end should be initiated as fast as possible.

On September 23 Brooks passed Schurz' message on to Meeker, in the form of official instructions:

Secretary telegraphs from Denver that two Ute Indians, Bennett and Chapman, have been identified. . . . Agent Meeker should be instructed to arrest and turn them over to civil authorities. . . . You will act on Secretary's suggestion, calling on military for assistance if necessary.

Deep in the wilderness of the White River country, far from the flurry in Washington and the tempest in Denver, Agent

Meeker had returned to agency matters and attending to the business details that were part of running an Indian agency, with or without plowing. In a short letter written to the Indian Office on September 24, he was concerned with the dwindling supply of paper bags in the agency stockrooms. The goods for which he said he had made "due requisition" were then on wagons between the railroad and the agency, or had already arrived, but no invoice of paper bags had been received. "It is of greatest importance," he wrote, "that the needed supply be forwarded."

The goods now arriving at the agency were partly the regular annuity supplies for the Indians, and partly agricultural equipment and supplies needed for further development of the Plan. Meeker was especially eager for the arrival of the new steam-powered threshing machine he had ordered—he felt sure that this marvelous object would excite the awe and respect of even the most unco-operative of the Indians.

Between reading and writing of letters on such pressing details of agency business, Meeker received and read, on September 25, a dispatch from Major Thornburgh, en route to the White River Agency from Fort Steele:

> In obedience to instructions from the General of the Army, I am now en route to your agency, and expect to arrive there
>
> on the 29th instant, for the purpose of affording you any assistance in my power, and to make arrests at your suggestion, and to hold as prisoners such of your Indians as you desire until investigations are made by your department. I have heard nothing definite from your agency for ten days, and do not know what state of affairs exists; whether the Indians will leave at my approach or show hostilities.
>
> I send this letter to Mr. Lowery, one of my guides, and desire you to communicate with me as soon as possible, giving me all the information in your power, in order that I may know what course I am to pursue. If practicable meet me on the road at the earliest moment.
>
> *Very respectfully, your obedient servant,*
> T. T. THORNBURGH
> Major, 4th Infantry, Com'd'g Expedition

« II »

The plow lay on its side in the middle of the field where the new worker had left it. It had lain there for many days, its two wooden handles sticking up from the ground like the feelers of a grasshopper. No one had come out to get it and take it back to the place where the Agent kept such things, and it lay there, gathering dew in the early morning, gathering dust under the tall sun.

No one came out—not one of the Maricat'z from the agency had walked that far from the buildings. They hardly came outside, and the Agent had been seen only once or twice during the past days. The workers pounded and scraped at the wood for the new building, but they did not come toward the fields or toward the river where the carniva were. Only once in a while one of them would look down that way, his hand shading his eyes, as though he expected somebody to come up and talk to him.

The Agent had talked a great deal during the summer. He had told the People to do things—he had told them to move down to the agency, he had told them to move away; he had told them they must have wagons for their work, he had told them they could not have wagons; he had told them they were good people, and the next day he had told them they were bad people. But now he told them nothing. Nobody—not Quinkent, not Canávish —knew what the Agent wanted the People to do, for he had not talked to anyone.

So the People went on and did the things they had to do each day; they played games in the evening and they slept at night. The children played and the women worked. And in a day— perhaps less than a day—everybody forgot about the Agent and the agency. The things that went on at the agency had nothing to do with the People—it was as though they were going on in some faraway Maricat'z place. It was like the old days that nearly everybody could remember, not so very long ago.

These days were deep and still like sleep, but those few who listened could hear a stirring far under the ground. They could hear it and they could feel it, as though the beginning of some sickness moved deep inside, ready to bite its way upward; and the still sky was stretched tight, like the cover of a drum; and something thumped very softly on the drum—beating all the time.

The women did their day's work, but they worked a little too fast and went at things a little too hard—pana burned on the fires, buckskins were scraped too hard and too long until thin places wore through; they pulled the threads too tight on their beadwork and the beads sometimes popped off. The children made more noise than usual as they played, and at night when they came to the carniv to go to their blankets, they were still full of play and would not go to sleep. The dogs barked a lot; they barked at everything.

Nicaagat and his friends met at his carniv or Sowówic's and talked and watched the women work in the garden, gathering the vegetables to put away for the winter.

Nicaagat told about his last talk with the Agent, before the council about the plowing. The Agent had called him to talk about the plowing, but he had wanted to talk about their trip to see the Governor.

The Agent was angry about that. He had told Nicaagat it was not his business to go around finding out what his agent had written. He said Nicaagat was a man who could not write, and what he said could not mean anything; but a man who could write could make his words travel far. Nicaagat asked the Agent:

"Why do you call me in here to talk if what I say is no good and means nothing?"

Then the Agent began to talk about the plowing, and Nicaagat said there should be a council of all the People called to talk about it; and the Agent again was angry. He said that the plowing was the business of Washington and that the time was short. He said that it would take too much time if all the People tried to settle it. But after a while the Agent told Nicaagat to call the council.

It was now many days after that big council, and still no plowing was done. Nicaagat wondered if the Governor had sent words to Washington and there was going to be a new agent again.

The tight, quiet days moved on. The time was drawing near for the passing out of the presents from Washington, and over the whole country there was a slow movement toward the agency, as the deer and antelope and elk begin to move down toward the lower country when the first snow clouds settle over the high mountains.

One day Nicaagat rode down to the agency to look around, and he saw that many more carniva had grown up there. Around the agency there was a great deal of motion and color, and he saw that many men and women were sitting around in little groups, playing games and talking, while children and dogs ran and played among them. They were waiting for some sign from the Agent that the presents were ready to be given out.

Nicaagat looked around at the People and he felt it—stronger —in the ground and in the sky.

He went over to one of the groups of men who were not playing any game and sat down. They had been talking about the Agent, but now they said nothing.

"I think one of you has something to say about this Agent," said Nicaagat.

"It is nothing," said one of the men.

They were all very silent for a while, but one of the men who always liked to be telling something finally spoke up.

"This Agent says we will not get anything from Washington for a long time. He says we are bad people and that some of us have been stealing from the agency."

They had not wanted to tell Nicaagat because they thought he might be angry with them for talking of trouble; but now it was out and they all spoke at once.

"He says perhaps soldiers will come here and put some of us in prison. He says they will put only the bad ones in prison, but he has said we are all bad, and he will tell the soldiers this."

"He has said they will put chains around our necks and around our hands," said another. "He has said they will hang us up on trees."

Nicaagat listened; then he said: "Perhaps one of you has heard the Agent say these things."

And around the circle each man said, "*Cut'z,* I have not

heard him, but I have heard this from others."

"If you have not heard the Agent say this you should not be talking about it," Nicaagat told them. "You are talking in a way to cause trouble."

Nicaagat got up and left the group, and as he walked toward the Agent's house he saw one of the white workers coming toward him.

"Will you get these Indians out of here?" the Maricat'z said when he was close to Nicaagat. "The Agent don't want them hanging around his house."

Nicaagat saw that this was the man who helped to pass out the presents from Washington; he asked when these things were to be given out, thinking maybe he would have something to tell the People that would stop this talk about trouble.

"Two moons," said the Maricat'z. "Now get these Indians away from here. They make too much noise and they steal everything we lay down."

"You see some of dem people steal somet'ing?" Nicaagat asked.

"Don't have to," said the white worker. "All we have to do is miss something and take one guess as to where it went."

The Maricat'z started to walk on, but Nicaagat stopped him and asked where the Agent was now.

"Maybe go see, talk to Agent," he said.

"Mr. Meeker don't want to see anyone today. He ain't feelin' well."

The sun was slanted against the red and yellow cliffs as Nicaagat rode back toward his own carniv. Along the trail between the agency and the village up above, he met other families coming down to get the things from Washington. The men and boys, riding ahead and driving the pack horses, would stop and talk, wanting to know if the presents had come from Washington. Many of them came down from the high forests, and they brought the fall color with them. Between hunts of the summer they had gone to the stores, and their women had made fine things for them to wear out of the colored cloth they had bought. Long, fresh hawk and eagle feathers shone in their hair, and many of them wore the white weasel furs hung from their necks on the beaded buckskin suncircles that are given from father to son. Some of the ponies' bridles were covered with bright silver ornaments, for after the presents from Washington were given out, there were always games and dances.

Nicaagat would repeat to them what the white agency worker had said about the passing out of the presents. They would be puzzled, then they would go on their way, for they meant to see for themselves and to talk to some of the others about it.

Soon after he came to his carniv and was settling down for a smoke and to wait for the food to be ready, Acarí and Sowówic came over and sat with him. A little later Colorow rode past, his big belly bouncing over the tight line of his pants drawn close around his waist, and Nicaagat called out, "Maiquas."

"Maiquas," answered Colorow as he rode back to dismount. He was going to his carniv to eat, but he wanted to know whether Nicaagat might have some tobacco.

Colorow carried two pipes, and one had a very large bowl. This was the pipe he took out as Nicaagat handed over his tobacco pouch.

They talked about their visit with the Governor. Nicaagat said he could not forget what the Agent had said about it: "Is it your business to go around finding out what I have written?" It had been a long time since they had talked with the Governor, and he had told them he would write Washington about taking this Agent away. And now this Agent was talking even worse than he had before. The camps were filled with talk of soldiers.

Going to the Governor had seemed at the time the thing to do, but now something more had to be done. This Agent's writing had, indeed, traveled far.

There was a long silence. Acarí was drawing slowly on his pipe, letting the smoke curl up his nose. Colorow, who was probably thinking more of his belly than of agents and soldiers and governors, was watching Nicaagat's piwán, who squatted in the brush *wikki-up*, bending over a large pot, from which a smell of good cooking meat mingled with the smoke.

Then Nicaagat said that he was going to leave again in the morning. He was going up to the railroad and to that place where the soldiers lived. He would talk to their general and tell him the truth about things on Smoking Earth River; then perhaps the general would pay no attention to any writing the Agent might send him. He, too, would know that it was lies.

"Unh," said Sowówic and Acarí. They knew that Nicaagat could talk to soldiers.

« III »

Major Thornburgh's orders were positive; they were all that was positive about this expedition.

Commanding a detachment of 190 officers, soldiers, and scouts, Thornburgh had only a vague picture of the conditions or incidents that were taking him to the White River Agency. Although Agent Meeker had suggested that 100 men would be enough, it was these uncertainties that caused Major Thornburgh to decide to take nearly twice that number, with a supply train of twenty-five wagons carrying rations for thirty days and forage for fifteen days.

With his two companies of cavalry, commanded by Captain J. S. Payne and Lieutenant B. D. Price, and the long trailing supply train, Major Thornburgh left Fort Steele on September 21. A Lieutenant S. A. Cherry, stationed at Fort Russell, had been ordered to join the expedition at Rawlins, and Major Thornburgh had appointed Lieutenant Cherry adjutant of the command.

They took the military road south, across the rolling, high prairies of southern Wyoming, toward the distant hulks of mountains that lay in Colorado. The first night out of Rawlins they camped at Fortification Creek, where Major Thornburgh left Lieutenant Price to establish a supply camp.

That night, with the Ute country at least two days' march ahead, Major Thornburgh made his first attempt to get some clear information on what awaited his command at the end of their march. He wrote to Agent Meeker and sent the letter ahead with one of his scouts, Lowery. He inquired about conditions at the agency and requested Meeker to meet him on the road.

The answer to the largest uncertainty of all lay with the Utes themselves. No soldiers had ever before marched into their country. It was not as though the troopers were marching into Cheyenne or Sioux country. Marching against these tribes, the soldiers would have known that the only thing they could expect was a fight, and they would have endless records behind them of experience in fighting Cheyenne, or Sioux. They would know the tactics and fighting style, the methods of attack, and the meanings of signals and approaches. But the Utes were a military unknown. Less than a generation ago they had fought fiercely against the plains Indians, but during the past decades of settlement the Utes had been assumed to be a degenerate, peaceful people.

Major Thornburgh was forced to rely heavily on his scouts for advice about the Utes, and the scouts were not backward about telling him everything they knew or had heard rumored, and perhaps more. The chief scout, Joe Rankin, was particularly talkative and full of authoritative advice, and it was seldom necessary to solicit his opinions.

Rankin, who had for a time ridden the mail route between Rawlins and White River, had come to Thornburgh highly recommended for the post of chief scout on this march. Rankin was well known around Rawlins and Fort Steele. He and his brother ran a livery stable in Rawlins, and Joe was a familiar sight on the streets and in the saloons, dressed always in the fanciest and most expensive of buckskin frontier costumes. He was man of vast self-confidence, never hesitant in offering his views on almost any subject, and fond of a good fight. Rankin usually won his fights, since he reputedly chose his opponents wisely—usually men who were small, overloaded with liquor or, if possible, both.

At this particular point in his career, Rankin was an expert on the Utes. He rode close to the officers, presenting them with a scout's picture of the entire Ute reservation, border to border. When he was not lecturing on the Utes or anticipating the conflict which he felt sure would come, he was telling long stories, designed to entertain the officers, of the various humorous or heroic incidents in the life of Joe Rankin.

Out of the supply camp on Fortification Creek, the road led

down that creek for several miles. The landscape changed, with great round hills, topped with patches of pine forest. The hills grew into low mountains. By mid-afternoon of their third day out from Fort Steele, Major Thornburgh's command rode out on the bank of the broad Bear River. Here the Major decided to make camp and await an answer from Agent Meeker.

« IV »

The road from the agency up to Bear River led through the upper valley, where the old agency had been, and out through the narrow canyon which the Maricat'z named Coal Creek Canyon. Nicaagat and his piwán drove two pack horses, loaded down heavily with their camp; and the sky was cracked with morning when they came to the mouth of the canyon. There Acarí and Sowówic rode out of the dark and fell in behind them. They had said nothing the evening before, but Nicaagat had known that some place along the trail his friends would be waiting to ride with him.

The pack horses, under their great weight, moved slowly, and the sun climbed fast. It was in the middle of the sky when they stopped at one of the forks of the Smoking Earth River to rest and water their ponies; and while they waited there, great round clouds began to grow up out of the mountains. Soon rain was sifting over the far slopes like gray dust. Nicaagat said it would be well to hurry on toward Bear River, away from the rain, before it made the trail muddy and slippery. He told them he wanted to spend tomorrow night with the storeman, and go on up to Fort Steele the next day.

They pushed the horses, and moved faster through the afternoon. The rain only brushed them, scattering the trail dust with dark little round holes.

That night they made a hurried camp. They were all up and out of their blankets before sunrise, munching on pieces of jerky, pausing to get a quick drink of water at the stream before saddling their horses to start on. The sun rose in a clear sky, with no sign of the storm that had passed them the day before. They pushed on without stopping, over the sharp ridges, down into the little bowl-like valleys.

Soon they were in the country of brush-covered hills, and the forests and green grass were behind them. From the top of one of the hills they saw the Bear River, and Peck's store below.

When they walked into the store they saw the storeman standing there alone. He smiled and put out his hand to Nicaagat. Acarí and Sowówic went outside to water and take care of the ponies.

The storeman started asking Nicaagat how things were at White River, and how the Agent had been treating them lately; but Nicaagat did not have time to answer. Acarí and Sowówic came back through the door, saying they had seen a soldier outside. They were very much excited. So was the storeman when Nicaagat told him what his friends had said.

Then Acarí said there was only one soldier outside there, and another Maricat'z dressed in fine fringed buckskin, and that both these Maricat'z had called out to Acarí and Sowówci and motioned them to come over.

The storeman turned suddenly and scurried out the door behind the counter, which led through to his house.

Nicaagat went outside with Acarí and Sowówic to see about this. The two whom Acarí and Sowówic had told him about, the soldier and the other white man, were down by the river watering their horses. The man in buckskin saw them come out of the store. He hollered something at them, then both he and the soldier started up the slope, toward the store.

The man in buckskins walked toward them holding his hand over his head and shouting, "How," which was the way some white men greeted people. When he was close to them he began to talk, and his words were like Maricat'z baby talk. He was asking questions about what they were doing at the store and how many Indians had come with them.

The soldier who, Nicaagat saw, was some kind of an officer, although not an important one, came up behind the other one. He spoke in a quieter voice and did not ask any rude questions. He held out his hand to Nicaagat and said his name was Lieutenant Cherry.

The one in buckskins never stopped talking, although no one, including the officer, was listening to what he said. This kind of Maricat'z—the kind that talk too loud and do not even use their own language right—it was better not to talk to, unless a person wanted to make jokes on them and laugh at them.

The officer told Nicaagat he and the other one had come to the store from their camp down the river. He said many soldiers from Fort Steele were camped down the river. Nicaagat asked what the soldiers were doing there, but the officer did not answer this. Instead he told Nicaagat that their commanding officer was at this camp down the river, and he asked Nicaagat to come with him to talk to this leader of the soldiers.

Nicaagat told his friends what the officer had said. Sowówic said he did not want to go where there were many soldiers. He wanted Nicaagat to talk to this one and find out why the soldiers were here. Nicaagat explained that with soldiers a man must talk only to the general—that the others knew nothing.

Nicaagat turned to the officer and told him that he would not come to the soldiers' camp now. He told the officer to go on back to the camp and tell the commanding officer that Nicaagat and his friends would come soon. The soldier and the one in buckskins went back to their horses. Nicaagat watched them out of sight down the river, then he turned and went back into the store. The storeman was there with his wife, who was holding her little boy in her arms and crying. Nicaagat told them not to worry, that there would be no trouble.

The sun was getting low, and Nicaagat said it would be well to hurry. They would be able to tell more about this business if they came to the soldiers' camp before dark. Then they would see whether there were many soldiers, or only a few. They went outside to their horses, mounted, and started down the river.

Only a short way along the trail, in the thinning daylight, they could see a wide scattering of big fires—big, the way all white men build fires.

Suddenly a soldier stepped out on the trail in front of them, pointing his rifle. Nicaagat remembered guards outside the camps of General Crook. He stopped the others.

The sentry looked at them, one after another, holding his

rifle at his hip. Nicaagat explained that he had talked to the officer down at the store and that he had come to see the big officer here. The sentry pointed at one of the fires and let them pass.

They rode on toward the fire the sentry had pointed out. Four men sat there, and one of them was the Major. He looked something like the Governor, except that he had a bigger beard, which formed around his face like a cloud.

"Hello," said the Major. "You people must be from White River. Lieutenant Cherry and Mr. Rankin here told me they had seen you down at the store awhile ago."

As they got down from their ponies, Nicaagat caught a look at the others sitting around the fire, all of them watching him closely. The same officer he had talked to down at the store sat there, and beside him lay a big, thin dog, shaped a little like an antelope. The soldier kept his hand around the dog's neck, as though to keep him from jumping forward.

There was also the man in fine buckskins. Nicaagat caught a glimpse of the black, drooping mustache and the narrowed eyes; suddenly he realized where he had seen this man before. It is hard to recognize a white man, unless you know him well.

"I am Major Thornburgh," the Major was saying. "These two

men are Captain Payne and Lieutenant Cherry. May I ask your names?"

Before Nicaagat could answer the Major, the one in buckskins spoke up in his loud voice: "Hell, Major, they won't tell yuh their names. That there big tall one's Captain Jack. He's a big chief down there."

"Thank you, Mr. Rankin," said the Major, without looking toward Rankin. "You must be Ute Jack, the one who scouted for General Crook."

"General Crook, me, good friends."

"Good," said the Major. "We were just talking over our visit to your agency. Since you have ridden with the army, you will be able to understand something about our march."

"Careful, Major," the man called Rankin muttered, as though by talking without opening his mouth too far nobody but the Major could hear what he said. "This is a tricky one. Smart. Speaks good English. He'll carry it all back."

Nicaagat noticed by the Major's face that he was a little bothered by this Rankin's talk, but he answered in a voice that did not show it.

"I don't believe there will be anything to hide from Captain Jack and his friends, Mr. Rankin. I know of no secrets we have."

The Major nodded his head at Nicaagat, as though he now wanted him to talk.

"Why soldier come here?" Nicaagat asked.

"Because I have received orders to take my command to your agency."

"Who tell you take soldiers dere?"

"My orders are from General Pope."

"Why dis Pope want soldiers dere?"

The Major thought a moment, as though putting words together in his head.

"There have been reports—some from your Agent, some from settlers, and some from Denver and Washington—that a few of the White River Utes have been bad and have caused trouble. We are only coming down there to see if there is any trouble."

"Ain't no trouble dere," said Nicaagat.

"That's just what we are coming down for—just to see. If

there is no trouble everything will be all right. We will go away again."

Nicaagat looked around him. Dark was coming fast, and for a long way down the river toward the hills there were fires burning. Beside each fire were some soldiers. There were many soldiers here.

"You want to see about dis trouble?" he said. "Why all dese soldiers want to see too?"

Again the Major hesitated, thinking. Finally he said, "The orders I have told me to take troops because we have heard about a message from your Agent, saying that his life and the lives of his family and employes are in danger from the Indians."

There had been lies about the fires in the trees and the burning of the houses. There had been lies about the People hurting the white settlers. Now such lies as Nicaagat had never heard were coming from this Agent.

Acarí and Sowówic had been listening to what the Major said and they had been able to understand some of it; but Nicaagat translated the Major's words to them to make sure they understood it all. Both Sowówic and Acarí were troubled by what the Major said about the Agent. There had been a great deal of talk among the People all this summer about the words the Agent had been writing on papers about them and sending out to many places. The People were both angry and afraid when they talked of this writing of the Agent, for it is well known that a Maricat'z can bring bad, even death, to people by writing his words on paper.

Nicaagat did not reply directly to the Major about these lies of the Agent. As he thought about it, a trooper rode up, carrying a paper, which he handed down to one of the soldiers sitting on the ground, then rode away.

"Army horse lean and skinny," said Nicaagat, watching the trooper as he rode away into the dusk. "All the time dey run around, carry lies."

The man called Rankin made a funny noise, as though he had started to laugh and stopped before the laugh got all the way out of his mouth.

"What do you mean, 'lies', Jack?" asked the Major.

"Dis Agent write lies. Soldier come when dey hear lies. Dey come long way."

"Then perhaps you can tell me something about this trouble," said the Major. "A telegram from your Agent says he has been beaten up by one of the chiefs. We understand he is lying in his bed now, seriously injured, and that his family dare not go out of the house because there are Indians all around outside."

Nicaagat told his friends what the Major had said this time about the Agent. Again both Acarí and Sowówic had understood enough to the Maricat'z words to know something of what the Major had said. Acarí was anxious to talk about it—too anxious to wait until the talk with the Major was finished.

"This Agent is a strange man," Acarí said. "For many moons he has complained that the People stay away from the agency. He said he wanted them all to come and live near him. Now, because the presents from Washington are to be given out soon, many of the People have come to the agency; so the Agent tells the soldiers to come because the People are waiting outside his house to hurt him."

"This general has heard all these lies," Nicaagat told them, "and for this he is coming to the agency. But I think this general is a man who wants to know the truth. Maricat'z believe papers more than they believe spoken words; so it is better that I not try to tell him these are lies. It is better that I tell him to come to the agency and see for himself."

"But this may make trouble," said Sowówic. "If all these soldiers come down to our country it may make trouble. Soldiers are not like ordinary men; they chase after the women like crazy people."

"I must talk some more to this general now," Nicaagat said.

He turned to the Major: "I show you how iss no trouble down dere," he said. "I show you dis Agent ain' beat up. You come. Maybe three, four soldiers come too. Others dey stay here. Lot of soldier come to agency, women get scared, children get scared. Young men, maybe dey want to fight. Maybe old ones say, 'No fight,' but maybe young men don' hear old men. Maybe trouble."

The Major glanced at the soldiers sitting off at one side. Then

174

he began to feel inside his coat, and his hand brought out some cigars. He gave one to Nicaagat and one each to Acarí and Sowówic. They took matches the Major offered and lit their cigars, then the Major lit one for himself.

"I think I should talk this idea over with my staff," said the Major, without taking the cigar from his mouth. "Tomorrow night we shall be camped on Williams Fork. Meet me there and I will tell you what we have decided."

Nicaagat drew in smoke from the cigar. It felt good, down inside him. Smoke was meant for talk of this kind. Now all he had seen in the past two days passed before him—the still, cold air before dawn; the warm sunshine, the dust, then the thumping raindrops from the early fall storm; the crying eyes of the storeman's wife, and now the dark that had settled over the whole country. And always, all through these days, as in the days that went before, the sickness deep in the ground, gnawing its way upward.

Soldiers were here, on their way into the country of the People. He, Nicaagat, had ridden with soldiers into the Sioux country, into the Cheyenne country.

"I will do what I have to do," the Major added. "I hope, as you do, that there will not be bloodshed."

Nicaagat had thought little about war since he had ridden with General Crook, into the country of those other people.

"You soldier," Nicaagat said to the Major. "I Indian. Your Washington iss my Washington too. One time I see dis man President Johnson. He say, white man no fight Indian, Indian no fight white man, Indian no fight Indian. Den I say, dis iss all right. We no fight. Some other Indian fight white man, but Ute don' fight. Ute do what Washington say; be friend with white man. Now I don' know why you come with soldier. Washington don' want fight. I don' want fight. Ute don' want fight."

Rankin made another loud noise like a laugh.

"We don't want any trouble if we can help it," said the Major. "We have to take that chance in carrying out orders. I too feel that the Indians and white men are brothers under one flag. As I told you before, I sincerely hope that there will not be bloodshed."

"One time I see war," said Nicaagat. "One time when I am with General Crook I see Indian, soldier fight; and I see blood on ground. I look at dis blood and I say, 'Maybe Indian, soldier sit down and talk first dere don' be dis blood. Dere don' be fight.'"

The Major listened, nodding as Nicaagat talked. When he was finished the Major said:

"Many people have said what you just said. Jack. Great men have said it; yet here we are—soldiers, uniforms, guns. No matter what some may say, how often they say it, or how well it sounds, there is still need for soldiers and arms because it is man's nature to fight. Many times brothers by blood have fought and killed each other."

Acarí was listening closely to the Major's words. He said in a soft voice to Nicaagat and Sowówic, "What is this that general is saying? Brothers kill brothers! This is not good talk."

Nicaagat understood something more about this. In the white man's Book, which he says was written for him by God, there is something about brothers killing brothers. Nicaagat reached far back into the days when he was a young boy and those Maricat'z with whom he lived talked to him about their Book, their God, and their Church.

"Dese brothers fight, kill, iss not good brothers," Nicaagat told the Major. "If dey good brothers, one say, 'Why you mad, brother? What iss wrong? Why you fight me?' Den dey talk about dis fight. Dey see fight iss no good. Pretty soon, no fight."

A change seemed to come over the Major. For a long time he had been like many other men—like all men who could talk and laugh, and be friends. Now he sat up very straight, his eyes looking out over Nicaagat's head.

"I have my orders; I must obey them," he said.

Nicaagat stepped closer to him.

"Dis iss all I want," he said. "You come down dere with me. We have talk—good talk. If dere iss good talk, dere iss no blood."

"I am sorry, Jack; my orders do not include talk. As I told you before, I will give you my answer tomorrow, at Williams Fork."

Nicaagat turned to go. "There is no more to say," he told his friends. "We must wait now."

But as they were walking toward their ponies the Major called out, "Captain Jack."

When Nicaagat turned around he saw that the Major had again changed. He was not sitting up so straight, and one arm was thrown over his knees.

"I just want you to know that I still feel that we are all brothers. We do not hate your people; if there is fighting, some of us on both sides may be killed. We are still brothers." He stopped. He seemed to be having trouble putting words together. The Maricat'z language is bad that way. "That's just— the way things are. It's my orders."

Rankin was snorting with laughter. He did not even try to hide it now.

"You and your friends are welcome to stay here with us tonight," said the Major.

"No. We go now."

"Good night, Jack."

"G'bye."

The man called Rankin was still laughing as they rode away.

« V »

As the party of Utes rode out of the camp of Major Thornburgh's command, and the sound of their horses died away, Captain Payne spoke up.

"You're not serious about this, are you Major?"

"About what, Captain?" asked Major Thornburgh.

"About going with those fellows into their agency, with only a small escort, sir."

"I told them I would think it over and give them my answer," said Major Thornburgh. "I have not decided yet."

"But Major Thornburgh, sir," protested Captain Payne, "it's obviously a trap. It's another Modoc trap. You'll be another Canby."

Major Thornburgh was visibly tired after his talk with the Indians. He did not want to have a conference on this, or on anything else, tonight. He wanted to write his dispatch and go to bed.

"Colonel Canby," he answered shortly, "did what he thought to be right. If I am to become another Canby, as you suggest, it will be for the same reason."

"If you'll pardon me, sir," said Lieutenant Cherry, "I think we missed a good opportunity there. Those fellows came here to spy. We should have taken them as hostages."

Major Thornburgh's tired eyes looked over at his young adjutant.

"My orders say positively to avoid encounters if possible," said the Major. "If I had taken those Indians prisoners, and if a fight were to follow, for any reason whatever, I would be blamed—by my superior officers, by the Department of Interior, by the entire government, and all the settlers of this area, to say nothing of every newspaper in the country."

Captain Payne persisted. "We might consult our scout, Mr. Rankin, on the nature of the country around Williams Fork."

Rankin spoke up eagerly, "I'll tell yuh, Major," he said. "There's high bluffs all around that camp ground. And timber. If you left the command there, them sneaking Injuns would ambush 'em sure as hell. It'd sure be the place to do it."

"I believe, sir," said Captain Payne quickly, seeing that Rankin intended to go on talking, "that if those men do come to Williams Fork we should hold them and march on into the agency. We would be close enough then that we would not have to hold them long, and with chiefs as hostages, the Indians would surely not attack us."

"I'll consider it," said the Major.

"Y'can see now, Major," Rankin burst in, "they don't amount t'nothin'. There ain't no fight in them Utes. It's their little tricks yuh gotta watch out for. I think we can just go right on to the agency, without worryin' none about a fight. Even if we do have a brush with 'em, it won't amount to nothin'. They got no guts."

Major Thornburgh covered a yawn. "We have a long march ahead of us tomorrow, gentlemen. I would like to get some sleep. And now, before I go to bed, I have a dispatch to write, if you will excuse me."

One by one they got to their feet and walked away toward their own tents. Cherry and Payne walked away together, talking earnestly. Joe Rankin strolled off toward one of the campfires, where a group of soldiers were talking loudly.

The two vertical creases in Major Thornburgh's forehead deepened as he sat alone by the fire, thinking. He reached beside him and picked up his writing box, opened it, took out a paper and pen and ink, and began to write.

His telegram, addressed to his department commander and dated September 26, would go out from the Peck store by mail carrier in the morning.

> HAVE MET SOME UTE CHIEFS HERE. THEY SEEM FRIENDLY
> AND PROMISE TO GO WITH ME TO THE AGENCY. SAY UTES
> DON'T UNDERSTAND WHY WE HAVE COME. HAVE TRIED TO
> EXPLAIN SATISFACTORILY. DO NOT ANTICIPATE TROUBLE.
>
> T. T. THORNBURGH, MAJ. 4TH INF.

« VI »

Acarí and Sowówic rode on into the village by the Smoking Earth River, growing now with families awaiting the passing out of the presents from Washington. At the mouth of the canyon which opens into the upper park Nicaagat and his piwán had separated from them. He said he was going down to the Agent's house to tell the Agent he had seen soldiers on Bear River.

For the first time since Bear Dance all the families who belonged with the Nüpartka band of the People were gathered in one village. Tonight was the time for dancing and singing of the songs celebrating the end of summer, before the snow comes. The best of the meat from the last hunts would be offered, and the women would bring out the last of the cakes they had made from dried and pounded nuts and berries gathered in the First Fall Moon.

Now, as the day became older, the young men were wandering around restlessly in groups, not stopping for games or talk among the older men. They were not pushing, shouting, and wrestling as they usually did when the People were gathered

179

for feasts and dancing. There was little laughter. Already some of the young faces were beginning to show ceremonial paint, matching the bright trees and brush of the high country.

Smoke climbed straight upward in the still air, like the trunks of many trees; and as Acarí and Sowówic approached the village they saw the carniva stretched far up toward the wrinkled, dry country and down toward the river. Beyond the great village, quiet under the warming sun, were the buildings of the agency.

The older men were gathered mostly down close to the river, beyond the log house Washington had built for Canávish and beside the long racing track. Sowówic and Acarí rode through the village toward the river, where they dismounted to sit with their friends.

Most of the men were smoking their pipes, and all were listening to Quinkent, who had just begun to talk.

When he heard about the soldiers coming, Quinkent had gone and talked with the Agent, and he was telling of this talk now. He said he had asked the Agent to make a paper to tell the general to come to the agency without his soldiers. The Agent had said he would not do this. Quinkent had then asked the Agent to go with him to meet the soldiers and have a talk. Then, Quinkent said, the Agent seemed to be angry about something and would not talk any more.

Word of their visit to the soldiers had traveled ahead of Acarí, Sowówic, and Nicaagat; now, when Acarí and Sowówic joined the group, all the People were anxious to hear what these two had to say of the soldiers.

Sowówic first told them that Nicaagat had gone now to have a talk with the Agent. Then he told of Nicaagat's talk with the general, what this general had said about brothers fighting brothers, and how the general had said he might come in to the agency for a talk and leave his soldiers in a camp outside; but that he had not promised to do this—that he had not known what to think of the idea, and that he would give his answer tonight.

Acarí and Sowówic then heard from the others that Colorow had gone out with the Little Boy and a white man from the agency to see the general, and that Colorow would perhaps have some word from this general when he came back.

There was nothing more to talk about now, until Colorow came back, and this would probably not be until long after the sun went down. They sat and waited for Nicaagat to return from his talk with the Agent.

After a while Nicaagat rode down from the agency buildings and dismounted. He sat with the group for a long time before he spoke, and they all waited, eager to hear what the Agent had said to him about the soldiers.

At last Nicaagat spoke. The Agent had told him he knew nothing of these soldiers. The Agent said some general had told them to come here, and that an agent could not order them to go back. Nicaagat told the Agent of his talk with the Major, and he asked the Agent to send a paper telling the Major to come on to the agency with only a few of his soldiers. But the Agent would say nothing.

"I told the Agent then that we should all talk some more about this—that I had told this general the same: that with good talk there will be no trouble. Then the Agent got up from his chair. He said to me, 'All right, you can stay there and talk,' and he went into another room and shut the door."

The sun dropped into the desert and dark gathered in the village. The fires burned up brighter as the women, bringing food down from the carniva for the feasting, piled wood on them. The medicine singers came with their small drums, and a group of dance singers rolled out the great drum. Many of the young men were showing long stretches of bare skin and wearing their fur neckpieces and bonnets in place of the single, down-pointed feather.

The sky was black, and every man, woman, and child carried a full belly from the feasts when Colorow rode alone into the village. Circles had already begun to form around the drums, beating softly, slowly; the dances were slow in getting started tonight.

A group of the older men gathered around Colorow when he got off his pony, Colorow said, "I have seen this general," and he had his face heavy, as though with some deep trouble, and turned away from them to lead his pony to the corral.

When Colorow had something important to say he always

liked to make people wait awhile. The more important it was, the longer he waited to tell it. But this business with the soldiers was too serious for Colorow to be making a game of it. As soon as Nicaagat came to push his way into the circle, Colorow began to talk.

Colorow said he had told the general not to come with his soldiers, and when Colorow said this the general had a great deal to say. He said he would come to the agency and he would fight. He said the People were his brothers but it was his business to kill his brothers when he was told to do it. Colorow told the general not to bring his soldiers across the Little River, which is where Washington had said the country of the People began. Then the general told Colorow that he would make a camp on the Little River the next night.

The general also talked about the fires and such things as the papers had been saying. He said he had some Maricat'z with him who were not soldiers and these were coming to catch the men whom the Agent had said were bad men and to put them in prison.

Mumbling arose again. These wagons must be carrying those things the Agent had talked about, and maybe even worse things.

At this Nicaagat stood up and said he was going to his carniv, for tomorrow, he said, he was going to meet that general again, at his camp on the Little River.

Fires burned up bright: not the cook fires that are the center of a family; these were the fires that eat up a great deal of wood and call many people together.

Songs moaned above the drumbeats; something in the shrill voices that climbed above the long songs made Acarí and Sowówic turn and look toward the dance. One circle was breaking apart, then another. The drums beat faster. The women broke away and formed their own line.

Acarí and Sowówic felt the drums in their chests beat harder and louder.

"My son, your sons are in that dance," said Acarí softly. "The old men have given the dance to the young ones."

After the Meeker tragedy, Coloradoans demanded that the Utes be removed from the Western Slope, but Indians in ceremonial dress were still "colorful," and these tribal members were invited back to Denver for the National Mining Exposition. They were photographed by William Henry Jackson on September 21, 1882, three years after the Thornburgh battle at Milk Creek. Courtesy of the Colorado Historical Society. F-42387.

This 1897 photo looks south on Meeker, Colorado, and buildings constructed by the army garrison under the command of General Wesley Merritt, who established his "Camp on White River" to enforce the banishment of Northern Utes to Utah. Courtesy of the Denver Public Library. X-12375.

Utes struggled to adapt to a new world on the Uintah & Ouray Reservation in Utah, but when President Teddy Roosevelt ignored their pleas to stop allotting reservation lands in severalty, many tribal members fled north to be with the Sioux only to be returned by armed guard. This unidentified Ute man was probably photographed by Fred Garrison of Rifle, Colorado, ca. 1915. Photo in the collection of Andrew Gulliford.

Despite being banished to Utah, Northern Utes frequently returned to the White River to hunt and they camped near Meeker, Colorado, where they were welcomed by townspeople. Photo ca. 1910 from the Wildhack Collection donated by the Meeker Chamber of Commerce to the Colorado Historical Society. F-15899.

At this spot Chief Douglas and other warriors surrendered their female prisoners to General Adams a month after the Thornburgh incident. The Ute prisoner surrender tree of October 25, 1879, was photographed on Grand Mesa in Mesa County on May 10, 1924. Photo courtesy of Museum of Western Colorado. F-230.

Utes pose with their lawyer as they try to get treaty rights restored. Courtesy of the Colorado Historical Society. F-44,345.

At Milk Creek, Rio Blanco County, Colorado, where fifty Ute warriors held off the U.S. Army between September 25 and October 5, 1879, stands the stone monument to Major Thomas Tipton Thornburgh and twelve other soldiers who died. The Northern Ute defenders also lost 37 men and twelve million acres of western Colorado. To the right of the original memorial, in 1993 the Ute Tribe erected their own taller monument "dedicated to the Ute Indians who were involved in the Battle of Milk Creek." Photo June 1995 by Andrew Gulliford.

Monument marker on the spot of the Thornburgh battleground marking the
battle between September 29 and October 5, 1879. In 1993, the Ute Indians
placed a commemorative marker of their own to honor their ancestors who
had defended their homelands. Photo courtesy of the Denver Public Library.
X-30693.

The women formed into two long lines, limping under the heavy loads they had always carried away from the wars of the old days. The song leaped high, fell, and leaped again:

"*Tsiúta . . . tsiúta . . . tsiúta . . . .*"

The songs of the People seldom have words. Songs need no words, for the music speaks. But when a people are coming to war it is a time when they should celebrate themselves. They sang, over and over, the word by which the Shoshoni have named the People:

"Tsiúta . . . tsiúta . . . tsiúta . . . ."

The older men—those who were not singing or beating the drums—gathered to one side.

Nünt'z, the life, the spirit of the People and of the men and women who come together as One, was in the dancers. The young men had taken it from their fathers and grandfathers, who had worked to give it to them, little by little, year by year.

"Tsiúta . . . tsiúta . . . tsiúta . . . ."

Through the night the dance grew—became great and whole —as the older men watched. A few of the young dancers dropped out after a while, to come and talk with their fathers. Sowówic and Acarí, who had found Canávish, saw their sons coming toward them and said to the m'sut t'quigat:

"Here are our sons. Your sons are with them. Now you will give to your sons the power and wisdom of Quigat, the great bear, which they will surely need."

Acarí said, "My son, Sáponise, is with the sons of Sowówic and your sons. If you will give them the power and magic of your pöorat, I will give the best of my ponies."

"And I," said Sowówic, "have many fine ponies. I will give you the best of them."

Canávish led the two fathers, their sons, and his own sons to his carniv, near the dance ground. He laid out his fire in the center of the floor. Soon the carniv was filled with the warm, red light. Canávish took out his stone pipe and smoked to the powers; then he passed it around the circle.

When the time of silence was over, Canávish spoke to the young men. He told the story of War:

A long time ago Sunáwiv, the God, lived in a great carniv on top of the greatest mountain. His suits were all of white buckskin, made thick with beads; and inside that carniv were many bags, full of his fine things. When he became lonely in his carniv on the tall mountain, he made a brother for himself, to sing and dance and tell stories with him. This one was Sunáwigá, whom the Maricat'z call Holy Ghost.

Sunáwiv told his brother that he must not pry into things while He was away hunting. But as soon as the God left the carniv, Sunáwigá, who always thought he had to see everything, went creeping inside. He found some little buckskin bags tied up tight; and he could hear voices inside. He thought they said: "Let us out! Let us out!"

So Sunáwigá started pulling those bags open. Inside were men—all the men of the world, of all sizes and colors, each kind in a separate bag. Sunáwigá did not know it, but Sunáwiv was keeping the men in those bags, waiting for them to get ripe; and when they were ready Sunáwiv would put them in their places over the world, in such a way that they would never fight each other, each wanting what the others had.

But Sunáwigá was the one who was always spoiling everything, and one by one he opened the bags. The little men hopped out and ran away. As he was opening the last bag, some people jumped out who were much noisier than the others. These were the Sioux. They made so much noise that Sunáwigá was frightened, and shut the last bag tightly. Then he heard Sunáwiv coming back, so he ran away and hid.

When the God came into his carniv he knew that Sunáwigá had been poking into things again. He called his brother to him and said: "Now you have done what I told you not to do. You have let those men out of the bags before they were ready, and they will make wars. You will have to fight them all by yourself."

Then Sunáwigá was very frightened. He begged the God to help him fight those Sioux, and at last Sunáwiv said he would help. He told Sunáwigá to set to work making arrows.

Sunáwigá made many arrows because he was very much afraid; but Sunáwiv made only one arrow, and for the point he used the leaf of a cottonwood tree. Sunáwigá asked him,

"Brother, how will you fight all those people with only one arrow?" But the God said nothing. He only took his arrow outside and, with the point, drew a circle around the carniv. Wherever the arrow point touched, there came a great crack in the ground.

Sunáwiv then said, "Brother, do you see this crack in the ground? You and I can jump back and forth across this crack, but those people can not. There is one thing you must remember: if you finish fighting and jump back across this crack, you must not turn and look at me."

Then they heard those Sioux people coming and they went out to fight them. Sunáwigá fought hard, and soon he shot away all his arrows. He jumped back across the crack.

But as he stood with his back to the God, he could not help wondering how his Brother was fighting all those Sioux with only one arrow. He had been told not to turn around, so he bent down and peeked between his legs. He saw Sunáwiv shoot his arrow once, and a hundred Sioux fell. Then He reached behind His back and drew out another arrow.

But when Sunáwigá looked, it spoiled the magic. One of those Sioux people shot an arrow into the knee of the God, so that he could not jump back across the crack. Then all those Sioux jumped on the God and tore him into little pieces, which they carried off in all directions.

Then Sunáwigá felt bad, and he was frightened that his Brother was with him no more. He called to the ants and commanded them to gather up all the pieces of his Brother's body and lay them on top of their ant hills. The ants did not want to do it, but Sunáwigá made them. When the pieces were all in one place, Sunáwigá laid them out in order. Then he wept and danced and called out: "Oh, my Brother, be back in your body. Come back and be with me again!"

But Sunáwiv spoke down from the sky: "I will not come back. You have disobeyed me again, and you have spoiled everything." He was very angry.

Sunáwigá pleaded a long time, calling to the sky; and at last Sunáwiv came down. He told His brother that He was going to change him into Yorowit'z, old Coyote, because he had spoiled

185

everything, and that now he could always call to the sky, asking his Brother to come back. Sunáwigá did not like being changed into old Coyote, and he said, "If I am to be Coyote, all the animals must be like me. They must not speak any more, but always hunt and kill each other. They should not be able to dance and sing."

Sunáwiv said: "It shall be this way."

Then Sunáwiv opened that last bag, which Sunáwigá had closed up tightly after the Sioux jumped out. Inside were all the others of those tribes who lived in this land before the Maricat'z came. At the very bottom of the bag were some that Sunáwiv had saved to take out last. These were Nünt'z, the People.

When Sunáwiv took them out, he told them that they were His People. He said that when bad things happen to the world they must not be afraid, for they would be all right.

Then He said to them: "There are only four things you have to fear: Fire, Flood, Wind, and War.

"You will carry with you always a little piece of 'rabbit brush,' and when Fire comes you will crouch down behind it. It will grow big, so that the fire burns over the top of it, and does not hurt you.

"You will carry with you always some little feathers from certain birds, and when Flood comes these feathers will grow to become a boat, to carry you over the water.

"Against Wind you will carry with you always a little stone, and your women may cover these with beads to make them look pretty. When Wind comes these stones will become heavy, and hold you down.

"But against War I can give you no protection, only what is in your hearts."

« VII »

His meeting with Captain Jack's party on Bear River was the only communication Major Thornburgh had had with the White River Agency since he left Fort Steele. The next evening, in the camp at Williams Fork, the midway camping point between

186

Bear and White Rivers, the letter from Meeker, so long awaited by Major Thornburgh, arrived.

September 27, 1879

Sir:

Understanding that you are on your way hither with United States Troops, I send a messenger, Mr. Eskridge, and two Indians . . . to inform you that the Indians are greatly excited, and wish you to stop at some convenient camping place, and then that you and five soldiers of your command come into the Agency, when a talk and a better understanding can he had.

This I agree to, but I do not propose to order your movements, but it seems for the best.

The Indians seem to consider the advance of troops as a declaration of real war. In this I am laboring to undeceive them, and at the same time to convince them that they cannot do whatever they please. The first object now is to allay apprehension.

Respectfully,
N. C. MEEKER, Indian Agent

Major Thornburgh talked with the employee and with the two Indians who accompanied him. One of the Indians was Agent Meeker's interpreter, through whom Major Thornburgh hoped he could send word to the Indians, convincing them that the coming of the soldiers meant no trouble for them and that the soldiers did not necessarily have to fight.

The second Indian, a fat, large-faced, sullen man, claimed to be a big chief, and was introduced as Colorow. Major Thornburgh found Colorow not nearly so approachable as Jack. When he was offered some tobacco for his pipe, Colorow grew even more surly, refusing to smoke with the Major. He mumbled something about a cigar. The officers had smoked the last of their Havanas the night before; Major Thornburgh tried to explain this to Colorow through the little interpreter, but the big Ute acted as though he did not believe anything that was said to him.

Colorow asked much the same questions Jack had asked on Bear River; but Colorow was not so easy to talk to. His voice was gruff, his expression one of distrust and disapproval, and his questions short and curt. The Major tried to explain this expedition to him as he had explained it to Jack and the others; he repeated his hope that there would be no fighting, but he tried also to make it clear that he and his command would fight if it became necessary.

Major Thornburgh and his officers held a short conference; then the Major wrote his answer to Agent Meeker:

> Headquarters, White River Expedition
> Camp on Williams Fork, September 27, 1879.

Mr. Meeker,
U.S. Indian Agent,
White River Agency:

Sir: Your letter of this date just rec'd. I will move my command to Milk River or some good location for camp, or possibly may leave my entire command at this point, and will come in as desired with five men and a guide. Mr. Eskridge will remain to guide me to the agency.

I will reach your agency some time on the 29th instant.

> *Very respectfully, your obedient servant,*
> T. T. THORNBURGH
> Major, 4th Infantry, Comd'g Expedition

The next day the command marched about eleven miles and made camp at a spring, where there was plenty of grass for the horses. When the camp was ready Major Thornburgh again called his officers and scouts into conference.

"I have been thinking of this matter all day," he said. "I am satisfied that, under my orders, I have taken a little too much responsibility in consenting to keep the command so far from the agency. I ask your advice."

Between the present camp and the agency the road passed through a long broad valley, through which Milk River wound. After crossing the river into the reservation, the road rose gently to a pass between level ridges, and then passed through a deep, narrow canyon, called Coal Creek Canyon, beyond. This canyon opened out into another valley, where the old agency had stood, and passed through a narrow gateway into Powell's Valley below.

It was Coal Creek Canyon which worried the scouts. There, they told the Major, would be where the Indians would attack, if they had that in mind. The Utes would not meet the soldiers in an open valley. They would set an ambush trap in the canyon.

Captain Payne, the senior ranking officer, came up with what seemed to Thornburgh the most acceptable plan.

He suggested that the command should go through all the forms of making camp on Milk River, as the Indians had requested; meanwhile, Major Thornburgh with five soldiers would proceed openly to the agency, as agreed.

"Then," Payne continued, "as soon as it gets dark, I will take the cavalry column and carry it through the canyon and place it near the agency. The Indians will see you going to the agency and follow you, supposing that you are carrying out your program, and we can get through the canyon without trouble. Then the whole command will be within supporting distance of the agency."

After a little more discussion of the plan, Major Thornburgh wrote a letter to Agent Meeker and sent it on with Eskridge, the agency messenger:

> Headquarters, White River Expedition
> Camp on Deer Creek, Sept. 28, 1879

> *Sir:* I have, after due deliberation, decided to modify my plans as communicated in my letter of the 27th inst. in the following particulars:

> I shall move with my entire command to some convenient camp near, and within striking distance of your agency, reaching such point during the 29th. I shall then halt and encamp the troops and proceed to the agency with my guide and five soldiers, as communicated in my letter of the 27th inst.

> Then and there I will be ready to have a conference with you and the Indians, so that an understanding may be arrived

at and my course of action determined. I have carefully considered whether or not it would be advisable to have my command at a point as distant as that desired by the Indians who were in my camp last night and have reached the conclusion that under my orders, which require me to march this command to the agency, I am not at liberty to leave it at a point where it would not be available in case of trouble. You are authorized to say for me to the Indians that my course of conduct is entirely dependent on them. Our desire is to avoid trouble, and we have not come for war.

I requested you in my letter of the 26th to meet me on the road before I reached the agency. I renew my request that you do so, and further desire that you bring such chiefs as may wish to accompany you.

T. T. THORNBURGH

Maj., 4th Inf., Comd'g Expedition

Mr. Eskridge arrived at the agency with this message on the morning of the twenty-ninth, and Meeker sent off a dispatch reporting on the situation to the Indian Bureau at Washington:

Major Thornburgh, 4th Infantry, leaves his command fifty miles distant and comes today with five men. Indians propose to fight if troops advance. A talk will be had tomorrow. Captain Dodge, 9th Cavalry, is at Steamboat Springs with orders to break up Indian stores and keep Indians on the reservation. Sales of ammunition and guns brisk for ten days past. Store nearest sent back 16,000 rounds and thirteen guns. When Captain Dodge commences to enforce law, no living here without troops. Have sent for him to confer.

Then Meeker wrote a letter to Thornburgh:

U.S. Indian Service
White River Agency, Col.
Sept. 29, 1879—1 p.m.

Major T. T. Thornburgh
White River Expedition, in the field, Colorado:

Dear Sir: I expect to leave in the morning with Douglas and
Serrick to meet you. Things are peaceful, and Douglas flies
the United States flag. If you have trouble getting through
the cañon let me know. We have been on guard three nights,
and shall be tonight, not because we know there is danger,
but because there might be. I like your last programme. It is
based on true military principles.

Most truly, yours,
N. C. MEEKER, Indian Agent

But this last letter from Meeker never reached Thornburgh.

7. THE BATTLE

WHEN THE sky above the tallest mountains was gray with morning, three young men rode out from the village. The cold air, full of threats of early frost, stirred against their bare skin, and their high spirits were quieted only by the heavy, old wisdom of the dance, which still beat loud inside each of them.

They were riding into the long canyon, which rises to the pass separating the Smoking Earth River from the Little River, and they pushed their ponies up the steep side of the canyon's doorway, so that they could take the high trail and look down on the road, which led from the agency far up across Bear River and the Snake River—to the railroad and the place where the soldiers stay.

Single file, their ponies, pawing, pushing, panting, strained to the top. Then the rider in the lead stopped. The others drew in behind him, and above the heavy breathing of the ponies, they heard the noise. It was like little thunder up ahead in the canyon.

One dismounted, then the other two. They crept toward the rim of the canyon and peered over a standing rock, and while they watched, the thing dragged itself around the bend of the road and lumbered down the canyon, like a great grizzly bear.

The big, thick body swayed down the road. In front walked two mules, and on top of the thing sat two Maricat'z.

The three young men stared at it for a long time, no one of them wanting to make a guess what it might be. They studied it, and at last one of them said:

192

"This, I am sure, is something that belongs with the soldiers; but it goes faster than soldiers, and so it is far ahead of them."

Another said, "Those soldiers have only wagons filled with chains for our feet and legs—no, we have heard nothing of this sort of thing with the soldiers."

There was another long, thoughtful silence. Finally the one who had first spoken made an idea that filled them all with a strange excitement:

"That is not ropes and chains. Perhaps that is something the Agent and the soldiers are going to use to kill the People. That is something the Agent did not talk about, and the general did not talk about. It is something bad."

"We cannot talk about this," said another quickly. "We must go down there and tell those Maricat'z they must make this thing go back—away from our country."

They left their ponies standing, reins dragging, on the slope, and the three slid cautiously down the steeper slope to the road. There they crouched behind a huge rock that had broken away from the canyon rim and thundered down many snows ago. Around the edge of the rock they could see up the road, and they watched the thing rumble toward them. Some parts of it were shiny, other parts flashed with bright color. Something like a big snake curled back over one side, poking its head inside its own body.

The three young men, in their excitement, had left their rifles in the scabbards on their saddles, but one of them carried a revolver, with the belt across his bare chest, Mexican style. As the thing rumbled nearer, this one shook his revolver loose in its holster and stepped out on the road. The others followed.

They saw that one of the Maricat'z was holding lines and driving the two mules. He had a big, black beard. Sitting beside him was a smooth-faced one, not quite a man.

None of the young men had any Maricat'z words. The one with the revolver began making sign language, telling the Maricat'z to go back. The boy seemed to stiffen, as though he were afraid, but the one with the beard laid a hand on the boy's arm.

Then the hand of the bearded one shot behind him and the stock of a rifle appeared.

The revolver made a big noise in the narrow canyon, and the mules reared back in their harnesses. The boy grabbed at the reins as the bearded head snapped backward and the Maricat'z rolled off and onto the ground.

The mules squirmed and danced, the bits stretching their mouths; and with his free hand the boy, his eyes wide and staring, picked up the rifle which had fallen in front of the seat. Another noise from the revolver filled the canyon.

The boy did not fall to the ground like the other Maricat'z. He stretched out on the seat, his feet still hanging down.

Now one of the young men was holding the mules. Another had taken out his knife and was cutting the harness straps. All three shrieked as the mules galloped free toward the open park, out of the mouth of the canyon.

Barking and yelping like Old Coyote just after he has played a bad trick on somebody, the one with the revolver shot fire twice into the old dry hay in the bed of the wagon. As the flames began to spurt up, another pulled the body of the boy from the seat and laid it on the ground beside the man, and the yelping of Old Coyote turned into a fast hopping song.

The young men sang and rocked backward and forward. The fire burned up, a cool, transparent yellow against the blue morning sky. The dancers were circling the wagon, lifting their legs high. Heat waves rippled outward, and the hopping, flinging bodies were soon shining with sweat.

The flames ate long, black gashes in the old wood of the wagon bed. A great piece of board fell off and sprayed the dancers with sparks. Then came a ripping, splintering, and a great wonderful crash. The thing fell through to the ground in a shower of fire. Old Coyote shrieked, yipped, and howled. He was joined by a screeching mountain lion, and the song burst apart with the flames, which stretched out now, full length, long and yellow, to curl around the big body of the threshing machine.

« II »

The road on which the Maricat'z ran their wagons passed through the park where the agency had been, out through a narrow winding canyon, and climbed to the top of the pass; here a man could rest his pony and look out far in all directions; here the wind blew most of the time. Then the road dropped down out of the wind, winding one way, then the other, and came out into a great open valley. There the land was shaped like a bowl, and the bottom of the bowl rippled with many little hills.

Through the middle of the big bowl below the pass, a little river flowed. The Little River was what the People called it; but one time, not long ago, when a Maricat'z was bringing his wagon along that road, he had some trouble in the middle of the Little River. Nobody knew just what his trouble was, but after a while his wagon turned over. The wagon was loaded with many shiny little cans, and these cans were filled with milk. Some women were at the Little River that day, and they took some of these little cans back to their carniva. The next day other women came to the Little River, and for many days after that women were carrying this milk to their carniva. After this story had been told many times, the Little River began to be called Milk River, and this was the name the Maricat'z knew it by.

Washington had called it the Milk River when he said that all the land south of there belonged to the People, and all the land north of the river belonged to Washington, but the People could always hunt on the land that belonged to Washington. This was all right: if the People could hunt on that land, it was all right for Washington to say that it was his.

Now the soldiers were coming. Nicaagat had told the general he would meet him at Milk River, and the general had said he would camp there with his soldiers.

Many of the young men had said, "We will not let the soldiers cross the Little River."

Before dawn, as the dance was finishing up, the women rolled the sides of the carniva, packed the camps, and went away. The women, the children, and the old men crossed the Smoking Earth River and rode south into the hills. Far out of sight of the agency, as the white dust of dawn mixed into the black sky, the women put up the carniva again and made a new village. Quinkent and a few others stayed at the old village, near the agency. The other men rode out toward the Little River.

As the sun came up on the morning of September 29, the low hills along the Little River were filled with men of the People. There were little bursts of laughter and low singing; the young men were still filled with the dance.

The older men sat in small circles around little morning fires in the brush back from the river and talked. Canávish told stories of his young days: of wars with the Arapaho. He told of the days when the People were good friends with those who lived far south of the tall mountains, in the country where there is little water. He told how the People and these others, who were called Apache, joined together and gained many ponies, until some Maricat'z in long black dresses came with crosses in their hands and talked in soft voices, until at last the People and the Apache were fighting each other.

Colorow sat playing monte by himself, pretending not to be interested in the talk of the older men; but when a loud burst of laughter would come from the young men behind one of the nearest hills, he would look up.

The sun was moving toward the middle of the sky, shaking the long, curved lines across the faces of the bluffs that rimmed the valley bowl. The bluffs, gray in the early morning, now shown with many colors as the shrinking autumn sun lifted over them.

Then the older men noticed that the talking, singing, and laughing had quieted, and as they watched the hills where their sons were waiting, they saw one of the young men come running toward the river. The first soldiers had been sighted, far up across the valley where the road came out of the hills.

Colorow gathered up his cards, knocked the deck against his hand and slipped it into his pocket. He yawned, lifted his big body from the ground with a groan, and, like a great brown porcupine, lumbered off toward the hills where the young men lay waiting.

Nicaagat was on his feet. Shading his eyes, he peered across the wide bowl, and where the hills began he saw the first of them. Two men—two soldiers—riding side by side; behind them came two more, then two more. As he watched they became a long line, snaking down the road. There were many of them.

He was seeing soldiers again, riding in cavalry formation; the old scenes came back. He had looked at them too often these two days since he talked to the Major. He did not talk; he did not tell his friends.

Not so many snows back—two, maybe three—he had gone with General Crook to fight the Sioux. He knew when he came back, he would be an important man among the Nüpartka, who were not his own people but the ones he had chosen. He talked to that general every day; he did not talk to any of the other soldiers—only to the general.

One day they had come upon a village of Sioux, the band of the great chief called American Horse. The women and children had hidden in a cave up the wash, but the soldiers turned their cannon on the empty village. Then they dragged the heavy gun up the wash and sent fire into the cave—men, women, and children flopping and squirming in the smoke and dust, like fish scooped out of a stream; and that night, after the fight was over, a Maricat'z, who was not a soldier but a scout like Nicaagat, went to the place where those dead Sioux lay. Nicaagat went with him. They found the bodies of American Horse and his chiefs, and the Maricat'z showed Nicaagat how to take off the scalp locks. The People had never done this.

Now, here on the Little River, in the country of his own people the line of soldiers, a cloud of dust rising over them, came down the road.

The Major had said they would stop and make camp here. Nicaagat would talk to the Major again. It would be all right. . . .

As the soldiers came nearer, Nicaagat looked around him. His friends had gone. He was standing alone.

Suddenly the moving line of soldiers halted. Then a strange thing happened. The long string was breaking into pieces, like a line of marching ants hit by a puff of wind—scattering out across the face of the bowl. They were still far away. The faces were tiny white dots, but the straggling line moved forward, toward the river.

Nicaagat had waited beside the road to meet the Major, but now the soldiers had left the road and were scattering off to one side. He ran to his pony, mounted, and rode fast down the river, searching the nearing body of soldiers for the Major's face.

As they came closer to the river, the soldiers leaned back on their reins and their horses lifted their legs high—all but a few at the far end of the line, who pushed on until they had splashed into the water.

The small group of soldiers who crossed the river ahead of the others were led by the young lieutenant who had been sitting with his dog in the Major's camp the night Nicaagat was there. Riding at the rear of the group was that one who had laughed: the scout Rankin, with the big black mustache. He was still wearing his fine suit of light buckskins; a few of the young men who walked out to the top of the hill, as though to meet the first soldiers, all eyed the fine suit, each of them thinking he would like to have it for his own.

When the lieutenant saw the young men walk out into the open on top of the hill, he held up his hand to halt the soldiers. Then they all dismounted and stood facing the young men—so close they could have thrown stones at each other, or almost reached out to touch hands.

The rest of the soldiers, riding slowly, were crossing the river now; and a great thundering filled the valley as many wagons rolled out of the hills toward the river.

Nicaagat could see the Major now, and he thought the Major could see him. The Major was splashing across the river with the other soldiers, and Nicaagat pulled in his pony and raised his hand. He never knew whether the Major had seen him—whether the Major was coming across the river to talk to him, or whether he raised his hand in answer to Nicaagat. At that moment the valley was filled with a new sound. It burst the still air, then rolled up the sides of the bluffs; and floating between the small line of soldiers and the group of young men on top of the hill was a little yellow-white puff of smoke.

For a moment everything was still. The young men stood like rocks on top of the hill; the soldiers were stiff beside their horses.

It was the one in fine white buckskins who moved first. He jumped on his horse, wheeled around, shouting: "Warned ye . . . hills is full . . . in them hills."

198

The soldiers, leaving their horses, dropped to the ground and started crawling toward the hill, rifles cracking. The young men were out of sight now.

Nicaagat opened his mouth. He tried to shout. Then he did shout, "Hold on! Hold on!" But the fight had started. Firing came from the young men now—from both sides. The talk was finished; it had done no good.

Nicaagat was off his horse and on his belly in the brush, and over the sight of his rifle he could see a horse running fast away from the creek. Crouched over the horse was the white buckskin suit, and Nicaagat felt his rifle jerk against his shoulder. But the horse, carrying the one who had laughed at the Major and Nicaagat, ran on.

The whole world seemed full of guns shooting and men yelling. The soldiers, still trying to ride forward across the river, were shouting and scattering, their horses turning, rearing, and dropping from under them. Several mounds of blue Army cloth rolled on the ground and lay still, and from the little hills, like the steady beating of many drums, came the rifle fire of the young men.

Colorow lay on his side, his elbow pushed into his fat body and his hands holding the great rifle that made more noise than any other. Around him lay many young men, sighting and shoot-

ing over the top of the hill. They shouted taunts, which the soldiers could not have understood if they had heard them. The soldiers, mad and riding in all directions, were very funny.

The wagons, with more soldiers walking beside them, still rolled down the road and were coming near the river. Colorow studied them. Then he pointed to them with his lips and chin and said to the young men nearest him:

"In those wagons is food for the soldiers. If we have those wagons, our bellies will be full and we will all feel good. But those soldiers will have nothing in their bellies, and after a while they will go home."

Several of the young men ran down the hill to where they had left their horses. Others saw them and followed. Soon there were many, riding out of the hills fast, toward the wagons.

Now all of the soldiers, except those with the wagons, were across the river. The Major, who was on his horse surrounded by many soldiers, turned and saw that the young men were riding toward the wagons, and he shouted at the soldiers around him.

Nicaagat, still watching the Major, saw those soldiers ride fast toward the wagons and the young men, shooting as they went. Some of the young men fell from their horses, and the rest turned and rode back. From the hills around the river, every gun seemed to be aimed at those soldiers with the Major who were trying to stop the young men from getting the wagons. A horse pitched up in the air and a soldier rolled over on the ground. The wagon train was stopped, and the drivers were fighting to hold the squirming mules.

Then the Major stood up high in his stirrups and plunged headfirst to the ground, where he rolled over once, turning his face up to the high sun.

Sitting alone, Nicaagat took out his pipe and tobacco and made ready to smoke. His rifle lay on the ground beside him, and he looked around at the valley that reeled and seethed and stunk of powder smoke. He struggled to stand up. Then, with his rifle under his arm and his smoking pipe in his hand, he walked away, like a man sick with too much whisky.

The soldiers still held the wagons, and now they began to roll again, turning off the road down toward where the scattered

200

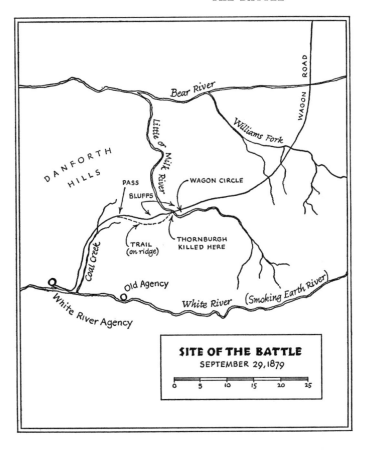

SITE OF THE BATTLE

SEPTEMBER 29, 1879

0   5   10   15   20   25

soldiers swirled around like little sticks in a crazy river; and behind the nearest hill, Colorow and Canávish brought the young
men together and got them ready for a great fight. There was
shouting and singing when everybody heard that the big general
was killed; and now, Colorow said, all of the young men would
rush down there and kill all the rest of those soldiers.

But the wagons were doing a strange thing. Straight down
below the hills where many of the young men were gathered for
the big fight, the wagons had stopped, and now the long, straight
line was curling around itself. In this place where the wagons
stopped the bank of the river was high and pushed back from
the water. It was hard to see down into that hole from the tops
of the hills.

When they saw the wagons forming a circle down in that
hole, the young men rushed over the hill; their bullets flew in
front of them, with little songs to sing to the soldiers. The young
men were spreading out far around the river, each one trying to
find a place where he could sight his rifle into that hole. Some
soldiers fell, but most of them—hunched over their crazy, foam-
ing horses, or running on foot—got back to the wagons, which
were now drawn up in a tight circle in the bottom of that hole.

On top of his hill, Colorow muttered some bad words in
Maricat'z and laid down his rifle. The soldiers were safe in that
hole now, and there could be no more fighting until dark, when
it would be easy to crawl closer through the brush. Beside him,
Acarí also dropped his rifle and stretched his cramped hands.

Someone came silently out of the brush and sat down beside
them. Acarí turned, and saw that it was Canávish. He was staring far out to where the hills touched the sky, and he looked
tired and very old.

After a long time Canávish said: "I have seen my son."

Acarí was puzzled. "You have two sons," he said, not quite
sure what Canávish meant to say.

"Now I have one," said Canávish.

Acarí quickly turned his face away. Canávish would have to
be alone now. He would have to be alone for a time, and cut off
his hair; only slowly as the shorn hair grew out long again would
things become right again for him. Lying on the ground beside

Canávish's limp hand were two rifles instead of one. The second gun was the fine new rifle of Tatit'z.

Then Canávish took up his long Sharps rifle and went away, leaving the new rifle lying on the ground. Acarí knew that it was meant for his own son; that was the right thing to do with a possession of someone who has died. They watched Canávish pick his way around the side of a hill to find a place where he could shoot into that hole. Many more soldiers would be killed by that rifle. Canávish had magic in his eye.

The dust thinned through the still air, which now smelled like the stinking springs from gun smoke; but the shooting and the yelling had stopped, and a great quiet settled over the bowl. Then a cold wind, which smelled of coming snow, stirred the brush and chilled the bare, damp bodies of the men in the hills. The dust and the stink went away with the wind. The shadows stretched slowly out toward the hills, and there was nothing left of the fight except the many who lay still along the flat land beside the river. The young men had spread out around the hole and lay waiting.

Then a thin, long feather of smoke rose above the circle of wagons. It thickened until it hung in big, solid clouds. A family of tiny flames gathered in the brush around the wagons.

Some of the young men had set fire to the brush on the windward side of the hole, hoping to drive the soldiers out; then the soldiers themselves set fire to the other side, so that there could be no sneaking up on them through that brush at night.

A great laughing and shouting came up from the hills. They saw the soldiers again, coming out from the wagons and even up over the rim of the hole. They were dancing around in the smoke and waving and slapping blankets at the flames.

Colorow rolled over on the ground, shaking, like a man who is dying of a great sickness in his middle.

"Aheeeeeeee . . . aheeeeeeeee!" he shrieked. "Aheeeeeeee! The Maricat'z have set themselves on fire!"

It was the finest joke of the day. The soldiers, when they set their fire, had not seen that the breeze was changing. Now there was fire all around the wagons. One of the wagons was already on fire. Hopping and dancing out in the open like crazy men, the soldiers would have been easy to shoot, but the joke was too good and the men in the hills could only laugh and roll on the ground.

Colorow sat up, weak from so much good laughing. Beside him, Acarí was holding his stomach, still trying to laugh, but looking a little sick.

"Aheee!" said Colorow. "It is a fine war dance. The soldiers are crazy. They fight and they are beaten, but they dance now."

It did not take the soldiers long, swinging blankets, sticks, and shovels, to put out the fire. They crept back into the circle of their wagons, while the men in the hills sang songs to them.

The sun was dropping toward the rim of the highest bluff, and its shadow crept out across the floor of the bowl. There was still work to be done, and this was work the young men did not like.

The soldiers had taken most of their horses inside the wagon circle with them. Some horses, and the mules that pulled the wagons, were tied outside. It would have been better if the young men could have crept up at night and taken them away, for some were fine horses; but with the brush burned away, they knew they could not do this. Some of the soldiers might use those horses to get away in the night and bring back more soldiers, so the animals, in plain sight over the tops of the wagons, would have to be killed.

Quietly, with no singing or shouting, the young men went to work. They sighted their rifles at the horses and shot them. They soon discovered that if they shot a horse in a place that would not kill it right away, that horse would jump and plunge around inside the wagon circle, and cause a lot of trouble for the soldiers.

Soon the space inside the wagon circle was like a burning ant's nest, with horses screaming, kicking, plunging, and rolling all over the place.

Everyone was glad when there were no more horses to be shot. They lay and waited for the sun to go down, then most of them went to the bottom of the hills to light cook fires.

The night was clear and dark and still. The little fires burned straight up, and the young men crouched over them, cupping their blankets to catch the heat. Many of the older men had started down to the big camp, carrying with them the ones who were hurt and the ones who were dead. Both would be given over to their families, who would do the proper things for them.

A few of the young men crept out to the river on the other side, and came back with many fine things: soldiers' clothes, guns, caps, money; games were played around the fires most of the night, while they took turns watching from the tops of the hills. There were a hundred—maybe more—soldiers in that hole, and they could not get out. The young men of the People and some of the older ones—no more than fifty in all—had fought that day on the Milk River, and the fight had ended with a fine joke. Everyone's head was full of that day, and no one talked or thought about tomorrow.

« III »

At the White River Agency, Monday, September 29, 1879.
      Narrators:[1]
      Miss Josephine Meeker, daughter of the Agent.
      Mrs. Arvella Meeker, wife of the Agent.
      Mrs. S. F. Price, wife of the carpenter at the agency.

The day was bright and warm, with the color and freshness of late September, and a hint of October breathing down from the mountains.

A new week had begun, and the employees of the White River Agency resumed their race with the season. The new building, which was to be a storehouse for the winter harvest from the new fields of Powell's Valley, was ready for roofing. There was coal to get in from the mines up in the canyon, for nights were growing longer and colder. Forage for the milk herd had to be stored, and there was still more fall plowing and planting ahead.

The work seemed harder than usual because all the men of the agency had been taking turns at night watches since Friday.

[1] From the statements given at Greeley, and the Washington testimony.

Last night the Indian camp had seemed especially noisy; but the Indians had seemed restless ever since first word of the approach of troops had reached the agency.

At the camp of Douglas, down toward the river and within sight of the agency house, a group of Indians were gathered, talking and smoking. On a tall pole above Douglas' lodge flapped a tattered American flag.

Josephine: On Sunday night a war dance was held at Douglas' camp, which lasted most of the night.

Father thought to take the family and all the employes, go out to the troops, and come in with them; but he knew now that if he did that, everything in the agency would be destroyed, and that he would be held responsible for everything there. He decided to remain.

On Monday morning Douglas made a speech to his men at his camp. He talked so loud we could hear him at the agency. I think it was agreed that if any of the Utes were killed by soldiers, the Indians would fire on the agency.

Before noon Mr. Eskridge, who had taken the last message to Major Thornburgh, returned with a letter from him to father. Father repeated it to me: that Major Thornburgh, anticipating trouble, was then upon day and night marches, forcing his way through as speedily as possible; but that he wished this news kept entirely secret from the Indians—he did not wish them to know he was coming on the reservation.

He wished to induce Douglas and the principal chiefs to meet him on Milk Creek, to hold a council there; all the troops would meet them, and then they would take care of them and march on to the agency. He thought in this way to avoid difficulty, as he would bring the principal chiefs in with him.

Major Thornburgh wished Father to return an answer immediately. Mr. Eskridge was prepared to return as soon as he had eaten his dinner, and he wished an escort to go with him. The Agent asked Douglas to send some men with him, but Douglas at first refused.

Mrs. Price: Douglas was talking with Mr. Meeker; he wanted five soldiers to come in; Douglas wanted Mr. Meeker to go back to the soldiers instead of dispatching Mr. Eskridge. Mr. Meeker told him he was not able to go.

Josephine: After a little, having gone home and talked the matter over, Douglas came back and said he would send two good men. He sent Ebenezer and Antelope (Jane's brother-in-law). I put them up some dinner.

Mrs. Meeker: At about 11:30 Mrs. Price and I were looking out at the window and could see a good way toward the cañon. We saw an Indian coming on the dead run. Mrs. Price said, "Just see that Indian run; it must be he has news." He never broke his stride, and rode straight into Douglas' camp. He must have brought the news that the soldiers were attacking the Indians.

Josephine: We did not think much about it, because we did not know much about runners at that time.

Between twelve and one o'clock, as soon as he finished dinner, Mr. Eskridge left with Ebenezer and Antelope. In about fifteen or twenty minutes, one of these men was seen to return to the camp.

Mrs. Meeker: At dinner time, just after we finished up, Douglas came in and took some victuals from the table. Several other Indians came around, and we gave them a piece of bread or something of that kind, and they were talking and laughing.

I did not mind anything about them, of course, as they are in and around there every day to meals. We always expect to have a kitchen full of Indians, more or less, and squaws and children; I never thought anything about it.

Mrs. Price: When Douglas came in he was laughing and talking with Josie and me, and shook hands with us. He seemed to be in good spirits. On Saturday he had taken his little boy from school; he said the reason was that he was afraid the soldiers were coming in.

Josephine: Douglas was in very high spirits. He promised to bring his little boy back to school that afternoon; that he wanted him to learn to read and write; that the Agent was pretty good; that all the squaws were pretty good. He seemed to be very much pleased over something.

Another Indian came in to borrow matches while I was washing dishes. I gave him some, and he laughed and said, "Me now going to smoke." He excited my suspicions because he had such a sneaking laugh. I said to mother, "I'll warrant he will set something on fire."

A few moments later one of the Indians came in and patted the heads of the children in the window.

About this time Father came in and wanted to find the keys to lock up the employes' room, where all their guns and the government guns were kept.

Mrs. Price: After dinner when the men got out to work, Mr. Price, Thompson, and Frank Dresser were working on the new building. After talking with us, Douglas went out and laughed and talked with the men. Then he left the boys, and started down to his camp.

I went out after May, and saw 20 or 25 Indians coming up with their guns to meet Douglas, then all came on together; Pow-vitz, Douglas, Ebenezer and Antelope. Ebenezer said something to me in Ute as I went into the house with my girl, and I did not understand. He went to hitch up his horse, and then they fired at the men on the building. An Indian was about 10 feet from me when he fired at Price, Frank, and Thompson. He crippled Frank in the leg.

Josephine: It was about 15 or 20 minutes after Douglas had gone out when we heard very suddenly several guns fired off. I ran and looked out of the window in the direction from which the sound of firing came, and I saw the Indians firing at the employes, who were running in every direction and trying to escape.

Mrs. Price: I ran in the house, picked up the baby, went to my bedroom, and Frank Dresser came in. I gave him a gun. Just as we got to my bedroom door both windows were smashed in. Dresser shot through the window and hit Johnson's brother.

We ran to Josie's bedroom and hid under the beds, but Josie said, "It is not safe here; let's go to the milk house," and so we did.

The shooting kept up for quite a while. We did not want

to look out. Frank looked out once on the north side, but he could not see anything. He put up the bread jar and some cans and things, to keep the Indians from seeing in there.

Josephine: As soon as we saw they were fighting, we took the children and went into the milk house, locked the door, bolted the outside door, and sat on the floor.

We sat there all afternoon. At intervals it would be perfectly quiet, and then again the firing would break out. It was evident that they were carrying off the goods, and that when they would see a man they would shoot him.

Every little while a heavy gun would go off, and Frank would say, "There goes a government gun." He had been to the employes' room to get the guns, but they were all gone—government guns and all were stolen.

Frank said he thought he heard Douglas, and when the firing would stop he said, "Douglas has got them quieted down; I heard Douglas talking to them pretty loudly." He had so much faith in Douglas.

Around sundown—about five o'clock—we discovered that the house had been fired. Then our room commenced to fill with smoke and we ran out. The Indians were so busy carrying off blankets and goods that they did not see us at first. We ran into father's room. Everything was just as he left it: a book lay open on the desk where he had been reading; nothing was disturbed.

Mrs. Price: We first thought of secreting ourselves under Mr. Meeker's bed. I said, "No, that will not do."

We looked out to the north. The blinds were open. The Indians were busy taking the blankets, shirts, and everything else they could. I said, "Let's try to escape to the north, in the sage-brush." Frank said, "Let's go now, while they are so busy," and we went.

I ran outside of the fence; Josie, Mrs. Meeker and Frank opened the gate and went into the field, and I crossed over through the wire-fence. Then they saw us; we had not got ten steps from the corner of the fence before they saw us and fired, and hit Mrs. Meeker.

The bullets whizzed by my head and hit beside me. They

shot at Frank, and as he would take a step the dust would fly.

Josephine: Mr. Dresser ran across the field, he being able to run much faster than we could, as, on account of my mother's being lame, we could not move very rapidly. The Indians discovered us, began firing at us, and came running up, calling to us to stop. One bullet from their guns hit my mother, but did not seriously hurt her, as it made but a slight flesh wound.

Mrs. Meeker: We were running away and had got into the sagebrush; when the ball struck me I dropped on the ground so that I would not be so much of a mark, and as I lay there I saw them capture Josie and Mrs. Price. I thought they would not see me, but as soon as they had captured the others they came to me.

The one who came after me thought I was wounded as I lay on the ground. He said, "I am heap sorry; I am heap much sorry." He was a young, smart, good-looking Indian, who spoke English pretty well.

He said, "Can you get up?" I said, "Yes." He said, "Will you go with me?" and I said, "Yes, sir"; he gave me his arm just as nice as anybody, and took me to Douglas.

Josephine: The Indians called to us to stop. Pah-sone called to me and said, "Come to me; no shoot you." I said, "Going to shoot?" He said, "No." I said, "Better not." He said, "Come to me." I looked back; one had hold of Mrs. Price and one had hold of mother.

They took us down toward the river where each one of them had his pile of goods. Pah-sone placed me on the blankets he had stolen.

Douglas came and tried to take me away from Pah-sone when we were going to the river. He tried to push Pah-sone away and tried to take me away by the arm, but Pah-sone pushed him away, and they had it pretty hot in Ute. I thought they were going to quarrel, but Douglas turned away and went off.

They asked mother if she had any money, and allowed her to go back to the agency for money and some other things.

Mrs. Meeker: In the first place I asked Douglas if I could go and get Spirit Book. He wanted me to get medicine. They would not let either of the others go back. Douglas said for me to go and get my medicine book.

The house was burning, and this Indian with me did not like to go in. All the time while I was in the building he kept saying, "Hurry up, hurry up; got to go a great ways tonight."

I got the Pilgrim's Progress; the medicine book I gave to the Indian; he said he laid it down, and I guess he let it go. He lifted the medicine chest and said, "No carry." I got my shawl, blankets, and hat that I have worn since. I thought of getting some other things, but knew it would not do. There was $30 there; I counted it; some of it was in silver. I handed it to this Indian and he took it to Douglas.

When we were going back I saw Mr. Meeker stretched out on the ground. He had been shot in the forehead.

Blood was running from his mouth. His head was leaning back, and he was lying very straight, as if laid out; with his hands right down beside him, just as if laid out.

I was a little ways from him the moment I saw a man dead there, and I thought I would go a little nearer and see if it was Mr. Meeker, and I went right up to his head. The Indian was ahead of me; and as I stooped to kiss his face the Indian turned around and looked at me.

I thought it would not do, and I started on and did not say a word to him, or he to me.

Josephine: The Indians all this time were busily occupied in stealing goods, and most of the buildings were on fire. They gathered together all the goods they could get hold of, took the agency's saddles and all the agency's teams they could catch, and packed them heavily with government goods—flour, all kinds of blankets, and everything else.

Pah-sone packed his things on a government mule, and I was put on a horse with the little Price girl tied on behind me in a blanket. An Uncompahgre Ute whom we did not know took Mrs. Price. She was taken to another camp. I did not see her at all.

Just at dark, we started across the river directly south.

Mrs. Meeker: Douglas asked me many times where the Agent

was, and kinda laughed. His breath smelt strongly of whisky.

He said: "Your father dead. I had a father once. He too is dead. Agent no understand about the fight Indians make."

The other Indians all took out bottles of whisky, which they held up between their eyes and the moon as they drank, to see how much was left. Douglas as he rode along sang what seemed to be an obscene song to a pretty melody in slow measure. When he finished he asked how I liked it.

My limb ached so terribly that I could scarcely sit on the horse. Douglas held it a while; then he strapped it in a kind of sling to his saddle.

As we rode, a villainous looking Indian trotted alongside and slapped me on the shoulder, and asked if I would like to be his squaw, and he made indecent proposals. Douglas listened and laughed. He said the Indian was an Arapaho, and I would kill Utes if I married an Arapaho.

We rode four or five miles and then stopped. It was in a little cañon, with high rocks all around except where we went in. They had us dismount and lay down, and they put a gun to Josie's head.

They stopped to search us, and see if we had anything— even searching our shoes. I had a needle-book in my pocket. This Indian took that and looked at it and kept it, but gave me back my pocket handkerchief. Those were the only two articles I had with me.

As I lay on the ground not knowing when I should be butchered, I thought of my young daughter who was not far away, and wondered if she had already been slaughtered. My face was partly covered, but suddenly I heard Douglas' voice standing close by me, with the muzzle of his gun pointed directly at my face. I involuntarily cried out and said, "Oh!" Josie heard me, and her voice came out of the night, saying, "Don't be afraid, Mama, I'm all right."

Douglas lowered his gun, raised it again, and took aim. I said nothing and he walked away. An Indian standing near by said, "Douglas no hurt you. He only playing soldier."

They asked Josephine if she was afraid, and she said, "No."

She thought the Indians were not pleased because Douglas failed to frighten her. They all laughed at him.

Then they saddled their horses, and Persune led Josie's horse to her and knelt down on his hands and knees for her to mount from his back.

We then moved out to Douglas' camp, I think 10 or 20 miles. We got in a little after midnight.

Josephine: The reason why it took us so long to get there was that the squaws, during the day, had moved the camp, and the men with us took us several miles out of the way. I think we were but a short distance across the mountains from where the fighting with the troops was.

Mrs. Price: After I left the river with this Uncompahgre Ute, he riding on the horse behind me, he pulled out a gold watch which I recognized as belonging to Mr. Post. He put the guard over my head and strung it around my neck, saying it was my watch.

When we arrived at the camp that night, a squaw came and took my little boy from the horse, and cried over him like a child. I dismounted and sat down in Pah-sone's camp.

I wasn't at all hungry, and when they offered me coffee, cold meat, and bread, I could not eat. After a while the squaw got over her weeping, when they talked and laughed.

All I could understand was when they repeated the soldiers' names and counted what number of men they had killed at the agency. They said they had killed nine. At first they said ten, and I told them differently, as I thought Frank had escaped. They asked me how many, and seemed to accept my statement as correct.

They spread some blankets for me to lie on, but I could not sleep. The moon shone very brightly, and everything looked ghastly.

Josephine: Pah-sone had blankets from the agency, and he spread them for my bed, and made some for a pillow. Two squaws danced at the foot of the bed after I got in it. At a certain point in the song, all the men laughed. Pah-sone sent them away with blankets.

The same night Pah-sone took me for his squaw. Of course they were drunk, and we dared not refuse them to any great extent. A good many times I pushed him off, and made a fuss, and raised a difficulty. He did not threaten to kill me, only once: I asked him if he wanted to kill me. He said, "Yes." I said, "Get up and shoot me then, and let me alone." He turned over and did not say anything more that night.

It was done while his own squaws were in the tent. The other Indians did not seem to think it was very wrong; they thought it was a pretty good thing to have a white squaw. His squaw told me I must not make a fuss about it; it was pretty good. I think she felt sorry for me, but she did not dare do anything for me.

Jane said: "Well, I cannot help it, because these Utes want to take you and protect you." I told her I did not think much of his protection.

She says, "We will give you enough to eat, and you will not starve while you are with us. If he wants to protect you I cannot help it."

« IV »

Colorow sat behind a little hill that would hardly have been high enough to cover his belly if he had decided to lie down on his back. He sat very still, staring at the ground, as though no thought and no word could ever bring even a touch of a smile to his big, sullen face. His friends had tried all morning to talk to him, joke with him, or draw him into a game of cards; they had finally given him up and gone off a short way to arrange themselves in a circle around a blanket for a little monte.

Colorow would only say that he was hungry. As soon as dark came he was going out alone to attack those soldiers and send them home. Sitting here all this time and keeping the soldiers in that hole had only kept him from getting enough food to fill his belly, and tonight he was going to send those soldiers home.

His friends had left him there behind his little hill; for when Colorow was hungry and you could not feed him, you had better let him alone.

It was true that these past days on the Little River had not been nearly so exciting as the first one. It was only a matter of sitting on the top of the hills and watching that hole. Since this was a war camp there were no women in it, and the men had to live on jerky and cold bread which was sent to them from the big village. The soldiers could not get away, and they would not come out and fight; but some had to stay here to watch them, and this is the sort of business that makes any man tired.

From the tops of the hills you could almost see into the soldiers' hole. At night the soldiers had taken the dead horses and piled them up inside the circle of wagons. They had thrown dirt over these horses and made a good fort, and inside the fort they had dug pits where they could hide better when the men in the hills started shooting. From a narrow crack in the wall a faint path threaded down to the Little River. The soldiers had worn that path as they went to the creek for water at night.

Sometimes, from one of the hills, a man would see something move inside the wall. Then he could shoot. Maybe, after a long time of quiet, a man would shoot just to make some noise. But it was mostly just waiting and watching; and those who had to stay waited eagerly for some of those who had gone to the village to come back and take their turn at guarding the soldiers.

The village had been moved far below the Smoking Earth River, across the broad hills and down toward the Big River. Those who stayed to guard the soldiers heard something of this village. It was not like other villages. The games were the liveliest anyone had ever seen, for many fine things had been picked up in the fight with the soldiers and in the fight at the agency, while the flames stretched high into the sky over the agency buildings.

Every day and every night there was dancing, for all were happy that the soldiers were safe in the hole, where no one need be afraid of them. People shouted with laughter at the stories—the good, funny joke stories—which the men told of the fight, acting them out as they were told, sometimes wearing clothes they had taken off the soldiers.

There was feasting in that village, almost like the feasting after Bear Dance; all of the presents from Washington which the Agent had been holding were in that village now, and the women had even brought out many of the good things they usually saved for the long, dark snow nights.

The three Maricat'z women who used to live at the agency now lived at that village. The old one, who was called the mother of the Agent, had been taken into the household of Quinkent; they said she was very funny, and acted mad and scared all the time. The piwán of Quinkent did not like having her there, for she wanted to be waited on all the time, but Quinkent thought having the piwán of the most important Maricat'z was a fine thing, and worth all the trouble she caused. The daughter of the Agent was now the piwán of Pásone, and many of the men said he was acting in a very unmanly way toward her; he listened to what she said all the time and tried to do everything the way she told him. But it was his own business, if he wanted to behave in a foolish Maricat'z way. The women were saying that she might die soon, since she ate very little and would drink no coffee, but the other Maricat'z woman said she always did that way. That woman was living in the camp of Canávish with her two little children, and the women of his family liked to play with those children and teach them songs.

Some who came back from the village told all about this, and others left the Little River to go and see for themselves.

Little had been seen of Nicaagat during these past days. He would visit the place where the men were holding the soldiers in that hole, stay for a while, and then leave. Something seemed to be giving him much trouble.

Among the People, such things often happened to those men who were leaders—the leaders in hunting, in war, or the talking leaders. At such times as their own troubles took up most of their power, they had nothing to give those who followed them; and at such a time a man must be mostly by himself. Whatever might be troubling him was his own business, and none of his friends ever tried to question what it might be. Usually, after a time of being alone, this man would return to his people with his power restored.

It was said that Nicaagat went to the camp of the women one day and talked to Canávish, who now spent his days sitting by his carniv, talking little and mourning for that son who was killed by the soldiers. Nicaagat had asked Canávish to take all of the Maricat'z women into his house, so that they could be together and not scattered among the camps. He had then gone to the daughter of the Agent, at the carniv of Pásone. It was said that he had tried to explain to her that her father, the Agent, had written lies about the People and had brought soldiers to their country, and for this reason he had died. He had also told her the thing many of the older men felt—that he was sorry this thing had happened. But the Agent's daughter had not seemed to understand, and Nicaagat had gone quietly away by himself again.

Only a few men needed to stay on the hills around that hole, but when the fight began it had been Colorow who became the leader, and now Colorow had to stay there, while others came and left, taking turns watching the soldiers. Colorow was not happy. He thought of the white settlers' cabins on Bear River, and the Maricat'z women who kept great kettles on their stoves. His great belly ached, with nothing inside it but dry jerky and cold sourbread—food of which few men ever complained because it was the diet of men who fought in wars. He thought of his piwán: his mind saw her scrape the ashes of the fire away and pull out a fat roasted prairie dog and chip the black, burned crust of skin away from the shining, steaming meat.

The monte game broke up. Two of the players—Yaminatz and Acarí—came back over and sat down with Colorow.

"The soldiers are still in that hole," said Acarí. This was the way a man started talk about the soldiers. It was the only thing a man could say about them; if another man wanted to keep on talking about the soldiers, he had to think of something new to say, and this was not easy. Yaminatz, who had not wanted this fight to happen and who had said little these past days, was the one to make the talk start this time.

With the others, Yaminatz was staring down at the hole where the soldiers were hiding and at the stout, firm wall they had thrown up around them. The soldiers had made a good wall out of their dead ponies. It was a wall that would stop bullets, but soon that wall would begin to smell bad. Then it would not be such a good wall any more.

217

"This will not be so bad," Colorow still sat staring at the ground and his face hardly moved as he spoke. "This bad smell will bring many flies—big, fat, blue flies. Those flies will get even fatter on those dead horses, and when the soldiers run out of food, they can roast them."

Yaminatz and Acarí laughed at this joke, but Colorow did not laugh. He only said again that he was going down to that hole as soon as the sun and the light went away. Those soldiers down in that hole would be very frightened. They would be so frightened of Colorow that they would climb over their wall of dead ponies and go home. They would have to run all the way home, with no ponies to carry them.

Since the first day of the fight, Colorow had told of many ideas he had of going down to the soldiers by himself—to attack them, to scare them away, to shake hands with them and tell them to go home. So far as anybody knew Colorow had not left his hill in all that time, except when he smelled something being boiled over one of the fires. Yet from behind that hill Colorow had directed the fight that drove the soldiers into that hole and kept them there all these days and nights.

They sat and talked, and for a long time nothing moved but the circling sun, which poured down through the still air and soaked the ground with gentle autumn warmth. Late in the day great clusters of dirty white snow clouds began piling higher and higher over the long range of hills. Some said it would snow that night; others said it would not. It made something new to talk about until dark, when a cold wind swept down and tiny specks sparkled around the cook fires.

Later, a few of the young men carried their blankets to the tops of the hills, where they huddled, watching the glow from the fires inside the hole. The icy wind was strong, and little pellets of sleet came at them like bullets. A rifle cracked somewhere near the hole, and they heard a dog scream with pain. A second shot brought silence. The young men puzzled over this strange happening and one said: "I think the soldiers are afraid and want to build their wall higher. They are shooting their dogs."

Maricat'z seem to enjoy going around shooting animals

whether they need them to eat or not. "Perhaps," another of the young men said, "this means that the soldiers are getting tired of all this waiting too, and are shooting their dogs."

A long time passed and they heard no more sounds from the camp. One of the young men sent a shot off in the direction of the hole, but this sort of thing was not much fun any more. They waited awhile longer, then one by one they slipped off to roll up in their blankets beside the dying cook fires.

The morning came behind gray clouds. The snow had stopped, but the smell of it was still strong. The men crawled out of their blankets and gathered around the fires of those who had coffee. Thoughts of another long day of watching and waiting were heavy on every one of them, and there was little talk.

Then came a shout from the top of a hill; another shout from another hill. Soon every man was scrambling for a place which would let him see out across the flat on the other side of the river.

Far out toward the hills the dust was again stirring up from the frozen ground. The morning was young and dimmed by clouds, but they could see that many men were coming on horses, a long way off. "Swerch!" somebody whispered, and every eye was strained to see if there were really more soldiers coming to help those in the hole.

"Aheeeee! Aheeeee!" shrieked several of the young men at once. "To-Maricat'z! The black-whitemen! The Buffalo Soldiers!"

The tiny specks came closer and closer. It was not hard to see, even in the dim morning light, that these were the soldiers with

black faces; and in the center of the line they could see the one white face of the general who always led the Buffalo Soldiers.

Not one man raised his rifle. They only watched with great curiosity as these strange soldiers came on toward the hole. The Buffalo Soldiers were something to wonder about and to laugh about—perhaps, sometimes, to be a little angry with—but they were nothing to be afraid of. They had been in the North and Middle Parks since the last snow; often that general who led them had told some of the People they must go away from the Parks and not come back, but none of the People ever went until they were ready, and that general and his Buffalo Soldiers did nothing about it.

They could see the soldiers inside the wall begin to move around, jumping up and down, and climbing to look over the wall as the white general got off his horse to go inside the hole. When he came out again, all of the Buffalo Soldiers got down, unsaddled, and went inside.

"Aheeee!" shouted one of the young men, as he put his rifle to his shoulder. "Aheeee!" shouted others. "Aheeee . . . aheeee!" They were filling the air with the little, stinking clouds of powder smoke. Down beside the hole the ponies of the Buffalo Soldiers jumped in the air like jack rabbits, rolled on the ground kicking. Many ran away—so far that the Buffalo Soldiers would never see them again.

"Aheeeee!" shouted all the young men. Now they had the Buffalo Soldiers in that hole; and, like the others, they had no ponies. They could not get away.

For a little while the soldiers down in the hole seemed to come alive again. They even sent a few shots up toward the hills, and each time a bullet thumped in the dust the young men shouted and sang and yelled. They made up words about the Buffalo Soldiers and chanted them over and over:

Soldiers with black faces,
You ride into battle behind the white soldiers;
But you can't take off your black faces,
And the white-face soldiers make you ride behind them.

As the day grew older the sun beat the gray cloud blanket to pieces, chased those pieces off behind the mountains, and hung bright in the blue sky. The sun was getting weaker every day as the snows moved down from the high country, but it soon warmed the valley enough that some of the men dropped their blankets from their shoulders and went to work with their paints, bringing faded colors back to their skin. For a long time the young men waited and watched anxiously. The coming of the Buffalo Soldiers had brought new interest to this game. They hoped that some of the Buffalo Soldiers or the other soldiers would now come out and start the game going again—like the first day.

The older men did not feel this way about it. They did not see any good in killing more soldiers, when the number of men killed was already even on both sides. All that was necessary now was keeping the soldiers in that hole until they got tired and wanted to go home. Then they could all go out and shake hands with the soldiers, and the fight would be over.

At last they saw two of the Buffalo Soldiers come out of the hole, and the young men began to wave and shout at them. But the Buffalo Soldiers were carrying only buckets; they were going down to the creek after water for those in the hole, and they did not wave back. They acted as though they did not even hear the shouting from the hills.

The Buffalo Soldiers had not come to fight; they had come to work for the white soldiers. The young men were very disappointed.

Then they saw something that made them all shout again and pick up their rifles. Many Buffalo Soldiers were coming out of that hole, and it looked as though they were carrying their guns on their shoulders. They were walking around the wagon circle toward one of the dead horses that had been shot earlier.

Again the young men laid down their rifles in disappointment. The Buffalo Soldiers were carrying shovels, not guns, and when they reached the first dead horse they began digging a hole. After they had finished burying that dead horse, they carried their shovels over to where another lay bloated and swollen on its side with its legs sticking straight out in the air. They worked fast under the high, warm sun and soon they had buried all the horses. Then they went back to the wall and began digging dirt and throwing it over that pile of dead animals.

The coming of the Buffalo Soldiers had put new life into the young men, but it had turned out to be a great disappointment. They began drifting back toward the level land behind the hills to start more games or gather in circles for talk. Little by little their thoughts again turned away from the soldiers and that hole to the big village and the fun those who had gone there must now be having.

The shadows on the brush were drawing out; more clouds were piling up in the north—gathering for talk about making more snow and sleet with the passing of the sun. But the sun was not too low to bounce from a shiny object far up toward the pass behind them. Every man looked up; they could make out four men on ponies, coming fast toward them. Now they could hear the yelps and whoops, and the young men set up a great yelling and shouting in answer.

Riding in front were Nicaagat and Sowówic, and following were Quinkent and Pauvit'z. The bright flash had come from the big silver sun which Nicaagat wore on his chest.

Those who had stayed on the hills gathered around them eagerly as they dismounted—all except Colorow, who looked up only briefly as the four rode into view, and did not leave his place behind the little hill. Quinkent grinned and his little eyes gleamed as he looked over the group of tired young fighters. Piah appeared from some place off in the brush, and began talking about the Buffalo Soldiers, as though the excitement of their coming were still new.

Quinkent, who, with Pauvit'z, was visiting the Little River battleground for the first time, was naked to the waist although he still wore the blue pants and big Maricat'z shoes he had always worn around the agency. The bare upper part of his body was painted and crossed with long yellow stripes, and his face and forehead were splendid with new paint.

After the greetings, the four newcomers pushed their way over to Colorow and sat down, while Colorow put on his angriest look and fixed his eyes on the ground.

Colorow, the great clown of the Nüpartka, had proved himself one of the greatest warriors of the People. He was admired
by all, yet when a man was with him he still found it impossible
not to think first of his great jokes and his talk that was big like
his belly. This had always been Colorow, and this was what
Colorow wanted to be still. As the great clown he had always
called himself the great warrior. Now the great clown had really
become the great warrior.

As the four who had just ridden in from the big village seated
themselves in the circle, Colorow began muttering something
about going out tomorrow and shaking hands with the soldiers.
Quinkent eagerly offered to go with him so that he could make
friends with the general and tell him that he must now take his
soldiers home. Colorow told Quinkent that the general had been
killed, but Quinkent knew something about such things. All of
the generals of the Maricat'z soldiers could never be killed, for
when one was killed they made a new general. There would certainly be a general down there in that hole with whom Quinkent
could make friends. Quinkent was the only one who believed
everything Colorow said, except, perhaps, for some of the little
boys and old women.

The shadow of the hill was edging around and stretching out,
covering the twisted clumps of brush one by one. A cold wind
was blowing again, straight down from the high mountains,
already white with new snow. Nicaagat began picking up sticks
for a fire, and Quinkent was pulling a blanket over his bare
shoulders.

Nicaagat's piwán had filled his saddle bags with meat and
pana and some coffee. Now they could make some hot food to
put inside them at the beginning of the cold night.

Colorow grunted like an old bull buffalo. Nicaagat had
spoiled his vision of a roasted prairie dog with talk of boiled
meat. It was better to have a roasted prairie dog in his head than
to have boiled jerked meat in his belly.

Acarí, seeing the look on Colorow's face, offered to take his
rifle the next day and shoot a prairie dog and roast it himself for
Colorow. But Colorow only grunted again. Tomorrow he would
want antelope, or perhaps buckskin or a fresh buffalo steak.

Besides, it did not look as though the sun would be shining to-morrow, so he could not sit in the sun and eat it. He dropped his head again and stared angrily at the ground.

Nicaagat, who still seemed in low spirits, was digging in his saddle bag for the food his piwán had packed. When the food was cooked, Colorow ate like a starved coyote, his sharp eyes always watching for ways to get more than was offered him. When the food was all gone he lay down on his blanket with a long sigh and a groan, while the others sat staring into the fire.

The hills turned into black shapes against the gray sky. The five men sat and talked as night came on and tiny specks of sleet began to rattle among the hardening leaves of the brush.

The wind stretched out, long and far, over the tops of the Shining Mountains and across the sea of land on the other side. It pushed itself along, twisting through the black sky; and inside it were many, many little winds that rode fast and aimed their arrows of sleet at the land. Then the long wind crawled like a great snake over the ridges, and the little winds danced out of the valley, over the black hills; and the air was still, with a cold that silently chewed and gnawed.

The sky had cleared and was seeded with the crazy scatter-ing of stars like huge drops of frozen water; the five men sat beside their fire, blankets cupped over them, and talked about the stars. Each one seemed to have other things to say, but no words to say them. "There is Old Coyote with his seven daugh-ters following. I can see Old Coyote well tonight—Surníyow, the 'One Who Sleeps with His Daughters.' That one is always mak-ing trouble."

One by one they gave in to the heavy sleep that settled over the camp, weighted with cold air, and soon they were lying like huge logs around the red circle of the cook fire.

Morning came with many colors—without clouds and with-out wind. The Little Summer began with the new day, and there was a bright cheerful feeling in all the camps.

Sometime during the still, cold night the eager desire for excitement of the other days had passed away from everyone. The morning sun soon warmed the valley, and the day passed quietly. In the afternoon a few more men, tired of the celebrating at the village, rode in and, finding things quiet and restful among the hills by the Little River, settled down with the others for a slow, lazy game or a quiet talk.

Fires burned up a little brighter that night, and most of the men sat up long after dark. Few felt like sleep. There was talk about the fall hunts and where would be the best places to spend the snow. The soldiers were nearly forgotten when they went to their blankets that night; but with the morning the long, slow days of waiting on the hills had ended.

The morning fires were burning when they heard the sound from far away. It was like some animal, lost and calling to the herd with the first light of dawn. Many recognized it as a soldier-horn, but the sound came from far beyond the hole by the Little River. Then one of the watchers came down from the top of a hill and told them: many more soldiers were coming—more even than had come the first day of the fight.

They left the fires and quickly climbed to the tops of the hills; from there they could see the soldiers, coming on in a long line across the flat, headed straight for the hole. They could hear the men inside shouting and yelling.

Two of the new soldiers got down from their horses and went inside the hole, but the others stayed outside.

For a little while—only for a little while—the waiting quiet returned. Then the new general and the other soldier came out. He began shouting at his soldiers; the faint sound of his voice rose up to the tops of the hills. Then the horn blew again. Yelling like crazy Sioux, the soldiers were riding fast toward the hills. The air was again filled with little singing bullets which thumped in the dust all around.

The young men sprang to their feet, dancing, chanting, yelling back at the soldiers. All of the old spirit, the old feeling, the fun of the great game was with them again. They sent shots back at the soldiers, and the noises of the guns came together like a loud, rolling thunderclap.

The rifle fire from the hills was too much for the soldiers. They slowed, stopped, and turned their horses back toward the hole, leaving, as before, a few lying still on the ground while their riderless horses galloped back with the rest.

The new soldiers were crowding into the hole with the others. The men on the hills waited. Then one of the young men rose up on his knees with a little yelp. The others turned and looked at him; his face seemed to be coming apart, and in that instant he fell over on the ground and lay still. A rifle cracked again somewhere near, and a bullet thumped beside the dead man, scattering his bare leg with dust and little chunks of dirt.

The others peered out over the top of the hill, and they saw the soldiers. They were not on ponies. They were crawling along through the brush on their bellies, and they dragged long rifles with them—not the short saddle rifles used by the others— the kind of rifles which, like the one used by Canávish, reached out a long way to hit the tiniest mark.

All the young men crouched down now, taking careful aim, and shot back at the crawling soldiers. There was no shouting, no singing now.

They began moving back, putting the tops of the hills in front of them to catch the bullets of the soldiers' long rifles. Whenever they saw a movement in the brush below, a speck of blue cloth, they shot at it. This was a new kind of war for the young men, a kind that makes a man stiff and cold, makes his skin creep over his body. This was the kind of war the old people talked about, with the Arapaho or the Sioux.

A long heavy stillness slowly settled in the warm air, under the bright sunshine and the wide blue sky. Only now and then came the crackling of brush—as though a fat, lazy snake moved unseen—and the boom of a rifle from below.

The sound of running horses, coming from the direction of the pass to the south, made many heads turn cautiously. Two men rode toward the bottom of their hills. At first it seemed they must be coming from the village, but it was soon plain that one was a Maricat'z, but not a soldier.

The two pulled in their ponies at the foot of the slope, where the morning cook fires still smoked; Colorow, Acarí, Nicaagat, and some of the older men went down to meet them.

The Maricat'z was a worker from the other agency, down toward the tall mountains to the south. The other was one of the People who lived near that agency, an old man called Sapava-

nero, the brother-in-law of Ouray. The white worker carried a
paper which he handed to Nicaagat, who saw written there:

Los Pinos Indian Agency
October 2, 1879

To the chief captains, headmen, and Utes at the White
River Agency:

You are hereby requested and commanded to cease hostilities against the whites, injuring no innocent persons or
any others farther than to protect your own lives and property from unlawful and unauthorized combinations of horse-
thieves and desperadoes, as anything farther will ultimately
end in disaster to all parties.

OURAY

Sounds of the fighting still came from the tops of the hills,
as the young men drew slowly back, shooting at the creeping
soldiers. The other men crowded around Sapavanero, who told
them that Ouray was angry about the fight and that Washington
had heard about it and was angry too. He thought that Washington wanted this fight to stop, and that probably Washington
would now send these soldiers home.

The Maricat'z had handed another paper to Nicaagat, and
this one read:

Los Pinos Indian Agency
October 2, 1879

To the officers in command and the soldiers at the White
River Agency:

Gentlemen:

At the request of the chief of the Utes at this agency, I
send by Jos. W. Brady, an employe, the inclosed order from
Chief Ouray to the Utes at the White River Agency.

The head chiefs deplore the trouble existing at White
River, and are anxious that no further fighting or bloodshed
should take place, and have commanded the Utes there to

227

stop. I hope that you will second their efforts so far as you can, consistent with your duties, under existing commands. This much for humanity.

Very respectfully, your obedient servant,

W. M. STANLEY
United States Indian Agent

Nicaagat began looking around the camps for a piece of cloth. The white worker helped him look. Soon they found a piece of white tent cloth and tied it to the end of a long stick; then they carried it to the top of the hill and set it upright behind a little pile of stones.

It was like some kind of magic. The soldiers stopped shooting, stopped crawling along on their bellies; and the young men, seeing this, laid down their rifles. Suddenly a strange new feeling came over the whole place—that battleground on the Little River—and everyone knew that the fight was over.

The Maricat'z worker got on his horse and rode down the hill to that hole, carrying the two papers. He stayed in the hole for a little while, then he came riding back to the hills where Nicaagat, Colorow, and the others were waiting.

The white worker told Nicaagat he had seen the general. That new general, whose name was General Merritt, had nothing to say about this note, but another officer said Nicaagat could come into the soldiers' hole tomorrow to talk. That was all. The general had been lying under a wagon and would not come out to talk to the white workers.

The change came too quickly. It took time for the young men to wash the fight from their minds—to think that they would go back to the village now, and to the little games of monte and the hand games, to gamble over a monte blanket the things they had won on the battlefield; back to the carniva and the women and children. They gathered in groups to talk about it; then one by one they found their saddlebags and blankets. Two of them rode out to round up the ponies and bring them in. There was a great deal of shuffling, scraping movement as they saddled up their ponies; the dust rose again, and the talk was broken and scattered like the chattering of many birds. In a little while most

of them were riding south toward the pass and the trail to the village. Nicaagat rode with them.

Colorow stayed. With a few of the young men he remained behind, watching from one of the hills, watching the soldiers. Many of those who had been so long in the hole were coming out, going down to the river to lie flat on their bellies and drink the clear, moving water.

A long time passed, and the soldiers did not start to go home. They seemed to be spreading out instead, making a wide camp along the river. Then some of the new soldiers got on their ponies. They were riding, but they were not going home. They were coming toward Colorow and the little group of young men with him. They were coming south, toward the hills.

Colorow and the young men drew back. They found their ponies quickly and rode away across the flat toward the ridges that held the trail leading to the village. Behind them came many soldiers—riding south, into the country of the People.

« v »

The town of Rawlins lay dozing in the lukewarm autumn sun, between its two bare hills, which gave it partial protection from the blizzard-driving winds that would soon blow across southern Wyoming. Nothing stirred, either on the shimmering, brush-dotted hills or among the cluster of wooden buildings in the hollow.

Then, loping down the dusty road, which became Rawlins' main street, came a rider on a tired horse. As the rider neared the town he leaned forward across the horse's streaked, sweating neck. The animal reached for more speed, but only tottered a little in its stride. Joe Rankin, his white buckskin suit grimy and sweat-stained, was riding back into Rawlins from the White River country.

In a few minutes sleepy Rawlins was awake, for Joe had a story to tell; and in less than an hour everybody in the settlement knew about the defeat of Major Thornburgh's forces on Milk Creek. An overwhelming army of Utes had ambushed the command in a narrow canyon. They had crushed Major Thornburgh's small force and were driving northward "on the warpath."

Joe had made the ride from the White River country to Rawlins in 28 hours. The whole distance, about 170 miles, in 28 hours—it was repeated over and over throughout Rawlins that day, for Joe, tired though he was, never tired of telling it. He told how he managed to sneak through the barricade with the command surrounded, and under deadly fire had escaped to spread the alarm and bring help.

He had stopped on Bear River and again at Snake River to change horses, and a small army of fleeing settlers followed a few hours behind him. Some had snatched up a few of their belongings and thrown them into wagons and buckboards. Others had only taken to their saddles, leaving their property and possessions behind for the savage Utes, who were surely close behind them. That day the population of Rawlins began to swell as though someone had mentioned gold.

Then Mr. Rankin rested. His mission was accomplished. The fight was on; the word was out.

A few hours behind Rankin came another messenger from the troops on Milk Creek. His story was a little less sensational.

He carried a message from Captain Payne, who had taken over
the command, addressed to General Sheridan at Omaha.

> MILK RIVER, COLO., SEPT. 29
> 8:30 P.M.
> VIA RAWLINS, WYO., OCT. 1
>
> THIS COMMAND, COMPOSED OF THREE COMPANIES OF
> CAVALRY, WAS MET A MILE SOUTH OF MILK RIVER BY SEVERAL
> HUNDRED UTE INDIANS WHO ATTACKED AND DROVE US TO THE
> WAGON TRAIN WITH GREAT LOSS. IT BECOMES MY PAINFUL DUTY
> TO ANNOUNCE THE DEATH OF MAJOR THORNBURGH, WHO FELL
> IN HARNESS; THE PAINFUL BUT NOT SERIOUS WOUNDING OF
> LIEUTENANT PADDOCK AND DR. GRIMES, AND KILLING OF TEN
> ENLISTED MEN AND A WAGON MASTER, WITH THE WOUNDING OF
> ABOUT TWENTY MEN AND TEAMSTERS. I AM CORRALED NEAR
> WATER, WITH ABOUT THREE-FOURTHS OF MY ANIMALS KILLED,
> AFTER A DESPERATE FIGHT SINCE 12 M. WE HOLD OUR POSITION.
> I SHALL STRENGTHEN IT DURING THE NIGHT, AND BELIEVE WE
> CAN HOLD OUT UNTIL RE-ENFORCEMENTS REACH US, IF THEY ARE
> HURRIED. OFFICERS AND MEN BEHAVED WITH GREATEST GAL-
> LANTRY. I AM ALSO SLIGHTLY WOUNDED IN TWO PLACES.
>
> PAYNE, COMMANDER.

With great relief the words "We hold our position" were
repeated throughout jittery Rawlins.

A second telegram from the Rawlins railroad station,
crowded now with eager news-seekers, carried the news to Commissioner Hayt in Washington and added, ". . . fear Agent
Meeker and employes all massacred, as trains and wagons trans-
ferring Indian supplies from here have all been destroyed by
Indians."

The news sped eastward from Rawlins, and down the track,
at Laramie City, where the next nearest army post was located,
another telegraph key clicked, and the message shot southward
to Denver and Governor Pitkin:

LARAMIE CITY, WYO., OCT. 1
THE WHITE RIVER UTES HAVE MET COL. THORNBURGH'S COM-
MAND, SENT TO QUELL DISTURBANCES AT THE WHITE RIVER
AGENCY, KILLING THORNBURGH HIMSELF AND KILLING OR
WOUNDING MANY OF HIS OFFICERS, MEN, AND HORSES, WHEREBY
THE SAFETY OF THE WHOLE COMMAND IS IMPERILED. I SHALL
WARN OUR PEOPLE IN NORTH PARK AND TRUST THAT YOU WILL
TAKE SUCH PROMPT ACTION AS WILL PROTECT YOUR PEOPLE
AND RESULT IN GIVING THE WAR DEPARTMENT CONTROL OF THE
SAVAGES, IN ORDER TO PROTECT THE SETTLERS FROM MASSACRES
PROVOKED BY THE PRESENT TEMPORIZING POLICY OF THE GOV-
ERNMENT WITH REFERENCE TO INDIAN AFFAIRS IN ALL TIME
TO COME.

COL. STEPHEN W. DOWNEY

The governor's office exploded into a frenzy of action. Pitkin sent for the editors of all the newspapers. He sent for the officers of the state militia. In a few hours Denver was under arms—a fortified city, looking tensely toward the wall of brown and white mountains to the west.

Government rifles came out of storage, bright and oily and coated with grease; crowbars struggled with nails that sealed the lids on ammunition crates, and the bark of drillmasters sounded in public buildings.

The Governor sent couriers to alert every town and settlement in the state not served by railroad and telegraph. Then he sent his telegram to the Secretary of War in Washington:

DISPATCHES JUST RECEIVED FROM LARAMIE CITY AND RAWLINS
INFORM ME THAT WHITE RIVER UTES ATTACKED COL. THORN-
BURGH'S COMMAND TWENTY-FIVE MILES FROM AGENCY. COL.
THORNBURGH WAS KILLED, AND ALL HIS OFFICERS BUT ONE
KILLED OR WOUNDED, BESIDES MANY OF HIS MEN AND MOST OF
HIS HORSES. DISPATCHES STATE THAT THE WHOLE COMMAND IS
IMPERILED. THE STATE OF COLORADO WILL FURNISH YOU,
IMMEDIATELY, ALL THE MEN YOU REQUIRE TO SETTLE PER-
MANENTLY THIS INDIAN TROUBLE. . . .

The fevered excitement that gripped the newly-civilized frontier city might have died a natural death in a few days, or perhaps a few hours, but the newspapers were good physicians—they kept it alive. The crisis persisted and grew, nourished by news that trickled in, some rumored, some on good authority. The task of the newspapers was an easy one; Denver was young and excitable.

Then came the story that all Colorado, all the West, and all the nation was awaiting. It covered an entire page in the *Denver Daily News*. The headline announced:

A SCENE OF SLAUGHTER

ARRIVAL OF TROOPS AT
WHITE RIVER AGENCY

The Horrible Scene that Met
the Gaze of Merritt's
Command

Discovering the Bodies of Father
Meeker and His Men

RAWLINS, October 13. (Special to the News)—I have just interviewed Mr. Webber, a courier who has just arrived from the White River Agency.

General Merritt

REACHED THE AGENCY

on the 11th inst., when a scene of horror and desolation met his view.

All the Agency buildings except one unfinished house were burned to the ground.

The remains of Father Meeker and all his employes were found and buried.

A chain was found around

FATHER MEEKER'S NECK,

his head smashed, a piece of barrel stave sticking in his mouth and his hand badly burned.

The women and children, families of the agent and employes, have all either been murdered and put out of sight, or else have been taken away as prisoners.

233

Eaton and Frank Dresser, two of the employes, were found

BURNED TO A CRISP

Sheppard was found naked, with a lot of paper sacks in his arms, his face eaten more or less by wolves, body partially burned, and

A BULLET HOLE

in his left breast.

Price was found naked, with two bullet holes in the left breast.

Another man, found naked, was burned so badly that he could hardly be recognized, but it is supposed to be Thompson.

E. W. Eskridge was found two miles this side of the agency, naked and shot through the head.

Mr. W. H. Post

FATHER MEEKER'S SECRETARY

was found one hundred yards from the agency house, toward the river. He was shot through the left ear and one shot below the ear. He was also stripped naked.

Harry Dresser's body was found about twelve miles this side of the agency, in a coal mine. He had evidently crawled in there after being wounded,

AND THERE DIED

Dresser had been sent from the agency to the command with a dispatch. The letter found on his person was from Meeker to Thornburgh, asking Thornburgh if he had had any trouble coming through the canyon, and stating there was no sign of trouble at the agency.

Reporters traveled out from the East, took their first look at the Rocky Mountains, drank whisky in the Windsor Hotel bar, and attended news conferences in the Governor's office. Governor Pitkin gave his statement to the press:

"I have thought for six weeks," he told reporters gathered around his desk, "that there was a liability of the White River Utes making trouble. I have written several letters to General Pope.

"I think the conclusion of this affair will end the depredations

234

in Colorado. It will be impossible for the Indians and whites to live in peace hereafter. This attack had no provocation and the whites now understand that they are liable to be attacked in any part of the state where the Indians happen to be in sufficient force.

"My idea is that, unless removed by the government, they must necessarily be exterminated. I could raise 25,000 men to protect the settlers in 24 hours. The State would be willing to settle the Indian trouble at its own expense. The advantages that would accrue from the throwing open of 12,000,000 acres of land to miners and settlers would more than compensate all the expenses incurred."

Raw materials for the news mills of Denver now flowed in from two principal sources: the officers of the forces fighting the Utes on Milk Creek, and the Los Pinos Ute Agency and mining towns in the nearby San Juan Mountains, more than 100 miles from the battlefield and the White River Agency.

When news of the Thornburgh battle was first received, General Merritt started for White River with 500 men, and railroads carried fighting forces into Rawlins from other Army posts of the West. The total forces moving against the Utes now numbered about 1,100 men; still they had not advanced beyond the entrenchments on Milk River.

At Los Pinos, Chief Ouray, friend of the white man, who had been notified of the trouble at White River while he was on a hunt, returned to his home immediately and called for a council of all southern bands of Utes. The chiefs, in a very short time, all agreed that they would take no part in the trouble at White River and that they would order all of their people to stay at home. Ouray immediately sent out an order to the White River people, carried by Joseph Brady, miller at the Los Pinos Agency, and Sapavanero, usually recognized as the chief next in importance to Ouray. News of these councils and of this order reached Denver, released through Ouray and Wilson M. Stanley, agent to the Los Pinos Utes. Meanwhile alarm spread through the bustling infant mining towns of the San Juan country.

Then a runner came in from White River and told Ouray that the White River Utes had obeyed his order and had stopped fighting. According to the reports, this runner told Ouray that the hostile Utes were moving back into their own country.

But the towns and settlements of Colorado continued to call for arms. Militia units drilled. And Governor Pitkin called more news conferences.

News from Lake City, Silverton, and the town of Ouray, the three largest mining towns in the San Juan country, where Governor Pitkin had considerable business interests, funneled through the Governor's office and into the Denver newspapers. One dispatch, signed by 12 citizens, read:

Lake City, Oct. 4, 1879

The Indian Chief Ouray has notified the whites to protect themselves, that he is powerless and can afford no protection. The town of Ouray is under arms, and the country is all on fire. We will do all we can, but want arms, can you send them? We must have protection of some kind.

And another message to Governor Pitkin from A. W. Hudson, a "leading lawyer and most reputable citizen" of the town of Ouray:

Your dispatch received at Animas City. Bands of Indians out setting fires on the line between La Plata and San Juan. They say they will burn the entire country over. Chief Ouray, from the Uncompahgre band, has sent out a courier warning settlers that his young men are on the warpath, and that he cannot control them. The Indians setting these fires, being off their reservation, cannot the people of these two countries drive them back? We don't want to wait until they have killed a few families, and if they understand we are prepared, there may be no outbreak.

Governor Pitkin dispatched his answer to Mr. Hudson:

Indians off their reservation, seeking to destroy your settlements by fire, are game to be hunted and destroyed like wild beasts. Send this word to the settlements. Gen. Dave Cook is

236

at Lake City in command of State forces. Gen. Hatch is rushing in regulars to San Juan.

Reports that all fighting had stopped continued to come from Agent Stanley at Los Pinos. He reported that no depredations had been committed by Indians, and that none of the Utes of Southern or Uncompahgre bands and only a part of the White Rivers were engaged in the fight with the soldiers on Milk River. His information came directly from Ouray and from the Indian couriers who had returned from Milk River.

"If we should take the statements of what newspapers here say," Agent Stanley wrote, "and especially the *Denver Tribune,* one would suppose that every Ute on the reservation was on the war-path, and half of the people in Colorado murdered and their property destroyed by fire and stolen by Utes. . . ."

On Oct. 15 Agent Stanley wrote Commissioner Hayt:

> I hope and trust the Indian Department at Washington will use every influence to see that the Utes have a fair hearing in this matter, that the world may know who is to blame, the Utes or the white cormorants surrounding them. I am absolutely disgusted at the conduct of the white people and am not at all surprised that the Indians do occasionally turn upon the traducers and robbers of their rights. The worm will squirm when tread upon and the noble horse defend himself when goaded to desperation, and why not an Indian, one of God's people, who is covered by the same divine mantle of charity that enrobes the whites, and are as devout worshippers in their simple way at the seat of justice and mercy as the white man, with none of the white man's hypocrisy and studied cant.

Shortly after this a dispatch to Governor Pitkin from one of his friends at Lake City, who "knew all the headmen" of the Los Pinos Utes, called for the removal of Agent Stanley from the Los Pinos Agency, contending that the Utes "cannot guarantee safety while he is there." Governor Pitkin sent this request to Secretary Schurz, stating further, "My advices indicate that many of the Uncompahgre Utes are at White River."

Secretary Schurz' answer to the Governor of Colorado did not mention the recommendation about Agent Stanley. Secretary Schurz wrote:

> Ouray informs us that his orders are being respected, and that there is prospect of ending the difficulty. Permit me to suggest that militia and armed citizens be strictly instructed to confine themselves to protection of life and property outside the reservation, if such should become necessary, which now seems improbable.

But Governor Pitkin, with his silver interests in the San Juan and his vision of 12,000,000 more acres of his new state opened for settlement, was a persistent man. His answer to Secretary Schurz again summed up the Indian situation in Colorado and repeated his offer of state aid:

> There is the most intense excitement throughout the State over the captivity and possible tortures of the female prisoners taken at White River. If there are enough regulars in the state to successfully overcome the Indians, would it not be well for General Hatch to march directly to the Uncompahgre Agency, and seize all women and children as hostages? If federal force too small, we can furnish enough additional troops in San Juan in a day. The barbarities practiced by the Utes have inflamed our people almost beyond the possibility of control.

Secretary Schurz sent an immediate answer to Governor Pitkin:

> The course suggested in your dispatch cannot be adopted. No effort will be spared to rescue those in peril. General Sherman tells me that the troops in hand appear sufficient for present purposes, and there is neither authority nor occasion for enlisting volunteers or state forces. You will recognize the importance of keeping militia and armed citizens away from the Indian reserve to avoid more extended and unnecessary complications.

238

8. DECISION

I

CHARLES ADAMS of Colorado and Secretary of the Interior Carl Schurz had a number of things in common.

As young men, both had left Germany after the unsuccesful revolution of 1848, speaking only the language of their homeland; both had learned English as they earned their American citizenships. Both were employed by the government of the United States, in positions dealing with, among other things, the Indian problem.

Each had been christened Karl, Adams having altered it to Charles when he dropped the family name of Schwanbeck, which was difficult for Americans to pronounce. He was often called General Adams, since he had been appointed, with many others, a general of the Colorado Militia.

Both were known as friends to the Indians. Schurz had had very little first-hand experience with any Indians; he saw in them basic similarities to the peasant populations of Europe—conquered, oppressed, exploited, people in need of a champion. Adams had served as agent to the Utes of Colorado, both at the Los Pinos Agency and at White River.

Now, with the people of Colorado and the United States Army at war with the Utes, Secretary Schurz selected Charles Adams as the special agent of the Interior Department, to rescue the white women captives from the hostile Indians.

This is where General Adams story begins:

239

Sometime in September last—I think it was about the 24th —I was asked by Governor Pitkin to come to his office and meet Secretary Schurz, who at that time was in Denver. . . . The question came up as to what could be done with the White River Indians, against whom a detachment of troops was then marching, and Governor Pitkin suggested that if I could go there in advance of the troops, probably the difficulty, if any difficulty there should be, might be avoided. The Secretary asked me if I could go. . . . I had to go to New Mexico about that time to attend to some cases in court . . . but I agreed that as soon as I could come back I would go, and do my best with the Indians.

It seems there was some charge that the Indians had burnt some grass and timber, and also houses, on Bear River, outside of their reservation, and that the soldiers were sent down to arrest the perpetrators.

I returned to Colorado on the 7th of October, and then first heard of the fight with the soldiers and also of the massacre of the agent. On the 14th of October I received a telegram from the Secretary, and also a telegram from my department, the latter detailing me temporarily to the Interior Department and the former giving me instructions how to proceed. I was to go to the Southern Ute Agency, see Ouray, the chief of the Utes, put myself in communication with the hostile Utes, and try to obtain the release of the women and children who were then supposed to be in their camp. If that was agreed to without any conditions, I was to ascertain whether the Indians wanted to prolong the fight, or whether they would be willing to give up the principal instigators of the massacre and resume their relations with the government. I started, taking two or three men with me, and also some Indian chiefs, and went to the hostile camp.

I think I arrived there on the 21st of October, about ten o'clock in the morning, at the small camp; there were only about ten or fifteen lodges of Indians there. A boy that we met about a quarter of a mile away told me that the prisoners were scattered—that is, one woman was in one house at the lower end of the camp; another one in the center, and another above.

I went to the lower end first, and by inquiring I saw Miss Meeker peeping out of a tent. I dismounted and asked her who she was, not knowing her personally at the time, and told her I had come to release her, and asked where her mother and the other woman were.

I then mounted again and told Miss Meeker to get ready to leave, if possible, that afternoon. I went up to the upper camp and found all the Indian men, probably about thirty or forty, in a tent together talking very boisterously. I went inside. I knew them all personally, but none of them would speak to me. I found at once that there was a certain hostility amongst them towards me, but was asked to wait; that they had sent for the principal chief, Douglas, that he would come very soon, and then we could talk the matter over.

I inquired for the other captives, and was told that they were hidden in the brush about 200 yards distant down a steep bank towards the river. I waited for about an hour, when Chief Douglas, with probably five or six other chiefs, rode up. He informed me that the soldiers were advancing from White River, and that the whites were hostile, and he did not see why he should give me those women. He asked whether I had any conditions to offer for the release of them. I told him I had not; but after he had given them up to me I might have something further to say. He drew a map on the ground, saying that the soldiers were building a wagon road and advancing rapidly towards Grand River. I told him that, from my understanding of the instructions from Washington, I had supposed that at the same time I entered their country the commanding officer of the soldiers had also received orders not to advance any farther from where he might be at the time. . . . He then asked me, "Will you go and see them, and if they are coming farther, stop them?"

I said, "I will go to their camp after you give up the women." He then invited me inside, into the lodge where all the others were talking, and I believe they talked there until about four or five o'clock in the afternoon, some in a very hostile, others in a peaceful manner.

241

One of the Indians I had taken with me could speak Spanish, and through him, as interpreter, I had several remarks to make to them, but always to the effect that they must first give up these prisoners without conditions, and then I might perhaps be able to do something for them. They said that they had not been willing to go into this fight; that the fight had been forced upon them; that the soldiers had come there without any cause whatever. I paid very little attention to their excuses at the time, but said that if these women were started on their way home I would then go to the main camp (this being only a small one) and get all the chiefs together and talk it over. So finally they agreed to give them to me.

They said: "We don't want to have anything more to do with the government. All that we want is that the soldiers shall not pursue us in our own country. We can live on game, as we have lived before, and do not desire to have anything to do with the government, but we give these women to you, and if you can do anything for us afterwards, all right."

So I immediately had the old lady, Mrs. Meeker, and Mrs. Price brought up out of the brush. I then said that I wished those three women to come together that night, Miss Josephine having been kept in another part of the camp, and that they should start the first thing in the morning. The Indians promised it, and I made arrangement for the saddles and animals for next morning, and then I immediately saddled up and went with Douglas down to the main camp.

Before that, when I first met Miss Meeker, I asked her the question, "Do you know who of these Indians killed your father and the other employes?" She answered No, she could not tell. I then asked her how the Indians had treated her. She said, "Well, better than I had expected." I asked her whether they had offered her any indignities to her person. She made the off-hand remark, "Oh, no, Mr. Adams, nothing of that kind."

Then later on when I met Mrs. Meeker, she asked me whether their release would make peace with the government for the Indians. I said, "No."

Mrs. Meeker was very willing to talk of who had abused

her, but Chief Douglas and other chiefs stood around her so close that with her I could not possibly speak about the murders, because if they had thought that I was making an investigation there I considered my life and the others in danger too.

But I got Mrs. Price, the other captive, accidentally alone, and I asked her the question whether any indignities had been offered to her. She said, "No." I thereupon wrote the dispatch to the Secretary that the women had been given up, and no indignities had been offered them.

My horse was waiting at the time. This dispatch was given to an Indian who was to carry it back to Ouray's house, probably 120 miles distant; from there to Lake City, from there to Del Norte, probably four or five hundred miles altogether.

I then went on with the Indians to the main camp, and reached there about 11 o'clock that night. All the chiefs had assembled. One had gone ahead and told them I was coming. . . .

The Indians were all in the tent of a chief called Sawawick, and in this tent we sat up all night, and they told me their story, and asked me to report that story to Washington.

Chief Jack was the spokesman that night. He said that he had tried his utmost to avert the fight, but that the agent had told him that the soldiers were bringing shackles and ropes, and that some of them would be hurt, and others taken out as prisoners; that they had also met Major Thornburgh, and asked him to keep his troops outside, as their women and children would become frightened if they all came there, and asked him with some of his men to come to the agency; and on refusing that, they proposed that he should come about half way between where he was then encamped and the agency, and that they would go back and tell their agent and some of their chiefs to come and meet him and talk the matter over, and see what he actually wanted; that instead of his doing as he had promised, they got notice in their camp that he was advancing with his whole command across the place where he had promised to meet them alone; that thereupon they withdrew to the side of the road . . . that the soldiers evidently came to fight them, because they were deployed in skirmish line and that then the soldiers commenced firing on them. That was their story in camp.

They also said that then, after some of their people had been killed, some of the young men rushed back to the camp and notified the others that the soldiers were killing their people, and that thereupon they had killed Mr. Meeker and the employes, laying all the blame on Mr. Meeker. I asked them the question why they had killed the freighters on the road, but they declined to answer. I found that it was better for me simply to listen to their story—to put no questions to them at that time. . . .

About ten o'clock next morning we saddled up, and rode up Grand River towards White River. I had asked for an escort of four or five Indians to go with me, inasmuch as some of the Indians were ahead on the road, and those, with two of the chiefs that I had brought with me from the Southern Agency, I thought sufficient. But when I started out the crowd kept increasing until there were about twenty-five men with me, and they kept very close around me, and from their whole movements I saw that I was more of a prisoner than anything else.

About noon that day, just after crossing Grand River, away ahead I saw an Indian coming toward us at a fast gait. Some of the Indians also saw him at the same time, and they galloped up ahead very fast. I then saw several loose ponies with saddles on, coming over the trail following the first one, and pretty soon two more Indians, mounted. I rode up leisurely; when I came up I found them gesticulating and talking very loudly . . . and it took some ten minutes before even the chief that came with me, Sapovanero, would speak to me.

All of them looked very morose and hostile; but finally after talking among themselves a while, Sapovanero turned around and said, "It is all right; the Indians and the soldiers have had another fight, and two Indians were killed and two white men; so it is all right."

He then explained that there had been a party of about twelve Indians some twenty-five miles from White River on the high peaks of the mountains watching the soldiers, and they had seen a party of seven come out from the camp, who had unsaddled and stopped for lunch, probably within 200 yards of the camp of the Indians (which was on a little creek) where four or five of them were, while the rest were up on the mountains. This party of seven, partly soldiers, partly citizens, were considered by them as being on a hunt, and they did not think any harm of it; but all at once two of the party started one way and five another, and one of the men came very close to the Indians and shot at a deer, which are very plentiful in that neighborhood. One of the Indians went up on a rock to see if the deer had been hit and the white man discovered him and killed him.

Then the other four immediately jumped for their arms and killed the white man as well as the officer with him, and then all the other Indians from the mountains joined in pursuit of the other five white men, intending to kill them. They corralled them in the ravine until night, and during that time another Indian was killed. That night they went back to the camp on White River.

That was their story of the affair in which Lieutenant Weir and Scout Hume were killed.

That night we camped on Grand River. The next morning we started on. About noon we met two or three other Indians who told the same story. They also had been in that fight.

Very soon afterwards, about the place where this fight had occurred, one of the Indians told me that he had seen the head of a horse some two or three miles in advance on the road, and he did not want to go any farther, and he asked me to go on alone. So I took my handkerchief out and tied it to a pole, and I went ahead to this place where the Indian had seen the horse, and found two or three loose horses only.

I sent word back to the Indians to come; that there were no soldiers here. I then rode ahead quietly, and just as these Indians, some 25 in number, were riding pretty fast to overtake me, I saw the soldiers ahead; in fact they were all around us at once. My Indians saw them in a moment and ran off to the mountains, leaving me alone. I kept on, but the soldiers did not seem to recognize me; at any rate they kept skirmishers all deployed, and kept coming closer and closer around me, and some of them were even dismounted and ready to fire, but fortunately an officer, who was a little ahead, saw me and came and conducted me to the commanding officer.

I learned that Col. Sumner had come to find the bodies of those who had been killed or that were supposed to have been killed the day before, and I told him I thought I could get the Indians to find them for him, inasmuch as they had talked the affair over very fully, although I had none of the Indians with me that had been in that fight. There were some threatening remarks made by some of the scouts to the effect that it would be a good thing to shoot us, but nothing of that kind happened.

I went back to get the Indians to come; Col. Sumner promising to take in his lines. He said he had been informed that there were more than 300 Indians in front. I told him that there were not more than 25, and that they would come with me. He did not seem to believe me. . . .

I went back and signaled the Indians on the mountain-side to come down, and one of them, the Chief Sapovanero, came down and met me on the road, we two all alone. I told him that the soldiers had simply come to find the bodies, and that if he would call the others down from the mountain they could all find the bodies, and we could all go to the camp at White River.

While we were talking I saw another company come right behind us, cutting us off from the road and from the other Indians on the mountain. The Indians on the mountain hallooed to the chief who was with me and he looked around and saw the soldiers, and at once accused me of betraying him. He hadn't time to get his gun out or I think he would have fired at me. He ran right back and almost through the soldiers and up to the mountain. I went after him and told him that if there was any treachery it was not on my part, and that if such was the case I would rather stay with the Indians than the soldiers.

Some of the soldiers came round and I rode up to one of

the officers, a sergeant, and asked him what he meant. He said he had not heard any orders to the contrary. I told him I had heard the bugle very plainly, sounding the retreat to the main column. I rode back to Col. Sumner, who was following me closely with his whole column, and asked him what this meant. He said there was a misunderstanding, that there was one company that had not heard the signal. The soldiers were then recalled.

I told Col. Sumner that the Indians were under the impression that I had used treachery, and I said that they must be disabused of that idea, and asked him to send an officer and a trumpeter with me to meet them, which he agreed to do. The Indians from the mountains were circling around, and they met me again about three miles off, standing in line. I rode up and explained everything, and in a few minutes they found the bodies. The bodies were buried, but the Indians would not come to White River.

Next morning I saw General Merritt and asked him what his instructions were. He said he had been advancing and had built his road in order to follow the Indians up south, when he received orders to stop until I should get through with my mission, and that he had come back to White River and made his camp there, and was waiting for further orders. . . . I told him what I had already accomplished, and wrote quite a lengthy telegram to the Secretary of the Interior, and showed it to General Merritt. He read it and said that under the circumstances he would have to stay where he was.

Before I entered the camp of the soldiers the Indians made me promise that I would come back that way and inform them of what the troops were going to do. . . . General Merritt and myself agreed . . . that I should go back and see that these women were actually sent off, as it might be possible that the Indians had kept them. . . . General Merritt promised that he would give ample time for me to get back which would take five or six days . . . and that then the War Department and the Interior Department together must decide.

I went back and met the Indians at the same place; they

had been on the mountains watching to see whether I would come back or not. I went with them back to their camp.

. . . We arrived back at the camp about noon the next day; stayed there all night; rode back about daylight towards the small camp; found that the Indians had kept their word, and that the women had gone; and then left and arrived next day at Ouray's house.

While at the Indians' camp . . . the Indians being so very anxious to make peace and to have no further trouble with the government, even the women and children coming to me crying and begging me to keep the soldiers away, I came to the conclusion that the matter could be settled satisfactorily to the government by the surrender of those Indians that were actually guilty.

. . . I don't think Mr. Meeker understood these Indians; I think he tried to do his best to civilize them. He was a great agriculturist, and he thought that he could succeed in forcing the Indians to work and to accept the situation as farmers, but he did not take in consideration that it is almost impossible to force Indians into that sort of labor all at once. At the Southern Agency a few of them had farmed, and by gaining something from it they had come to look favorably upon it.

For example, some of them raised a large quantity of potatoes there and got some money for the crop, and the result was that probably three-fourths of them asked me why I could not do something to get a large ditch cut for them in the Uncompahgre Valley, so that they all could go to work in that way. . . . There are only two or three little springs there to furnish water, and all the water that the Indians could get has been utilized. Ouray himself farms thirty or forty acres. If there was a large ditch cut for irrigating purposes a great many of them would farm, because the Uncompahgre Valley is very good agricultural region, but the White River Valley is unfit for cultivation.

The Indians say they told Mr. Meeker that . . . Agent Adams, Agent Danforth, and Agent Littlefield had tried it and had failed to raise anything, and why should he attempt it? and his answer, they said, was that he was a farmer, and we were not.

II

General Edward Hatch had two missions at the Los Pinos Ute Agency. The first was one of fact-finding and peacemaking, as a member of the commission investigating the recent White River Ute uprising. The second was that of representing the military arm of the government in what had become a moral conflict between the military and a civilian branch of the government.

General Hatch was an officer in the United States Army, and the Army did not like the idea of an investigating commission— not any part of it. The Army was an instrument of peacemaking, but not in this way. The Army was paving the way for advancement and civilization in the West, but investigations had no part in this work.

It was always the same: the military did the hard work— the dangerous and bloody man's work—and when the job was half done some civilian department of the government took over. It was the same, whether it was an uprising of rebellious Indians or trouble with the Mexicans on the Texas border.

This time it was the Utes. When the Interior Department had tried out all its theories on civilizing savages and had met disastrous failure, the Army was called to straighten out the mess; when General Merritt's forces were within range to do some good, the troops were called back. The military was subordinate again.

Now they had sent a commission in to investigate. They wanted to determine guilt—to get the facts, they said. After these Indians had ambushed Major Thornburgh's troops, who were on a peace mission, and after they had killed the agent and all his employees, burned the agency at White River, and made captives of three white women, the Interior Department talked of getting facts—of determining guilt.

General Hatch would represent the military on this commis-

249

sion. He would represent his branch of the government as well
as he could. As before, he would recommend that a new Army
post be established. The Army would probably gain that much,
but whether they would gain their just and reasonable end—the
turning over of the Bureau of Indian Affairs to the Department
of War—was doubtful.

General Hatch had been at the Los Pinos Agency just three
years ago, in the fall of 1876. His assignment then had been to a
commission created by Congress to attempt to persuade the Utes
to move to Indian Territory, or to consolidate their agencies at
White River and sell out this mineral-rich San Juan country. The
commission had failed. They had only been able to get the Utes
to sell a tract of land already occupied by farmers who were supplying produce to the mining camps, and this agreement had
come only after days of dogged talk with the head men.

In another house, isolated but not far from the Los Pinos
Agency, another member of the commission was getting himself
ready for the first day of the hearing.

He moved slowly and patiently, but his big, spade-tipped
fingers were deft as they worked with the collar button of his
white shirt, until it slipped into place. Then he began looping
the black string necktie until it was adjusted in a neat bow.

He lifted the coat of his black broadcloth suit and hunched
it on over his wide shoulders, shook it down over his hips, and
buttoned it. Then he stepped back and with a studious frown
looked himself over, top to bottom.

He ran his hand over the top of his head, down to his
shoulders, and lifted one of the long, black braids of hair, holding it up for a moment and rolling the silver band at the end
between his fingers. Then he let it fall back down over his chest,
where it belonged.

There was one thing he could do nothing about: the fine,
pale lines that crossed the firm flesh of his face, like many spider
webs. He rubbed his cheek hard with the back of his hand, until
the dark red blood glowed through the color that had soaked in
during the recent fall hunt. The net of lines only showed more
plainly, like aging white hairs. Perhaps he could get a better
sleep tonight. Those lines had come during the many past nights

of thinking about this business that was to begin today—thinking, through the gray light of half-sleep. There had been too many nights since Chipita, his piwán, had come to his fall hunting camp with the message.

Ouray, that man whom Washington had made chief of all the Utes, who lived in the kind of house white men build and who rode in a carriage behind a beautifully matched team, knew of another time when there had been many wakeful nights—when he had at last learned the key to the white man's ways; when he had learned how one man can be deceived by another.

He had learned, and he had taken the money from Washington every year. He had made a farm here in his own country, and with this came more money. He had sat in the churches and read their books. He had tried to stand with a foot on either side of the wall, and in this way he had led the People. He had always thought first of sparing them from being cut down by the white man's soldiers or being driven away to the white man's prison land, which Washington calls Indian Territory.

Now this thing had come, swiftly, suddenly; it had bounded like some cat animal into the middle of his sleep—into the warm sunshine and new snow, when the whole body and all its senses are sharp as the newly-frozen pine needles.

Ouray had made his home halfway between the two countries of the southern bands and the White River. He had hoped that this would help him in the work Washington had given him. With the southern bands it had not been so hard. They had lived close to the Quat'z, the Spanish people, and they had learned enough of white men's ways to understand when Ouray tried to teach them. With those on the White River it was different. They were far away, their eyes hidden somehow from the new things that were happening all around—far away, in a tall, deep land; far back with the Old People.

He went out to the stable where he lifted the harnesses from their place on the wall and quickly performed the task that had, many years ago, taken him painful hours to learn. He backed his two handsome blacks from their stalls and hitched them to the carriage.

The road, rough and full of holes at this time of year, looped out onto the valley floor and followed the river to the agency. It would take a little time to travel it—an hour, perhaps longer. He drove away from his house, past his acres of farm land—the fields that had yielded a good harvest this year: hay, potatoes; and the new field laid open to receive the seed of winter wheat.

The first home he had known was a carniv in a Ute village down near the great Taos Pueblo; Ouray, "The Arrow," a lonely little boy who was something less than the other little boys—less than any of the People. That man who was now dead—Guera Murah, a Jicarilla Apache who had been taken captive by the People in one of the old wars—was Ouray's father. To the People he was "that Apache." Ouray was only half a boy: only half of him belonged to the People. The other half belonged to nothing.

There were many Quat'z in that country, and in the place they called Taos, near the great Pueblo, were many Maricat'z. Ouray learned both Spanish and English; but, like most of the People who knew these languages, he talked Spanish whenever he had to use a language other than his own. Spanish, like the language of the People, would say what a man felt and thought. Perhaps this was why the Quat'z were easier to live among than most of the Maricat'z.

Ouray had learned both the languages well, and while he was still a boy the Maricat'z, when they had business with the People, sometimes asked Ouray to be interpreter; then one day, when he was a young man, they had taken him to Washington.

It was there that he met a white man who was one of the big leaders of his own people, and that man told Ouray that Washington wanted to make him chief of all the Utes and would pay him money for this. It was a strange idea: Washington did not make a tawacz viem. A man did not become a chief because Washington wanted it, or because the man himself wanted it. A man only became a leader of the People because he *was* the People. Before Ouray could answer that important white man, he was called over to a window. The ground below, as far as the eye could see, was covered with a huge village of tents, pushed so close together that they looked like young trees growing up on old, burnt-over land. This village, said the white man, was the place the Maricat'z soldiers stayed. Not all of the soldiers were here. Many were out fighting a great war.

Ouray had never forgotten those many tents at Washington. Later, many times, he told the People that the white man had enough soldiers to surround the country of the People three times. It was better to live in peace with the white man: to be his friend and try to make him a friend of the People.

On the seat in the rolling, swaying train, going away from Washington with the money they told him was his first pay for being chief of all the Utes, he saw nothing but the life he was going to make and the things he was going to do for the People, with his new friends in Washington. He was going home to the tall mountains.

It was some time, perhaps two snows, after this when the white men came with their tools they said were to measure the land for Washington and the papers that were to be signed. It was then that Ouray learned all about this thing they called a "treaty." The Maricat'z talked with fine words, and he wrote those fine words down. Then he took what he wanted, and he had given away only those fine words.

Still Ouray remembered the long, wide village of tents—the young new forest. It was better to live in peace with the white man. It was better to try to learn to call him friend.

Ouray's carriage slipped around a bend in the road over the dry cottonwood leaves, and overhead the fall wind tossed the half-bare cottonwood branches. Ahead were the buildings of the Los Pinos Agency.

As Ouray's carriage pulled into the agency yard, a group of about a dozen men, standing, some leaning, against the gray, weathered logs of an old stable, looked up. They were all white men; some wore the blue uniforms of soldiers. Several who knew Ouray waved; and one of these was Charles Adams, who, like Ouray, had first learned English as a young man. All of the People knew this man and they called him friend.

A short way off, toward the agency storehouse, stood another group. Most of these were men of the southern bands, but two of them were from White River. One, like Ouray, was dressed in white man's clothes. This was Quinkent, who would be called by his Maricat'z name, Douglas, during the hearing today. Ouray could also see Canávish, piwán to Tsashin, Ouray's sister. Canávish had cut off his hair, for Canávish had lost a son in the fight with the soldiers. Many years ago Ouray had lost a son in a fight with the plains enemy. That son had been captured, and Ouray had never seen him again, although even Washington had tried to find him.

Ouray had sent messages to the White River country to ask the leaders to come to the meetings at Los Pinos. He wondered now whether Nicaagat, Colorow, and some of the others would come. He was not surprised to see that Quinkent had come, for Quinkent was always glad for a chance to talk, especially if he thought some of those who listened would be important men of Washington.

Near the agency house was a hitching rail, shaded by big cottonwoods and a box elder, now giving up many of their dying leaves to the wind and letting through great patches of half-warm sunlight. At this rail Ouray tied his horses. Quinkent watched with bright-eyed interest as Ouray got down from his seat and tied his team.

He found the white men ready to start the meeting. General Hatch moved around briskly, attending to the posting of a guard at the door, seeing whether there were enough chairs inside the stable, where the hearing would be held. Ouray shook Adams' hand. General Hatch shook hands hurriedly and rushed away to talk to one of the others. Ouray also shook hands with Lieutenant Valois, a small man with grayish-dark skin whom Adams explained was going to be legal advisor for the commission. Adams also introduced two others: Mr. Caldwell, who was to write down what was said so that it could be sent to Washington, and Mr. Townsend, whom Adams called the official interpreter.

General Hatch opened the door of the stable and called the others to come in. A young soldier stood stiffly outside the door. The stable, a long room, had been hurriedly swept out. A fire rumbled and shook in the thin stove and already the room was hot. The old smell of horses seeped out of the floor and walls and mixed with the sweet smell of bats. A long table had been placed at one end of the room and behind it were several chairs. Mr. Caldwell, the stenographer, was already sitting down and spreading papers in front of him. Adams sat down and motioned for Ouray to take the chair beside him, and for the first time this morning Adams smiled a brief smile.

The others took their chairs, and General Hatch closed the door and sat down in the chair at the end of the table. The meeting was ready to begin.

There was a short silence—not like the long silences with which the councils open and which are for men to use to put their minds, thoughts, and feelings in order. It was a very short silence, and Adams broke it:

"I move that General Hatch be named chairman of this commission."

"I second the motion," said Lieutenant Valois.

A pencil scratched. Mr. Caldwell was writing, making some strange marks on the paper which were not Maricat'z letters. It was another way of writing, by which a man could take down what people said as fast as they said it.

"Are the Indians of the White River band ready to begin giving their testimony?" asked General Hatch.

"Two are here," answered Ouray.

"Only two?" asked the General. "You mean the others we requested to be here have refused to come?"

"Perhaps they are now on their way," said Ouray, wishing that Washington had sent somebody other than General Hatch for this business.

"You saw them, General," broke in Adams. "Douglas is outside now—and Johnson."

"Douglas?" said General Hatch. "That's Chief Douglas?"

"I pointed him out to you this morning," said Adams, a little impatience creeping into his voice. "Douglas is the first one we wanted to hear, so I move we call him in now. We will probably only have time today to hear him, and perhaps Johnson. I am confident that the others will be here soon."

Adams was not confident of this. Neither was Ouray. Both knew that the white man's way of measuring time out like ground corn, and fitting everything he does into this measured time, was hard for the People to understand; and they saw no good reason for trying to understand it. But both Adams and Ouray were anxious to get on with this business, and Adams knew that, if permitted, General Hatch would take time to make an issue of the others not being here.

"Have the guard call in Chief Douglas," said the General to Lieutenant Valois.

The Lieutenant went and opened the door. His thin voice drifted back to the table. Shortly after the Lieutenant was seated again, Quinkent, head high, strode into the room and stopped before the table, standing very straight.

"I suggest," said Adams, "that we also call in Johnson."

"We are not ready for Johnson's testimony at this time," said General Hatch.

"If you expect him to be here when you are ready for it, I suggest you call him in now."

The General hesitated. He was a man who liked to have even his smallest decisions stand without question.

"Have the guard call in Chief Johnson," he ordered finally.

Again Lieutenant Valois went and opened the door, spoke to the guard, and returned to his seat. Canávish did not come in immediately. It was a long time before the door opened again, and General Hatch tapped the table with his finger while they waited. When Canávish came in he did not come to the table. He went and sat on the floor against the wall at the other end of the room.

"Now we are ready to hear the testimony of this man, Chief Douglas," said General Hatch.

"Just a moment please, General," said Adams. "Let Ouray swear him in—with their own oath."

General Hatch's fingers again pounded the table while Quinkent turned sideways to the commission. He drew forth the feather which carried his name to Sunáwiv and he spoke the oath.

"It will have to be translated," said Lieutenant Valois when Quinkent had finished. "We will have to include it in the record, just as we would our own oath."

Ouray hesitated. It was a long gap between the Old Language and English. After a long while the words began to come.

"There is but one spirit governing the heaven and the earth; He looks down upon me and sees upon earth as well as in heaven. Therefore I cannot speak anything but the truth."

It was hard; it did not sound right in English. It did not say the same thing.

Then Quinkent turned. He looked out over the heads of the men at the table, and his eyes caught a glint from one of the dirty windows under the roof. Quinkent now had begun to speak. Ouray now found the English words he needed, and he interpreted, while Mr. Caldwell made his marks on the paper as each one talked.

It took a long time—all the rest of the morning and part of the afternoon. Quinkent, who loved words, used many. He spoke in the Old Language, and his hand moved in front of him as he told the story, which Ouray had heard many times before—part of it before the trouble at White River.

Quinkent told the story of the Agent, the land, and the People. He told how the Agent had plowed the land and turned the grass under; how he wanted to move their houses and kill their horses; how the Agent had told them that the land was not theirs but had been bought by Washington with blankets and other presents; how the agent had sent lies to Washington and to the papers; and how he had brought in soldiers to put them in chains and kill them.

When Quinkent at last said he was finished he turned and went back to sit on the floor, as a man would in a council when he was finished talking.

"Bring that man back here," snapped General Hatch. "I want to question him."

Ouray called Quinkent back. General Hatch leaned back in his chair, took a long cigar from his pocket and began slicing at the end of it with a little knife. He studied Quinkent; then he shot a question directly at him.

"Did you participate in the massacre?"

There was a silence.

"The General means," said Adams to Ouray, "the killing of the Agent and the employees at the agency."

257

Ouray told Quinkent what the General had said, and Quinkent answered that he knew nothing of that business.

The General asked his second question: did Quinkent know who "massacred" the Agent and his employees?

Quinkent answered that he had been in the storeroom when he heard the shooting. He saw the white women go and hide in the milk house, but he did not tell the others where they had hidden. He only went to his own carniv, where a young man who had been shot in the foot came to him. Quinkent said he took care of this young man.

General Hatch then asked whether Quinkent had taken any part in "plotting the massacre," and Quinkent answered, "No," in English. He added that he had nothing more to say. General Hatch frowned a moment, then waved his hand.

"That will be all."

The General pulled a watch from his pocket and looked at it. "We will not have time for more testimony today. I move we adjourn."

General Hatch looked angry. He did not seem to want the meeting to be over, yet all through the day he had seemed unhappy with this whole business—as though he wanted to push it through to some finish of his own making as soon as possible. Perhaps now General Hatch would go away by himself and Adams and Ouray could have a talk. Ouray could not see this thing as clearly as he thought he should, and he felt the need of a talk with a wise friend.

But that was not the way it happened. When the session was closed, and chairs began scraping on the floor, and Mr. Caldwell was rattling his papers together, General Hatch changed. He was smiling, puffing on his cigar, and making little white-man jokes with Adams, and the two of them went away together, talking and laughing. Quinkent and Canávish went out the door first, and by the time Ouray came out the agency yard was empty, except for Adams and General Hatch, who were walking toward the agency house, where they would have their supper and would sleep tonight.

Ouray stood alone, peering through the bars of sunlight that slanted low through the thinning trees. He was expected to eat with the white men at the agency house and to sleep there to-night; but he stood a long time looking at his carriage before he went to turn his horses into the corral.

Ouray ate at the table quietly, talking only a little—and about nothing in particular—to his friend Agent Stanley. He went to the room he always used when he stayed at the agency, and although the day had been full of painful confusion, he was tired and he slept well.

They opened the next session soon after breakfast. More men had come from White River during the night to talk in the meeting, and when the doors to the stable-room were opened again, four went in and sat on the floor. The commission again gathered behind the table.

Canávish was called. He took his oath from Ouray, then gave his name—both his Maricat'z name and his real name—to the commission. Lieutenant Valois then said, "State in your own way what you know about the trouble at the agency before and during the attack on Agent Meeker."

Canávish gave his answer; Ouray changed the words into the language of the white men.

"I do not know anything except what I knew from the agency."

"Heard from the Agent?" asked Valois, and Ouray passed the words on to Canávish.

"That is exactly what I said," came Canávish's answer through Ouray.

Canávish then began his story:

"One time I was in my house and Agent Meeker came to my house and told me to come here. The Agent told me it was better that I move from here. I answered that I could not move because the government had given us orders to build houses, and I already had my house built. How could I move? The Agent then left for the agency and I returned to my house."

Canávish paused while Ouray translated, and Caldwell's pencil crossed the paper several times, rapidly.

"After the Agent left for the agency I came out of my house and saw them coming with a plow and afterward plowing my land, the site where my house stood and around it. When I saw them plowing, I went to the man who was plowing and asked him why he was plowing there. The man said the Agent ordered him to. I then went to the agency where the Agent was."

Again Canávish stopped talking while the white men took his words from Ouray.

"The Agent was standing outside the house. I told the Agent that it was not right that he should order the men to plow my land. The Agent told me I was always a troublesome man, and it was likely I might come to the calaboose. I told him that I did not know why I should go to prison. I told the Agent that it would be better for another agent to come who was a good man, and was not talking such things. Then I took the Agent by the shoulder and told him that it was better that he should go. Without doing anything else to him—striking him or anything else— I just took him by the shoulder. I was not mad at him. Then I went to my house . . . that is all."

Lieutenant Valois opened the questioning.

"Where were you when Agent Meeker and the employees were killed?"

"I was in my camp."

"How far was that from the agency?"

"Traveling with lodges I could make it in about two days; traveling loosely, without lodges, in about one day."

"What direction from the agency?"

"South, in the direction of mid-day."

General Adams then took up the questioning of Canávish.

"Were you in the fight with the soldiers?"

"No."

"Were any of your sons in the fight?"

"No."

Adams continued questioning Canávish about the fight with the soldiers, about the trouble at the agency, about his sons and his family during the trouble; and Canávish gave back quick, short answers as soon as Ouray translated each question to him: "I was not there. . . . It is not true. . . . I do not know. . . ."

General Hatch shot his questions at Canávish.

"Do you know the names of any of the Indians engaged in the fight at the agency?"

"No."

"Do you know the names of any of the Indians engaged in the fight with the soldiers?"

"No."

"Do you know whether or not there was a fight with the soldiers?"

"No."

"Do you know that the agency was burned up?"

"No."

General Hatch sighed and waved his hand, motioning Canávish back to his seat on the floor. He called for more testimony, and Ouray called Sowówic forward and listened to his oath.

"State in your own way," directed Lieutenant Valois, "if there was any trouble between the Indians and Agent Meeker before the fight with the soldiers took place."

"The whole question was about the land and what the Agent said about our lands," came Sowówic's answer.

"What did he say about the land?"

"The Agent told me that everything we were getting from the agency, such as blankets, shoes, and clothing, were given by the government on account of the purchase of the land, as an equivalent for the purchase of the land—our entire reservation."

Lieutenant Valois began asking about the fight and the talk with the soldiers in camp before the fight. Sowówic told them about when he went to talk to Major Thornburgh with Nicaagat. Then they began asking him about the fight with the soldiers and the trouble at the agency, and Sowówic's answers were like those of Quinkent and Canávish—he knew nothing, saw nothing.

After this questioning had gone on for a long time Adams asked another question—not the kind that had been asked before.

"Was I ever in your tent on the Grand River?" Adams was speaking of the time he came to the camps to take the white women away, and the council he had with the men there.

"No," answered Sowówic.

Adams looked at General Hatch. Hatch looked back at Adams, then he motioned Sowówic away.

When all of the Indians were again sitting in their places on the floor, General Adams said to General Hatch: "The answer to that last question was not true. I was in his tent, and in his tent we held a council which lasted from eleven o'clock at night until six in the morning. Sowówic was present and agreed with the others about what was done; and today he comes here and says he does not know anything. He has not spoken the truth, and I believe that he does not want to speak the truth. I believe that none of them want to speak the truth, and it is therefore unnecessary to go any further. They have refused to mention a single name. I now refer the situation to Ouray, so that he may recommend to us some other course, whereby we can execute the orders of the government. The government wants us to find out who were engaged in the outbreak. If we cannot find out, we had better go home."

Ouray's voice was weary. "I cannot force them to say that which they do not wish to. For that I brought them here—that they might speak for themselves."

Ouray waited for Adams' answer, but he felt that the answer had already come in those words ". . . we had better go home." For a moment Ouray was again swimming in that great gulf between the two peoples—that gulf which was now like an empty ocean of black sky. Ouray, too, was thinking of home.

"Have you no men among those who are here who will speak the truth?" Adams asked.

"Among these, no," answered Ouray. "These are the ones who have come through the whole business."

The shrill voice of Lieutenant Valois cut the air like a bright flash—like a shining, sharp knife.

"No Indian would be safe from his own people, whether implicated or not, who testified against those who were guilty."

Ouray's voice was not so tired when he answered Lieutenant Valois: "Show me an act of law by which a man is compelled to criminate himself."

Valois said no more. Adams had not let his attention be driven from Sowówic and his answers to the questions.

"From my understanding," said Adams, "this man Sowówic had nothing to do with it, and unless he wanted to tell the truth he ought not to have taken the oath."

"He took the oath because he was ordered to," said Ouray.

"He said no to everything when he ought to have said yes, according to the truth. . . ." Then quickly Adams' thoughts seemed to drop Sowówic. He had some papers in his hand, and now he looked at them.

"I wish now," he said, "to offer the commission the testimony which I took at Greeley, Colorado, of the ladies who were captives. It was given under oath, and in our law the testimony of a woman is as good as that of a man, when given under oath."

"How is that under Ute law?" Hatch asked Ouray.

"The oath of a woman is almost worthless among my people." Ouray answered. "However, I am willing to have the testimony of the women read to me, and will reserve my objections until after I shall have heard it."

Adams began reading the testimony of Mrs. Price, the wife of the carpenter. It had been long, the talk he had with her at Greeley, and the reading took a long time. Adams read his own questions and the answers given by Mrs. Price. She had said a great deal about the trouble at the agency, but Adams had found it necessary to ask many questions before she would give the names of the Ute men she saw that day. She told of her captivity, and it was something about "outrages" that Adams seemed particularly interested in talking about.

He read:

Q. Did any of the Utes treat you badly or strike you?
A. No; none of them struck me.
Q. What did they do?
A. I do not like to say. You know them, of course, and can judge.
Q. This is an official investigation. I can not guess these things. It is your place to state, in order that we may know the extent of the crime, and who the guilty parties are.
A. It will not be made public in the papers, will it?
Q. Certainly not through this commission.
A. Well, this Uncompahgre Ute and Johnson outraged me.
Q. Johnson, the old man himself?

A. Yes, sir, the old man himself.

Q. Did any others outrage you?

A. Those two were all. . . . Johnson tried to make me believe that they would let Mrs. Meeker go, but would not let Josie and me go, and the children. . . . There is nothing further I wish to state; only I want to have those Utes taken and killed, and I want to have the privilege of killing Johnson and that Uncompahgre Ute myself.

Adams finished the reading of Mrs. Price's testimony. At the other end of the room a thin cloud of smoke hovered above the still, silent ring of men on the floor; they seemed far away from these words Adams had read from his paper. They might have been sitting around a monte blanket at a game ground or around a fire in some hunting camp, far from this stable, from this agency, from these Maricat'z. These were the People of the White River; the Nüpartka of Smoking Earth River, the People who lived in a tall, deep land and who would always be far away from such words, who would not understand or care to try.

The session was adjourned.

The commission assembled for the third day. Angry lines had hardened around General Hatch's mouth and eyes, and tired streaks had formed overnight in Adams' face. The business of the session was begun immediately. General Hatch asked Ouray whether he had any suggestions about further testimony, and how they might find out "the truth."

"I can do no more than I have, at present," Ouray said. "The Indians will not testify any more. If you give me time, say two or three months, I can find out the guilty ones and punish them."

"If we give you this time," said Hatch, "will you accompany us in the meantime to Rawlins to hear the evidence of the officers and soldiers?"

"No," said Ouray without hesitating. "I will go to Washington but nowhere else."

"Do you mean you prefer to go to Washington to settle these difficulties?" asked Hatch.

"Yes. I want to take other chiefs and go to Washington to talk over this matter. I know the Indians will not say any thing here, but believe they will speak the truth at Washington."

"How many chiefs do you want to go?"

"I think eight of the principal chiefs will be enough."

General Hatch picked up a pencil and began writing. When he had finished, he turned to Ouray. "I have written here," he said, "a dispatch to the Secretary of the Interior. I will read it for your approval:

" 'Chief Ouray this morning asks for time and believes it is in the interest of the government to take to Washington such chiefs as we may designate, not to exceed ten, including some of the White River chiefs. In the meantime, we will take such testimony as we can obtain here and elsewhere.' "

Ouray listened and approved the message to his friend in Washington, Secretary Schurz. General Hatch asked Adams to continue with the testimony of the women, and Adams began reading the statement of Mrs. Meeker, also taken at Greeley.

The story was much the same as that of Mrs. Price. Mrs. Meeker told of that day at the agency and of the time she had lived with the White River People. Again the word "outrage" was read:

" 'It was made known to me that if I did not submit I would be killed or subjected to something of that kind. . . . the women made all the motions of making a fire and burning me, and running in my way, and everything of that kind. . . . Douglas himself had not notified me that I would have to submit but all the rest had. His children said I had to be Ute squaw that night, and used indecent language. . . . I said I was going to wait for Douglas, he had taken me. I expect he wanted to have everything ready for him. I was made to understand I was to submit when he came. . . . Douglas I had connection with once, and no more; I was afraid he had disease. . . . Douglas told me to stay in his tent, and I stayed there. I was not going to be driven away by any of them. I did not know but that I should be nearly killed, but I got along in that respect better than the rest of them. . . . The children were cross, and all of them were cross. I do not know that his wife ever spoke to me. . . .' "

When the reading of Mrs. Meeker's testimony was ended, General Hatch asked whether there were more to testify today. Except for the white men and Ouray at the long table, the stable room was empty. Ouray rose and went to the door. He stepped outside a moment, and when he returned a line of men followed and formed their circle on the floor. There were those who had already been questioned: Canávish, Quinkent, Sowówic. Then there was another who had not been in the stable before. This was the man Ouray now called forward to speak the oath.

"State your name and what nation you belong to," sang Valois.

The huge, square face turned, the black eyes, under heavy eyelids, taking in face after face at the table.

"Colorow of the Nüpartka Utes," came the translation.

General Hatch began explaining this meeting and what the white men were trying to find out about the trouble at the agency and the fight with the soldiers. Colorow looked very solemn and wise.

Then he spoke, and Ouray changed his words into English: "I do not know how this thing came about. All of you ought to know better than I the reason the Agent asked for soldiers to come to the agency."

"Agent Meeker is dead," said General Hatch. "He cannot say; therefore I want you to tell for what reason he asked for troops."

"I know nothing about the agency troubles at all," came Colorow's words. "I understand about Jack."

"Let him go ahead and tell what he knows about that," Adams broke in, before Hatch could form another question.

Colorow began with his visit to the camp of the soldiers and his talk with the general. He told of the fight, and how the white worker came with the paper from Ouray and another paper for the soldiers, and the fighting was over.

"Many said it was very much like a fight between two drunken men who, when someone came and parted them, found that they had been fighting for nothing but foolishness," Colorow finished. "General Adams has been an agent of ours and is at this time an officer of the United States; General Hatch is also a high officer of the United States. You, Ouray, also are an officer over us, sent to settle this trouble and to part us who have foolishly gone to fighting; and I ask you all, what more can we do?"

Colorow had worn a sad and sorry look throughout the telling of his story. Now as he finished he looked humbly from one to another, and his eyes looked as though he were suffering great pain. The commission was silent. Even General Hatch seemed impressed, and had trouble bringing the properly severe expression back to his face.

Adams began questioning Colorow.

"Do you know that the Agent refused Jack and his people rations?"

"He never gave them any rations, that I know of," answered Colorow sadly.

"Did he ever issue them any goods?"

Colorow shook his great head in the manner of the white men. He was having no trouble understanding the questions, and this was apparent to all members of the commission, but he waited for Ouray to translate them and he answered in his own language.

"The Agent had made the women ashamed to come by his refusal to give them anything," came Colorow's answer through

Ouray. "It is a shame for a man who has anything to send his women to ask where they will be refused."

"What is your opinion:" asked Adams, "would there have been a fight if the troops had taken the main road?"

"If they had gone the main road I think there would have been a great difference in the way it turned out. Jack would have then been able to have met and talked with the general as he intended. I think there would have been no fight."

General Hatch seemed displeased with this line of questioning, and he tried to show his displeased face to Adams: but Adams was again shuffling papers in his hand.

"This is the last of the women's testimony," he said when Colorow was again seated on the floor. "This is the statement of Josephine Meeker, taken by me at Greeley; I will read it in full and it will be translated to those Utes present."

Adams began reading the words of the daughter of the Agent. Again the story of the trouble at the agency and of the captivity of the women unfolded—of the dreary days in the Ute camps and of "outrageous treatment at night."

" 'Pah-sone asked me the day before you [Adams] came what I was going to tell about the Utes. He said, "You go back and tell them that Utes are no good." I said no, I should not. . . . [About the outrages] we told Mr. Pollock when he interviewed us, and also Dr. Avery, a lady physician in Denver; of course we don't want the newspapers to get hold of it. . . . The Indians delight in telling such things. . . . you know how low they are.' "

Then: " 'I do not know that I can give you as correct a list as I gave Mr. Pollock, because I have forgotten. . . .' "

The sun was low and the room was filled with a bloody light when Adams finished. After another short silence, General Hatch pulled out his watch and frowned at it.

"We haven't much time," he said. "This session is away overtime now. But I want you to read off those names, Adams. . . . These are the names given by the women. These are the men whom they saw during the massacre and who mistreated them during their captivity."

Adams read the first name: "Chief Douglas."

The second: "Johnson."

Canávish sat and smoked his pipe; he gave no indication that he had heard his Maricat'z name. Quinkent sat frozen, staring at nothing.

There were more names: ten more. Adams read them off slowly. There was Pásone, who had taken the daughter of the Agent for his piwán. There were the old men who had stayed at the agency because they wanted neither to go to the fight nor go with the women's camp.

"This commission," said General Hatch, "will determine the extent of the guilt of these twelve men and will also determine if any more were involved. For that reason we are making no recommendations now as to the administration of justice."

Ouray thought he could see a hint of a smile on the General's face, but the hard lines hid it well. He thought of that other time he had looked at that face across a council table; when he had been able to say to him, "No," and again, "No," and the General had to give up and go home. He shot a glance at Lieutenant Valois, who was smiling openly.

Then Ouray spoke: "You say one time, General Hatch, that Ute Tribe is a nation. You say that when you are here trying to get some land from us. Now I say that the law of our nation does not accept the testimony of women."

General Hatch again turned his eyes toward Lieutenant Valois, but he turned them slowly this time, with an anxious question.

"Members of the Ute Tribe are wards of the United States," said the little legal adviser. "If they are to be considered, as you suggest, a separate nation, they may only be considered as a conquered nation."

"If we are a conquered nation, who has conquered us?" Ouray waited for an answer, but none came.

"You say the law of your nation, Lieutenant Valois," Ouray continued. "That is what you are on this commission for. I am here to represent the Ute People, and I say the law of my nation."

The red light of the old sun was leaving the room—drying dark, like old blood. Shadows filled the corners and blurred the faces of the white men; and a last strong ray caught the cloud of smoke above the circle.

"This session is adjourned," said General Hatch.

Lamps were being lit in the agency house as the members of the commission walked through the twilight toward their supper. Under the shadows of the big trees, a carriage, pulled by a pair of blacks, rolled down the road and toward the broad valley of the river the white man calls the Uncompahgre because he can not say the real word.

« III »

Ouray had come back. He rode in from the big valley when the morning fires were going to smoke. He sat high on the great buckskin horse that he once rode all the time, before Washington bought him the handsome pair of blacks that pulled his fine buckboard. There was no hat on his head; his black hair clung close to his massive skull and was smoothed down and greased, so that it shone in the sun. A long hawk feather swept down to his shoulder from the great silver sun in his hair, and the early morning sunlight found many colors in the thick beadwork of his buckskin suit.

For several days the white members of the commission had met in the old stable, discussed some routine matters, and adjourned. Ouray was absent. "Because of illness," the record said.

The hearings had been further delayed because one of the most important of the witnesses had not arrived at Los Pinos. This was Captain Jack, who was said to know more about the cause of the trouble and the fight with the soldiers than any other of the people from White River. This same day, it was learned, Jack had arrived.

Ouray dismounted, tied his horse, and walked toward the stable. The few men, the faces of the commission, chattered like a flock of well-fed crows around the door. Down at the other corner of the stable, standing close together as though to collect the warmth of their bodies against the cold wind, was a little group of men from Smoking Earth River. A head and a pair of wide shoulders stood above the group. This was Nicaagat, whom the Maricat'z called Jack.

As Ouray moved closer to the stable, General Hatch looked up and nodded once. Adams also looked up, smiled, and put out his hand to Ouray. Hatch was looking over the group at the other end of the building. He said to Ouray:

"Are all those men going to be sitting around in here today? All of them have already testified, except that big one."

"Those men came to this place to speak," said Ouray. "Some have already spoken, so they have come to listen. They are all part of this council." He turned to Adams.

General Hatch jerked open the stable door and mumbled something about getting started and getting this over. Ouray and Adams went in together, talking, followed by Lieutenant Valois, Townsend, Caldwell, and the men from Smoking Earth River. Hatch stood at the open door and his eyes followed each of the White River men through the door and across the room. He eyed the circle that was forming on the floor, then he closed the door and took his seat at the table.

Ouray was the last to take his seat. He crossed in front of the long table and went directly to the circle of the People.

Papers rustled at the table. Hatch muttered something to Adams, then drew a cigar from his pocket and pinched at the tip of it with his cigar cutter.

Then the paper-rustling, the talking, and the cigar-cutting stopped, and for a brief moment the room was still. Hatch laid his cigar between his teeth, lit it in the silence, puffed on it, and declared the session opened. Blowing out a long plume of smoke, he called for the next man to testify.

Some talk went around the circle on the floor, then Nicaagat and Ouray stood up together and came forward. Nicaagat turned sideways, pointed his feather, and recited the oath:

"There is but one spirit governing the heaven and the earth; He looks down upon me and sees upon the earth as well as in the heavens. Therefore I cannot speak anything but the truth."

"I want Jack to tell his story," said General Hatch, settling back in his chair. "How the Agent treated him, and all about the troubles at White River."

Nicaagat began the story. He began with his first meeting with Agent Meeker, at the site of the old agency, and he told of the talk they had then about the moving of the agency. Then he told what he knew, what he had seen, of the work at the new agency—the plowing, the fencing, the planting, the school.

"The great trouble with the Agent was that he would tell one story one day and another the next, so that we did not know how to take him or when to believe him."

He then told about the fires: about the time he was called to the Agent's house and the Agent told him about the burning of the houses on Bear River. After that, his visit to the store and what the storeman told him about the letters that had come to the store from the Agent; that these letters were on their way to Denver and Washington and they told many bad things about the People, how they set fires in the trees and were bad to the white settlers. These were the same stories told by the newspapers, and the storeman had urged Nicaagat to go to Denver and see the Governor.

He told them about the house of Thompson, which the Agent had said was burned, and which he saw was not burned.

"On arriving at Middle Park," he said, "we found the same reports about fires and such things that I had heard on Bear River. I then said we had better hurry up and get to Denver to see how things were there. Upon arriving in Denver I was very anxious to see the Governor before going anywhere else. Several men told me that they could not bring me to where the Governor was, but that it took a man of influence to do so; and some told me that Mr. Byers could take me to the Governor."

Nicaagat repeated, through Ouray, all the details of his two days in Denver and his talks with the Governor; how he left the Governor's office with the promise that the Governor would write the next day to Washington and get another agent for White River.

"I then returned to White River. When I arrived I went down to the agency, and the Agent received me by asking me what business I had running around, and what business took me to Denver. I informed him that I had seen papers in which he had given information about things that were not happening. He answered, 'Is it your business to go around finding out what I have written?'"

Nicaagat told them about this talk and about another talk
he had with the Agent a few days later. This one was about the
plowing of the land where those who stayed with Quinkent had
their houses.

"The houses were fenced in, corrals were built there, and yet
he wanted them moved. So he told me that all the site which he
had given the Utes for their houses he now wanted for himself
and for the agency."

Lieutenant Valois broke in: "Were any of the men excited
at that time about the agency?"

"No, not yet," Nicaagat answered. "They asked to what part
he wished them moved, and he told them above and below. On
my arrival the Agent told me a shot had been fired at one of the
employees, which went very close to him. I asked Henry Jim if
this were true, and Henry Jim said, 'Tatit'z was firing at a mark.'
I told the Agent that they were firing at a mark, and he said no,
they were threatening by firing. I told him not to get angry about
this; to let it pass by. I told him he was an employee of the government and that his business was to keep peace. I told him he
was getting old, and consequently got mad quickly; then I left."

Nicaagat went on, telling all the details, all the things that
happened which led him to decide to go to Fort Steele to talk
to the soldiers. He was telling about seeing the soldiers and the
sheriff from Snake River at Peck's store, when General Hatch
stopped him and asked that the session be ended. It was near
sundown.

The following morning the commission assembled at the
table quickly, apparently eager to hear the rest of Nicaagat's
story. Ouray again took his seat with the men on the floor, then
rose with Nicaagat and stood in front of the table.

Speaking through Ouray, Nicaagat began again:

"I asked the soldiers where they were camped. They told
me about two miles above. They told me I better go see the commanding officer. I told them all right, I go. I told them to go on
ahead and I would follow. I told the others with me that perhaps
the officer knew what brought him here, and would probably
tell me."

Nicaagat then repeated his words with that general who was

now dead, Major Thornburgh: what he told the Major about war, and what the Major himself had said about war, and how they agreed to meet later, before the soldiers came onto the reservation, and talk again. Then he told how that meeting failed, and the fight came.

He told his story up to the end of the fighting, when the white man came with the paper from Ouray, and they quit shooting and made a white flag. How they left that place, and the soldiers followed them, into their own country.

"I have nothing more to say," he finished at last.

General Hatch leaned forward and eyed Nicaagat. The long story, told through two mouths in two languages, had already taken most of the second day. Now Caldwell, who had written it all down, was flexing his tired fingers. General Hatch was ready with his questions.

"How many Indians in the fight with the soldiers?"

"Perhaps about fifty," Nicaagat answered in English.

"Were there any Uintah Indians there?"

"I think there were some there."

"Were there any Uncompahgre Utes there?"

Nicaagat hesitated. Questions like these were always among those asked after a man finished telling his story. There had been a great deal of talk among the People in the camps about these councils and what the Maricat'z were trying to do. The Maricat'z had said many times that in this trouble there were some bad Indians who must be found out and punished; but after the talks began the Maricat'z kept asking questions which tried to make a man say that all the People were bad and should be punished.

Nicaagat answered, "No."

"Weeminuches or Capotes?"

"At White River," Nicaagat answered, "Weeminuches and Capotes are hardly known." These bands lived far to the south.

General Hatch's eyes again probed Nicaagat's face, as though he were certain he would find his next question there.

"Did you tell Major Thornburgh when you talked with him that if he entered the reservation with his troops there would be a fight?"

"No," Nicaagat answered.

"Did you and the Ute warriors leave at the same time when they went to meet the soldiers at Milk Creek, and got into the fight with them?"

Nicaagat answered this in his own language. The words came through Ouray: "We did not start out together. The 'warriors,' as you call them, started out afterward."

"I wish to know," said General Hatch, "if you know who killed Meeker and the employees."

"No, I do not. The Indians had all scattered."

General Hatch waved his hand and Nicaagat went back and sat in the circle with his friends. The familiar darkness was creeping into the stable. This time it was the chill, blue dusk that made the country ready for new snow. A pool of darkness gathered in the center of the floor, and the circle was marked only by patches of light buckskin and slashes and tiny points of white beadwork. A black head with three round silver disks at one side of it nodded slowly, and a feather of smoke rose toward the ceiling.

Hatch's face, still white with the light from the dirty windows, moved. His mouth opened.

"This session is adjourned," he called out. The two groups of men stood up and seemed to melt together. They filed out through the door into the brighter dusk outside.

The next day a thin line of white faces formed along the table in the meeting room. The stable was again empty, except for those white men who sat down to the meeting table. There were no Indians there, and a few minutes after the session met it was adjourned. The names of those who met were listed on the record, which said: "Absent, Chief Ouray of the Ute Nation."

It was nearing the time when the sun passes close to death, when the white men believe Sunáwiv-ta'wat'z was born on earth. For many days the snow had covered the high country of the Smoking Earth River, but down in the valley of the Uncompahgre, where the warm weather stays long after the sun has gone into the south, there had been no snow yet. Now, when the night was black enough, a few white flakes sprinkled into the air. The stars were gone, but the snow came to take away some of the blackness.

In the morning a white land shone back at the weakening
sun. The trees began to drip, and blobs of wet snow thumped to
the ground. Down below the agency and the stable where the
hearing would begin again soon, the Uncompahgre River flowed
black between white banks.

They came out from the agency house and from the village
on the river, walking through the clean air, kicking their feet in
the thin skin of new snow. The stable door was open and heated
air rippled out into the morning.

The men took their seats: the white members of the commission at the table, Ouray and the men from White River in their
circle on the floor. As soon as everyone was in place, General
Hatch opened the session by asking for any further testimony.

No answer came. Every man in the room had, at some time
or other during the long days of this hearing, told his story. The
men from Smoking Earth River were tired of talking and they
had nothing more to say. They had told that to the Maricat'z
already, many times. The white men at the table, too, were tired
of talking; they wanted to go home.

General Adams spoke: "Chief Ouray, before the Indians give
their final answer I wish to speak a few words to them, and ask
you to do me the favor of translating my words to them."

"All right," said Ouray.

Adams stood up so that he could look down into the middle
of the circle on the floor. Most of them would understand his
words as he spoke them, although Ouray's translation would
make certain that all of what he said would be understood by
all of the men.

Adams looked around the circle. He knew all of these men.
Most of them he respected, and some of them he admired. They
all knew him as their friend, although at this moment Adams felt
very keenly the growing distrust among them of all members of
the Maricat'z Nation, all people of his race. He thought a
moment, trying to choose his words well, feeling now a great
responsibility to the people of two races.

The circle on the floor was wider today, although the men sat
close together, as though they were trying to form a tight, solid
band. The men of White River were there: Jack, Colorow,

Douglas, Sowówic, Acarí, Johnson. There were also some there
from the people of the Uncompahgre, including the two chiefs
Shavanó and Sapavanero.

"When I first came to your camp on Grand River," Adams
began slowly, "and after the white prisoners had been delivered
to me, I sat with you for a whole night in council, and you asked
me whether there was a way by which further fighting could be
avoided. I told you that the government would demand as
prisoners such of you as had been guilty of barbarous and
treacherous warfare; it might be possible that the government
would cease further fighting.

"You heard these, my words, and all of you made speeches
assuring me that you wanted peace, and asked me to go to White
River and stop, if possible, further advance of the troops. I went
there and sent a long telegram to Washington, representing your
side of the trouble, and the result has been that this commission
has come here to hear your testimony, and have such Indians
turned over to the government as may be identified as having
been engaged in bad work.

"We have been here now a month; have patiently waited
from day to day and week to week for your arrival and for your
explanations and have kept away in the meanwhile the troops
from your reservation, hoping and expecting that this trouble
could be settled without war. Some of you have come here and
have told a straightforward story, and we are well-informed as
to the causes of the trouble from your standpoint, and have heard
all the particulars of the fight with the soldiers; and while I think
that if the chiefs had exerted their influence better, the fight and
the subsequent murders might have been averted, still I consider
this part more the action of a lot of crazy and hotheaded young
men than the result of a preconcerted plan; and while the action
of these men may be overlooked by the government, I cannot
excuse the action of those cowardly dogs who went to the agency
and shot from the roofs of the houses, like birds from trees, the
white men who were not dreaming of danger, and who certainly
had given the Indians no cause to be killed, even if you will have
it so that Agent Meeker deserved death at your hands.

"What reason did there exist to kill those men that all un-

277

conscious of danger were driving teams to the agency, bringing you the very provisions and goods which the government furnishes you for the friendship it has towards you? This was willful murder, and you cannot expect the government to overlook it.

"If I or any other white man commit a crime against the laws, we expect to be followed and captured and tried by a jury of twelve men, who shall say whether we are guilty or not. If we defy arrest, the whole power of our state or government will be turned against us.

"In that position some of your people are today, and as we have been unable to learn from you the names of those that are guilty, we have been obliged to accept the testimony of the captive women, who saw these men named on the list, besides others whose names they do not know, with rifles in their hands before and after the killing; and myself and General Hatch now present that list to you so that those whose names are thereon be surrendered to us, so that they may be tried and punished if found guilty. I do not say that these men are guilty, but I do say that in absence of testimony from you we consider that there exists cause enough for us to demand these men for trial.

"Every man will have the right to be confronted with his accusing witness, and it may be that these captives, when confronted with these men, may fail to identify some of them; but with that we cannot now lose further time, and must ask for those as now implicated by that testimony.

"I will now further inform you that you cannot afford to refuse this demand of the government, for the people of this country would not support its government if it should not insist on this condition for peace; and I know that if we should leave here with your refusal, in a short time troops would come here and from all sides the guilty ones would be hunted down like wolves on the prairie or rabbits in their holes. You cannot afford to go to war with a nation of forty millions."

Ouray waited until Adams had finished to interpret the speech. He talked longer than Adams, for the language of the People uses more words than the language of the Maricat'z. At the end Ouray told Adams he did not think it was necessary to mention about going to war with the nation of forty million,

Poles leaning against a living tree are all that remain of a historic Ute wickiup structure in the Hogback Wickiup Village near Rifle, Colorado. Photo ca. 1980 in the collection of Andrew Gulliford.

Kenny Frost and Alvin Pintecoose, former Northern Ute Sun Dance Chief, study ancient pictographs and gather red, black, and yellow clay in sacred Shield Cave on the Western Slope. Photo July 1993 by Andrew Gulliford.

Shield Cave is so named because of numerous sacred shields painted in red on the cave's walls. The cave is now protected with restricted access, but time and weather will eventually deteriorate the images on the walls. For the Utes this is as it should be, and paintings made by a medicine man generations ago will fade as part of a natural cycle. Photo July 1993 by Andrew Gulliford.

The prehistoric and historic Ute Trail still exists between the Colorado River and the White River with a trailhead on Bureau of Land Management land near Dotsero. This view of the trail from the Flat Tops looks southeast towards the confluence of the Eagle and Colorado Rivers. Photo July 1995 by Andrew Gulliford.

Trappers Lake and the smaller lakes near it have long been special places to the Northern Utes whose ancestors lived there, knew the plants and the animals, and sung songs to keep everything in harmony. Photo August 1997 by Andrew Gulliford.

View of the Chinese Wall in the Flat Tops near Trapper's Lake. Utes would hunt the ridgetops during the day and return to camp at night. Photo in the collection of Andrew Gulliford.

As they have for generations, the northern Utes still have traditional gathering areas on the White River National Forest for harvesting special plants. Photo August 1997 by Andrew Gulliford.

Chief Ouray and his wife Chipeta met with white settlers at the Ute council cottonwood tree, which dates back to the 1880s, in Delta, Colorado. Chipeta was said to have been the only Ute woman permitted to sit in council meetings. A Ute trail from the Uncompahgre Plateau to Grand Mesa passed nearby. Photo September 1997 by Andrew Gulliford.

Low-lying stones mark an ancient vision quest site high on the Flat Tops Mountains. Utes who visit here leave offerings for the spirits and eagles have been known to fly low over this site. Photo August 1995 by Andrew Gulliford.

Clifford Duncan, Betsy Chapoose, and Kenny Frost on an archaeological reconnaissance survey of the White River National Forest sponsored by U.S.F.S. heritage manager Bill Kight. Photo August 1997 by Andrew Gulliford.

Southern Ute Kenny Frost works with other Ute tribal leaders to identify and preserve sacred sites and plant gathering areas on historic Ute lands now included in the White River National Forest. Here he holds large leaves of sacred Indian tobacco. Photo August 1997 by Andrew Gulliford.

since Ouray had said this same thing many times, and all the Utes understood it fully.

"Well, it is not necessary to say anything further," Adams said wearily. "I can only say, in conclusion, that I have come here as your friend, that nothing short of our demand will be accepted by the government, and that I hope you understand the situation fully."

One by one, the men on the floor spoke, the soft muted sounds of the ancient tongue rising like the sound of water. Each said only a little, and Adams listened to the tone—to the few Ute words he could understand. He felt that they had received his talk well, in the spirit in which it had been given, and were considering what he had said carefully.

But before the Indians had finished the discussion among themselves, General Hatch was on his feet; his voice came like the taste of metal on the tongue.

"You must now listen to what I have to say!"

He brought both hands down hard, flat on the table. He looked up and down the room, waiting for the silence his voice demanded.

"This is the decision of the government, and if complied with will prevent the final struggle with the Indians, which must, in the end, result in their utter destruction, forfeiture of all their treaty rights, and loss of their lands. As yet, only Chief Douglas and Johnson have come to the commission, of all the Indians who were suspected of the massacre of the agency people. Against them we have the evidence of the women belonging to the agency. I have come here, leaving my troops, with the understanding that the Indians found or supposed to be guilty of those murders would be surrendered and held for trial by jury. Of the Indians engaged in the fight with the soldiers there is no clear and sufficient proof of the individuals. Douglas, who is the acknowledged chief of the nation, must be held responsible, and he and the cowardly murderers of the agency people, who did the Indians no harm, should suffer.

"You know as well as I do that by surrendering these cowardly murderers you now have an opportunity to preserve the tribe, and it is better that these bad men should suffer the penalty of

the law, which upon conviction is death, than that the entire
tribe should suffer.

"We therefore demand that the following men be turned
over for trial, as the only way now offered to settle this trouble;
and it now remains with the Indians to comply with this demand.
They are as follows, from the list now held in my hands: Chief
Douglas, Chief Johnson, Wausitz (Antelope), Ebenezer, Pásone,
Ahuutupuwit, Johnny (son-in-law of Douglas), Serio, Crepah,
Tim Johnson, Thomas (a Uintah), Paruitz (Pauvit'z).

"I am now done, and await your answer."

Ouray translated, and when he finished no sound came from
the circle. Their eyes seemed to meet at a point in the center of
the circle, and the round band seemed to be drawing in tighter
and closer.

There was nothing but empty floor in the center of the circle,
yet all their eyes seemed fixed there.

Then, suddenly, something was there. The men stared at it,
lying on the bare splintery boards in the center. It was a knife
and it belonged to Colorow. He had laid it there, and now he
brought his stone pipe out from inside his shirt and laid it beside
the knife.

Each man around the circle brought out his own knife and
laid it in the center. One by one the pipes came out, and were
laid down beside the knives.

All the talk was finished. The time for decision had come. The
knife is war; the pipe is peace. There were no words.

The circle on the floor was no longer merely a ring of men. It
had become in itself a single thing: the great world-circle, the
Nation's sacred hoop.

The room was very still: even the fire in the stove no longer
popped and snapped. Outside the sun moved a little and shot a
slanting ray through the window, and the blades gleamed and
the white stone of the pipes lay like bones on dry, hot ground.

The straight line of men along the table was stiff and still.
They seemed not to be breathing. Each knew, separately, what
could happen if the knives were lifted from the center. There
were many Indians now at Los Pinos, and the white men
were few.

There was a motion in the circle. It was Ouray's hand that shot out, alone, and grasped his knife. Then his arm jerked; the knife thumped, point-first, into the soft wood of the floor.

Ouray was standing up, walking slowly toward the table. He looked into the frozen white faces. His own face gave nothing and asked for nothing.

"You are waiting for our answer," he said. "I will now give it." The eyes before him never moved.

"You, the Maricat'z, and Washington. You want our land; you want our country. You have tried before to get our country away from us, and us from it. You have tried to get it in pieces; you are now trying to get it all.

"We will not leave our country. We will fight. We will go back into our mountains and we will fight your forty millions. Our mountains will drive you away; you will die in our mountains."

He looked straight at Adams. "You, General Adams, were once my friend. Now you are my enemy." He turned to Hatch. "You, General Hatch, are my enemy. You, who have been here before with your commissions, trying to drive my people out with your talk and your lies."

His eyes swept the table again. "You are all my enemies, you five white men—no, four white men and one brown-faced little Frenchman. I have shaken hands with all of you and called you 'friend,' but you are my enemies.

"All of the people of Colorado and New Mexico are our enemies. We will not give these twelve men over to you to be tried by a court of Colorado, where no justice will be shown them. We will give over these men only if they can be tried in Washington, where I know I have at least one friend."

Ouray turned and walked back to his seat on the floor. Knives and pipes were put away. At the table chairs scraped and creaked as the white men let their tense bodies relax back into them. Slowly, quietly, fear left the room, to hover just outside, close by.

General Hatch found his voice again: "I have sent a message to your friend Secretary Schurz, asking that you and some other chiefs be allowed to testify in Washington. I will dispatch another, informing him of your latest request." 281

There was a long council in the circle of Indians. The white men waited, still tense and uncertain. At last two of the men got up from the floor and left the room.

Ouray said, "Two men, Jack and Colorow, have gone to bring in those you demand; but we will not give them up until we hear the decision of Secretary Schurz."

"The session is adjourned, then," said General Hatch, "pending the decision of the Secretary of the Interior."

« IV »

The rest is the story of process; the ritual adopted by the young nation during the first century of its life—ritual dedicated to that god they worshipped and gave the name of Progress.

The land held wealth, and that wealth belonged to any man who found it and was willing to devote his life and his soul to claiming it. There were obstacles, and these must be removed; and sometimes the process of removal was maddeningly slow. But performed properly the ritual guaranteed fulfillment. A man must have faith.

Just two days after Chief Ouray gave the answer of the Ute Nation to the commission at Los Pinos, the first dispatch was received from Secretary Schurz in Washington. The Secretary congratulated General Hatch and the commission on the "success achieved" and promised to lay Ouray's proposal that the hearings be continued in Washington before the Cabinet the following morning, then advise the commission of the decision.

The decision of the Cabinet was swift. On the following day General Hatch received another telegram from Secretary Schurz:

RECEIVE SURRENDER OF THE INDIANS DESIGNATED BY YOUR
COMMISSION WITH THE UNDERSTANDING THAT THEY WILL BE
GUARANTEED A FAIR TRIAL BY A MILITARY COMMISSION OUTSIDE
OF COLORADO AND NEW MEXICO. INFORM OURAY THAT HE WILL
BE RECEIVED HERE WITH FOUR OR FIVE UNCOMPAHGRES, THREE
SOUTHERN UTES, AND THREE WHITE RIVER UTES. TAKE CARE
THAT GOOD AND INFLUENTIAL MEN BE SELECTED, ESPECIALLY

FROM THE WHITE RIVER UTES. IT WILL PROBABLY BE DESIRABLE
TO HAVE JACK HERE. TAKE POSSESSION OF THE PRISONERS WITH
A MILITARY GUARD TO CONVEY THEM, IN THE FIRST PLACE, TO
FORT LEAVENWORTH.

CARL SCHURZ

But all of the decision made in Washington was not con-
tained in this telegram. Another dispatch came to General Hatch
from Secretary Schurz the same day. This one was marked
"CONFIDENTIAL."

IT IS PREFERRED NOT TO BRING THE PRISONERS TO WASH-
INGTON FOR TRIAL. FORT LEAVENWORTH WOULD IN MANY
RESPECTS BE MORE CONVENIENT. TRY TO ARRANGE IT SO, BUT IF
IT IS ESSENTIAL TO PROCURE THE SURRENDER, YOU MAY CONSENT
TO HAVE THEM BROUGHT FOR TRIAL TO THE DEPARTMENT OF
THE EAST, IN WHICH WASHINGTON IS SITUATED, IN WHICH CASE
THE TRIAL MIGHT BE HAD AT FORTRESS MONROE.

CARL SCHURZ

Since the main provision in Ouray's proposal was that the
accused Utes be tried in Washington, General Hatch and the
white members of the commission took great care that the information in this confidential dispatch not get into the hands of
Ouray or the other Indians. But as subsequent meetings were
held in the stable to arrange for the coming Washington hearing
and to accept the surrender of those Indians demanded for trial,
all the Indians began to show a mysterious reluctance to surrender the "guilty" ones. Even those of the White River chiefs
who were to testify at the hearings in Washington were hesitant
about appearing before the commission again.

Ouray made a trip to the camp of the White River Utes. Jack,
he reported upon his return to Los Pinos, had refused to go either
to Los Pinos or to Washington, although, Ouray told the commission, Sowówic and Colorow had joined him in trying to convince Jack that the trip to Washington was for his own good and
for the People's best interest. There were rumors that Jack was
gathering his followers to go through Utah to the Shoshoni
country and join Sitting Bull and the Sioux.

283

Ouray again visited the White River camp and came back with Sowówic. Still none of the accused White River men had surrendered.

All of the white members of the commission loaded their belongings and went on to a ranch on the Cimarron River, where they had agreed to meet with Ouray and the other Indians for the trip to Washington. It was the day after Christmas, and the mountain passes between Los Pinos and the Eastern Slope were filling up with snow.

Two days later Ouray arrived at the ranch on the Cimarron with a small band of White River and Southern Ute leaders. None of the "guilty" men on General Hatch's list were among them, except Douglas, who had come believing that he would go to Washington to talk at the hearings, not go on trial.

General Hatch was angry and disappointed. He first wanted to go back to the Los Pinos Agency and try to capture the fugitives. Ouray advised him against it, saying that there was too much snow in the San Juan country now, and that General Hatch might find himself snowbound there until spring. Ouray said he believed that those whom Washington wanted to put on trial had gone hunting toward the La Sal Mountains, in southeastern Utah. General Hatch knew then that it was hopeless to try to capture them. No posse, no army, no matter how large and well-equipped, could find men in that vast wilderness, crosshatched by canyons, unmapped, and unexplored.

The strange party of Indians and white men, bound for Washington, moved on in mule-drawn wagons to Alamosa, nearly snowbound at that time of year.

The train started off across the white prairies toward Washington. At Kansas City the train halted for a short time. Here Chief Douglas was taken from the train by General Adams and a military escort. His trip was cut short. His hope of visiting Washington and talking with the chief of all Maricat'z—the dream that had been with him for many years—vanished. He was locked up in Leavenworth Prison, and the rest of the delegation went on to Washington.

The Committee on Indian Affairs of the House of Representatives began the Washington hearing on the "Ute Indian Outbreak" on January 15, 1880. In a basic sense the Washington hearing was a continuation of those held in the stable at the Los Pinos Agency; but instead of the old, draughty stable, the testimony was taken in a hearing room in the nation's Capitol, through which the long line of witnesses passed, stopping to tell their stories to the congressmen. There were men of government and Eastern men of business, some of whom had never seen an Indian. They were sympathetic, and they were unsympathetic. At times it seemed that white men, such as Governor Pitkin, Commissioner Hayt, Captain Payne, were themselves on trial. William N. Byers, of Denver and Middle Park, told his story, and Miss Josephine Meeker again told the tale much of the nation had now already heard, of massacre and captivity.

Day after day the testimony was taken, while congressmen fired questions at witnesses. Then, one by one, the leaders of the Ute Nation sat in the chair and filled the room with the strange, singing language that had to be translated into Spanish, then into English.

The hearing ended on March 22. The official decision made in Washington was the decision made many years before in the office of the Governor of Colorado, in mountain mining camps, in the homes of Colorado's leading citizens, and in the editorial rooms of Denver newspapers—"The Utes Must Go!"

On June 15, 1880, Congress passed an act "to accept and ratify the agreement submitted by the confederated bands of the Ute Indians in Colorado, for the sale of their reservation in said State, and for other purposes, and to make the necessary appropriations for carrying out the same."

On June 21 a commission of five men was appointed to carry out this act. The commission met in Denver on June 28 and convened again at Los Pinos Agency on July 8.

Most of the Colorado Utes were to share the reservation of the Uintah Utes, in Utah Territory. The Colorado bands were to purchase the land from the Uintahs out of their tribal funds, and each family was to be settled on a separate piece of land. A small rectangle of desert in southwest Colorado was, as a special favor to Ouray, to be the reservation of the Southern Utes.

For three weeks the talks were held. Ute leaders held councils, then all Utes attended councils so that their leaders could explain the removal to them. There were conferences between Ute chiefs and the commissioners.

Then, reluctantly, one by one, the Ute men put their marks on the agreement, which turned their country over to the white man. The commission obtained the marks of a sufficient number of the Uncompahgre and White River Utes at Los Pinos, then met again at the Southern Ute Agency, across the San Juan range, to get the necessary signers from the southern bands.

"They acted without restraint and of their own accord," wrote George W. Manypenny, one of the commissioners. "It was, however, painfully evident that it was a fearful struggle for them to give up their country where they from infancy and their fathers before them had roamed at will over the mountains and through the valleys of Western Colorado. Moreover, they mistrusted their abilities to meet the responsibilities of the new mode of life outlined for them in the agreement. With a sad expression of countenance and with a voice which impressed every one present, Sapavanero, when about to touch the pen, said, 'It is the best we can do, though not what we want.' "

The commission was also directed to try to capture the White River men wanted for their parts in the killings at the agency and the captivity of the white women. None of the Indians knew where these men might be. Some, they said, were dead, and the others had gone they knew not where.

The Utes made a plea before the commission for the release of Douglas from Leavenworth Prison. They said he was not present during the massacre and was not guilty. Douglas, however, was not released until long after the removal, when he was declared insane and sent back to his own people.

The commission finished its work by September 6, 1880. The commissioners ended their report:

> The reports of the agents among the Ute Indians, made from year to year since our first treaty relations with them, bear evidence of their orderly disposition and desire to avoid complications and conflicts with the white people. Some of

them, it is true, committed deeds of violence deeply to be
deplored. In such cases, and they are but few, a careful investigation of surrounding circumstances will show that the
Indians were inspired by events that aroused their savage
passions and led them to commit the crimes referred to. In
our intercourse with them for several months during the past
summer and fall we can without hesitation confirm all that
their agents have said in relation to their disposition and general good conduct.

9. DEATH

THIS is the way it was:

A long time ago the Old People came to the Shining Mountains from a place that was far away. In that place they came from there were great waters, in which lived men with bodies like fish.

When they came to this land, they found a great, warm lake, beside which they made their homes. The bed of that great lake can still be seen in the land up northwest of the Big River.

The lake was full of big fish and snakes as long as a hundred lodge poles; and the air was as warm as the waters of the lake. Giant trees grew all around, and there were big deer and oxen with white horns.

One day the giant snakes that lived in the warm lake began to raise such a steam from their noses that the whole ground shook. The steam rose in clouds that became thicker and thicker, until the sun was hidden. The land became very cold.

Then the ground cracked, and the lake began to fall away, and fall away, for three moons, until one day it was not there any more. The Old People looked and they found that where the waters of the lake had flowed away there were now deep, wide canyons. And all the deer and big oxen with white horns wandered away to the east and died in the great cold. Many were killed in the tall mountains by the arrows of hunters.

One day many small people, whose faces were very light, came floating down the rivers in skin canoes. They built stone

houses in the cliffs, and they raised corn and beans and pump-
kins. They became friends to the People. They worked with
iron tools; and they taught the People how to make good spears
and bows and arrows, and how to scoop up the ground and
make vessels from it, and how to weave baskets.

Then came some others. These people were big and red, and
they fought the little people and killed many of them; and those
they did not kill they drove away to the south. The big people
followed to the south, and they were the Fathers of the Navajo,
Apache, and Kiowa.

All this time the country where the People lived was becoming drier and colder; and at last only the People were left to
live on the Big River and its branches. The People loved their
land, and they would not go away.

Then another terrible change came: melted rocks began
pouring out of the hills everywhere, flowing over the ground
like a flood and killing all the grass and trees that were left. As
it cooled it became rock again, and the country was like a desert.
But the People loved their land, and they did not go away. . . .

These are the first words. The story goes on and on—so long
and so far that one man can never tell all of it. It is the story
of the land that changes many times—a land with a face that
grows old but always becomes young again. It is the story of
the People, who lived with that land. They never went away:
when the land was sick, they watched over it; when the land
was cruel to them, they made better friends with it.

The Land is the body; the People are the spirit. When the
Land and the People are cut apart, this is death.

Now the Maricat'z have come, and they are not like those
others who came before. They do not go away. They stay; but
they do not live with the land. The Maricat'z must change
everything to their own way, like Old Coyote, the spoiler. The
white men fight the land: they fight against the land, like an
enemy, and they must believe their enemy is weaker than themselves.

The white man is like the tallest pine tree in the forest. He
is like the pine tree that grows taller than all others; but he must
grow still taller. He becomes angry with his roots, and with the

land that holds his roots. He is angry with the land that holds him down, while his head is higher than all others. He pulls and strains toward the sky. At last, that tallest tree must break his roots out of the land that holds them.

The Land and the People were cut apart. After the fight with the soldiers, after the great fires at the agency, after the white men's councils, the People were taken away; and the soldiers came in—to the Smoking Earth River, and on beyond to the big river. There were many who saw them come.

Those of the People who belonged to the Smoking Earth River scattered and went down into the desert. They broke apart and scattered, away from their tall mountains and deep valleys, where the hunters could always find game and the ponies could always find grass.

A new year had come, and was past its middle. The days were clear and yellow. Sunlight washed over the broad, broken desert, and the same little birds flew in and out of the brush. It was a good year for game, with plenty of rain and many days of sunshine. The snow had gone away from the mountains slowly, sending good, clear water down from the high country. But the spring had come without a Bear Dance, and the summer was passing without hunts.

The People who belonged to the Shining Mountains—the trees and the streams and the high grass—were broken apart and scattered over the long, wide desert: that land of rock ridges, dry washes, and low mesas, where bright, dead colors seep out of the earth.

Through these days the men of the Nüpartka still wore colors on their faces, but the red of the fire and the yellow of bright open sunlight were not with them. On the forehead of each man was a circle of black. From that circle of black a thin black slash darted across the face. It crossed the left eyelid, parting where the eye looked out from behind it, and it crossed the left cheek. It ended, pointing to the heart; for the head, covered by the black circle, was filled with sad thoughts, and in the heart, where thoughts are felt, there was bad blood.

The soldiers had come to stay on Smoking Earth River; they built their houses there. They took their rifles and rode out to hunt in the hills, and other white men came to kill the deer and elk and antelope. They piled the skins high on their wagons and went away, and the coyotes grew fat and the sky was heavy with buzzards.

The Nüpartka, who for as long as even the oldest of the old people could remember had lived and hunted in the tall mountains and deep forests north of the Big River, had scattered over the desert like game before a hunting party. Cut apart—cut away from their land—they waited, through a snow, through the spring without a Bear Dance. Still not knowing, still not understanding the ways and thinking of the Maricat'z, they hid in the unfriendly desert and waited.

Then, when the sun was again moving away to the low south and the Last Summer Moon hung in the night sky, those who had gone away to Washington came back. They rode out to the scattered camps to tell about it: the long, long Maricat'z talk, and the Maricat'z decision.

Four Nüpartka—Nicaagat, Sowówic, Quinkent, and the Little Boy—had gone away to Washington; now, in the Last Summer Moon, only three returned.

It was Quinkent who had many times told the People of his love for Washington; who, when he spoke of Washington, had held his arms out to show how this father held all the children—all the tribes, the Nünt'z, the Arapaho and Sioux, the Maricat'z—and gave them his great love and protection. Quinkent had gone away with the others, but he had never seen Washington. Those who returned told how Quinkent had been taken to one of the Maricat'z prisons, to live always in one small stone room.

When the long days of talk at Washington were finished, the men of the People were taken into another room. In that room sat a man who shook hands with them: they said this man was the President. He was a different man from the President Nicaagat and some of the others had talked with many years ago, who had wanted all tribes to live in peace.

This new President said the People must leave their country. They must give their country to Washington and the Maricat'z, who would give them money for it. Then the People must pay money for all the white men who were killed at the agency and in the fight with the soldiers; and they must take the rest of the money to buy a new country for themselves.

Then that President said to them all: "Now this trouble is dead. It is buried, and any man who tries to dig it up again will go to prison."

Now Maricat'z were coming to the Uncompahgre country, as they had come so many times before, bringing papers for the People to sign. But this time the People could no longer say "No" and "No"; they must sign.

The People knew what was in these papers because they were told about it by that man whom Washington called their chief; and after that man had finished talking to the People he went away by himself. He was sick.

When the others, one by one, made their marks on those papers, that man was not there to make his mark. When the Maricat'z heard that he was sick, they sent their doctors to him; but that man would not see the Maricat'z doctors.

Then that man sent out the medicine sign, and the healers of the People came to sing by his bed. They sang for many days, while he slept.

Then one morning he opened his eyes. He looked around him at those who were there to sing for him, and he said in a voice that was stronger than sickness:

"Ouray will never leave the Great Mountains."

Then he closed his eyes again, and went to the Old People.

« II »

The Ute Campaign
by Captain James Parker, Fourth Cavalry

In March, 1880, I was ordered to join Mackenzie's command at Fort Garland. . . . We learned about this time that the State of Colorado, desiring to develop its western territory and impatient at the outrages continually being committed on miners, teamsters, and settlers, had demanded of the general Government that all the Utes should be moved into Utah, to the Uintah Reservation of 270 square miles.

The Indians fiercely resented the demands of the Commission, and the whole summer of 1880 was absorbed in protracted negotiations; the troops, cavalry and infantry, under Mackenzie, standing idly by. These parleyings were conducted by the Interior Department; Mackenzie, under the War Department, having no part in them. They were finally apparently crowned with success. The Indians, in exchange for a certain sum of money, agreed to move to Utah the following summer. . . .

Accordingly, in October, 1880, we left the supply camp and proceeded on our return march to Fort Garland. The road back we found much easier, as the State of Colorado during the summer had made many improvements.

As the spring of 1881 advanced we heard rumors of threatened hostilities on the part of the Utes. Having signed the treaty to evacuate, they now claimed that they were deceived and did not understand the treaty. Accordingly, on May 9th, the command entrained for Fort Garland. . . . The Commission appeared, and began to parley.

The negotiations dragged on all summer without success.

Finally in September the Commission found that their efforts were useless, and notified the Government to that effect. The matter was turned over to the War Department to settle, and Mackenzie was ordered to take such steps as were in his opinion necessary and proper. . . .

Upon receipt of the telegram from Washington, the force of troops present, about ten companies of infantry and cavalry . . . was ordered to stand equipped with 200 rounds of ammunition per man and three days' cooked rations. This done, Mackenzie sent word to the chiefs to come in for a conference.

It took place the following morning. Mackenzie informed the chiefs that the matter had been turned over to him for settlement; they had promised to move to Utah, and he wished to know whether or not they were going. . . . The leading chief commenced an oration in which he denounced the whites for wanting to deprive the Indians of their land, and was proceeding to more violent expressions when Mackenzie, with his hat in his hand, stood up.

"It is not necessary for me to stay here any longer," he said.

"You can settle this matter by discussion among yourselves. All I want to know is whether you will go or not. If you will not go of your own accord, I will make you go. . . ."

After a debate lasting several hours they sent for Mackenzie. They proposed a compromise. They said they had concluded they must go, but first they wished to go back to their camp and talk with their old men. "No," said Mackenzie. "If you have not moved by nine o'clock tomorrow morning, I will be at your camp and *make* you move."

The next morning, shortly after sunrise, we saw a thrilling and pitiful sight. The whole Ute nation on horseback and on foot was streaming by. As they passed our camps their gait broke into a run. Sheep were abandoned, blankets and personal possessions strewn along the road, women and children were loudly wailing.

. . . It was inevitable that they should move, and better then, than after a fruitless and bloody struggle. They should think, too, that the land was lost beyond recovery.

And so as we marched behind the Indians, pushing them out, he [Mackenzie] sent word to all the surrounding whites, who hurried after us, taking up the land. . . .

Lawton's troop and mine camped on the north side of the river, while A. E. Wood's troop and Abiel Smith's troop followed

in the rear of the Indians. Our task at the mouth of the Uncompahgre River was to hold back the civilians. They followed us closely, taking up and "locating" the Indian land thrown open for settlement. For obvious reasons it was not desirable to let these civilians come in contact with the Indians; thus we were holding a crowd of these people on the south side of the Gunnison until the Indians had passed Kahnah Creek, thirteen miles distant.

. . . As we pushed the Indians onward, we permitted the whites to follow, and in three days the rich lands of the Uncompahgre were all occupied, towns were being laid out and lots being sold at high prices. With its rich soil and wonderful opportunities for irrigation, the Uncompahgre Valley—before a desert —soon became the garden spot of Colorado, covered with fruitful fields and orchards.

THE BETRAYAL OF JACK

by CHARLES WILKINSON

« I »

After the United States of America acquired the Southwest from Mexico through the Mexican-American War and the Treaty of Guadalupe Hidalgo in 1848, the United States had essentially no impact on the Plateau for nearly a generation. The country began to make its mark with the capture of Navajo resisters in Canyon de Chelly in 1864 and the resultant Long Walk and imprisonment at Bosque Redondo. Once the Navajo were returned to the Four Corners with the Treaty of 1868, however, John Wesley Powell's two visits notwithstanding, the nation kept a minimal day-to-day presence for another decade.

The nineteenth-century enterprises of the Mormons should be distinguished from those fostered by the United States. Although the Mormons were U.S. citizens, the settlement of their outposts on the Plateau was disconnected to any federal policy. To the American government, the Mormons were pariahs. From the Mormons' side, their efforts were inspired by their faith. To the extent statism was involved, the motivating force was not patriotism to the United States but a devotion to the brighter dream of Deseret. It is worth noting that the Mormon infusion had a piety, a gentleness, about it.

Then, beginning in 1879, the United States exercised its military might in western Colorado to accomplish an out-and-out conquest of the Ute Tribe. The exuberant, opportunistic land rush of 1881 that resulted bore no resemblance to the steady-as-you-go travails of the Hole-in-the-Rock Expedition.

The nation's role became ever more prominent. While the programs of Spain and the Church of the Latter-Day Saints were driven primarily by religion, now the dominant impetus was nationalism. Then, especially after World War II, industrialization became at least an equal force. The United States would be almost entirely successful in achieving its stated objectives. A century after the events in western Colorado in the late 1870s and early 1880s, the Colorado Plateau, for all of the notable staying power of its people and land, would be a significantly different place.

《 II 》

Morgan Bottoms, much of which is the old Carpenter family ranch, is an eleven-mile stretch near Hayden, Colorado, where the banks of the Yampa River are dominated by cottonwood forests. The groves cover hundreds of acres of land, mostly along the south bank but sometimes enveloping the river by spreading north of it as well. The lower valleys of the Yampa, just south of the Wyoming border, and the White, the next watershed to the south, form the most northeastern part of the Colorado Plateau. These rivers run east to west, rising in the Elkhead Mountains, Mount Zirkel Wilderness, and the Flat Tops, and then flowing down into the Plateau where they pass through small ranch towns – Hayden, Craig, Meeker, Rangely – and uncluttered rangeland to red-rock terrain where the waters pour into the Green River.

Each of the cottonwood groves at Morgan Bottoms is tall and dense. The canopy is multi-tiered, with the upper reaches composed of narrowleaf cottonwood trees. Midway, a graceful story of box elders spreads out its many wings, while lower down you see red-osier dogwoods. Hiking is a slow-moving proposition. Various shrubs and forbs form a tangled ground cover, with coyote willows thick near the river. The forest floor is within the Yampa's floodplain, and it is watered by the river's high runoff in spring and early summer. Gnats, mosquitoes, and other insects make pesky swarms in the marshy reaches. I have seen an unbelievable array of bird life there: a great blue heron, great horned owls, golden eagles, even an occasional bald eagle; mergansers, wood ducks, mallards; sandhill cranes in full flight with seven-foot wing spans, casually squawking out calls that sound like creaking doors.

Yet this profusion of vegetation and wildlife habitat was alien to my eye. Across the whole arid West, cottonwoods run along nearly every low-and middle-elevation river, stream, and creek, but the trees form thin ribbons, two or three deep, not unlike the buffer strips of Douglas fir or ponderosa pine that the Forest Service so assiduously leaves along highways adjacent to clearcuts. I'd never *been* in a cottonwood forest before.

I knew why this cottonwood forest, one of the few left in the West, had survived. Cottonwoods need high flows to deliver water to their big root systems and to create new, moist sandbars for young trees to take root. On almost all western rivers, dams block the spring runoff and have gradually killed off the downstream cottonwood forests, but, here, on the Yampa, there are no dams of any size, and the forest at Morgan Bottoms thrives. Still, cottonwoods usually come in thin strips, not forests, and so for me Morgan Bottoms took on a surprising, almost suspicious, cast.

For we all perceive the natural world in layers. We may take in nature in a literal way – vegetation, animal species, waters, soils, land formations – but we overlay those objective natural facts with our own memories, imaginations, fears, and dreams, and for us those overlays are as complex and real as the natural facts themselves might be.

There are many layers, some held by the public at large, some personal, over this part of Colorado. The issues swirling around the two coal-fired power plants that ship current to distant cities and, it now seems, acid rain to the Mount Zirkel Wilderness. The questions looming on top of the oil shale deposits of the Piceance Basin, deep below the White River, that may some day be strip mined. The stories and traditions of five full generations of ranch and farm families up and down the Yampa and the White. The perceived strangeness of full cottonwood forests on a western river. All of these, and many more, hover over the Yampa and White country.

Yet for me the thickest overlay on the Yampa and on the White, on the whole Colorado Western Slope, the overlay that has settled in and subsumed all the others, will always be the experience of the Ute, how they lived and loved and worshipped and how they rode through the high ranges and valleys for so many centuries. The Ute experience includes the horse and the elk and the buffalo and the eagle and the cottonwood forests, and it includes Nathan and Arvilla Meeker and Ouray and Jack and a great tribal land estate and a bad ending that even today, long after the cataclysmic events of 1879, lies heavily over the White-Yampa country.

« III »

The tenure of the Ute people in the region traces back farther than we can fully imagine. Some anthropologists think they migrated into the Colorado Plateau region between 1000 and 1300 A.D. Others believe that the modern Utes emerged from the Fremont people. The Fremont, who date back to about 4,000 years ago, lived both in villages and on the move, hunting and gathering, and leaving behind housing sites, baskets, pots, and magical pictographs and petroglyphs. In turn, the Fremont probably evolved from hunters and gatherers who lived on the Colorado Plateau beginning about 10,000 or more years ago.

That is the way non-Indian scholars assess it. The Ute themselves seem disinclined to join the debate in those terms. They hold by their own explanation. At the beginning of time, Sinawahv, the Creator, had all of the peoples of the world in a bag. He opened the bag and placed the Ute in their mountain, plains, and desert country, in the best place. By any account, the current of Ute blood runs very, very deep out here.

A dominant event in Ute history took place in the early 1600s, when tribal members acquired the horse from the Spaniards. Vast numbers of horses were later freed up by the Pueblo's revolt against the Spanish in 1680.

The Ute took immediately to this fantastic new animal and became extraordinarily mobile. Bands of Utes ranged from the Wasatch Front all the way to the Colorado Front Range – from present-day Salt Lake City to Denver. They established a lasting trail system, which included what is now Trail Ridge Road through Rocky Mountain National Park, the highest paved road in the United States. With the horse, the Ute traversed all the territory they wished, speeding across open plains, ascending to the high mountain hunting grounds, and dropping down into steep washes, draws, and canyons in that rough country. They were master horsemen. Just as a virtuoso pianist blends with an instrument, a Ute rider became one with his horse.

Ute people today understandably look back on this as the time of times in all the centuries since the Creator released them from the bag. To be sure, in many ways life was hard. The winters, even in the lower-lying valleys, were brutally cold. A head injury, broken leg, or tooth infection could be a life-threatening event. Loved ones were lost in battles with the Shoshone, Navajo, and plains tribes to the east. The Ute signed a peace treaty with the Spanish in the 1600s, but a treaty was of no use against the smallpox, measles, and other diseases for which the Ute lacked immunity.

Yet the horse shut down so many threats and opened up so many options, so many freedoms. The curse of hunger, or outright famine, was essentially eliminated by the large-area hunting now made possible. Relations with other tribes and the Spanish took a new posture. The horseback Ute could escape, pursue, and fight so effectively that the other cultures conceded the Central Rockies to the Ute as their mountain stronghold.

This was especially true for the White River Band of Utes, who lived in the White and Yampa River Valleys. The mountain buffalo inhabited the high parks across the mountain spine to the east. With the horse it became easy and productive to head up the Yampa in the late spring, summer, or early fall, cross the Continental Divide at what is now Rabbit Ears Pass, and drop down into North Park to hunt. Hunters could also ride up the White River, traverse the level plateaus of the Flat Tops, descend their eastern flank, and then move up the mainstem Colorado River and the Fraser River to Middle Park. Yes, the Creator had chosen well and blessed the Ute: other than parts of the Pacific Northwest, Ute country held more kinds of mammals, and in greater numbers, than anywhere in western North America.

The hunt was a time of heightened excitement. Ute hunters were splendidly arrayed in buckskins adorned with beads, fringe, paint, porcupine quills, and elk teeth. Eagle feathers flowed from their braided hair. Some of the hunting was done from stationary positions, behind cover, but when necessary the athletic hunters worked at top speed, united with their horses, using bows and arrows and, later, rifles. The whole community celebrated when the hunters returned in glory from a hunt, their pack horses trailing behind, weighed down with buffalo and elk meat.

What prizes the mountain buffalo were. They made a wonderful food – meaty, nutritious, delicious – whether cut into thin strips, smoked, and dried for the winter or put right on a spit. Their huge bodies yielded thick, versatile hides, which the Ute used for teepee exteriors (about ten hides were needed) and clothing. Sleeping robes made from the shaggy animals, along with the teepee fires, kept away the winter's bitter cold.

The women tanned the hides. They scraped the fat off the fleshy side with a deer-bone knife, soaked the skin overnight, applied a mixture having a base of boiled brains, sunned the hide for several days, soaked it again, stretched it (a difficult and tedious job), smoked one side over an open fire, and then finished the hide by softening it through vigorous rubbing with a stone or rope. These hides were warm, pliant, durable, and handsome when decorated with paint, beads, and fringe. Buffalo hides also were valuable in trade, allowing the Ute to obtain items from the south, such as clay pots, pipes, and bridles from the Apache and Navajo and steel fishhooks and brass bracelets from the Hispanics. The Ute preferred mountain buffalo, but the abundant deer, elk, antelope, and mountain sheep met the same needs.

The Ute made use of virtually the whole land, and the cottonwood forests at Morgan Bottoms serve as a good example. For fuel, the Ute preferred cottonwood, especially in the summer when light, rather than heat, was the main objective and the cottonwood could throw out its bright flame with few sparks and relatively low heat. The cottonwood was also best for smoking meat since the smoke, not the heat, dried the meat. Cottonwood leaves were suited for wrapping tobacco as the smoke coated the throat and added flavor to the tobacco. The smoke on the singers' throats enhanced the quality of their voices, giving a stronger range. The White River Utes put their sturdy, tightly-woven baskets (they rarely made pots) to many uses. Squawbush and willows were the key materials. They ate service berries raw, or cooked them and dried them into cakes. An important Ute food, found near Morgan Bottoms, was a succulent tuber of the carrot family that grows in northwestern Colorado and gave the valley its name: the Yampa plant.

Morgan Bottoms, then as now, was spectacular wildlife habitat. Because the deer and elk that wintered there were so plentiful, the Utes had relatively little to do with fish, but they did take some cutthroat trout, suckers, whitefish, and chub with spears, weirs, and Mexican-made fishhooks. The White River Utes prized eagles for their feathers and bones, which they used as whistles. Black bear used the thick underbrush of the cottonwood forests as cover. Ute dancers wore the bear skins during the Bear Dance, the major festival held in the early spring when the leaves began to turn green. Bear Dance celebrated a new, hopeful year and a good hunt.

Morgan Bottoms was one of hundreds of places integral to the Utes of Northwestern Colorado in their intricate life. They

camped there for extended periods and also used it as a stop-
over point along the Yampa corridor on the way to and from the
mountain hunts. A vivid reminder can be found just upstream
from Morgan Bottoms. On a vertical cliff up above the river
floor is a panel of Ute pictographs with many burnished-red
figures, including a rider on horseback.

This horse tribe controlled its domain, apparently with little
competition, for more than 200 years. Then events beyond its
boundaries began to take a toll. Americans discovered gold in
faraway California, and in 1848 the United States immediately
wrested away from Mexico territory that now comprises all or
part of seven states, including much of the Yampa and White
country. In 1859 and the early 1860s, gold was struck all along
the Colorado Front Range, drawing would-be miners from the
east and from the mining camps in California and Nevada. By
the late 1860s, although few Americans had entered Ute country
yet, the Ute were in a vise.

Ouray is renowned as the great nineteenth-century hero of
the Ute, praised in all of the history books, honored in all the
lists of leading figures in Colorado history. Raised partly in an
Apache family, he came to his own tribe as a young adult and
quickly assumed leadership in the Uncompahgre Band, which
was located in the Gunnison and Uncompahgre Valleys south of
the Yampa and White. In time, he came to be tacitly acknowledged as a spokesperson for the seven Ute bands at treaty time.
Federal officials respected him as an able diplomat, a man of
transcendent judgment, skill, and reliability. Ouray was
quadrilingual, fluent in Spanish, English, and his two Indian
tongues.

In 1868, despite relentless pressure for Ute land, Ouray was
the principal negotiator in perhaps the most favorable Indian
treaty in the history of the country. The Ute domain recognized
by this treaty encompassed 16 million acres – one-third of Colorado – 120 miles west to east, 200 miles south to north, from the
New Mexico border nearly all the way to Wyoming. Most of the
high mountains, the place of the summer hunts where the ani-

mals must have seemed limitless, were included. So were the lowlands, where the Ute and the big game wintered. The government assured the Ute they could hunt on aboriginal lands that lay outside the reservation, which included the White River watershed but not the Yampa. The Ute held the whole reservation in absolute ownership, guaranteed by the 1868 treaty – and by settled principles of United States real property law – forever.

Forever would not last long. The fury that would descend on the Ute Reservation in 1879 made that impossible. "The Utes must go!" the newspapers shouted. Even at the late date of 1880 and even under the most difficult circumstances, Ouray negotiated a far better resolution than seemed imaginable. The two reservations in southern Colorado and the one in northern Utah are just remnants of the old lands, but still they amount to nearly 1.5 million acres. Ouray earned all the accolades.

Although a master hunter and horseman, after the 1868 treaty Ouray gradually began to take on many of the trappings of the whites – their dress, wines, and cigars. He acquired a Mexican servant, worked at a formal desk, and took rides in a carriage given to him by General Edward McCook. He encouraged his people to farm. Ouray had his policy reasons – he felt that coexistence with the whites was essential and wanted to demonstrate some of the benefits of non-Indian society – but his assimilationist ways did not sit well with many Utes.

The pictures of Ouray display a figure of dignity and respect. His clothing is always neat and prim, his broad face open and soft, welcoming. One can see how he drew in the Indian agents, the Governor of Colorado, even Presidents of the United States. Ouray inspired trust, affection, and comfort in the new people who were so keenly interested in Ute land.

Not Jack. This ultimate leader of the White River Utes, who rode the White and Yampa River Valleys, was born Goshute and taken in for several years of his youth by a Mormon family in Utah. It was too shackling: the wrong clothes, the wrong schooling, the wrong God, the wrong land. He fled to the mountains in his teens and took up with the Ute, who were closely aligned

305

THE LAST WAR TRAIL

with the Goshutes. In the early spring, just as the cottonwood leaves were turning green, he lived the Bear Dance for days and a young Ute woman took him as her husband. He became a Ute: tribal custom was to take in Indians from other tribes and, if they became fully part of the society, grant them full tribal status.

Jack became so completely accepted by the White River Utes, the most unrelenting Ute band, because his personality so completely matched. He loved the hunt. He rode with abandon. He was fierce: photographs show a lean, leathery man with a hatchet of a face. Jack had no desire at all to be conciliatory. Yes, he had signed the 1868 treaty along with Ouray and seven other Ute leaders, but he did that out of strength: the treaty had set aside a reservation that included most of the hunting grounds and the United States guaranteed the Ute access to those traditional hunting areas, such as the Yampa Valley and North and Middle Parks, that lay outside of the reservation. And the treaty, which Jack knew thoroughly, stipulated that no white people, except authorized federal agents, could enter Ute country without permission of the tribe. Jack had no desire to settle down with white people as a fellow farmer. Jack felt that Ute country was for the Ute and for the Ute alone.

Some of the older White River Utes, believing that cooperation with the whites was inevitable and necessary, thought Jack too abrasive, but the younger people and most of the elders idolized him. He became spokesman for the White River Utes, the band most determined to hold on to the Ute way – the way of the horse and the hunt.

« IV »

The events of 1879 became inevitable on May 10, 1878, when Nathan Meeker arrived at the White River Agency as the new federal Indian agent, soon to be joined by his wife, Arvilla, and daughter, Josephine. Tension hung in the air like cottonwood smoke. The Ute felt violated by the 1874 Brunot Agreement, which had removed 4 million acres, including most of the San Juan Mountains in southwestern Colorado, from the reservation after gold and silver had been found in the San Juans. The white River Utes did not hunt much in those southern mountains, but they knew their band was directly threatened by the precedent of ceding Ute treaty land. They also hated mining: it promoted a sedentary lifestyle and was an affront to the land they revered. Why should a whole mountain range be given over to such people? Then, too, the 1874 agreement seemed a clear threat to the status quo that Jack, Ouray, and many other Utes had tried so hard to achieve. How firm were the solemn promises made in the great 1868 treaty?

Events had worsened after 1874. In 1876, Colorado became a state and this event seemed to signal to the non-Indian residents that local, rather than Ute, prerogatives were paramount. Frederick Pitkin, who made a fortune mining in the San Juans, was the Governor. Some people had been prospecting on the reservation, and others came through to assess its worth for farming. Jack had gone to Denver on behalf of his people to meet with Pitkin. The Governor's views were clear and oft-stated and he addressed the issue in his first inaugural address and regularly thereafter: Pitkin wanted the Ute out of Colorado.

In his own mind, Nathan Cook Meeker had nothing but the best interests of the Ute at heart. Idealistic through and through, Meeker became captivated by Utopian agrarian communities and after the Civil War began writing an agricultural column for Horace Greeley's *New York Tribune*. With Greeley's encouragement and financial backing, Meeker went West to Colorado and in 1869 founded Union Colony, one of the most famous communal farm societies. The nearest town was named Greeley, after Union Colony's benefactor. The colony's prospects were promising and irrigation canals were built, crops raised, and produce marketed in Denver.

Meeker's own star, however, fell. Horace Greeley died, and his estate called in as a debt the seed money that Greeley had advanced to Meeker. Soon thereafter, the members of the colony voted Meeker down as leader. He was out of a job and, even worse, was bereft of a pulpit for his fervid views on the verities

307

of farming and the hardworking, worthwhile communities that it built.

Senator Henry Teller of Colorado saw the right fit for Meeker and arranged for his appointment as Indian agent at White River. The sixty-year-old Meeker plunged in, full-spirited and determined to assist the Ute in making the necessary transition to a civilized – that is, an agricultural – life. His way of using the land was better than the Ute's way, and he was determined to convince them of that truth.

Meeker's first move was to relocate the White River agency about fifteen miles downstream to a site (now the town of Meeker) where the valley widened out and the level ground and good topsoil would make for much better farming. There were political rivalries among Ute leaders, and Quinkent and Canalla, both older and more conciliatory toward the whites, were willing to move. Jack was adamantly opposed. The new location was further from the mountains and the hunt, and he argued strenuously that the treaty had mandated that the agency be at the existing site. The treaty had no such requirement on its face, although the provisions regarding the agency were sufficiently extensive (requiring, among other things, the construction of several buildings) to suggest that the original site was to be permanent. Also, Jack, as a treaty negotiator, may have known of unwritten assurances made during the negotiations. In any event, Meeker was not to be deterred. In an action that probably seemed to him routine rather than momentous, the federal installation was relocated.

The summer of 1879 came in hot, dry, and tense. Governor Pitkin was beginning his second term and Ute removal remained his top priority. Many fires broke out on the tinder-dry western slope of Colorado and homesteads were lost. Pitkin trumpeted as "facts" the complaints of settlers that raiding parties of Utes had set the fires.

> Reports reach me daily that a band of White River Utes are off their reservation, destroying forests and game near

North and Middle Parks. They have already burned mil
lions of dollars of timber, and are intimidating settlers
and miners. . . . These savages should be removed to the
Indian Territory, where they can no longer destroy the finest forests in this State.

Never mind that it was common knowledge in Colorado
and across the West that miners and loggers were notoriously
careless and that their fires ravaged the forestlands. Never mind
that the reports of Ute aggression from white settlers were not
substantiated and never would be, even after federal investigation. At least one Ute hunter was shot down as an arsonist in
the West's version of a lynching. Good. Fair recompense. The
Ute did not belong in Colorado.

Nathan Meeker was growing increasingly jittery. The fires
and the pressure from the Governor and the settlers – which
built up even more in the spring of 1879, when gold was discovered on reservation land to the south and miners promptly
rushed in – were part of it, but there was more. He wasn't gaining the respect of the Ute. Moving the agency headquarters had
caused deep bitterness. Quinkent and Canalla had relocated
their camps to the new agency but Jack and his followers had
remained ten miles upstream. Further, the annual shipments of
food and goods such as blankets and clothing guaranteed by
treaty were late. The goods were important to the Ute; tribal
members could use them and Ute hunters could trade them to
settlers for rifles and ammunition. The delay in the arrival of
the annuities was not Meeker's fault (the Union Pacific rail shipments to Fort Steele, 150 miles north, were being held in a
warehouse pending government payment), but he was tarred
with blame regardless.

Meeker's own personal foibles added to his problems. He
insisted that the Ute call him "Father," which plainly irritated
them. Behind his back, and a few times to his face, they called
Meeker – who to the white man's eye was handsome, erect, and
dignified – an "old lady" because he seemed so out of place and

inept in Ute country. Also, fearing conflicts with settlers, he told the Ute that they should not leave the reservation, which was contrary to federal policy and assurances given at the time of the 1868 treaty. Meeker saw himself as a good man headed in the best direction for both the Ute and his own people, but he knew that his problems were spiraling, and began to fear for his own safety and, worse yet, for that of Arvilla and Josephine.

The Indian agent had been able to put nearly 200 acres under the plow. In early September, he ordered two additional parcels to be plowed and made ready for irrigation the next spring. One of the areas was a track where the younger Utes raced their horses. The other was the field where Canalla, the old medicine man who had tried to cooperate with Meeker, pastured his ponies. Meeker's mandate threw the Ute into an uproar. They didn't like plowing to begin with – it tore up the earth and was a symbol of the new life the white people were trying to force on them – and these were not places where plowing made any sense. The races were good for the young riders and showed off the magical skills of the horse. Canalla needed the pasture for his many horses. Still, this was not a time to anger the white people. Danger was in the air. There was a great deal of talk among the Ute, some with Meeker, much more in the teepees with elder-stem pipes and the tobacco wrapped in cottonwood leaves.

Meeker decided to go ahead with the plowing. Canalla, who was not a volatile sort, went to the agency and confronted Meeker, who was having his lunch. Pushing and jostling ensued between the two older men. Canalla pushed Meeker through the open door and the agent landed in a heap outside the building. His body seemed not to be hurt, but his dignity was. On September 10, 1879, Nathan Meeker shot out fateful calls for assistance to Governor Pitkin and the Interior Department. The telegram to Washington reported:

I HAVE BEEN ASSAULTED BY A LEADING CHIEF . . . FORCED OUT OF MY OWN HOUSE, AND INJURED BADLY, BUT WAS RESCUED BY EMPLOYÉS . . . LIFE OF SELF, FAMILY, AND

EMPLOYÉS NOT SAFE; WANT PROTECTION IMMEDIATELY; HAVE
ASKED GOVERNOR PITKIN TO CONFER WITH GENERAL POPE.
N.C. MEEKER, INDIAN AGENT

Interior referred the matter to the War Department, which
on September 15 ordered troops to be dispatched to Meeker's
aid. The nearest installation was Fort Steele, under the command of Major Thomas T. Thornburgh. Thornburgh, out on an
elk hunt, did not take immediate action. The Indian forts in the
West had become somewhat low-key operations in recent years
– the Sioux and the Nez Perce had been subdued, and the operat-
ing assumption was that the last Indian war had already been
fought.

But enough telegrams, reports, and rumors were flying
around Colorado and Ute country in particular that Jack became concerned. He decided to travel north to Fort Steele to
talk matters through. Jack and ten of his men headed up Coal
Creek Canyon to the divide between the White and the Yampa.
This divide, where Milk Creek begins to flow north, was the
northern boundary of the reservation. When the riders dropped
down into the bottomlands of the Yampa, they learned that federal soldiers were in the area. The Utes sought out Major
Thornburgh's camp.

On September 26, Jack and Thornburgh discussed the situation at length. Jack said that he and the Ute wanted only peace
and to be left alone: "I told them that I never expected to see the
soldiers here. I told him we were all under one government,
Indians and soldiers, and that the government at Washington
ordered us both; that we were brothers, and why had they come?"
Thornburgh truthfully said that he, too, wanted peace and that
his orders were to avoid combat. He related the federal
government's concerns about the fires, concerns that had been
aggravated by still more reports from Pitkin.

Jack, exasperated because he thought he had cleared up the
matter of the fires just a few months earlier with the Governor,
explained that the fires absolutely were not set by Utes. Further,

ever precise, ever focused on the hard-negotiated treaty, the Ute leader argued that any entry into the reservation would be in violation of the treaty and an act of war. Ute land was, according to the treaty, "set apart for the absolute and undisturbed use and occupation" of the Ute. The treaty also said that "no person... shall ever be permitted to pass over, settle upon, or reside" on the reservation without Ute consent.

However, Thornburgh also had some treaty words on his side. There was an exception for "officers... of the government as may be authorized to enter upon Indian reservations in discharge of duties enjoined by law." Thornburgh showed Jack his official orders. Jack understood Thornburgh's point, but pressed his own position that there was no reason that federal troops should encroach on Ute land. The Ute had never engaged in combat with the United States. The fires were not set by Utes. Canalla had done no harm to Meeker.

The next morning, Jack returned to Thornburgh's camp to offer a compromise. Leave your troops in the Yampa Valley at least fifty miles from the agency, well north of the reservation line, and proceed with just five men to the agency. You can investigate the circumstances and will see that there are no possible grounds for bringing in your army. Jack hurried back to the agency on the same day, September 27, and Meeker promptly sent Thornburgh a message by runner supporting Jack's proposal, urging the Major to proceed with just five men, and saying that "the Indians are greatly excited" and "seem to consider the advance of troops as a declaration of real war."

Thornburgh initially acceded. He seemed satisfied with the talks with Jack. After their first meeting, the Major wired his superior:

> HAVE MET SOME UTE CHIEFS HERE. THEY SEEM FRIENDLY AND PROMISE TO GO WITH ME TO AGENCY. SAY UTES DON'T UNDERSTAND WHY WE HAVE COME. HAVE TRIED TO EXPLAIN SATISFACTORILY. DO NOT ANTICIPATE TROUBLE.

On September 27, Thornburgh wrote to Meeker that he would follow Jack's plan: he would camp down on Milk Creek, well north of the reservation, and then "come in, as desired, with five men and a guide."

But after discussions with his officers and scouts, Thornburgh's hierarchical sense of duty prevailed. He had been ordered to proceed with troops to the reservation. Leaving his army fifty miles distant did not conform with his orders.

On September 28, Thornburgh formally reversed himself and sent a letter by horseback messenger to Meeker, saying that he would enter on to the reservation, leave the force "within striking distance of your agency," and then come in with a guide and five soldiers.

Meeker replied on September 29 at 1:00 P.M. It was an ambiguous response. He endorsed the march onto the reservation: "I like your last programme, it is based on true military principles." But he also downplayed any trouble and sent a clear signal that he was safe:

> I expect to leave in the morning with [two Ute leaders] to meet you. Things are peaceable, and [Quinkent] flies the U.S. flag. If you have trouble in getting through the cañon [on upper Milk Creek] today, let me know in force. We have been on guard three nights, and shall be tonight, not because we know there is danger, but because there may be.

Perhaps something in Meeker's letter might have caused the Major to reconsider his decision to march his troops into Ute country. We do not know, for Thornburgh never received the message.

A mixture of fear, despair, and determination had settled in among the Ute. No one knew what Thornburgh had in mind, but they did know from Jack's reports that he and his troops had reached the Yampa. And every single Ute knew in vivid detail, just as though it were yesterday, the horrors of the Sand Creek Massacre of 1864, when Colonel John Chivington led his murderous charge on Black Kettle and the Cheyenne. Two hundred

Cheyennes, most of them women and children, were slaughtered. Thomas Thornburgh was not remotely a John Chivington, but the Ute did not know that. They knew only that he was marching toward their land for no apparent reason.

On September 27, young Ute men began to move up toward the headwaters of Milk Creek, at the north edge of the reservation, and made camp on high ground above the trail over which Thornburgh might be advancing his troops and wagons. Most of the old men, women, and children moved their camps out of the agency and across the White River. Dancing and singing went on nearly all night.

Jack, who spent the night near the agency, was on his way before first light on September 29. He rode up past the autumn-yellow cottonwoods along Coal Creek as he had a few days before, but this was different from that exploratory mission. His scouts had reported that troops were moving up Milk Creek. The Ute leader could not be sure whether Thornburgh would honor his request to leave the troops on lower Milk Creek, but Jack's approach remained the same as it had been over the past few days, over the many years that he had held responsibility for his tribe's future. Look for solutions but be firm. See that the treaty is honored. Preserve Ute land. Preserve the hunt.

Jack crossed over Yellowjacket Pass, rode through the narrow Milk Creek canyon, and arrived at the large bowl just below. He found, as he knew he would, some fifty Ute young men camped at the high edge of the bowl among the sparse junipers. Jack's wife and children had come over from their camp. The young men, many in their early teens, were singing solemnly. Most wore Ute war paint, yellow and black. They were edgy. Jack and Colorow – another Ute leader – gathered with the young men. They talked, telling each other what they knew, and waited to see what would appear on the trail down below.

At midday, Major Thornburgh and an advance column broke into view on the sagebrush-lined trail at the far end of the bowl. They proceeded on, followed by a long line of soldiers. Now it was clear that Thornburgh did not intend to abide by

314

Jack's request. Jack directed his wife and children to return to the camp. Thornburgh waved to the Utes and Jack waved back. Wanting to confer with the Major and slow things down, Jack told his men to hold their fire and moved his horse down the side of the bowl toward the troops.

A shot – no one knows whose – exploded and filled the bowl with instant sound and history. Jack shouted out to both sides, "Hold on, hold on," but full-scale combat was already raging. Within minutes, Major Thornburgh was dead, shot in the head. The Utes kept his troops pinned for five days until relief forces rescued them. In all, thirteen United States soldiers were killed and forty-three wounded. Thirty-seven Utes died.

At the moment firing broke out, Ute riders raced down Coal Creek to the agency to warn of the danger. When the riders arrived at about 2:00 P.M., Quinkent and about twenty other Utes, furious at Thornburgh's march on Ute land and releasing more than a year's pent-up anger at Nathan Meeker, took immediate action. They killed Meeker (who had just dispatched his ambiguous letter to Thornburgh), all seven other agency employees, and three other white men. They drove a stake through Meeker's mouth so that, as they said, his lies would finally cease, even in the afterlife. Twelve Utes, led by Quinkent, then kidnapped sixty-three-year-old Arvilla Meeker, Josephine Meeker, and a Mrs. Price, holding them for twenty-three days. The hostages initially reported that their captors had treated them well. Later, Mrs. Meeker testified that Quinkent had forced her into sexual intercourse on one occasion. Josephine said that she suffered the same from a Ute named Pah-sone.

Outrage and panic over the battle, the killings, and the kidnapping spread all over Colorado, on front pages, in public lecture halls, over dinner tables. Governor Pitkin fueled the anti-Ute hatred with his telegrams to the Western Slope: "Indians off their reservation, seeking to destroy your settlements by fire, are game to be hunted and destroyed like wild beasts." In the months to come, Josephine Meeker made sure the furor did not die down. She took to the lecture circuit and gave detailed descriptions, far more lurid than anything she said to federal officials, of the indignities she suffered during her captivity.

Federal hearings were promptly held in Colorado and Washington to investigate the situation. Ouray, who had been at his home in Uncompahgre Park at the time of the battle and who struggled to keep both sides calm during the ensuing days and weeks, acted as what amounted to chief counsel for the Ute.

The proceedings, especially those in Washington, seem generally to have been open and fair, thanks in good part to Ouray's vigorous and skillful representation. Jack and the other Ute soldiers were exonerated (the Battle of Milk Creek was seen as a misunderstanding, ripening into combat, between two governments). The killings at the agency and the treatment of the three women were viewed differently, and Quinkent was sent off to prison for a year. But the investigations, which drew out all of the tangled circumstances of this clash of irreconcilable cultures and could theoretically have created the basis for an understanding and resolution of the Ute's situation, were of little moment. Passions – that is, the passions of the settlers, whose passions counted – were too high. It was impossible for the Ute to remain in Colorado.

When the Utes were ordered back to Washington for the hearings in early 1880, they were told that they would have to negotiate still another "agreement." All the Utes knew what this meant. It would be much worse than the Brunot Agreement in 1874. All the land – almost all of it, anyway – would go. So would the hunt. Jack balked. He considered travelling to Dakota Territory to join Sitting Bull. In the end, Jack did go to Washington.

The final 1880 agreement, passed by Congress in June, erased the treaty signed twelve years earlier. The Southern Utes were to be located on a strip of low-lying land in southern Colorado, adjacent to New Mexico Territory. The government would try to find unoccupied land for the Uncompahgre Utes in the Grand Valley (this arrangement proved unacceptable to the settlers and the band was moved to the reservation of the Uintah Band of

Utes in Utah). Years later, a reservation was set aside for the Weeminuche Band in barren country in southwesternmost Colorado. As for Jack and the other White River Utes, the 1880 agreement was terse: "The White River Utes agree to remove to and settle upon agricultural lands on the Uintah Reservation in Utah."

Of course, for all of the Ute these terms were dictated, not negotiated. Jack was present but refused to sign. A photograph shows him gaunt and glowering, the leader of horse people who had lost the hunt forever.

General Ranald MacKenzie was sent out with troops in May, 1880, to oversee the removal of the White River and Uncompahgre Utes to Utah. The government soldiers rounded them up and brought them to the junction of the Grand (later named the Colorado) and the Gunnison Rivers, now the site of Grand Junction. The Ute tried to resist one last time, saying they would not go. Utah was not their kind of country. That land already belonged to the Uintah Band and no additional land had been set aside for the White River Utes. The White and the Yampa country was their home. General MacKenzie explained again and again that the move was inevitable.

In the spring of 1881, the despondent Ute failed to hold the Bear Dance for the first time since the Creator opened the bag. Talks were held during the spring and summer of 1881. General MacKenzie had two difficult jobs, marching the Ute out and, in the meantime, restraining the rapidly gathering numbers of settlers wanting to stake their claim on former Ute lands. He became more and more insistent with the Ute. They wanted permission for one last hunt on the Yampa to put in meat for the winter. He refused. The Ute needed to be on the Uintah Reservation before winter broke and the settlers needed to beat winter as well.

In late August, 1881, the Ute and their persistent military keepers began final preparations for the move. MacKenzie held the settlers at bay. On September 6, the Ute moved out. On the last day the sky was marked by two large, separate clouds of dust. One was created by the White River and Uncompahgre Utes, slowly pushing west with their military escort and what was left of their belongings and their ponies. The other was created by the land rush of anxious settlers, released from the soldiers' restraint by a bugle call, pounding into the Grand Valley, now free of the Ute, to open it for settlement and farming.

« v »

For the White River Utes, who in their tenacious way have rebuilt their lives at the Uintah Reservation in Utah, the issue in northwestern Colorado now is not the land or even the hunt, but rather the truth. The memories of the White River Utes are strong, and they have not forgotten 1879 or the long, glorious time that came before.

In the fall of 1993, Ute people came back to the place of the Battle of Milk Creek to dedicate their own monument, which tells the story of 1879 as they believe it, and their monument now sits next to the one the non-Indians erected to honor Major Thornburgh and his fallen soldiers. It was a powerful ceremony that drew a gathering of more than 1,000 people, Ute from Utah and southern Colorado, National Public Radio and Channel Four from Denver, numerous citizens from Meeker and the surrounding area, and many from around Colorado, including myself and my son David. We all listened hard to the speakers, trying to search out meaning from their words about the whirl of events that descended upon this place more than a century ago. Luke Duncan, erect and dark and in braids, said simply, "We were removed to a country not our own. We still feel that loss today. It was very cruel." Then the eight Ute men seated around the deer-hide drum pounded out an honor song and the old sharp sounds pierced the autumn air of the White and Yampa country once again, and the overlay of the Ute experience hung thick over the sagebrush and juniper bowl.

The first settlers and those of us who followed have made many mistakes out here, but we have done some things right, too. The mountains are mostly within the national forest system, kept open for the public. In turn, major blocks of those national forests have become part of our wilderness system. These include the Flat Tops, the elevated plateaus where the Ute's hunting trails ran.

Then, too, there is evidence of our care for the land in the cottonwood groves at Morgan Bottoms, where some of today's old trees may have been alive when Jack still rode the Yampa. Those forests surprised me simply because they are so rare. We have taken out almost all of the cottonwood forests, all across Colorado, all across the American West. At least these, which the Ute used so fully, remain vital because dams do not capture the nourishing spring floodwaters.

Still, for whatever restraint we may have shown toward the Ute's ancestral lands and whatever good we may have done, we must remember the betrayals.

For we betrayed Jack and the Ute people in so many ways. We took away the land and the buffalo. We took away the hunt. We betrayed the trust lodged in the great 1868 treaty, a device of our making that embodies the solemn word of nations. Jack tried to hew to those words, those promises, in a precise and honorable way, but the promises were stamped out by an on-rushing society that would not pause to negotiate.

We betrayed Jack in other ways. In our stampede to assimilate the Ute, we changed nearly all the Ute's names, including his. Nicaagat. It is a song of a name, with the "c" and the "g" pronounced with a soft guttural clip, with all the syllables pronounced equally, flowing like mountain water over pebbles. Ni-ca-a-gat. It means "leaves becoming green," the time when the cottonwoods come out, the time of the spring Bear Dance when he met his wife. Jack. Nicaagat.

And, in the end, we betrayed Nicaagat by driving a wedge between him and his people. Back in 1879, at the end of the commission hearings in Colorado, General Hatch announced that there would be no charges with respect to the battle with Thornburgh's troops but that Quinkent and the other men involved in the killing of Meeker and the abduction of the three women must stand trial. Ouray, old and dying, outfitted once again in

319

his buckskins in defiance of his former white friends, flashed out a last burst of rage. There would be no trial of Utes in Colorado. "[A]ll the people of Colorado and New Mexico are our enemies." The government, on the word of Interior Secretary Carl Shurz, whom the Ute trusted, agreed to a trial outside of Colorado. But the Ute would have to produce Quinkent and the others.

The Ute leaders at the hearing went into council. They agreed to the trial. They selected Nicaagat and Colorow to bring Quinkent in, which they did.

Quinkent's followers, who were few, never forgave Nicaagat. Most of the White River Utes revered him, but it seems that Nicaagat could never again be safe among the Ute. In a sense, his destiny had become entwined with that of Ouray, who at times slept with guards at his door as a precaution against rivals who objected to his attempts to appease the whites. Nicaagat struck out with his wife and children, probably for the mountains, never to return to his people.

And we need to assess still another betrayal, that of ourselves as well as Nicaagat. Conquerors, as well as the conquered, are diminished when a trust is broken. We know now that we came on too hard and fast for the Ute. We could have accommodated settlement by non-Indians and also allowed for the White River Utes to hold good land in the Yampa and White country. We could have allowed for the hunt.

Betrayals, and all the lasting things that we learn from them, die out when our memories die. This is why the forceful but careful and restrained, even gentle, reminders from the modern Utes matter so. So, too, do the high, wild Flat Tops and the green expanses at Morgan Bottoms tell it straight, that these are healthy natural systems and that our ethics must run to them as well as people. Those places hold our memories, they keep us fixed on truth, on Nicaagat, who may or may not still travel down the Yampa from the mountains, past the red horseback pictures drawn by his forebears, past the trees whose leaves turn green at the time of the Bear Dance, riding with precision, riding with his best eagle feathers and his finest pony, back from the hunt.

INFORMANTS

Ute

SAPONISE CUCH: Chief of White River Utes at Whiterocks, Utah, 1948. As a young warrior of about fifteen, he participated in the fight with the soldiers. Through the translation of Mrs. Tavapaunt, he told the whole story of the trouble, the battle, and the removal. He died at Whiterocks in the spring of 1949.

MRS. HARRIET TAVAPAUNT: Granddaughter of Tim Johnson, great-granddaughter of Canávish. From her was obtained most of the material on stories and customs; she spent many patient hours instructing me. Her daughter, Arita, her son, Reid, and her husband, Ray Tavapaunt, also gave invaluable help and information.

MRS. LULA MURDOCH: Whiterocks, Utah. Related stories, tales, and information on customs, mostly contemporary.

ANDREW FRANK: Present chief of the White River Utes, Whiterocks, Utah.

CHARLEY JOE: White River Ute, Whiterocks, Utah.

CHARLEY COLOROW: White River Ute, Myton, Utah.

HENRY MAY: Leader of band of "runaway" Utes in Allen Canyon, Utah.

TONY BUCK: Titular chief of Southern Utes, son of Buckskin Charley, Ignacio, Colorado.

REX CURRY: Business manager of the Tribal Council, Uintah and Ouray Ute Tribes, Fort Duchesne, Utah.

White

HARRISON HAYES: Settled with family on Snake River in 1875; was fourteen in 1879 when his family left their ranch for Rawlins because of the uprising. Now living near Baggs, Wyoming.

ZEB WISE: YZ Ranch, Meeker, Colorado. His father, who was an interpreter for the Utes, came into Colorado in 1880 and settled near the agency site; present ranch includes site of the Thornburgh Battle. Mr. Wise himself remembers most of the principal Utes in the story and was entirely in sympathy with the Indians.

MRS. ONEY MORGAN ST. LOUIS: St. Louis Ranch, Snake River, Colorado. Her family was one of the earliest in Routt County, Colorado; she was born there around 1875.

ROBERT MARRIMON: Indian trader, Whiterocks, Utah. His father was a trader there before him. His mother, the elder Mrs. Marrimon, also gave helpful information.

MRS. HENRY WAP-SOCK: Teacher at Indian school, Whiterocks, Utah. Married to a White River Ute, Mrs. Wap-Sock gave much useful information, especially regarding medicine practices and religious beliefs.

FOREST STONE: Uintah and Ouray Indian Agent at Fort Duchesne, Utah.

MR. AND MRS. AMOS WALTHER: Ouray, Colorado.

BIBLIOGRAPHICAL ESSAY

2. THE NATION : I

A detailed account of the holding up of annuity goods and supplies for the White River Ute Agency came out during the "testimony in relation to the Ute Indian Outbreak," taken by the House Committee on Indian Affairs at Washington. During the investigation of the "outbreak" the House committee showed great interest in the general handling of the Ute problem by the Indian Bureau, thus creating, in many respects, an investigation within an investigation. Because of a delay in the payment of freight charges to the Union Pacific Railroad, later blamed on a teamster who held the contract for transporting goods to the agency, the White River Utes received virtually no supplies for two years. Indian Commissioner Hayt presented a day-by-day report of conditions and activities at the agency and at Rawlins between September 27, 1877, and August 1, 1878, before the House committee, and the narrative of this section is based largely upon this report.

That the meeting between Nicaagat (Captain Jack) and Quinkent (Douglas) took place sometime around November 18, 1877, is clearly indicated by telegrams, included in Hayt's report, sent from Rawlins to the Indian office by both Jack and Douglas. Douglas' telegram was sent from Rawlins on November 13, and Jack's telegram was sent by Captain Nash of Fort Fred Steele, near Rawlins, on November 17. Hayt's report shows that although Douglas made a plea to the Bureau for release of the goods held at Rawlins, it was Jack who was responsible for the supplies being turned over to the Indians from the stocks at Fort Steele.

The split of the Nüpartka band between Jack and Douglas was apparent at this time, although it developed into a much wider rift after Meeker became agent. Hayt's report to the House committee notes in several instances that Jack's and Douglas' "bands" were camped on the two different rivers. Background on Jack and Douglas as used in this and succeeding chapters was drawn from material given by modern Ute informants.

Jack's friendship with Agent Danforth, White River agent before Meeker, is mentioned in several of Danforth's letters. Mr. and Mrs. Danforth believed in gradual adoption of useful white customs by the Utes but were interested in retention of basic Ute culture. In general, Jack's ideas were much the same.

Douglas' speech on "agents" was reported by Daniel W. Jones in his *Forty Years Among the Indians* (Salt Lake City, 1890). Jones, who heard Douglas make this speech at a tribal council in Utah, said it was a "favorite tirade" which he translated and recorded verbatim.

Acarí was the father of Saponise Cuch. Sowówic was noted by Meeker as "Jack's right-hand man." Photographs or clear physical descriptions of these two men were not available to me. Saponise gave me some background on them, but because of the Ute tabu against talking of persons who are dead, particularly relatives, Saponise was reluctant to talk at length to me about his father, even though the pressure of this particular tabu seems to relax as people grow older. Colorow was one of the best known of the Utes of this period because of his habit of going to white settlers' homes and "scaring" the inhabitants into giving him food. Sidney Jocknick, in his *Early Days on the Western Slope* (Denver, 1913), claims that Colorow was a Comanche who joined with the Utes because of their "fat living" during the Denver days. I was never able to substantiate this. A number of Colorow's descendants, including a son, Bob Colorow, are living at Myton and Whiterocks, Utah.

2. THE NATION : II

"Lo, The Poor Indian" was published as a chapter in William B. Vickers' *History of the City of Denver, Arapahoe County, and Colorado* (Chicago, 1880). Vickers opened the chapter by quoting Governor Pitkin's speech on the Utes before the Colorado Legislature. Information on Ute treaties and special commissions to the Utes came from George W. Manypenny, *Our Indian Wards* (Cincinnati, 1880), and Charles J. Kappler, *Indian Affairs, Laws, and Treaties* (57 Cong., 1 sess., *Sen. Doc.* 452).

2. THE NATION : III

Indian informants who contributed most to my knowledge of the Ute Bear Dance are Mrs. Harriet Johnson Tavapaunt, Ray Tavapaunt, Arita and Reid Tavapaunt, and Mrs. Lula Murdock. Robert Marrimon, owner of the Whiterocks Trading Post, furnished some important details on this ceremony with other valuable information on Ute culture and language. Bear Dance is still held every spring on the Uintah and Ouray Reservation. Principal reading sources for Bear Dance are Frances Densmore, *Northern Ute Music* (Bureau of American Ethnology *Bulletin No. 75*, Washington, 1922); M. K. Opler, "The Southern Utes," in Linton (ed.), *Acculturation in Seven American Indian Tribes* (New York, 1940); and V. Z. Reed, "The Ute Bear Dance," in the *American Anthropologist*, Vol. IX (1896).

The historical sketch of the Ute Nation was pieced together from information given me by the above named Ute informants and by a number of other Utes. A good description of the Utes in their earliest contact with European culture appears in an article in the *Western Humanities Review*, Spring, 1951, entitled "The Yuta Indians Before 1860."

Saponise Cuch, whose father, Acarí, was a close friend of Nicaagat and who, at the time I talked to him, was the only living Ute who had known Nicaagat personally, gave me an outline of Nicaagat's life before coming to White River. Saponise said Nicaagat definitely was a Gosiute, but there are a number of other rumors about his background. Wilson M. Rankin pieced together an account of Nicaagat's life for his book, *Reminiscences of Frontier Days* (Denver, 1935). His life is also dealt with in *The Ute War* (Denver, 1879), by Thomas F. Dawson and F. J. V. Skiff; *Massacres of the Mountains* (New York, 1886), J. P. Dunn Jr.; and in Jocknick's book. Most of these accounts agree, except in certain minor details, with that of Saponise. Considering the white men's bias and their tendency to accept rumor for truth, knowing the deeply-rooted Indian *mos* of truthtelling, I have, in such cases throughout the book, favored the word of my Indian informants over that of the whites. Rankin gives the name of the Mormon family who raised Nicaagat as Norton and states that he was baptised into the Church of Jesus Christ of Latter-day Saints in Salt Lake City. While living and working in Salt Lake City I attempted to trace him further through the church records, but was unsuccessful. Nicaagat may have been baptised in a smaller Utah community, in which case it would probably not be recorded.

3. THE PLAN : I

Biographical sketches of Nathan C. Meeker appeared in many newspapers at the time the "massacre" was reported. A particularly useful one was printed in the *New York Tribune*. Most general histories of Colorado and all writings on the Ute War deal to some extent with the life of Meeker. Accurate historical material on the Union Colony is given in *A History: Greeley and the Union Colony* (Greeley, Colorado, 1890), by David Boyd, and *The Union Colony at Greeley, 1869–1871* (University of Colorado *Historical Collections*, Vol. I, 1918), by J. F. Willard. "Letters of Horace Greeley to Nathan C. Meeker," printed in an article by O. M. Dickerson in the *Colorado Magazine*, Vol. XIX, Nos. 2 and 3 (March and May, 1942), were useful in understanding life and problems of the Union Colony and the personal relationship between Meeker and Greeley.

The article entitled "Lonely," which was printed in the *Gree-*

ley Tribune in mid-May, 1878, and which is excerpted here, is highly descriptive and covers Meeker's first weeks at the White River Agency.

Meeker's first annual report to the Office of Indian Affairs was dated July 29, 1879. In it he first summarizes the groundwork for his project with the White River Utes. He also deals extensively with the problem of the Indians leaving the reservation. This condition is either mentioned or dealt with in detail in subsequent letters to the Indian Bureau. A letter from Hayt to Meeker, dated February 12, 1879, and a circular prepared by Commissioner Hayt for all Indian agents are excerpted in this section to show Hayt's attitude toward this problem and its solution. The section closes with an excerpt from the July 29, 1879, report.

3. THE PLAN : II

Material on Quinkent was much easier to obtain than on Nicaagat. Present-day Utes will talk about Quinkent much more readily than about Nicaagat. I was never able to discover the reason for this. Information on Quinkent came freely from the Utes, although none of my informants, except Saponise, ever knew him personally. All writers on the Ute War deal more freely with Douglas than they do with Jack. My white informants who knew Douglas include Zeb Wise, Meeker, Colorado; Harrison Hayes, Baggs, Wyoming; and Mrs. Oney Morgan St. Louis, Little Snake River, Colorado.

All informants, both Ute and white, definitely give the impression that Douglas was considered somewhat mentally unbalanced. ("Douglas" was pronounced "Dugeris" by the Utes. Our consonant sounds of *l* and *r* merge in the Ute language.) Douglas' relationship with Meeker, the nature of his support of Meeker's plan for the Utes, and his inducing some men of his "band" to work for Meeker for wages is thoroughly dealt with by Rankin, Jocknick, Dawson and Skiff, Dunn, and other writers on the Ute War. It is verified by all of Meeker's early letters, some of which are reprinted in this book. The specifics of his

327

method for getting Indian workers for Meeker and the attitude
of the other Indians, as described in this section, were given
by Mrs. Tavapaunt and other Ute informants. Mrs. Tavapaunt
told of Douglas' using "magic" and supernatural powers to im-
press his followers, as in the case of the eclipse of the summer
of 1878. For a time, according to Mrs. Tavapaunt, he carried
a live grasshopper around with him from which he claimed to
draw magic power, pertaining mostly to control of the weather.
Later he attempted to build a religion around the grasshopper.
Communication with the dead was another of his claims. Mrs.
Tavapaunt told of an incident wherein Douglas angered her
great-grandfather, Canávish, by telling him he saw Canávish's
grandfather floating in the sky.

"Curtis" is Uriah M. Curtis, who spent much of his life
among the Utes and was one of the interpreters favored highly
by the government. The story of his expedition with the Utes
into the Sioux country was told in Rankin's book.

The Utes' impressions of the Meeker women and their re-
lationships with them are taken from material contributed by
Ute informants.

3. THE PLAN : III

Meeker's letter, of December, 1878, to Senator Teller is reprinted in part here because it so clearly summarizes the progress of Meeker's Ute program and shows his changing attitude
toward the Indians.

3. THE PLAN : IV

The episode with which this section is totally concerned—Nicaagat's visit to the agency and his talk with the Agent over the
removal to Powell's Valley—is taken from Nicaagat's account
before the investigating committee at Los Pinos in November,
1879, and at the Washington hearing that followed. All of the
dialogue which Nicaagat repeats to his friends is written as he

reported it during the hearings, with the exception of Colorow's remarks.

Colorow's taunt to Nicaagat about the Agent being his "grandmother" was a stock joke among the Utes. It was repeated to me in various forms during my stay on the reservation. It is the richest kind of humor among the Utes to give the title of a relative, particularly an older one, to any person.

Colorow's story about the selling of the land was told to me by Charley Joe, whose son-in-law is Charley Colorow, a grandson of old Colorow. It is repeated here as nearly verbatim as possible.

4. TALK : I

With the rumors, then the accepted reports of Utes deliberately setting fire to forests in attempts to drive out settlers, the real trouble between Ute and white man began. In this section I have tried to show, through excerpted letters and telegrams, the source of these reports and the resulting interplay between Denver, Washington, and the White River Agency, eventually involving the Army.

Letters excerpted to show progress of Meeker's work at the new agency are: to Hayt, April 7, 1879, quarterly report; to Hayt, July 7, 1879, monthly report.

Telegrams from Pitkin to Hayt and from Hayt to Meeker were sent on July 5, 1879, as indicated in the text. Letters excerpted for Meeker's report of fire conditions are: to Hayt, July 2, 1879; to Hayt, July 7, 1879, monthly report; and to Hayt, July 15, 1879.

All letters at this time between Meeker and others concerned in these fire reports indicate that Meeker had never considered any possibility of untruth, deliberate exaggeration, fabrication, or ulterior motive. He seemed primarily impressed with this opportunity to gain support of the Army, the Indian Bureau, and the state of Colorado in keeping the Utes on their reservation.

By this time he had dropped his original complaints, so far as they appear in his letters, but his original motives for keeping the Indians at home had not changed.

4. TALK : II

My information for this section was drawn from both white and Indian sources. The basic narrative of the section was clearly sketched in Meeker's letters. Ute informants, principally Saponise and Mrs. Tavapaunt, gave me material for a remarkably clear picture of Quinkent, his motivation, and the part he played in the incidents leading up to the battle and "massacre."

4. TALK : III

The brief outline of the life of Major Thornburgh is taken from an article printed in the *New York Tribune* shortly after the Thornburgh battle on Milk Creek. The letter from Meeker to Thornburgh from which the excerpt used is taken was written in March, 1879. Thornburgh's letter to General Crook is used in full, but letters from settlers enclosed in Thornburgh's letter are excerpted, excepting the first one.

4. TALK : IV

I have told, in the first part of this section, the Utes' version of the fire stories. The account is based on information gathered from talking with Saponise and from remarks made by Nicaagat, Sowówic, and Ouray at both the Los Pinos and Washington hearings.

Colorow's visits to the agency, his behavior when seeking food, and the description of the agency workers who went into the coal mines in Coal Creek Canyon are reconstructed from descriptions by Meeker and the Meeker women as told in Dunn's *Massacres of the Mountains,* Dawson and Skiff, Jocknick, Rankin, and various letters of Meeker. Colorow was also described in his visits to the homes of settlers by Mr. Hayes and Mrs. St. Louis. The story of the ranchers who grazed their cattle on reservation lands and of what happened to them was printed in Jocknick's book.

Nicaagat's conversation with Meeker on the burning of the houses on Bear River is taken from the account he gave of the incident before the commission at Los Pinos. He also told the commission in detail of his visit to the store on Bear River (which was called Windsor or Peck's Ford; the name of the storekeeper referred to was Peck, but Nicaagat did not give this name for the record) and his decision to go to Denver to see the Governor. No sources other than Nicaagat's testimony were used.

4. TALK : V

This account by R. D. Coxe, member of Sheriff Bessy's posse, is excerpted here. It is printed in full in Vickers' history.

4. TALK : VI

Nicaagat described in detail, including dialogue, his visit to the Governor in his testimony at both hearings. Some dialogue and other details are taken from the testimony of Governor Pitkin and Byers at the Washington hearing and from the news story of the interview which appeared later in the *Denver Times*.

5. THE LAND : I

Meeker's early letters and reports from the agency indicated that he expected to bypass what he called the "herding stage" and bring the Utes directly from the "hunting stage" into the "agricultural stage." Placed in chronological order, his letters clearly map decided changes of viewpoint on this prospect, and the fact that he permits such changes in his attitude to come with experience is, I believe, definitely to Meeker's credit.

At this point he had apparently accepted the need for the Indians to become cattle raisers before they became general farmers. As he notes in his second annual report (dated August 16) to the Indian Bureau, excerpted here, the Utes have a natural talent for livestock raising. This is very apparent to the observer of the modern Ute.

331

Meeker did not seem to realize, however, that the necessary shift from horses to cattle involved a basic cultural change. Even less-educated persons were well aware of this at the time and attempted to warn Meeker of the possible trouble he faced.

In order to trace the development of the horse problem as Meeker saw it I have, in this section, gone back and excerpted Meeker's monthly report of March, 1879, and the monthly report of April, 1879, both addressed to Hayt.

It is important in this connection to trace Meeker's relationship with Canávish (Johnson). His letter to the *Greeley Tribune* was dated October 2, 1878, and was printed in full by David Boyd. A short excerpt from the monthly report to Hayt, dated February 3, 1879, and another from the monthly report dated March 3, 1879, tell Meeker's side of the incident with Johnson involving the horses. In closing the section I again excerpted from the report of August, 1879.

5. THE LAND : II

The first real rift between Quinkent and Meeker occurred over the Agent's wanting to plow the land he had given Quinkent's people for homesites. Quinkent began his testimony at the Los Pinos hearing with an account of this trouble, starting with the complaints registered by Jane through her husband, Pauvit'z.

The story of Tatit'z shooting at the plowman was told me by Mrs. Tavapaunt, whose grandfather was Tim Johnson. The dialogue between Tim and Tatit'z which leads to the shooting is reconstructed from Mrs. Tavapaunt's account. In general, the wording of the dialogue is her own.

5. THE LAND : III

I have reprinted Meeker's letter to Hayt (September 8, 1879) in full that he might tell his story, in his own words, of the trouble over the plowing and the shooting at the plowman.

5. THE LAND : IV

The first part of this section is based on Quinkent's testimony before the commission at Los Pinos. All the dialogue between Quinkent and the Agent is recorded in Quinkent's testimony. The council is taken from the testimony of Nicaagat, Quinkent, Henry Jim (the "Little Boy"), and Sowówic at the Los Pinos and Washington hearings.

5. THE LAND : V

All of the background on Canávish, Tsashin, and their sons, Tim and Tatit'z, was furnished by Mrs. Tavapaunt. Although she never knew her great-grandfather, Mrs. Tavapaunt was close to her grandfather, Tim. All of the information used in this section was passed down through Tim.

Mrs. Tavapaunt instructed me in the manner that is used in instructing sons and daughters who have passed puberty. I was not a student; I was a pupil. Having done a good deal of book research on the Utes, I believe that I was the first white person to hear and record the Ute creation stories and the nature of the Ute religion. I had often questioned Mrs. Tavapaunt directly on the "beliefs" of the Utes and received no answers. When she finally began instructing me properly, she prefaced each story with, "This is the way it was."

The instructions which Canávish gives his sons in this section is a part of the instruction which Mrs. Tavapaunt gave me. She received it from her grandfather who had received it, with his brother, from Canávish.

Canávish's two meetings and his conversations with Meeker are taken directly from Canávish's testimony before the commission at Los Pinos. Some details were furnished by Mrs. Tavapaunt.

6. THE TROUBLE : I

Letters and telegrams included in this chapter are arranged in an order to demonstrate the activity which followed Meeker's telegram of September 10, 1879, reporting the Johnson incident to the Bureau of Indian Affairs.

6. THE TROUBLE : II

In his testimony at Los Pinos and at Washington, Nicaagat described his talk with the Agent before the council on plowing, his conversation with the group of Indians near the agency, and his talk with the white agency employee W. H. Post. Colorow and Sowówic, in their testimony, both gave vivid descriptions of the feeling among the Indians at this time.

6. THE TROUBLE : III

The story of Thornburgh's march is told by a number of writers and historians, all of whom furnished material for this section. They include Elmer R. Burkey, "The Thornburgh Battle with the Utes on Milk Creek," in the *Colorado Magazine*, Vol. XIII, No. 3 (May, 1936); Philip H. Sheridan, *Record of Engagements with Hostile Indians* (Washington, 1882); A. M. Startzell, "Thornburgh Massacre at Meeker," (MS in Colorado State Historical Society Files); and Wilson M. Rankin, *Reminiscences of Frontier Days*.

In their testimony taken and recorded at Washington, Captain Payne and Lieutenant Cherry gave detailed accounts of the march.

Scout Joe Rankin, who later became the popular hero of the "Meeker Massacre," was well described by Wilson M. Rankin, his cousin, in his book and by Harrison Hayes, a white informant, who, as a cowboy in the Rawlins area, was well acquainted with Rankin and his brother, who ran a livery stable at Rawlins.

6. THE TROUBLE : IV

In his testimony both at Los Pinos and at Washington Nicaagat described in great detail his trip to Bear River and his talk

334

with Major Thornburgh. The dialogue is almost entirely that which Nicaagat reported in his testimony, with a few pieces taken from the testimony of Lieutenant Cherry and Captain Payne. There was no actual conflict between these reports, except that Cherry and Payne omitted entirely any mention of the exchange between Nicaagat and the Major on war and the killing of brothers by brothers. Nicaagat made it clear in his testimony that he considered this exchange an important event in the chain of circumstances which led ultimately to the battle. Sowówic did not mention his visit to the soldiers' camp in his testimony, and Acarí did not testify at either of the hearings, so this section was written entirely from the viewpoint of Nicaagat.

6. THE TROUBLE : V

Most of the dialogue in this section was reported by Payne and Cherry in their testimony. Bits of it were taken from the writings of Burkey, Sheridan, Startzell, and Rankin.

6. THE TROUBLE : VI

Colorow's conversation with Major Thornburgh was reported by Colorow in his testimony at Los Pinos.

The events leading up to the war dance and the dance itself were described to me by Saponise, who took part as one of the "young men." At this point in his narrative Saponise said, "The older men did not want to fight, but the young men told them that if Washington was sending soldiers into our country, Washington must want us to fight." Saponise indicated that the war dance was spontaneous when he emphasized that no plans had been made for war, that the feeling of war just grew up among the young men and that an actual decision to fight was never made or spoken, until the first shot was fired. The words and form of the war dance chant were published by Frances Densmore in *Northern Ute Music*.

The creation story told by Canávish was one of those told me by Mrs. Tavapaunt. As with the other stories, this one was told her by her grandfather, Tim Johnson. I have preserved her wording of the story as much as possible.

6. THE TROUBLE : VII

Information for the narrative and direct quotations in this section came from the sources on the Thornburgh march and battle, including Burkey, Sheridan, Startzell, and Rankin. The quotations are written as reported by Payne and Cherry in their testimony.

7. THE BATTLE : I

Most of my material for this account of the threshing machine incident was furnished me by Zeb Wise, a rancher near Meeker. Mr. Wise came to the White River country with his father shortly after the battle. He learned the Ute language and became a close friend to many of the White River Utes, including some of those named in this book. Mr. Wise told me this story as it was told him by the Indians, and he showed me the large rock in Coal Creek Canyon where the three young Utes hid as the wagon approached them on the road. The teamster who was killed was named Isaac Goldstein and was known as "The Jew" throughout that area. His young companion was a youth who had just come to Colorado from New England. Another account of the threshing machine incident appears in *Tread of the Pioneers* (Steamboat Springs Colorado, 1944), by Charles H. Leckenby, editor and publisher of the *Steamboat Pilot,* at Steamboat Springs, Colorado.

7. THE BATTLE : II

Saponise described the battle to me in detail. At the time he talked to me he was the last Ute alive who had participated in the battle; I estimated that he was about fifteen years old in 1879. He said that most of the young men who fought were about the same age as himself.

To augment Saponise's information on the battle I have used the testimony of Nicaagat, Colorow, Sapavanero (who was one of the carriers of the message from Ouray to the Milk River battlefield), and Ouray, taken both at Los Pinos and Washington. Some details were also furnished by Zeb Wise, who, as I noted before, spoke Ute, was sympathetic to the Utes, and knew most of the men who participated in the battle.

In general, the story told by Saponise and the testimony of the Utes agrees with the accounts of the battle from Captain Payne, Lieutenant Cherry, and other members of Thornburgh's command; but there were some very important contradictions. For example, both Payne and Cherry estimated the number of Indians engaged in the battle at between three and four hundred. This estimate was accepted by the Army and by most of the writers and historians on the Ute War. Nicaagat was asked for an estimate of the number of Indians engaged. His answer was, "Perhaps about fifty." This was the estimate given me by Saponise. Considering the actual total number of White River Utes, the latter estimate is undoubtedly correct.

A claim popular with the Army, government officials, and various citizens of Colorado was that the fighting force of all the Ute bands participated in the battle. This is denied by Ouray and by Agent Stanley, both of whom were on the Uncompahgre reservation at the time of the battle, and by all Indians who testified.

There are probably two reasons for the exaggeration of the number of Utes engaged in the battle and the claim that all bands participated: first, the Army was obviously trying to save face by claiming that the troops were outnumbered, and, second, Colorado was by this time openly trying to get rid of its Indians. Seeing the Ute War as a good final argument to this end, Coloradans wanted at the outset to see all bands implicated.

Details of Nicaagat's experiences while riding with General Crook as "Ute John" were taken from John G. Bourke, *On the Border with Crook* (New York, 1902); from John F. Finerty, *Warpath and Bivouac* (Chicago, 1890); from Rankin's book; and from Saponise and other Ute informants.

7. THE BATTLE : III

For this section on the "massacre" and the capture of the women at the agency, I have excerpted the testimony of Josephine Meeker, Mrs. Arvella Meeker, and Mrs. S. F. Price taken by General Adams at Greeley and again, in the case of Josephine, at the Washington hearings. I have arranged the excerpts in chronological order to form a narrative.

7. THE BATTLE : IV

Again Saponise was my principal source for description of the battle and the war camp of the Utes. Testimony of Nicaagat, Colorow, Sowówic was less valuable as a source for this section than for Section II of this chapter because their testimony dealt largely with the beginning and the end of the battle and siege rather than the middle. The description of the women's village and of the white women captives is reconstructed from Saponise's remarks, although Saponise spent all his time at the battlefield and heard about the goings on at the village only as indicated here. Saponise also remarked on the behavior of Colorow, Nicaagat, Quinkent, and others as I have reconstructed it here. This information was augmented by Zeb Wise, Harrison Hayes, and other informants who knew of the battle through hearsay.

Joseph Brady, a miller at the Los Pinos Agency, Sapavanero, who was considered first subchief under Ouray, and other Indians from the Uncompahgre carried the messages to the White River Utes and to General Merritt. Brady and Sapavanero both testified at the Los Pinos hearing and described the battle at the time in which they saw it. Their testimony was used in the last part of this section. Nicaagat, Colorow, and Sowówic also described the bringing of the messages from Los Pinos and the end of the Milk River battle. Colonel E. V. Sumner, in his article "Besieged by the Utes," in *Century Magazine*, Vol. XLII (October, 1891), described the coming of General Merritt's forces. As an officer under General Merritt, Colonel Sumner gives a detailed description of the last skirmish, the erection of the truce flag, and the pursuit of the Utes into their own country. Colonel Sumner's article definitely gives the impression that the overwhelming force of General Merritt's troops attacking the hills actually brought about the truce. The testimony of the Indians, Mr. Brady, and Saponise's information definitely refutes this. It was the note from Ouray and the implied promise in Agent Stanley's letter to General Merritt that the soldiers would cease fighting if the Utes stopped that actually prompted the truce. Colorow's testimony indicates that he was surprised that the soldiers advanced on his small rear guard after the bulk of the Ute forces had retreated.

7. THE BATTLE : V

Harrison Hayes was living and working on Little Snake River at the time word was received of the "Ute uprising." He and other settlers in that region fled to Rawlins. Mr. Hayes described to me the coming of Joe Rankin with word of the Thornburgh battle and the general exodus of white people from southern Wyoming and northern Colorado to Rawlins. Mr. Hayes told of seeing Peck, the Bear River storekeeper, in Rawlins and recalled that the Pecks' young son was dressed in a small suit of fringed buckskin. I have tried to get into the first part of this section the feeling of panic in Rawlins and the area south as Mr. Hayes described it to me. Mrs. St. Louis was a young girl living with her family on Little Snake River at the time of the uprising. Her family, the Morgans, also went to Rawlins, and Mrs. St. Louis told me what she could personally recall of the flight.

Most of the books and articles on the Ute War contain a more or less vivid description of the reaction in Denver and other settlements in the Colorado mountains. Amos Walther, now a retired banker in Ouray, Colorado, was a young man working in Denver at this time. He described the Denver panic to me. Mrs. Walther was a young girl living in the town of Ouray at the time, and she described the false panic there. Mrs. Walther told me it was generally accepted among the white people in the San Juan settlements that all of the men of the Southern Ute bands were on their reservation and showing no hostility toward the whites, although citizens of Ouray insisted on posting a guard at the mouth of the canyon in which Ouray is built. Mrs. Walther said she heard her father remark, as he left the house to take his turn at guard duty, "This is a lot of foolishness."

Newspapers of Denver, other western cities, and even the newspapers of New York City were carrying long stories about the battle and "massacre." The *New York Tribune*, Mr. Greeley's newspaper, printed an editorial sympathetic to the Utes. Editorials in western newspapers cried loudly and variously for Ute blood in the spirit of the familiar slogan, "The Utes must go!"

Governor Pitkin's statement reprinted in this section was given to the *New York Tribune* and was printed in the form of an interview, giving the reporter's questions and the governor's answers. I omitted the questions here and reprinted in full the governor's answers.

8. DECISION : I

Because of General Adams' position with the Indians and his comparatively neutral and liberal attitude, I have chosen to use his testimony, given before the Washington hearing, to fill this particular gap in the story of the Ute War. If it were not for General Adams' testimony, a gap would definitely exist here. Very little was told me by my Ute informants about the captivity of the women and the conditions of their release. The Indians who testified at Los Pinos and in Washington had little to say about this phase of the conflict. White writings, testimony, and documentary evidence on the procedures of making peace with the Utes and procuring the release of the women captives is almost useless as truthful, factual evidence since most of the whites concerned were motivated almost entirely by a desire to see the Utes removed from Colorado or exterminated. To this end, the captivity of the women was used, as was noted in earlier chapters, to promote a chivalrous hysteria and a strong anti-Ute sentiment.

General Adams, despite his respect for the Utes and their

respect for him, presented this testimony with very little bias. I consider it accurate and am therefore offering it here verbatim, with only a brief introduction to sketch General Adams' background and show the interesting parallel with that of Carl Schurz, who is remembered today mostly for his interest in justice for the Indian.

I have cut portions of General Adams' testimony which I consider repetitious or not particularly valuable to the narrative.

8. DECISION : II & III

These two sections are based generally on the record of the Ute Commission at Los Pinos as published in 46 Cong., 2 sess., *House Exec. Doc. 83*. All of the dialogue in these sections is taken directly from this record, except where otherwise noted.

There is a great deal of background material on Ouray in various publications, most of which I found useful in making the sketch of Ouray at the beginning of Section II. Most of the material for this sketch came, however, from Ute informants. Mrs. Tavapaunt and her sons and daughters are extremely proud of being related to Ouray through his sister, Tsashin, Mrs. Tavapaunt's great-grandmother. They talk freely of Ouray, and the Tavapaunt children showed me papers they had written on Ouray for school projects. Mrs. Walther gave me a vivid description of Ouray, having visited at his house with her parents as a little girl. Mr. Walther moved to the Western Slope after the death of Ouray, but he knew Chipita well.

Writings which were particularly helpful for personal and biographical background on Ouray include *Our Indian Wards*, by George W. Manypenny; Jocknick's book; Major Thompson's article in Vol. VII (May, 1930) of the *Colorado Magazine*, entitled "Major Thompson, Chief Ouray, and the Utes," as related to T. F. Dawson; and various Congressional records of commissions which interviewed Ouray prior to the Ute War, as listed in the bibliography.

Some descriptive details, the general mood and tone of the hearing, and references to attitudes on the part of various participants are drawn from information given by Saponise and other Ute informants and in writings on the Ute War, all of which dealt more or less with the hearings at Los Pinos.

Especially useful as source material for these sections on the hearings was Jocknick's book. Mr. Jocknick, having been an employee of the Uncompahgre Agency and a correspondent for newspapers in the towns of Ouray, Silverton, Lake City, as well as Denver, was actually much closer, both geographically and in understanding, to the hearings than to the actual battle and "massacre"; and his book dealt proportionately more with the hearings than most writings. The newspapers in the above towns were vitally interested in the progress of the hearings and printed some detailed reports.

According to Jocknick's account, the official record failed to report some of the statements and happenings during the hearings. The final speeches of General Adams and General Hatch were printed in full in the record, but the final answer of the Utes, spoken by Ouray, was printed only in part. The paragraph which begins, "All of the people of Colorado and New Mexico are our enemies," was recorded as the Utes' final answer to the demands of the commission. All of Ouray's speech which precedes this statement is taken from the Jocknick account, which also describes the crisis with the knives and pipes as it is set down in this section. Ute informants furnished me with some of the details of this incident, and the tension and anxiety which was created among the white men present is described in Dunn's *Massacres of the Mountains* and Dawson and Skiff's *The Ute War*.

8. DECISION : IV

The first part of this section is an account of the balance of the Los Pinos hearings. I made no attempt to give testimony, questioning, or remarks in direct quotes because substantially all the testimony had already been heard and was recorded in the preceding sections. All dispatches and letters used here appeared in the official record of the Los Pinos hearings.

I have summarized the Washington hearing briefly. In many

ways the details of this hearing would be a reiteration of the story which has already been told, and in some respects it is another story, which makes good reading for anyone interested in the Indian affairs of this period.

The account of the signing of the removal agreement is taken directly from the official report of George W. Manypenny, who headed the commission. The quotations included are from this account.

9. DEATH : I

The story of the geological history of the Ute country and the early history of the Utes which begins this section was reconstructed from material given me by various Ute informants, particularly Mrs. Tavapaunt, and from an account in *The Ute War*, by Dawson and Skiff. It leads directly into a description of that period between the end of the Los Pinos hearings and the signing of the removal agreement. This part of the section was told almost entirely by Saponise, and much of it is written in his own words. The quotation from President Hayes, which begins, "Now this trouble is dead," are the exact words quoted by Saponise.

Mr. Walther described the black face painting. He was at the Uintah and Ouray Agency in Utah when the removed Colorado Utes were brought there. He said the men were still so painted when they arrived and added that this indicated "bad blood in the heart."

The brief account of the death of Ouray is based largely upon material given me by Ute informants, upon the account given in Manypenny's report of the removal commission, and from an article entitled, "The Death of Ouray, Chief of the Utes," by Mrs. C. W. Wiegel in the *Colorado Magazine*, September, 1930.

9. DEATH : II

This account of the Ute removal, written by Captain James Parker, of the Fourth Cavalry, is excerpted from his book *The Old Army* (Philadelphia, 1929).

343

BIBLIOGRAPHY

PART I: Meeker Massacre and Ute War of 1879

Baker, James H. *History of Colorado*. Denver, 1927.

Bourke, John G. *On the Border With Crook*. New York, 1902. (Tells about Scout 'Ute John' on Sioux campaign.)

Boyd, David. *A History: Greeley and the Union Colony*. Greeley, Colorado, 1890. (Contains Meeker's letters to the *Tribune*.)

Boyd, James P. *Recent Indian Wars*. Philadelphia, 1892.

Burkey, Elmer R. "The Thornburgh Battle with the Utes on Milk Creek" (based on correspondence in files of Colorado State Historical Society, Denver), *Colorado Magazine*, Vol. XIII, No. 3 (May, 1936).

Cheyenne Leader (newspaper), Cheyenne, Wyoming. Editorial: "The Utes Must Go!" October, 1879.

Chicago Tribune (newspaper), Chicago, Illinois. General accounts and interview with Governor Pitkin, September and October, 1879.

Clark, J. Max (member of Union Colony). *Colonial Days*. Denver, 1902.

Colorado State Historical Society. *History of Colorado*, Vol. I. Ed. by S. H. Baker and LeRoy Hafen. Denver, 1927.

Cowan, Bud (settler who moved to Meeker, Colorado, with family in 1879). *Range Rider*. Garden City, New York, 1930.

Craig, Katherine. *Brief History of Colorado*. Denver, 1923.

Dawson, Thomas F., and F. J. V. Skiff. *The Ute War*. Denver, 1879. (Newspaper's account.)

Denver Times (newspaper), Denver, Colorado, August, 1879.

Dickerson, O. M. "Letters of Horace Greeley to Nathan C. Meeker,"

Colorado Magazine, Vol. XIX, Nos. 2 and 3 (March and May, 1942).

Dunn, J. P., Jr. "White River Agency," *Massacres of the Mountains.* New York, 1886.

Finerty, John F. *Warpath and Bivouac.* Chicago, 1890. (Crook's Sioux Campaign, and 'Ute John.')

Goodykoontz, Colin B. "The People of Colorado," in Vol. II of *Colorado and Its People.* Ed. by LeRoy R. Hafen. Denver, 1948.

Greeley Tribune (newspaper), Greeley, Colorado. 1870–80.

Hall, Frank. *History of the State of Colorado,* Chap. XXIV of Vol. II. Chicago, 1918.

Haskell, T. N. "Fate of the Meeker Family" (verse), *Young Konkaput, King of the Utes,* Denver, 1889.

Haydon, W. "Uintah and Ouray Agency," *Report on Indians Taxed and Indians Not Taxed.* Eleventh Census, U. S. Department of the Interior, Census Office. Washington, 1890.

Jocknick, Sidney (employee at Los Pinos Agency in early 1870's). *Early Days on the Western Slope.* Denver, 1913.

Kappler, Charles J. (ed.). *Indian Affairs: Laws and Treaties,* Vol. I. (Statutes, Executive Orders, Proclamations, and Statistics of Tribes, to December 1, 1902.) 57 Cong., 1 sess., *Sen Doc.* 452.

Kelsey, D. M. "The Utes," *History of Our Wild West.* Chicago, 1901. (Sensational style, very confused.)

Kimball, Maria Brace. "The Thornburgh Massacre," *A Soldier-Doctor of Our Army.* Boston and New York, 1917. (Dr. James Kimball was the army surgeon with the Merritt expedition.)

Leadville Eclipse (newspaper), Leadville, Colorado. September and October, 1879.

Leckenby, Charles H. *The Tread of Pioneers.* Steamboat Springs, Colorado, 1944. (Personal accounts from white settlers in Middle and North Parks.)

McReynolds, Robert. *Thirty Years on the Frontier.* Colorado Springs, 1906.

Manypenny, George W. *Our Indian Wards,* Chap. XIX. Cincinnati, 1880. (Sympathetic and clear account by member of last Ute Commission.)

Meeker, Nathan Cook. *The Adventures of Captain Armstrong.* New York, 1856.

———. *Life in the West, or Stories of the Mississippi Valley.* New York, 1868.

———. "The Utes of Colorado," *American Antiquarian (and Oriental Journal)*, Vol. I, No. 4 (April, 1879).

Monroe, A. W. *San Juan Silver.* Grand Junction, Colorado, 1940. (Account from miners' viewpoint.)

New York Tribune (newspaper). October through November, 1879.

Nixon, Elizabeth. "The Meeker Massacre." Unpublished Master's thesis, Colorado State College of Education, 1935. (The author used material in collections at Greeley, Colorado, talked with the Meeker family, saw private letters and scrapbooks.)

Parker, James. "The Ute Campaign," *The Old Army.* Philadelphia, 1929. (A brigadier general's firsthand account of the Ute removal of 1881.)

Parkhill, Forbes. "The Meeker Massacre and Thornburgh Battle," *Westerners, Denver Posse.* Denver, 1945.

———. *Troopers West.* New York, 1945. (Fiction.)

Parsons, Eugene. *The Making of Colorado.* Chicago, 1908.

Quiett, Glenn C. "Reclaiming the Desert," *They Build the West.* New York, 1934. (Story of Union Colony and Meeker's role in its establishment.)

Rankin, M. Wilson (cousin of Scout Joe Rankin). *Reminiscences of Frontier Days.* Photolithographed in Denver, 1935.

Ripley, Henry and Martha (settlers near town of Montrose, Colorado). "Indian Troubles," *Hand Clasp of the East and West.* Denver, 1914.

Rocky Mountain News (newspaper), Denver, Colorado. August through November, 1879.

Salt Lake Herald (newspaper), Salt Lake City, Utah. October through November, 1879.

Sheridan, Philip H. *Record of Engagements with Hostile Indians, 1868-1882.* Compiled at Headquarters, Division of the Missouri, from official records. Washington, 1882. (Records of Thornburgh fight and death of Jack.)

Sherman, William T. "Annual Report to the Secretary of War," *Messages and Documents, War Department, 1879-80,* Vol. I. Washington, 1880.

Smiley, J. C. *Semi-Centennial History of the State of Colorado,* Chaps. XXI and XXXII of Vol. I. Chicago, 1913.

Startzell, A. M. (one of Thornburgh's troopers). "Thornburgh Massacre at Meeker." MS in Colorado State Historical Society Files.

Stone, Wilbur F. *History of Colorado,* Vol. I. Chicago, 1918.

Sturgis, Thomas. *The Ute War of 1879: Why the Indian Bureau*

Should Be Transferred from the Department of Interior to the Department of War. Cheyenne, Wyoming, 1879.

Sumner, E. V. (Col.). "Besieged by the Utes," *Century Magazine*, Vol. XLII, No. 6 (October, 1891). (Account of Merritt's expedition by the officer in charge of the scouting party, Weir incident.)

Thayer, William M. *Marvels of the New West.* Norwich, Connecticut, 1887.

Thompson, James B. (Major). "Major Thompson, Chief Ouray, and the Utes" (as related to T. F. Dawson, May 23, 1921), *Colorado Magazine*, Vol. VII, No. 3 (May, 1930).

United States Congress:

    45 Cong., 3 sess., *House Exec. Doc. 1, Part 5.* "Report of the Secretary of the Interior," Vol. I. Includes Annual Report of White River Ute Agent Nathan C. Meeker.

    46 Cong., 2 sess., *House Exec. Doc. 1, Part 5.* "Report of the Secretary of Interior," Vol. I. Includes Report of the Commissioner of Indian Affairs containing: "Reports of U. S. Indian Agents for 1879"; "Report of the Ute Commission"; "Copy of the Agreement with Capote, Muache, and Weeminuche Utes, Washington, December 27, 1878"; "Executive Order from the President Affecting the Colorado Ute Indian Reservation."

    ———., *House Exec. Doc. 83.* "White River Ute Commission Investigation, Ouray, Colorado, 1879."

    ———., *House Misc. Doc. 38.* "Testimony in Relation to Ute Outbreak, Taken by the Committee on Indian Affairs, Washington, 1880."

    ———., *House Report 1401.* "Agreement with Ute Indians of Colorado." Includes the statement of the Secretary of Interior and the general discussion, Washington, May 11, 1880.

    ———., *Sen. Exec. Doc. 27.* "Information in re. Payments Made to Ute Indians, in Accordance with Agreement of September 3, 1873."

    ———., *Sen. Exec. Doc. 29.* "Information in re. to Number of Mining Camps Located on Ute Reservation."

    ———., *Sen. Exec. Doc. 31.* "Correspondence Concerning the Ute Indians in Colorado."

    ———., *Sen. Exec. Doc. 169.* "Letter of Secretary of Interior Relative to Affadavits by or on Behalf of Settlers on Uncompahgre Park, Colorado." Includes letter of Hon. C. H. McIntyre on settlement of Uncompahgre Park.

46 Cong., 3 sess., *Sen. Exec. Doc. 31.* "Letter of Secretary of Interior Transmitting in Response to Senate Resolution of January 27, 1881, a Copy of the Report of the Ute Commission and Copies of Correspondence Between Department of Interior and Governor of Colorado."

Ute Massacre! Brave Miss Meeker's Captivity! Her Own Account of It . . . . Philadelphia, 1879.

Vickers, William B. *History of the City of Denver, Arapahoe County, and Colorado.* Chicago, 1880. (Vickers was secretary to Governor Pitkin and was able to include important private letters and papers in his book.)

Wastrous, Ansel. *The History of Larimer County, Colorado.* Fort Collins, Colorado, 1911.

Wellman, Paul I. *Death on Horseback.* New York, 1934. (An account of the Ute War entirely from Army records. Has good bibliography.)

Wiegel, Mrs. C. W. "The Death of Ouray, Chief of the Utes," *Colorado Magazine,* Vol. VII, No. 5 ,September, 1930). (Based on story told to Indian Service employee by old Indians.)

Willard, J. F. *The Union Colony at Greeley, 1869–1871* University of Colorado *Historical Collections,* Vol. I. Boulder, Colorado, 1918. (Complete documents of the Union Colony.)

PART II: Historical Background

Alter, J. C. "Father Escalante and the Utah Indians," *Utah Historical Quarterly,* Vols. I and II (1928–29).

Burton, R. F. *The City of the Saints.* London, 1861.

Campion, J. S. *On the Frontier.* 2nd ed. London, 1878.

Coues, Elliott (ed.). *Expeditions of Zebulon M. Pike.* New York, 1895.

———. *Journal of Jacob Fowler.* New York, 1898.

Dellenbaugh, Frederick S. *Breaking the Wilderness.* New York, 1905. (Dellenbaugh was a member of the Powell expedition of 1871–82.)

De Smet, Pierre J. *Letters and Sketches, with a Narrative of a Year's Residence Among the Indians of the Rocky Mountains.* Philadelphia. 1843.

Dodge, R. I. *Plains of the Great West.* New York, 1877.

Doolittle, J. R. *Conditions of the Indian Tribes.* 39 Cong., 2 sess., *Sen. Report 156.*

Farnham., Thomas J. *Travels in the Great Western Prairies . . . and the Rocky Mountains . . . .* London, 1843.

Gregg, Josiah. *Commerce of the Prairies.* Philadelphia, 1844.

Hafen, LeRoy. *Colorado Gold Rush; Contemporary Letters and Reports, 1858–59.* Glendale, California, 1941.

Heap, G. H. *Central Route to the Pacific.* Philadelphia, 1854.

Howard, Sarah Elizabeth. *Pen Pictures of the Plains.* Denver, 1902.

Humfreville, J. L. *Twenty Years Among Our Savage Indians.* Hartford, Connecticut, 1897.

Iseley, Jeter. *Horace Greeley and the Republican Party.* Princeton, New Jersey, 1948.

Jones, Daniel W. *Forty Years Among the Indians.* Salt Lake City, 1890.

Otis, Elwell S. (Lt. Col.). *The Indian Question.* New York, 1878.

Palmer, W. R. "Utah Indians Past and Present," *Utah Historical Quarterly,* Vol. I (1928).

Parker, Rev. Samuel. *Journal of an Exploring Tour Beyond the Rocky Mountains.* Ithaca, New York, 1838.

Pattie, James O. *Personal Narrative . . . .* Cincinnati, 1831.

Powell, J. W. *Exploration of the Colorado River.* Washington, 1875.

Richardson, Albert D. *Beyond the Mississippi.* Hartford, Connecticut, 1867.

Ruxton, G. F. *Adventures in Mexico and the Rocky Mountains.* London, 1847.

Tierney, Luke. *History of the Gold Discoveries on the South Platte River.* To which is appended "A Guide to the Gold Mines on the South Platte," by D. C. Oakes and S. W. Smith. Pacific City, Iowa, 1859.

Willison, George F. *Here They Dug Gold.* New York, 1931.

PART III: Ethnological Background

Bancroft, Hubert H. *Wild Tribes.* Vol. I of *The Native Races.* San Francisco, 1882.

Barber, E. A. "Gaming Among the Utah Indians," *American Naturalist,* Vol. XI (1877).

———. "Language and Utensils of the Modern Utes," United States Geological and Geographical Survey of the Territories Bulletin. Washington, 1876.

Beals, R. L. *Ethnology of Rocky Mountain Park: the Ute and Arapahoe.* Berkeley, California, 1935.

Chamberlain, R. V. "Some Plant Names of the Ute Indians," *American Anthropologist,* n.s., Vol. XI (1909).

Clark, W. P. *The Indian Sign Language.* Philadelphia, 1885.

Cooke, A. M. "The Northern Ute," *American Anthropologist,* n.s., Vol. XL (1938).

Densmore, Frances. *Northern Ute Music.* Bureau of American Ethnology *Bulletin No. 75.* Washington, 1922.

Douglas, F. H. "The Ute Indians," Denver Art Museum *Indian Leaflet Series,* X (1930).

Gottfredson, Peter. *History of Indian Depredations in Utah.* Salt Lake City, 1935.

Harrington, John P. "The Phonetic System of the Ute Language," University of Colorado *Studies,* Vol. VIII, No. 3 (1911).

Hodge, Frederick W. (ed.). *Handbook of the American Indians.* Bureau of American Ethnology *Bulletin No. 30,* Part 2. Washington, 1910.

Hrdlicka, Alex. "Southern Ute," Bureau of American Ethnology *Bulletin No. 30,* Part 2. Washington, 1910.

Hurst, C. T. "A Ute Shelter," *Southwestern Lore,* Vol. V (1939). Colorado Archaeological Society, Gunnison, Colorado.

Kroeber, A. L. "Notes on the Ute Language," *American Anthropologist,* n.s., Vol. X (1908).

———. "Ute Tales," *Journal of American Folk Lore,* Vol. XIV (1901).

Lowie, R. H. "Shoshonean Tales," *Journal of American Folk Lore,* Vol. XXXVII (1924).

Mason, J. Alden. "Myths of the Uintah Utes," *Journal of American Folk Lore,* Vol. XXIII (1910).

Murdock, G. P. "Utes," *Ethnographical Bibliography of North America. Yale Anthropological Studies,* Vol. I (1941).

Opler, M. K. "The Southern Utes," in Ralph Linton (ed.), *Acculturation in Seven American Indian Tribes.* New York, 1940.

Reagan, A. B. "The Bear Dance of the Ouray Utes," *Wisconsin Archeologist,* n.s., Vol. IX (1929).

———. "Mortuary Customs of the Ouray Utes," *El Palacio,* Vol. XXXI (1931). Santa Fé, New Mexico.

———. "Some Games of the Northern Ute," *Northwest Science,* Vol. VIII (1934). Moscow, Idaho.

———. "Some Names of the Ute Indians," *Proceedings* of the Utah Academy of Arts and Sciences, Vol. XII (1935).

Reed, V. Z. "The Ute Bear Dance," *American Anthropologist,* Vol. IX (1896).

Schoolcraft, H. R. *Information Concerning the History, Condillons And Prospects of the Indian Tribes of the United States.* Prepared under act of Congress, March 3, 1847. Philadelphia, 1856.

Selman, Mormon V. *Dictionary of the Ute Language.* Provo, Utah, n.d.

Steward, J. H. "A Uintah Ute Bear Dance," *American Anthropologist,* n.s., Vol. XXXIV (1932).

"Ute," Bureau of American Ethnology *Bulletin No. 30,* Part 2. Washington, 1910.

INDEX

Acari: fires at Hayden settlement, 108f.; interview with governor, 115–20; effort to stop soldiers, 169ff., 180

Adams, General Charles: agent at White River, 79–80; rescue of agency women, 239–49; White River uprising investigation, 253–82

Army post commanders, duties: 95

Bear Dance: participants, 29–31; preparations, 35; dancing, 36ff.; feasting, 40

Bessey, Marshall: arrests Utes for arson, 110–14

Brooks, E. J.: Ute depredations, 87; troop protection for White River agent, 155f.; "Ute Difficulty," 159

Buffalo Soldiers ("Black-Whitemen"): 93, 105, 139; at Little River, 219ff.; war-dance chant concerning, 220

Byers, William N. (Pius): Pikes Peak gold rush, 6; first Denver newspaper, 8; Colorado development, 48; complaints against Utes, 86; Nicaagat's interview with governor, 115–16

Canávish (Johnson): medicine man, 38; becoming civilized, 123–25; the big joke, 143ff.; legend of Creation, 148–49; anger at agent, 151–53; legend of war, 183–86; son killed, 202; agency woman captive, 216; White River uprising investigation, 259–61, 286f.

Cherry, Lieutenant S. A., expedition to White River agency: 166, 178ff.

Cheyennes: Sand Creek battle, 22, 26

Chivington, Colonel J. W.: Sand Creek battle, 22

Colorado: territorial charter, 8; state, 9; Indian problem, 21, 25–26; large-scale irrigation, 48; forest fires set by Utes, 86; call for arms by settlers, 236; reservation for Southern Utes, 285; taking over Indian land, 294–95

353